FAITH, HOPE, AND LOVE

Dr. Wells Thoms bids farewell to a man returning home after his hospital recovery (Church Herald, *29 May 1970*)

FAITH, HOPE, and LOVE
The Hakeem's Journey
The Adventures of Pioneer Missionary Physician
Dr. Wm. Wells Thoms, FACS, in Arabia before Oil

David G. Dickason

© 2022 All rights reserved

A. C. Van Raalte Institute, Hope College
Van Raalte Press is a division of Hope College Publishing

Theil Research Center
9 East 10th Street
Holland, MI 49423

PO Box 9000
Holland, MI 49422-9000

616.395.7678
vanraalte@hope.edu

Jacob E. Nyenhuis, PhD, LittD
    Editor-in-Chief and Publisher

JoHannah Smith
    Project Editor

Russell L. Gasero, Archivist, Reformed Church in America
    Layout and Design

Cover images: *top, l-r:* A young landmine victim receives the gift of a donkey to carry him home up into the high mountains; Shaykh Hamid bin Hamid and son, 1949; Dr. Thoms and pharmacy assistant Malallah examine a patient's X-ray; *bottom*: Dr. Wells Thoms and Sayyid Ahmad bin Ibrahim, Oman's minister of the interior and de facto prime minister (1939-70), with his security detail. The minister was treated by Wells after an assassination attempt.

Printed in the United States of America

Library of Congress Control Number: 2021944146

To Lowey

The Missionary Memoirs Series of the Van Raalte Press, No. 3

This series is dedicated to publishing the heretofore untold stories of missionaries of the Reformed Church in America and the Christian Reformed Church in North America and Hope College alumni who worked to proclaim the Christian Gospel both at home and abroad. These books are the recorded accounts of their experiences, transformational for themselves and for the people of the countries where they served.

Series Editor
    Donald A. Luidens, PhD
    Director, Van Raalte Institute

Project Editor
    JoHannah M. Smith
    Van Raalte Institute

Editor-in-Chief and Publisher
    Jacob E. Nyenhuis, PhD
    Director Emeritus, Van Raalte Institute

Editorial Board
    The Albertus C. Van Raalte Research Professor
    and the Senior Research Fellows of the Van Raalte Institute

Contents

	List of Maps and *Photo Courtesy Abbreviations*	viii
	Acknowledgments	ix
	Preface	xiii
1.	Too Lucky in Love	1

Part I: Faith

2.	Madonna and Child	17
3.	Van Ess-ing	27
4.	Mesopotamia, Land of Legend	37
5.	Land of "Two Seas"	51
6.	Manama Memories	67
7.	Bitter, Bitter Tears	77
8.	Of Beards and Brains	85
9.	The Story of a Book: The Eleventh Century Speaks to the Twentieth Century	97
10.	The Ins and Outs of Bahrain	103
11.	Fast Dhow to Doha, Qatar	111
12.	Bahrain Blues	123
13.	Road to Riyadh: Oases of Al-Hasa and Katif, 1934-35	131
14.	Riyadh	147
15.	The Little Fort: Kuwait	163

Part II: Hope

16.	Glimpsing the Sultanate	187
17.	Muscat and Matrah Matriculation	203
18.	Home Again	219
19.	Hospital Snapshots: The General (Men's) Hospital, Matrah	229
20.	Hospital Snapshots: The Women's Hospital, Muscat	247
21.	The Interior of "Old Oman" and Points South	257
22.	Headwinds and Tailwinds of War	269

23.	Coastal Epidemics	281
24.	Dhofar	291
25.	Hospital Snapshots, 1942-69: The Sharon Thoms Memorial Hospital for Contagious Diseases	307
26.	Relief, Rest, and Relaxation	313
27.	Hospital Snapshots: Transition and Development	329

Part III: Love

28.	The Other Wise Man	357
29.	Epilogue: Journey's End	365
	Afterword	371
	Endnotes	373
	Glossary of Foreign Terms	401
	Bibliography	409
	Index	429

Maps

Al-Hasa Oasis 1937	135
Riyadh, Sa'udi Arabia, 1937	148
Kuwait 1947	167
Muscat 1765	194
Extent of the Sultan's Influence 1928	209

Photo Courtesy Abbreviations

WWT	Wm. Wells Thoms
SJT	Sharon J. Thoms
MTC	May DePree Thoms Collection
WTC	Wells Thoms Collection
RB	Russell Block
HD	Col. Harold Dickson
PD	Public domain
LD	Louis Dame
JD	Jane Dieulafoy
SST	Sultan Sa'eed bin Taymur
TH	Timothy Harrison

Acknowledgments

Some books require a "village" of people to bring them to completion. This book would certainly have been quite different without the help of so many. I happily acknowledge the many people in Oman and the Arabian Gulf countries who extended a warm welcome on my visits before and after the oil era. His Excellency Shaykh Abdallah bin Mohammed al Salimi, Oman's minister of *awqaf* and religious affairs, was most hospitable. His Excellency facilitated not only my visit to Oman to obtain oral histories but also my other visits to sites and people important to Dr. Wells and Mrs. Beth Thoms. To meet so many people who had either worked with or knew Dr. Thoms and to reaffirm these friendships was a great pleasure. Among many others, are included: Abdulla Khoda Rasoon, Gharib and Hassan Qambur al Mas, Yacoob Meerok, Shahoo Noor Mohammed al Zaydjali, Dr. and Mrs. C. Thomas, Muneer Toprani, Diyab Sakhar al-Aamri, Yusuf and Laila Haider, Suleiman Salim al-Khusaibi, Ghulan Rasool al-Zadjali, Abdul Baqi Abdullah, Mohamed Mansoor al-Maymani, Yousef Khudarasoon-Abdulla, and Dr. Achamma and Dr. T. P. Varghese. The Al Amana Centre (Matrah, Oman) deserves special mention. Staff members Tony Abraham and Bridget Ganguly extended hospitality beyond any reasonable expectation. Al Amana's directors, Rev. Michael S. Bos (now senior pastor, Marble Collegiate Church, New York) and Rev. Douglas Leonard (now senior pastor, Hopewell Reformed Church, Hudson Valley), also assisted.

I have benefited greatly from direct contact with all members of the extended Thoms family, including Dr. Wells Thoms and Mrs.

Beth Scudder Thoms, as well as Dr. Nancy Thoms Block (and Rev. Russell Block), Dr. Peter Thoms, Dr. Norman Thoms, and my wife, Lois Thoms Dickason. Without their knowledge of family lore, this book would have been incomparably poorer. The letters, documents, and photographs they made available have proved essential in recounting Wells Thoms' story. Other members of the family in the Midwest also shared valuable information, including the late Reverend Lewis R. Scudder III and Nancy Scudder, who assisted in interpreting Arabic and Arab culture and transcribing tape recordings. Lew's knowledge of the Arabian Mission, expressed in his sweeping history, *The Arabian Mission's Story*, provided an excellent point of departure for this work.

The Arabian Mission colleagues of Wells and Beth Thoms also provided supplemental insights, particularly Rev. Jay and Midge Kapenga, Rev. James and Joyce Dunham, Dr. Harvey and Margaret Doorenbos, Rev. Harold Vogelaar, Dr. Bern Draper, and Dr. Donald and Eloise Bosch.

Not least is the support of the Arabian Mission Writers Guild, whose members (Donald Luidens, Paul Heusinkveld, Peter Kapenga, Paul and Rebecca Armerding, and Charles Gosselink) provided ever-cordial encouragement as this project progressed.

The comments and suggestions of many others have also proved important as the manuscript edged to completion, including those of H. Byron Earhart (professor of comparative religion at Western Michigan University), Dr. Azzam Kanaan (CEO of KNI Southwest Michigan Imaging), Mr. Peter Kapenga (principal emeritus, Al Raja' School, Bahrain), Ms. Lois Veldman (retired missionary educator), Dr. Donald Bruggink (professor emeritus of Western Theological Seminary), and Lois Thoms Dickason. "Beta Readers," for whose reactions I am grateful, include Wilma Rowe, Prof. Ed Meader, Lois Young, Otis Rowe, Dr. Richard Hodgman, Dr. Jerold Veldman, Dr. Cherian Thomas, Dr. Kalindi Thomas, Charles Gosselink, and David Bosch. All enriched the final product. None bears responsibility for remaining infelicities, misinterpretations, or errors.

I am particularly grateful for the support of the staff and the resources of the A. C. Van Raalte Institute and the Van Raalte Press in Holland, Michigan. Dr. Donald Luidens (the institute's director) made special efforts to escort this manuscript to press. Dr. Jacob Nyenhuis (editor-in-chief) also tracked and nudged the project forward. Dr. Donald Bruggink (senior research fellow) enthusiastically affirmed my progress and thinking at every stage of the project. Not least, JoHannah

Smith (project editor) assured the quality and finish of this book, for which I am most thankful.

Rev. Jhonny Alicea-Báez (director of Global Mission, RCA) provided permission to access archival materials. Archival and library support was provided by many more and is gratefully acknowledged, including Russell Gasero (Archives of the RCA), Geoffrey Reynolds (Joint Archives of Holland), Lori Trethewey (Joint Archives of Holland), Debbie Ussher (Middle East Center Archives, St. Antony's College, Oxford University), Eileen Hicks and Paul Lierman (Penney Photo Services, Penney Farms), Greg Anderson (the W. E. Upjohn Center, Western Michigan University), the Hartford Seminary Archives, the British Library, the UK National Archives, and the Western Michigan University Libraries.

Finally, given the lack of standardization of Gulf Arabic phonetics in English, I have provided my own version of how Gulf Arabic names, places, and phrases sound in American English. The initial use of an Arabic term is identified in the text; for reminder definitions, please see the glossary.

Preface

Imagine a world composed of Mark Twain's *A Connecticut Yankee in King Arthur's Court* jumbled together with *Grey's Anatomy*, the *Injeel* (the Gospels of Jesus), the Pentateuch/Torah, tribalism, homeopathy, the four humors of Greek medicine, the gurgling Waters of Paradise, European imperialism, parching heat, hellish deserts, the Ottoman Empire, blood feuds, British Common Law, and absolute monarchies. Throw in folk medicine, pain therapy, Dr. Harvey Cushing and modern allopathic medicine, Abu Sina (Avicenna) and ancient Arab medicine, petroleum prospecting "fever," and good-old self-reliance. All this and more formed the everyday world in which Wm. Wells Thoms thrived for more than forty years.

Dr. Wells Thoms profoundly affected the lives of an untold number of people in the Persian/Arabian Gulf region.[1] Fifty years after his departure, this extraordinary man is still revered in the southeastern Arabian kingdom of Oman. For Muslim Arabs to remember and talk about a non-Arab, particularly a Christian missionary, in such salutary ways is most unusual. Some of the stories they tell of him are even

---

[1] As with many labels, the name tells a lot politically. Long called the Persian Gulf, the body of water separating the Arabian Peninsula from nearby Iran (née Persia) has been variously labeled depending on one's political vantage point. For the purposes of this volume, the neutral term "the Gulf" will be used, being mindful of the competing political entities.

true—others have evolved into legend. Today, few Omanis remain that knew Wells personally. Nevertheless, stories about him still abound. In light of this undimmed afterglow, it seemed more important than ever to distill his life into a book.

As I set out on this task, I wondered how hard writing a biography could possibly be. Does one not just write the facts? Will they not simply organize themselves into compelling prose? Wells' life story stretches across ten countries and almost a hundred years. The petroleum age in the Gulf, the distant echoes of World War II, and the end of the British Empire all disrupted his life in midcareer. As I plunged further into my investigation, I found that research on the history, politics, religion, and culture of Gulf countries, of course, had to come first, and I realized that Wells' biography might stall because of its ungainliness and complexity.

With all of this in mind, I wrote a nonfiction story, and although some components of my retelling might stand up in court, others might not. We never possess quite enough rock-solid information to be certain of our facts. No matter how many documents or letters we have, there is never sufficient evidence to corroborate the full story. Gaps explicable and inexplicable appear in any person's life journey. Moreover, between the cover pages of a biography, every life must inevitably be compressed.

The story of Wells Thoms—larger than life, in so many ways—must be shaved down to book size. Understanding his life and times requires remembering, and memory is tricky. The remembering and reintegration of events in this book constitute an effort to recreate as seamless a story as possible. In accord with acceptable standards of biography writing, there should be few situations or events that do not fit consistently and plausibly with other events and with the story's general frame of reference.[2] Thus, this biography strives to be complete and authentic.

This biography is also a social history of the Arabian Gulf on the eve of its petroleum-based renaissance. It contributes to historical understanding in ways a conventional history might not. In parts, it is narrative nonfiction, that is, based on actual events that occurred, preserved in letters and other documents created either at the time they occurred or on later recollection. Key personalities in Arabia and the Gulf played outsized roles in their communities and countries in those days, whether they were Arabs or foreigners, and Wells Thoms was a friend and confidant of many of these key personalities.

2 Popper, "Historical Explanation."

An understanding of Arab societies in the years before petroleum is essential in order to appreciate the context in which Wells and Beth Thoms served. A collective forgetting of this era has occurred among many Arabs not only because of the disruptive impact that oil royalties have had on their way of life but also because most Arabs of the prepetroleum generations have now died. Perhaps it was simpler when traditional Arab culture and values were more prominent in daily life. Gulf peoples today are vastly more westernized, cosmopolitan, sophisticated, and educated than in the decades before World War II. At the same time, many countries are, paradoxically, more religiously oriented.

Because of this collective amnesia about the Arab past, some attempt to reconstruct the pre-oil era in idealized ways. The reality is that the Arab past was neither golden nor wayward. People did the best they could, often in extremely difficult circumstances. The past was neither worse nor better than the present. It was what it was, and it reminds us of the extent to which Arab Gulf societies have changed.

Poverty—so widespread in the days before the disruptive effect on the local economies of Japanese cultured pearls, before oil riches swamped the region, and before all Gulf economies were so grimly squeezed by the worldwide Great Depression of the 1930s—no longer beclouds most Gulf Arab countries. These early twentieth-century decades, ones during which Wells served so faithfully, were a time of enormous economic hardship throughout the region and had an impact on the daily lives of all with whom Wells and Beth and other missionaries came in contact.

Readers may find it incomprehensible that Wells and Beth Thoms would practice medicine (essentially pro bono) for a lifetime among people so unlike themselves. Dr. Thoms could have pursued a successful medical career in the United States. There is no doubt that he would have become much wealthier monetarily if he had done so. Wells and Beth would have been highly respected in any community in America. It seems counterintuitive that they would sacrifice creature comforts, friends, income, and other advantages in return for hardship postings in Basrah, Bahrain, Kuwait, and Oman. Yet, they did just that, and they deemed their life in Arabia to be rich beyond compare.

This volume portrays the times, places, and people with whom Dr. and Mrs. Thoms interacted during their forty-year careers in the Middle East. Sincerely trying to understand the times and people of this era means that this book does not preach one position or persuasion over another. My effort does not unfairly favor the Arabian Mission of the Reformed Church in America (RCA) nor Protestant Christianity more generally—even though the Thomses were devoted Christian medical missionaries, supported by the RCA. Their record does not require burnishing or tarnishing.

Readers will find supplemental endnotes arranged by chapter in the back matter, a glossary, and an extensive bibliography. It was essential to cross-check all my information as much as possible against accepted authority to avoid writing a hagiographic biography based on family lore alone. The test of plausibility underlies all my narratives. We can but try to remember past times constructively, with affection and goodwill toward all the players in the drama.

CHAPTER 1

Too Lucky in Love

*I've thought over your proposal,
and if it is still open, I accept.*

Ann Arbor, Michigan, summer 1929

The conductor's "All Ab-o-o-a-rd!" and the piercing "thweet" of his whistle interrupted their tender, bittersweet embrace. With a wrenching goodbye, Wells waved her train into the distance and returned to the Phi Chi fraternity house.

As he entered the hall, the housekeeper intercepted him and asked, "Didn't you see this letter? It's from India. It's been here a couple of days. I wondered if you had missed it."

"Thanks."

That's odd, Wells thought, taking the limp khaki-colored envelope and turning it over in his hands. Mother didn't go to India this year; it wasn't her turn as a missionary to vacation there. He examined the envelope that sported a smeared postmark that nearly obliterated the British India stamp. He slowly slit it open and unfolded the contents, a single thin foolscap sheet. Written neatly it said:

Dear Wells,

I've thought over your proposal, and if it is still open, I accept.

Beth

Wells Thoms read and reread the note a half dozen times, trying desperately to comprehend its few words. Then its implications exploded like unstable gunpowder. He now had two fiancées.

Wells never dreamed he would be engaged to two beautiful, young women. And never, ever two at the same time. Now, however improbably, it had happened. It almost took his breath away. He had never heard of such a predicament among his acquaintances, and it made him feel even worse thinking he had invented, no matter how unwittingly, a new wrinkle in the vocabulary of love triangles.

His mind raced, one thought cascading after another. He needed help. He needed to turn the clock back. He needed a miracle. He did not know what he needed. Maybe Beth's letter changed nothing. Maybe it changed everything. "Okay, okay, don't panic. Let's review. Think," he told himself. He subsided into a reverie:

Beth ... three-plus years ago ... could be the soulmate I always hoped for. Loyal ... independent ... deliberate ... smart ... athletic ... wonderful. I was head-over-heels about her. After she graduated from Oberlin College, she went to India for a year to help her parents. It has dragged into three years. Meanwhile, I finished medical school, did my internship and surgery residency. ... India and the British Raj ... worlds away ... too far. ... Letters take more than five weeks. One letter every two or three months was not a real conversation. ... When she left we were on hold. I proposed anyway ... did not want to let her exit my life ... she didn't say no ... just an indefinite maybe. ... Now, it is a yes.

I wanted to marry Beth so much. ... "When you make up your mind, let me know. I'll be waiting for you," I remember saying. ... She was supposed to return in a year. ... Then that lady missionary teacher in India died. ... Beth accepted the mission's three-year teaching contract offer. ... Three years. An eternity. ... Fewer and fewer letters. ... After two-plus years, was she saying "no" without actually saying so? ... Seemed like it. ... I started halfway looking for someone else. ... Now I know she wasn't sending a message ... just big gaps in between those ever-so-polite letters.

Then came my internship at Gorgas Memorial Hospital in

Panama.... Gorgas with its great reputation in tropical medicine. ... My Hope College buddy, Harry Brinckman, and I went there together.... The best part was that as US Public Health Service employees, Harry and I received $100-a-month salaries plus room and board.... Almost too good to be true.... What a great time we had.

Panama... and Alma.... So attractive.... A nurse, a no-nonsense professional on the job ... a great sense of humor ... very poised.... Off duty, she was completely different.... Her cheerful manner ... that blond hair and those eyes, such sparkle.... I liked her right away.... One thing led to another.... Suddenly, it was personal.... Charmed ... she got under my skin ... captured my heart.... It was reciprocal ... like a cliche movie romance.... Some rough spots though, like our differences in background and hopes for the future.... But, they would smooth out, wouldn't they?

Could not forget Alma after returning to Ann Arbor.... Then the unexpected thoracic surgery opportunity came my way. ... A wonderful opportunity. My future would be set, our future would be set.... I popped the question.... Alma said yes, and I thought it was just swell.... So happy, I brought Alma from Panama to meet my family and see Ann Arbor.... Everything went perfectly.... The future looked so bright.

And now this: "If it is still open, I accept."

Wells rocketed back from his reverie. Without realizing what he was saying, he mumbled aloud: "My word is my word. I am not a cad. I did not deliberately create this problem. I have got to do the right thing." He had given his word twice, of course, but that was beside the point. What on earth was the right thing to do? The answer came with clarity: "Yes, yes, that's it. My more recent pledge to Alma tops my earlier proposal to Beth." But he did not quite believe himself.

Ethel "Beth" Talcott Scudder

Beth Scudder's parents were missionaries in India; in fact, she came from one of America's legendary Protestant missionary families.[1]

---

[1] The saga of the Scudders of India, Arabia, and Africa began when Dr. John Scudder, progenitor of this missionary line, went to Ceylon (Sri Lanka) in 1819. He subsequently transferred to Madras (Chennai), in India, in 1834, when the East India Company could no longer prevent Christian missionaries from entering its territories. Scudder's seven sons returned to India as missionaries

Three generations of her forebears had served as doctors in India, where Beth was raised. Wells and Beth had met as children in South India, where they both attended Highclerc School in the hill station of Kodaikanal.² Their paths diverged after high school, but they ran into each other again in 1922 when Wells had a summer job as an attendant on a Hudson River Day Line cruise boat in New York City. Beth and her relatives signed up for an excursion on his ship.³

Wells was instantly smitten by the poised coed whom he had remembered as just a skinny school girl. She seemed to radiate energy despite her apparent reserve. Whether Beth realized it or not, she had thrown Wells for a loop. By the end of the all-day excursion, however, they had exchanged only pleasantries. Afterward, Wells realized he did not even have her address. The following summer, while deep in his medical school responsibilities, Wells discovered by chance that Beth was attending Oberlin College. He wrote immediately. She answered by return mail. A regular correspondence ensued. Wells squeezed in as many trips to Oberlin as his studies would allow, and occasionally, he welcomed her to Ann Arbor. When Wells discovered Beth was planning to travel cross country to San Francisco with her aunt and uncle and then take a ship to India after graduation, he borrowed a buddy's Buick Roadster and intercepted them en route. He rashly proposed marriage as they trailed her uncle and aunt from campground to campground across Indiana and Illinois.

Lithe, athletic, vibrant, Beth had had several promising, down-to-earth, Midwestern beaux. Although she idealized farming and reveled in the feel of rich, loamy soil between her fingers, Beth was not sure she wanted to live in the Midwest. Despite her affection for a set of Oberlin women friends⁴ and her enjoyable time as a summer counselor at Harkness Camp (an Ohio YMCA/YWCA retreat for Cleveland inner city kids). Beth did not really understand or appreciate Midwestern mores.

---

and helped to form the Arcot Mission of South India. Beth had grown up in this family enterprise. See Scudder, *A Thousand Years in Thy Sight*. See also endnote 1:1, p. 373.

2   See endnote 1:2, p. 374.
3   Coincidentally, Wells discovered that the cruise boat's cook, Henry, was a young man he had known in childhood. The British Royal Navy had freed Henry from slavery when he was a boy and placed him in the Arabian Mission Freed Slave Boys School in Muscat, Oman. At the time, the school was being run by Wells' uncle James Cantine.
4   Their informal club of eight coeds named themselves the Sapphires—"Saps" for short—and were lifelong friends.

Scudder women were fearless. Hers was a family of liberated women. Beth knew their reputation all too well. Her idol as a teenager, Dr. Ida S. Scudder, had founded India's first women's medical college in 1900.[5] Beth wondered if she, too, should pursue a career and, if so, then in what field and where? With a degree from Oberlin College and a teaching certificate, with a physical education major, she was obviously prepared to become a teacher. Should she be a homemaker and raise a family instead? Or should she seek to do both? Uncertain of her future, she elected to take a year back in India to think things over. That year stretched into three. After three years in India, however, she still did not have a goal or a consuming focus in her life.

During an Indian wedding ceremony, Beth had a sudden epiphany. Wells Thoms, with his energy, creativity, charisma, machismo, exuberance, sense of humor, and star quarterback's sixth sense, was the one. To accept his proposal seemed absolutely right, so off Beth sent her attenuated letter, even though she had lingering reservations. She was no good at gushing nonchalantly or sparring verbally. She could not pretend their relationship had grown more intimate since she last saw Wells. Her words plopped onto the page resisting elegant sculpting and harmonious charm. She had already pared her letter to a minimum of words. If she did not say yes now, she never would. So, into the post went the ever-so-blunt message, "If it is still open, I accept."

Default decision

Wells had started medical school with one career objective in mind: he wanted to become a medical missionary like his parents. Specializing in tropical diseases had taken him to the Panama Canal Zone. Then Dr. John Alexander, a noted thoracic surgeon, offered him a coveted position on the staff at the University of Michigan hospital, possibly upending his initial plan. As Wells contemplated the dilemma of his two fiancées, he began to question that marvelous opportunity. Had he really abandoned his original idea? What was his life purpose—stimulation and "kicks," prosperity, security, unconventionality, fun? Did morality or faith count? Yes, of course they did, but what were the metrics for degrees of morality and faithfulness?

---

[5] Ida S. Scudder was Beth's father's cousin. Everyone who knew her called her Aunt Ida. Today the medical school and hospital complex she founded ninety miles west of Chennai in Vellore, Tamilnadu, is one of India's equivalents of the Mayo or Cleveland Clinics. See Wilson, *Dr. Ida*.

To put self-interest ahead of the people I love is not fair, he thought. I should select my wife on her own merits, not on the career I want. Because Alma and Beth are both so wonderful, and because I really cannot decide, I am going to stick to my original inclination—it has to be Alma, not Beth.

The next day, he wrote Beth. How could he sugarcoat the message? Better he should express himself unequivocally. Better to be direct than to pussyfoot around with the old, "It's not you, it's me" ploy, because of course that was not true. What had happened had happened. Nor could he write Beth a chatty letter saying their courtship had been just great, but now it was over. As he composed his fateful letter, he felt as if he was engraving his epitaph onto the paper. He felt sick:

Dear Beth:

Sorry, it's too late. I'm engaged to Alma, an American nurse at Gorgas.

Wells

Beth replied, "with heavy heart" (as she wrote in her diary), congratulated him, and offered them her best wishes. Why oh why, she wondered, had she waited so long to respond? And so, it seemed, that was that.

Plan A

Wells' original career trajectory seemed so straightforward. It was to follow in his parents' footsteps and pursue a life of discipline, even hardship, practicing medicine in the Persian Gulf as a member of the RCA's Arabian Mission. The life of a Christian missionary doctor offered little prestige, recognition, or material reward. It came equipped with difficult desert living, among strangers in places far away from friends and family in North America. The food would be odd, and the cultures and the language very different, difficult, and demanding. There would be uncertainties, risks, and real danger. The weather in the Gulf was one of the most stressful anywhere in the world. None of the conveniences of life then available in the United States or the Panama Canal Zone existed in the Gulf.[6] Plan A, as Wells came to think of it,

---

[6] Most countries of the Gulf region today have very high standards of living, access to the latest in fashion and technology, low energy costs, and superb health care. Theirs has been a "renaissance," triggered by the revenues of vast petroleum and natural gas reserves. Our story, however, refers to the time when petroleum and

fulfilled his parents' vision and call—and that had felt incredibly right. He had longed to follow this path.

In pursuit of his vision, he had talked with Dr. Paul Harrison, one of the Arabian Mission's pioneer physicians, a fellow of the American College of Surgeons. Harrison encouraged him and spoke enthusiastically about medical mission work among the Bedouin nomads of Arabia, whom Harrison greatly admired. This role was definitely not for a social climber, said Harrison. He himself had turned down an appointment at Boston's Massachusetts General Hospital and work with the stellar neurosurgeon, Dr. Harvey Cushing, in favor of healing the sick in Arabia. Cushing could not understand why Harrison had turned down Mass. General—then the most advanced medical institution in the United States.

Wells thought his decision would have been easier if the Holy Spirit would have just thwacked him on the side of his head. Or had He? Wells just did not know. Was he crazy to think that setting up a medical practice in Arabia was his lifelong calling? Becoming a medical missionary did not rank even at the bottom of most people's priority list.

Wells had thought Beth would be perfect for a Plan A life. Wells and Beth were both third-culture kids, born and raised outside the United States by parents who were born-and-bred Americans. The America that Wells and Beth knew was one they had learned about while growing up in Arabia and India in the age before radio. At best, Wells and Beth had a Norman Rockwell-like, *Saturday Evening Post* cover image of the States. They both felt comfortable among people of diverse backgrounds and languages. Beth spoke Tamil, a South Indian language, fluently. Wells had grown up speaking Arabic. Wells believed they could live almost anywhere, that Beth would prefer a Plan A life. That she was not trained in healthcare, however, as was Alma, was a drawback.

Plan B

In contrast to the uncertainties of Plan A, Plan B was the more conventional one. It centered on a medical career in the United States. The practice of medicine at the University of Michigan with Dr. Alexander would have enticed any young doctor. The prospect of advancing thoracic surgery, living comfortably, enjoying good times

---

natural gas had not yet transformed living standards in the Gulf, a time when traditional Arab tribal cultures and customs prevailed.

in Ann Arbor (a cultural Mecca even then), basking in the prestige of the medical school, and taking in Big Ten football games was quite enticing. How could Wells turn Dr. Alexander down? Every time Wells thought about Plan B, Alma seemed a perfect partner. He had really come to love this poised blonde with the fair complexion and penetrating blue eyes. She had intelligence, grace, and conversational ability that would be perfect in Ann Arbor's university community. She was playful, animated, intelligent, and relaxed away from work. He prized and loved her greatly.

Unforgettable memory

Reading Beth's letter repeatedly in the weeks after he turned her down, Wells argued within himself. Have I done the right thing for both Alma and Beth? There does not seem to be any right thing I can do for them. What a headache. Wells re-examined his once-clear plans in light of the new career that awaited him. Plan A versus Plan B. During his ruminations, his conscience would not leave him alone, and a single dream haunted him.

He would awaken from restless, fantasy-filled sleep every night, with the same, crystal-clear memory from his boyhood in Oman, in southeastern Arabia. In his dream, Wells was about nine years old, walking slowly with his father through the city gate of Matrah, the main seaport of Oman. The gate boasted heavy teak doors, locked every night to keep out intruder brigands.

Outside this imposing structure, a dozen or more people dressed in filthy rags squatted on the ground. Their emaciated, dirty, deformed faces, hands, and limbs shocked the nine-year-old Wells. Some had no nose, fingers, or ears. All had ghastly ulcers and oozing sores. Ghoulish to look at, they were completely impassive. In total silence they sat, with unwashed begging bowls at their feet. They waited patiently for food, coins, or cast-off clothing to be tossed at them from a distance by merciful townsmen. The beggars gazed at him empty-eyed, saying nothing. In his nightmare, Wells would turn to his father and ask: "Father, why doesn't someone help these people? Why are they suffering so, living in this way?"

His father would answer each time in the same manner: "These people have leprosy, a disease that has been in existence since biblical times.[7] Their fingers and toes become stinging hot and then numb,

---

[7] Leprosy today is known as Hansen's Disease, named after the Norwegian doctor who had spent his life studying it.

and they lose the use of their muscles. They lose their sense of touch. They do not realize it when they burn themselves or stub their toes. They develop sores that do not heal. They are malnourished and near starvation. The disease cuts off circulation to parts of their body, like their noses, so that their appendages do not feel pain as we do. Their noses and ears can just wear away from inadequate circulation."

"It's just awful, Father. Can't you help them?"

"No, my son. There is no known cure for leprosy. These people have been cast out of their families, their homes, and their villages. People here think leprosy is contagious. I cannot bring lepers inside the city wall to my little hospital. It is forbidden for them to be inside the city wall. If I brought them inside, I would offend everyone. Our medical practice here would stop entirely, and we would not be able to help any other people. We would have to leave the country. If I brought them to the hospital, how would I treat them in any case?[8] Begging at the city gate is the only thing left for them."

"Where do they live?"

"Up the wadi,[9] just there," his father would say, pointing. "They have no houses or tents. They sleep among the rocks or in little, cave-like depressions in the hillside. They have no possessions, except what they wear or carry.

"Perhaps when you grow up you can become a doctor," his father would conclude. "Maybe there will be new treatments available, and you would be able to help them."

Wells would wake in the depths of the night, chased into consciousness by this nightmarish conversation, indelibly etched into his memory.

Blissful agony of love

His was a double dilemma: Alma or Beth, or neither? Plan A or Plan B, or some yet-unknown plan? But this was not simply a logical, rational decision to be made. Wells was entirely human. How could he know the future? He reasoned, if he could make up his mind about which career he wanted, it would be much easier to discern who the right partner would be. Both career options were honorable, but which one was more truly in his heart of hearts? Or was the Holy Spirit calling him in some other direction?

---

[8] The original hospital in Matrah was in a house known as Beit al Baranda (veranda house), a museum today. It is located inside the city walls and close to the seafront.
[9] *Wadi*: valley.

One Sunday morning, Wells found himself in the First Presbyterian Church near the University of Michigan campus. The speaker, a missionary from India, gave an impassioned sermon, challenging students to pursue lives of Christian service. Wells, lost in thought and prayer, unexpectedly heard the closing lines of the Scripture reading in a new light:

> Lord, when saw we thee hungry, and fed thee? or athirst, and gave thee drink?
> And when saw we thee a stranger, and took thee in? or naked, and clothed thee?
> And when saw we thee sick, or in prison, and came unto thee?
> Verily I say unto you, inasmuch as ye did it unto one of these my brethren, even these least, ye did it unto me.[10]

Wells had always intended a life of service and had heard these words many times. That Sunday, however, they resonated in a new way. Suddenly the phrase, "Inasmuch as you did it unto one of these my brethren, even these least, ye did it unto me," captured his attention.

He recalled those dark hours of the night when nothing intervened between him and his inner self. He saw those silent lepers outside the gate. They were real people with names, like Latifa or Abdur Rahman, whose very identities had been taken from them when they became disfigured outcasts and had lost their last shred of dignity and humanity. Though discarded, they were not abstractions. They lived without hope of any kind. Were they not the least of these? Wells realized that many of them would be dead by now. On the other hand, Arabia and the Gulf in the 1930s were not very different from the way they were in 1910. Other leprosy victims would have replaced them at the gate. He shuddered at the thought.

In the next few weeks, a stark realization came to Wells. Plan A was overtaking Plan B. His father's challenge was becoming his own overpowering longing. He finally admitted he would have to tell Alma of his desire to pursue Plan A. He needed a fully committed partner in Arabia. He knew the toll that could be exacted, and he did not want Alma to be blindsided or think he had deliberately deceived her. She would have to want to go to Arabia, and she would have to freely accept the challenges, privations, and risks.

---

[10] Matthew 23:37-40 (American Standard Version, 1901).

Whenever he broached the issue, however, she made it clear that she would not accept those conditions, not even with reservations. She had said so again on her last visit to Ann Arbor when he proposed to her. Wells' dream of Arabia was his alone.

The more Wells considered Plan B, the more life in Ann Arbor grew less enticing. The more he envisioned the future, his commitment to Beth and to a Plan A, the more life in Arabia came into view.

Ultimately, Wells' feet propelled him to the Western Union telegraph office in Ann Arbor's railroad station. In a haze, he printed his short message in block letters and handed it to the telegrapher.[11] The operator carefully tapped seven words to Beth in Morse Code—dit-dah-dah, dit-dit...

WILL YOU MARRY ME STOP LETTER FOLLOWS STOP

WELLS.

Ever economical, Beth answered the next day: dah-dit-dah-dah, dit, dit-dit-dit...

YES STOP BETH.

Western Union's words were not cheap, not even for affairs of the heart.[12]

Wells somehow broke off his betrothal to Alma, but how he accomplished that task, the records do not report. It could not have been easy or pleasant, no matter how judicious his words. Repudiating a pledge of lifelong love and care would have been deeply wounding. It must have been a nightmare for Alma, as it was for Wells.

"How could Wells ever think of this?" she would have cried. He would try to explain. It was not because he was boorish, malicious, or indifferent. He felt compelled to renege on his proposal because, if he had chosen Alma and Plan B, he would have been haunted the rest of his life by the road he had not taken. Alas, such tragic choices and rationalizations mere humans were never intended to make.

Wells was caught in verbal brambles until the final, short drumbeat of a letter he had to write:

---

[11] Principal towns of the world were connected only by telegraph, over relatively slow lines by modern standards.

[12] The very day Beth's parents announced her engagement to Wells at a public reception in Vellore (Tamilnadu), Beth received Max Webster's proposal of marriage in the mail.

I'm so very, very sorry. It is my fault. But it cannot be. It must be over between you and me. It was so beautiful, and I wanted us to walk together through the years in an unbreakable partnership. You see, whether it is my destiny, my fate, or my call, I have had such vivid and recurring nightmares about failing to go to Arabia, I must go there. I would never ask you to accompany me where you do not wish or feel led to go. Arabia is not part of your destiny, I am sure. You have told me so yourself many times.

I did not manipulate your love for selfish purposes. I wish you the most wonderful life imaginable. Were it in my power, I would grant that (and more) to you. You are the priceless gem that some man, far more worthy than I, will value properly. May you find the life of satisfaction all people crave.

Wells

As he signed the letter, Wells rubbed his eyes and put his head in his arms on the table. How difficult, how impossible it was. Tears dripped onto the stationery even as he folded and inserted the small pages into the stamped envelope and sealed and addressed it. When he dropped the letter into the postbox, its old wrought-iron handle clunked definitively. There was no going back. He turned resolutely to Plan A and to Beth.

In later years, Wells referred as seldom as possible to this painful and bittersweet but so-beautiful-while-it-lasted episode that had almost kept him from Beth, Arabia, and his true calling. Wells always tried not to second guess—even though he had doubled back on that rule just this once. He was no fan of Monday-morning quarterbacking. There was no room to retread what might have been.

On July 5, 1930, Wells Thoms and Beth Scudder, serenely happy, walked out of the little church in Sleepy Hollow, New York, as a married couple. Their witnesses were Beth's Oberlin College friends, the "Saps," and surrogates for both their families. They honeymooned simply at a friend's rustic cottage on Round Pond, New Hampshire.

Mission welcome

The RCA's Board of Foreign Missions was delighted to appoint children of fabled RCA missionary families to active mission service. Given that diseases of the eye were so widespread in Arabia, the board asked Wells to take accelerated training in ophthalmology and eye surgery, and because there were no laboratory technicians in the

Arabian Mission hospitals at that time, the board also requested that Beth undertake lab technician training.

Although they were enthusiastic about their new missionaries, the board had little cash; the financial crash of 1929 had depleted their reserves. So, as they completed the requested medical training, the newlyweds were forced to live in a tiny studio apartment in New York and subsist on a skeletal budget. Given the privations of the Great Depression, they were fortunate the board could stick to its commitment to appoint them as missionaries to Arabia once their advanced training was completed.

Beth and Wells were deliriously happy knowing they were embarking on a meaningful life of service patterned on the example of Jesus Christ.

Part I: Faith

*"Nothing which is true or beautiful or good makes complete sense in any immediate context of history; therefore, we must be saved by faith."**

---
* Niebuhr, *The Irony of American History*, 63.

CHAPTER 2

Madonna and Child

In the 1930s, the Handley Page HP-42 was the world's premier airliner. With an enclosed cockpit, it was a biplane that flew slower than 100 mph and was considered to be the "Concorde" of its day.[1]

Jerusalem, spring 1931

Arabic language training brought Wells and Beth to Jerusalem in 1931, the first overseas leg of their missionary journey. They studied in Jerusalem under the tutelage of an esteemed scholar, Mu'allim Bargouti of the Mosque of the Dome of the Rock.

Jerusalem, with only fifteen thousand residents at that time, was a wonderful place to learn Arabic. To American Protestants, the Holy Land had always been a grand and glorious abstraction, but the reality that met Wells and Beth struck them profoundly. Jerusalem occupied an amazingly small area. The region had come under British and French control when it was "liberated" from the Ottomans after World War I, and the political situation was complex. The British and French dominated both the resident Palestinian Arabs—both Muslim and Christian—and the indigenous Jews. The native Eastern Orthodox Christians were a puzzle to Western Christians, especially to Protestants. Eastern Orthodoxy had been handed down from the

---

[1] See endnote 2:1, p. 374.

earliest traditions of Christianity and had changed little over the centuries. Despite the Crusades, Eastern Christianity had been little influenced by Western Roman Catholicism, and it had not experienced the reforming effects of Luther, Calvin, or Wesley, among others.

British prime minister Arthur Balfour's announcement that the British would establish a homeland for the Jews in Palestine was the cause of much apprehension and uncertainty while Wells and Beth sojourned in Jerusalem. The British had also made pronouncements supporting preference toward Palestinians. These opposing official statements made imperial policy ambiguous at best and spineless at worst. The great British Empire extended from Whitehall to Shanghai to Sydney and beyond. It had brought an unprecedented era of law and order (if not peace) to much of the world. Fully aware of the tensions around them, Wells and Beth believed it was not their place to take the empire to task for its Palestinian muddle.[2] They did not have access to the halls of imperial power. Their call was to a section of Arabia on the outer rim of the empire, so they soldiered on in the classroom, mindful of the uncertainties but not absorbed by them.

In September Beth and Wells interrupted their time in Jerusalem with an excursion just north of Palestine to Beirut, Syria (not yet Lebanon). The reason for the trip was to take advantage of the superior hospital facilities at the American University of Beirut. There, on September 15, 1931, they happily welcomed their firstborn, Nancy Fisher Thoms. She was easy to love and the first of several children Wells and Beth had hoped to have.

Christmas 1931

"How about going by plane to Baghdad?" Wells asked Beth. "I just learned at Thomas Cook's that Imperial Airways has the newest, biggest, and best airliner flying the leg from Palestine to Baghdad and India. It is a scheduled service with reasonable fares, not like the flight of the Graf Zeppelin that only hovered over Jerusalem last spring.[3] That flight showed only the German flag in these parts but did not land. We could get to Baghdad in a day or so by plane. It would be preferable to both the exhausting trip by Nairn bus or the month-long voyage

---

[2] Nor could they have foreseen the much-intensified, Israel-Palestine impasse that has occurred since their deaths.

[3] The Graf Zeppelin made two flights to the Middle East. The second one in April 1931 made a ceremonial pass over Jerusalem without landing before proceeding to Cairo and returning to Germany.

Graf Zeppelin above Jerusalem, April 1931 (WWT)

through the Suez Canal and around the Arabian Peninsula by the P&O to Bombay and then onward by BI (British India) ship to Basrah."[4]

The desert "highway" that the Nairn bus took was not a highway at all, as Beth knew from having traversed it on her return from India in 1929. Most of the route from eastern Syria to Baghdad was a naturally hard-packed, desert "pavement." Buses bounded along the track and sometimes got stuck in sand or mud. In hot weather, the desert evaporative coolers on the buses provided a modicum of air-conditioning, until their onboard water tanks ran dry. There were no food or bathroom facilities along the way. It would have been a relatively short but difficult trip with a young baby. It did not have much allure. Nor did an extended boat ride.

"If we choose to fly, we'll have to go from here via the meter-gauge Jezreel Valley Railway to Haifa and then on to Semakh, where the aerodrome is. Because Semakh doesn't have a hotel, we'll have to take a short detour by car to a hotel in Tiberias, on Lake Tiberias[5] itself. It would be an amusing jaunt, almost like traveling by

SS Strathaird, P&O Line, ca. 1930 (PD)

---

[4] P&O, the Peninsular & Oriental Steamship Co., had the Royal Mail contract to haul mail to India and Australia. The BI, the British India Steam Navigation Co., linked British colonial ports and dependencies in Asia and Africa. The British Empire was truly a maritime one, and these companies were key reasons the empire succeeded.

[5] In biblical times, Lake Tiberias was called the Sea of Galilee.

train in South India," explained Wells, referring to Beth's childhood travels in India.

Aeroplane. The prospect shocked Beth at first. As she and Wells talked about it, the idea changed from an outlandish notion to a logical choice. Most important to Beth and Wells was the welfare of two-month-old Nancy and the need to transport her to Basrah, Iraq, with minimal stress. They opted to take the aeroplane.

Basrah bound

Beth sat in their small pension perched on the shore of Lake Tiberias drinking in the December morning sun with a mug of hot tea. She was smiling contentedly about the impending flight, firmly convinced their travel choice was infinitely better than taking either the Nairn bus across the desert or the P&O boat through the Suez

A Nairn bus at a desert stop, ca. 1929 (PD)

As she watched in reverie, an Imperial Airways Short Brothers flying boat that had originated in Genoa, Italy, splashed down onto the sea in front of her. Lake Tiberias served as Imperial Airways' Middle Eastern "hub"—the place where land plane flights for India and Africa met seaplane flights from London.[6] All flights used visual flight rules. No planes flew after dark or when visibility was poor. As a result, it was a multiday trip to span the empire. As the rowboat stroked across the water toward the landing, Beth wondered whether any "big fish" from Europe had been netted.

Imperial Airways Flying boat, Lake Tiberias, ca. 1930 (PD)

The mission of Imperial Airways was to speed the delivery of government messages. London was gaining tighter control over its colonies and mandates—by the Cable and Wireless company's telegraph

---

[6] Imperial Airways soon switched its hub southward to the Dead Sea after complaints that the sanctity of Lake Tiberias from the time of Jesus of Nazareth was being violated by the intrusion of the flying boats.

HP-42 Hanno at Semakh, 1931 (PD)

for most urgent matters, by air mail for very important matters, and by sea mail for business and personal matters. The plane was undoubtedly filled with highest-value mail and freight. The passengers could be governors, viceroys, judges, generals, business tycoons, or *burra mems*.[7] All were treated deferentially by the waiting Airway staff, fed unimaginably well, and lodged in comfortable guest houses en route. Only children of VIPs traveled by airplane, so Nancy would be in a league all her own, as would Beth and Wells.[8]

The next day, the Thoms trio motored to the landing ground outside Semakh on the south shore of Lake Tiberias.[9] The plane had been fueled and was being loaded with mail and refreshments. They boarded this newest of world airliners, a veritable Concorde of its day.

Wells was excited to fly on the Hanno (nickname of the Handley Page HP-42). Its pilot proudly declared it was the first airliner to have an enclosed cockpit. Until then, pilots sat in open-air cockpits and wore leather helmets and goggles and leather jackets and gloves.

---

[7] *Burra mems*, the wives of the highest-ranking men in government service, were exceedingly influential because they often controlled social networking in colonial stations. Promotions often depended on whether one was perceived as a pakka (gentleman) or a *kaccha* (yeoman) in the pecking order maintained by these influential women.

[8] Wells, Beth, and Nancy were among the first few hundred travelers to fly this leg of the Imperial Airways route to the Orient.

[9] The Palestinian fishing town of Semakh (meaning "fish") no longer exists.

In Wells' mind, it was a fanciful Heath Robinson codebreaking machine—seemingly overdesigned and underpowered, with almost a box-kite design. Hanno seated passengers only in its forward section. A biplane with four engines, with tail ailerons and triple rudders, it was touted as crash proof.[10] It did not fly faster than one hundred miles per hour and had an effective altitude ceiling of nine thousand feet. It was not pressurized, nor was the cabin heated or cooled. In sum, it was luxurious.

Flying the furrow

Flying by compass and line of sight over the desert could be confusing. With few visible landmarks, the desert presented the eye with a numbing sameness for long stretches, and the horizon was frequently obscured. Planes easily wandered off course. Dust and sandstorms reduced visibility and wreaked havoc with engines. Planes either diverted away from storms or waited on the ground for them to pass. There was no alternative in this age of fair-weather flying. The fail-safe solution for the pilot of the Hanno was to follow a plowed, six-foot-wide furrow in the desert below, all the way from Syria to Baghdad. Where the desert pavement was too hard to excavate, a white stripe would be painted. Planes of all nations diligently "flew the furrow" from Damascus to Baghdad after World War I.

Hanno lumbered down Semakh's unpaved strip, accelerated slowly, and with a last ungainly bound lurched into the air. The pilot turned north up the rift valley, the plane clawing for altitude. Lake Tiberias was several hundred feet below sea level, and Hanno struggled to reclaim the altitude the flying boat had so readily sacrificed the day before. Reaching the required elevation, Hanno turned east across Syria. A winter storm on the horizon ended the day's flight at Rutbah Wells, in Anbar Province, Iraq. Passengers went into the fort, where they discovered clean, comfortable accommodations and a hot dinner. At Rutbah there were wells with potable water only forty-five feet below the surface, so it made a good middesert stopping point. Imperial Airways had cached fuel supplies below ground as well.

Wells was famished when they arrived in Rutbah. During the flight, the plane had bucked and bounced mightily on tremendous

---

[10] In 1936 the Horsa made a very hard landing in the desert west of Bahrain, injuring passengers and crew. All were transferred to the Bahrain mission hospital for treatment. The Horsa continued in service for several more years. In 1940 the Hengist disappeared over the Gulf of Oman without a trace. No HP-42s survived World War II.

thermals. He was a poor traveler and had upchucked his full English breakfast soon after takeoff. The steward saw him turning green and expertly slipped a basin in front of Wells saying, "Think nothing of it, sir. Happens to the best of us." Wells ate nothing the rest of the day.

It was Christmas Eve, and Rutbah seemed an unlikely place to celebrate Christ's birth. After their excellent multicourse dinner, Beth and Wells walked atop the walls of the fort. Stars glowed brightly in the clear, cold, desert night. Below them, in the distance, they saw that their plane was guarded from marauders. It was protected by French Mandate Zouave sentries, as were other planes from France, Germany, and the Netherlands.

After their evening wall-top stroll, Wells and Beth rejoined their fellow travelers—all men—sitting in the open square of the fort. Together they sang Christmas carols, each serenading in their own language: "Stille Nacht, Heilige Nacht," "It Came Upon a Midnight Clear." "Il Est Né Le Divin Enfant," "O Little Town of Bethlehem," and "Angels We Have Heard on High." It was not lost on these travelers "sweetly singing o'er the plain" that, as Beth cradled Nancy in her arms, they were looking on a contemporary "Madonna and Child." With the stars glimmering in the night sky, their thoughts turned nostalgically toward absent loved ones, remembered family Christmases, and the first Christmas, long ago.

Ancient Ctesiphon ("Tisphon"), 1924
(MTC)

Kerbela, Iraq, 1926 (MTC)

Central Baghdad, Iraq, 1929
(MTC)

The next morning, Hanno sputtered back to life and soon lifted skyward sluggishly to plow on to the furrow's end. The flight took them almost due east, just south of Ar Ramadi and nearly over Al Fallujah and then across Baghdad to the Hinaidi Aerodrome on the eastern edge of the city. If they drifted from the furrow and missed the city, pilots would look for other important landmarks, like the Imam Husayn Shrine of Kerbela or the Great Archway of Ctesiphon, to find their destination.

After relaxing and sightseeing for several days in Baghdad, Wells, Beth, and Nancy settled into a railway sleeper compartment for the final leg of their journey—an overnight, meter-gauge train ride to Basrah. "It's just like the South Indian Railway," exclaimed Beth. Although sulfurous coal smoke and soot filtered through the loose, rattling windows, they fell asleep to the reassuring lullaby of hisses and chuffs and the thin wispy whistle of the steam locomotive as it gently carried them to their new Basrah home.

CHAPTER 3

Van Ess-ing

"Who lusts after me?" called out the unwitting missionary nurse into the blackness of the night.

Basrah 1932

"We've come to Basrah to study with the greatest contemporary Western scholar of Arabic," announced Wells to the other missionaries sitting around the living room of the home of John and Dorothy Van Ess. "Rev. John Van Ess, renowned educator and linguist, has been in the Middle East since before World War I. He knows the difference between the Arabic of the Gulf and the Arabic used in the eastern Mediterranean. We learned some of those distinctions in Jerusalem while we were studying formal, newspaper Arabic. We must now focus on the Arabic spoken by people every day so we can function effectively in our work in the Gulf."

"Yes," affirmed John Van Ess, picking up the theme of linguistic idiosyncrasies while ignoring the apple polishing of the youthful Wells. "The Arabic of the Gulf has been infused with many non-Arabic words over the centuries. It is a patois quite different from classical Arabic. There are many words that have crept in from Persian and the languages of traders and migrants to the Gulf, the languages of India such as Baluchi, Gujarati, Sindhi, and Marathi, and others from Malay and African dialects related to Swahili. To top it off, there are words from English as well. Many Arabic words have migrated back into these other languages, too."

Turning to Wells, Van Ess said, "We'll start your formal language studies when I return from opening the school day for my young men—boys really." Van Ess rose, nodded a farewell, and left the room. Most of the other missionaries mumbled their goodbyes and followed him to the school.

As she poured one more cup of coffee for herself, Beth commented to Dorothy Van Ess, "It's kind of you to let us live with you while we learn Arabic." Then, unable to hold back her curiosity about this unusual couple, she let flow a torrent of questions. "How did the two of you meet? Were you childhood sweethearts? How did you and John happen to settle in Basrah?"

Dorothy smiled warmly, "Oh, John came to Basrah long before I did. Although he says he is from Grand Rapids, Michigan, his family emigrated from the Netherlands when he was a boy, and they spoke Dutch at home. He became a Dutch Reformed pastor after college, but he has always loved teaching and learning, and he wanted to be a missionary. Given his studious nature and his aptitude for Arabic, the mission board let him travel widely throughout the Middle East to see where and how the mission might best focus its efforts. He saw an absolute lack of modern, Western education and thought there was a wonderful opportunity for schools to teach contemporary subjects, as well as Christian ethics and values, without demeaning local knowledge or Islamic virtues. Because he came here before the First World War, a school in Basrah needed formal approval from Ottoman authorities. He applied for and received a *firman* (a permit from the caliph in Constantinople—today's Istanbul) to set up a school for the boys first and later a school for the girls.[1]

"John and I met here in the Gulf. He came in 1902, and I arrived in 1909. He was already in Basrah when I began learning Arabic in Bahrain. We met at the annual mission retreat shortly after I arrived. Something clicked, and we married in 1911. John had already opened his boarding school for boys, Medrissa el Raja' el Aali,[2] in Basrah. He was working hard, too, on developing his textbook, *Spoken Arabic of Mesopotamia*. It was first published in 1913 by the Oxford University

---

[1] See endnote 3:1, p. 375.
[2] The School of High Hope.

Press and has been reprinted several times since. You will probably use it in your language training.

"I am from the eastern United States and attended Swarthmore College, and I wanted to do more with my life than be a homemaker. John helped me to start the Medrissa el Raja' l'il Benaat,[3] a companion school for girls, because coeducation was out of the question. From here, it is just up the Ashar Creek, so I commute to work by *bellum*,[4] Basrah's equivalent of Venice's gondolas.

"John's Arabic is elegant," Dorothy continued. "Everyone loves the fluidity of his expression in both classical and colloquial Arabic. He's admired by well-educated Arabs, as well as British Arabists, like Gertrude Bell and St. John Philby. John is frequently asked to speak at public events. It is very odd because, even back in Ottoman days, he was always the only non-Muslim on the dais, and he was always the featured speaker. When King Feisal I died, John was asked to speak at his memorial service in Zubayr's leading mosque and to deliver a eulogy for the king. Perhaps you know Zubayr is a conservative Sunni[5] Muslim town not far from Basrah.

"John wondered whether it was a wise idea. His beautiful Arabic was given as the prime reason for asking him to speak. They told him, 'You are a missionary, and we trust you. He who is true to Allah will not betray Abdullah.'[6] He was still reluctant to speak because, of course, as an unbeliever in Islam, he would be making a major speech in the central mosque of a key Sunni Muslim city. Some Muslim mourners could have taken offense. He finally did it and did it very well, so I'm told."

Learning Arabic

One morning, John began his lessons with the pronouncement that "Arabic is the language of the angels.[7] But native English speakers often find it difficult to think in and pronounce Arabic simultaneously."

---

[3] The School of Hope for Girls.
[4] These gondola-like boats served as taxis, lorries, and pleasure craft. Manned by an oarsman.
[5] The Way—the main sect of Islam.
[6] A well-known Arabic proverb meaning that the person who is true to God will not betray his community. Literally: "He who is true to God will not betray the slave of God [Abdullah]."
[7] John Van Ess started his chapter, "The Language of the Angels," with this quote from Muhammad ed Damiri: "Wisdom hath alighted upon three things—the brain of the Franks [Europeans], the hand of the Chinese, and the tongue of the Arab." Van Ess, *Meet the Arab*, 42.

Warming to his subject, he continued, "It sounds so very different from our Irish-accented American English. I had an advantage because my family spoke both Dutch and English at home. I have often thought the guttural sounds of Dutch, coming from the back of the throat, may have made it easier for me to learn Arabic.[8] Arabic is endlessly fascinating. It has all the dignity of Latin, the variety of English, the beauty of Italian, the sonority of German, the flexibility of Greek, and the bewilderment of Russian.[9]

"To begin with . . . you cannot begin a word or syllable with a vowel. . . . You notice that when you try to say a word like 'sea-eagle,' there is a slight break between the two words as the throat opens to utter the word 'eagle.' . . . That feather-light sound, he [the Arab] calls a consonant, and it is known as a *hemza*. Then he has all the rest of our consonants plus some of his own. He has two kinds of *t* and two of *s* and three of *dh*. Then he has a vigorous gargle, and a high-pressure puncture, and a strangling *q* and a sort of vomit-like gag. . . . To learn some of these sounds, you listen to the bulbul[10] and practice his twitter, and to get the puncture effect, you must have had your throat properly dried out with desert sand, but to learn the gag you must literally sit at the knees of the camel and listen while he audibly and grouchily resents his burden."[11]

John expanded further, "Just before I arrived, Harry Wiersum[12] wrote a little essay on learning Arabic. Arabic is very daunting, and I wondered if I would ever come close to fluency in it." Then John shared the following, written by Henry, to make Wells and the other novices feel better, but at the time, they found it quite depressing.

> The verb and the noun require the most attention. A mere glance at the verb makes one stagger. We are told that some verbs have regular forms, while others—and they, alas! are the verbs in common use—depart from the ordinary, each forming a category by itself. The conjugations are most prolific, being no less than seventeen in number. This, though at first sight it appears gigantic, yields very nicely to the rules, so that it is a most

---

[8] There may have been some truth to this statement. Other missionaries of Dutch descent that developed excellent spoken Arabic, include Samuel Zwemer, Dirk Dykstra, Everdene DeJong, and Maurice Heusinkveld.
[9] Van Ess, *Pioneers in the Arab World*, 32.
[10] A songbird, sometimes known as "the nightingale of the east."
[11] Van Ess, *Meet the Arab*, 43.
[12] An early missionary to the Middle East.

interesting process to see how the same [three-letter] root yields so many different shades of meaning. As a matter of interest and curiosity, I have made the following attempt:

Katala	He killed
Kattala	He slaughtered
Kaatala	He fought
Aktala	He feigned death
Takattala	He was slaughtered
Takaatala	He fought a duel
Inkatala	He was killed
Iktatala	He lay killed
Iktalla	He was mangled
Istakatala	He sought death

It is a matter of comparative ease calmly to sit in your study and dig out the various shades of meaning which the peculiar form of the word suggests, but it is quite a different matter when you sit among a group of men rapidly chatting in a noisy bazaar; while, if you would make your first attempt at joining in the conversation, it would take you all day to get started.[13]

With these warnings echoing in their minds, Wells and Beth buckled down to language study. Wells agreed that, yes, Arabic was difficult. He was betting that common folk would not use very elegant Arabic. Theirs would be a sort of bazaar patois, a simplified Arabic with words borrowed from other languages. He was confident he could learn to treat patients with mostly colloquial Arabic. He suggested this shortcut to John Van Ess, who chuckled and launched into a legendary story about Mary Van Pelt, a mission nurse then in Kuwait.

"Just when you think you have it figured out, Arabic will surprise you. Mary learned how confusing Arabic is, with amusing results. When called upon to go to a Kuwaiti home in the middle of the night to attend a woman in childbirth, she thought she had the directions right. When she stood in front of the house she had intended and found the door fast closed against her and no lamp of welcome lit in the courtyard, she became anxious for her patient. In the middle of the narrow canyon of an alley, with her small lantern clutched in her hand, in a commanding voice, she demanded, '*Min yuhibbu-ni?*'[14]

"When she got no response, she called out ever more loudly,

---

[13] Wiersum, "First Experiences in Arabic."
[14] Scudder III, *The Arabian Mission's Story*, 347.

thinking she was asking, 'Who wants me?' What she did not know is the verb *yuhibbu* means 'want' or 'need' only when referring to things, such as food or clothes. When referring to people, its meaning changes dramatically. What she was really calling out again and again, in colloquial terms, was 'Who lusts after me?' She should have been asking '*Min yureed-ni?*' 'Who needs me?'

"A groggy male voice soon called from an upper floor, '*Ana, insha'Allah.*' 'I, God willing.' Shortly after that awkward exchange, Mary found the mother in labor and delivered a healthy baby. Only as she told others about her middle-of-the-night excursion did she learn what she had really said. All had a good laugh because her listeners had made their own linguistic faux pas."

Van Ess visitors

One evening after supper, Dorothy said to Beth and Wells, "Every Thursday you'll get a sabbatical from Arabic lessons. John, of course, has his school duties. On top of them, on Thursdays, the weekly 'fast' BI ship arrives in Basrah from Bombay and a few intermediate ports.[15] Inevitably, several of its passengers intend to visit John just as soon as they get off the boat. John, you see, is something of an 'institution,' and many want to try their ideas out on him and get his suggestions. He knows nearly all our visitors pretty well, so we have to adjust our weekly schedule to fit the ship's stay. We plan a large luncheon, not knowing who specifically will arrive on the boat. It's unthinkable not to feed visitors, and if you eavesdrop, you'll get a short course in current affairs."

Curious, Beth queried, "Have you been surprised at some of your visitors?"

Dorothy replied, "We have been more-or-less continuously surprised. In recent years, we haven't given it much thought. Our Thursday visitors have included Sheikh Mubarak the Great of Kuwait, Sheikh Khaza'al of Mohammerah,[16] T. E. Lawrence, Percy Cox, Arnold Wilson, H. St. John Philby,[17] British generals and high-ranking officers, Talib Pasha, Harold and Violet Dickson, assorted Maharajas from India, ministers of the new Iraq government, and even a female spy intent on spiriting away US Government secrets that John and I didn't know we had possessed.

---

[15] "BI" referred to the British India Steam Navigation Co. (or BISN). See endnote 3:15, p. 377.
[16] At the time, Mohammerah was part of Iraq; it is currently in Iran.
[17] See endnote 3:17, p. 377.

"Gertrude Bell, until her death, came to visit us regularly for long stays. I think she got tired of being the only woman among all those British administrators in Baghdad. We had such a good time when she visited; she was very refreshing. She would come by train from Baghdad and stay with us. She was a leading Arabist and the highest-ranking woman ever in British government service until that time.[18] We had many conversations about the future of Iraq—or the British Mandate for Mesopotamia, as it was called then. Gertrude knew Sunni Islam well. Iraq is heavily Shi'ah[19] Muslim, however, and Gertrude was not very sympathetic to them. John, on the other hand, knows both Sunni and Shi'ah Islam well, but he has always been much more attuned to Shi'ah belief and practice and to the idea that a republic would require popular Shi'ah support so they would believe they had a stake in a democratic government. Gertrude believed that Feisal I would make a good king for Iraq, even after his unsuccessful stint in Syria in the French Mandate. Feisal was a Sunni from the Hashemite family of the Sherifs[20] of Makkah. He was an 'outsider' both in terms of his branch of Islam and in his lineage from the Arabian Peninsula. John differed with Gertrude and favored Sayyid Talib, a Westernized Shi'ah of the family of the *naqib*, or governor, of Basrah."

With a sigh, Dorothy continued, "John supported Feisal's rule, despite his misgivings, and he sincerely appreciated everything Feisal was able to accomplish. John met with him from time to time, too. At his last meeting with him, King Feisal said: 'You are one of the few who have come to this land to give and not to get. By the milk of your mother, swear to me that you will always tell the Arabs the truth about themselves.'"[21]

After a thoughtful silence, Dorothy resumed, "John has written several Arabic grammar and textbooks. In fact, they are used by the British to teach Arabic to their own administrators. When they pass their Arabic exams, they proudly exclaim they had 'Van Essed.' Gertrude Bell admired John's book and penned him a jingle:

> V is for Van Ess, he once wrote a book.
> Perhaps you have seen it, or a copy you took.
> He deserves a gold medal, without any doubt,
> Not for what he put in, but for what he left out.

---

[18] See endnote 3:18, p. 377.
[19] Branch of Islam, perhaps 15 percent of all Muslims, found principally in Iran and Iraq. They recognize Ali as the legitimate successor to the prophet Muhammed.
[20] Ruling authority.
[21] Van Ess, *Pioneers in the Arab World*, 123.

John responded with a witty ditty for Gertrude on her next visit:

> G is for Gertrude, of the Arabs she's Queen,
> And that's why they call her Umm al Mumineen.[22]
> If she gets to Heaven (I'm sure I'll be there.)
> She'll ask even Allah "What's your tribe, and where?"[23]

"It was so sad," Dorothy mused. "Gertrude's star rose under Percy Cox and Arnold Wilson's sponsorships. Her influence waned after Cox retired. While we were on furlough in the United States, Gertrude met her end. Nobody seems to know whether it was accidental or purposeful. She paid a great personal price for her professional achievements, not counting her untimely end."

Wells and Beth understood that John Van Ess was a celebrity. It was a heady experience to see a missionary so widely appreciated in Arab and secular European communities and to know he did not have to sacrifice his integrity or his calling to preach the Word of God.[24]

Mastering Arabic

Beth had never before heard the sounds of Arabic. She was a diligent student and made slow but steady progress. "You learn Arabic so easily," Beth complained to Wells. "It's just not fair. I have to learn it by its logical structures, and that makes it is easier for me to read it than speak it."

"Remember, Beth, I heard spoken Gulf Arabic when I was a boy. It's quite different from the Arabic we learned in Jerusalem. Part of my learning is really relearning."

In later years, Wells was able to banter, joke, and pass news easily with people in the mejlises[25] or in the suq[26] of the great and small. Beth became an excellent teacher of Arabic to those who did not know how to read or write the language.

---

[22] Mother of the Faithful.
[23] Van Ess, *Pioneers in the Arab World*, 97-98.
[24] When she recalled John Van Ess in her retirement years, Beth noted that John was a free-lance ambassador, without portfolio, who practiced "soft diplomacy." Largely unrecognized as a representative of the US government, he was a genuine American hero. He was a forthright "man of the cloth" who endeavored mightily to not betray his God, his country, or "Abdullah."
[25] *Mejlis*: reception room in home, or hall for official gatherings.
[26] *Suq*: bazaar or marketplace.

In good time, they both passed the second-year language exams required of all novice missionaries. They, too, had "Van Essed."

CHAPTER 4

Mesopotamia, Land of Legend

If it's a boy they say,
"Praise God, you have a son."
If it's a girl they say,
"Praise God, the mother is well."

The Garden of Eden

One evening, Dorothy Van Ess remarked, "Beth, were you aware that we in Basrah live almost inside the original Garden of Eden?" Beth looked up from her Arabic text, surprised at the reference to the biblical site.

"Yes," John Van Ess chimed in, "the Bible is pretty clear about some of it. Dorothy and I have explored the idea of the Garden of Eden literally and figuratively. We are inspired by what we have unearthed. We do not, however, claim any one perspective on the Garden of Eden as the sole truth because of the deep antiquity of Mesopotamia's history, its relation to ancient Jewish culture, and the metaphorical nature of ancient legend. The specific facts are lost to memory, but the stories remain. According to Iraqi popular culture, the garden itself was located just up the Tigris River at al Qurna. The tomb of the Old Testament scribe Ezra is located there, too. There is even a tree some

Tomb of Ezra (Iraq), ca. 1926 (MTC)

claim was planted by Adam. Whether true or not, the stories inspire reverence."[1]

John paused to reflect on what he had just said, then continued with a chuckle. "We speculated once that the 'Tree of Life' was the date palm.[2] It grows so majestically, with its feet in the floods and tidewaters of Mesopotamia and its crown reaching to the scorching sun. Its dates feed people and animals so well. When you look around, Arabs even seem to subsist on dates. We've also speculated that the Tree of the Knowledge of Good and Evil was the grapevine. The temptation to excessively tipple the fermented juice of the grape may have represented one step too far in the direction of human irresponsibility, perhaps resulting in lackadaisical care for the plants of the garden.

"So, expulsion from the garden was possibly either literal or ecologically based or maybe both. Perhaps God's expulsion of Adam and Eve from the garden came because they did not flush away the salts in the soil with plenty of fresh water from the rivers each year, just as parts of California, Egypt, and India suffer now.[3] The build-up of salts in the soil would have decreased yields of the domesticated plants, perhaps to the point that people had to leave the original Garden because they could not support themselves there any longer. The Fall would then have come because God gave humans free will and

---

[1] Hamblin, "Has the Garden of Eden been located at last?" Hamblin's research corroborates the Van Esses' understanding. See Van Ess, *Meet the Arab*, 229. Their discussion of the garden is on p. 7. See also, endnote 4:1, p. 378.

[2] See Moldenke and Moldenke, *Plants of the Bible*. This is a masterful evaluation of ancient biblical zoo-geography and possible Edenic species. Now out of print.

[3] The area of "India" he referred to is present-day Pakistan and northwestern India.

the capacity to choose, and their own poor choices forced them to leave Eden. We humans are our own worst enemies, you know. Our strengths are our weaknesses—and the opposite may be true too, paradoxically. There is truth in more than one interpretation of this sacred legend, just as there are two creation stories in Genesis that do not conflict with but complement each other."[4] Again, he paused to let that sink in for his listeners.

"This area is still called Eden today—the word comes from old Babylonian meaning 'plain' or 'flat place.' Today the Marsh Arabs, known as the Ma'adan—'from Eden'—with their distinctive way of life, live there. I had an opportunity to explore the marshes back when the Ottomans still controlled Iraq—before Dorothy and I were married. On one of those trips, I went with Major Wilcocks, a British irrigation engineer, or maybe he went with me because I already knew several of the shaykhs.[5] Did you know, Wells, that the Euphrates is ten meters higher in average elevation than the Tigris on the other side of the marshes? Conceptually, it is not difficult to think of sending Euphrates water across lower Mesopotamia toward the Tigris to irrigate huge areas. Wilcocks—knighted by King George—believed he had found the four rivers draining the garden in the al Qurna area. No one else had been able to identify them until he did. That's a story for another day, though. I have letters to send on tomorrow's BI boat to Bombay, and I imagine you do, too."

Dakhil[6]

One afternoon, Wells and Beth picnicked with John and Dorothy on the grand waterway that ran alongside Basrah, the Shatt al-Arab. They took the mission's flat-bottomed bellum. As the cooling afternoon breeze wafted across the water and their boatman poled them leisurely, John barked at Wells, "What's the most important Arabic word after the required greetings when you are traveling in Arab lands?" Wells looked perplexed, so John answered his own question. "It's dakhil." Floating on the river had reminded him of an experience he had had as a young man that he thought would prove instructive to Wells and Beth.

---

[4] Genesis 1:1-2:3 and Genesis 2:4-25.
[5] *Shaykh*: clan leader.
[6] *Dakhil*: literally, "inside." It entails the implication of required hospitality toward and protection of strangers.

"Dakhil means 'inside' or 'inner,' implying 'an undeniable request' from those even temporarily on the 'inside.' It requires your host to give hospitality and respite no matter who asks for it. It does not matter if you are an enemy or a crook. You, the outsider, deserve a few days inside your host's establishment to recover from your travels before anything happens. I have traveled through Syria and Turkey, through the desert regions of Mesopotamia, and through the Iraqi Marshes. Dakhil worked everywhere, and I did not have to brandish a gun to force myself on anyone. Of course, I did not know how to use a revolver," he added, chuckling, "and I would not want to use one even now. A Turkish officer gave me a revolver for self-protection before I went into the marshes. It was really only for show. It was not so much that I trusted the Lord to protect me, but rather that I trusted the Lord would stimulate goodness in my fellow man. Of course, it is preferable to be an invited visitor; that way, you are expected and will be welcomed, even if your host does not know just when you are coming."[7]

"Did you ever find yourself in a situation when dakhil did not work?"

"When I went across the marshes back in 1909, I had my doubts.[8] The Ma'adan there speak a very different dialect and do not share the same values as other Arabs. They are known as ruffians, robbers, and rogues who prey on river traffic, although they largely leave the 'smoke boats'—the paddle wheel steamers—alone. They certainly were suspicious of me and suggested they might do me violence if they were not satisfied with my bona fides. I told them I was a doctor, but a medical doctor, I certainly was not. I had purchased medicines before I made my trip, though, because I knew I might get sick and that many people would be ailing simply because there were no modern medical services in the marshes.

"I did wonder if they were going to honor the dakhil custom. It did not work unequivocally since they tested my medical expertise first. I had brought the obvious medicines—quinine powder, aspirin, opium, and derivatives like morphine—along with soap, bandages,

---

[7] Van Ess, *Meet the Arab*, 93-96. Van Ess holds forth on the Ma'adan and the magical quality of dakhil as the expectation of protection, which in the desert is never to be refused by Bedouin (Bedu) nomads.

[8] Van Ess explored the Marsh Arab homeland in 1909. See also, Thesiger, *Marsh Arabs*, 256. Thesiger's is a much-later account (1951-58) than that of Van Ess, whose travels through Ma'adan country were much riskier than in Thesiger's time. In modern times, Saddam Hussein drained the marshes to gain control of this area and force the Marsh Arabs to settle down.

tincture of iodine, and the like. The shaykh presented me with a sick man—apparently with a major gastrointestinal problem. Who knows? Maybe it was dysentery. I didn't think the man had cholera, or I might not be here today to talk about it. I gave the patient an oral dose of opium. This calmed his gut, and he went to sleep almost immediately. The community agreed this was a good sign.

"I had lots of patients after that, and dakhil was honored. In fact, the shaykh later offered me his daughter as a bride in hopes I would stay in the community as their resident physician. Marsh Arab women are very attractive, quite beautiful in fact, and are not veiled or secluded from men like most other Muslim women. Getting married was not high on my priorities list just then. Making sure not to offend him or his daughter, I pleaded my need to purchase more medicines since my supply had run out. I said, ingenuously, that I might return later *'insha'Allah.'*[9]

"You know, *'insha'Allah'* is a nice term, if not used too frequently," said John. "Up until this century in the West, we always used the Latin phrase *Deo volente*, which has the same meaning—'God willing.' If not overused in trivial ways to demean God, these phrases respectfully acknowledge that we are guests in God's world. I like them both."

"Didn't the Turks prevent you from entering Marsh Arab country?"

"No. The Turks were quite terrified of the Ma'adan and left them alone, although they pretended to pursue them on the main rivers. The Turks would have been terrifying oppressors if they had ever caught anyone, but the Marsh Arabs seemed more afraid of their own people. Each of my Ma'adan guides would take me only to the next settlement, which seemed to be the horizon of their knowledge of the marshes and the limit of their courage. No amount of persuasion would convince them to lead me farther. So, I was handed from one guide to the next, and, of course, I had to offer a small tip, *baksheesh*, to each to take me to the next island settlement.

"I will say the food and the mosquitoes were ghastly, and I contracted a type of dysentery. I would have had more mosquito bites except various shaykhs invited me to sleep in their main hall, the *mudhif*, of the community. These splendid buildings are round, arching, reed structures, but they were more distinctive to me because they gave a little protection from the flow of mosquitoes through their doorways. Owing to the plentiful supply of reeds, new shelters were

---

[9] If God wills.

built frequently, so I didn't have to worry about mosquitoes burrowing through the thatch or breeding there. Anyway, the tobacco smoke from my pipe hung indoors and drove a good many off. I had a particularly grim Christmas dinner."

Dorothy emphatically broke in on John's soliloquy, "More than once, you have reminded me what a terrible Christmas dinner you had in the marshes—just rice and a thin soup. I felt sorry for you until you mentioned it once too often, and then I realized you were playing the old sympathy card. Who else ever did what you did in crossing the marshes? You didn't mind at all being a modern-day explorer. You enjoyed that meager Christmas repast just so you'd be able to rub it in later. You loved being off among the Marsh Arabs by yourself. So there."[10]

"Touché." said John with a grimace. "I'm going to ration my stories in the future. Even the best ones can be mined too frequently."

Sharon John and Marion Thoms

"Oh-h-h-h!" exhaled John Van Ess one evening after dinner. "Interesting as all this governmental finagling is, I would love to be a simple school headmaster once again. You know," he said to Wells, "some of this can be laid at your father's doorstep."

"How's that? I know my father and mother lived here in Basrah, but that was before my time. My sister Frances[11] was born here."

"Well, your father[12] was very much an activist on behalf of the Arabian Mission. He didn't see any reason to soft pedal the goals of Christian missions in favor of business or politics. He came into the mission early, and at that time, major initiatives were instigated more often from the field than from our New York board headquarters. As you know, the mission founders, Zwemer and Cantine,[13] had strong personalities of very different types. I think we'd have to say Zwemer was the more outspoken churchman. Your father was an early recruit of Zwemer, and your parents were perhaps the first doctor couple to serve in the mission. Your father was committed to the modern age and

---

[10] Van Ess, *Pioneers in the Arab World*, 37.
[11] Frances Thoms Scholten.
[12] Dr. Sharon John Thoms. At the time, Sharon was often a man's name. To further confuse matters, his wife, Dr. Marion Wells Thoms, had what was often considered a man's name.
[13] Samuel Zwemer and James Cantine were fellow seminarians at New Brunswick Theological Seminary when they decided to become missionaries to the Moslem world.

Military governor Mughsin Pasha, Basrah Wilayat, 1900 (SJT)

modern medicine; he loved the latest contraptions and technologies. He saw no reason not to use diplomacy to benefit the mission. I met him and Mrs. Thoms when I arrived in the Gulf in 1902. I didn't know him well, but he had energy, drive, and ideas."

"I have heard from Frances about my parents' time in Basrah," Wells said. "Her memory comes from what she was told and from old letters and photos. As you know, both our parents died before we kids had much chance to know them. My father was keen on photography in those days; he used dry plates and slow exposures. He actually took photos of family, friends, and Basrah at the start of the twentieth century."

"Yes," said John. "I'm told Customs used to open all dry photographic plate boxes to make sure they didn't contain contraband books. Of course, they destroyed all he plates by exposing them to light. Your father's friend was the military governor of the Basrah Wilayat, Mughsin Pasha; they were neighbors just down the Ashar Creek from here, toward the old city of Basrah. Your father taught him photography. When he heard what was happening to the shipments, Mughsin Pasha issued an order that no more searches of photographic plates be carried out. The governor of a *wilayat* in the Ottoman Empire had the final word on matters of strategic importance."

The governor's gift (front) 1900 (SJT)   *The governor's gift (back)*

"I didn't remember his name, but we have a photograph of him in formal dress that my father took," said Wells. "The occasion for this was the birth of Frances. The governor was curious to know what a Western baby looked like, even if she was a girl. He had seen only adult foreigners until then. Dad agreed to introduce him to Frances, and on the appointed day, he came for tea. Frances awoke from her nap, and my mother dressed her beautifully. My parents had decided she needed to be presented to the governor on a velvet cushion, and this they did—she was truly a precious little thing. The governor melted at the sight of her; he was quite serious about wanting to meet her and had planned his own little ceremony. He carefully placed a necklace around Frances' neck—really a ribbon to which was attached a gold coin of the Ottoman Empire. I've been told the coin was dated 1839 according to our Western reckoning. The governor had a jeweler solder a gold loop onto the coin so the ribbon could slide through it."

"I didn't know about that event. A very tender moment." After a brief silence, John continued. "You know, I think our mission effort has been distinguished from the beginning, in that we have always been here with our families and our children. This is a big difference between us and the British, Germans, and French. They generally don't raise their children here. There has always been a huge gulf between European Imperialists and the native peoples they ruled. The fate of the families of pakka—high-ranking empire builders—was never linked in any way to the fate of the indigenous peoples they governed. British children were mostly sent to boarding schools in England. Places like

Eton and Harrow and schools associated with famous cathedrals were and are fine institutions, but sending their children away meant that the Europeans in the colonies didn't fully understand the family experience. Our School of High Hope, for instance, was never asked to accommodate English children. There's another downside to the European pattern. Those European children grow up emotionally starved when separated from their parents during their formative years, and it preys on many English mothers living overseas with their husbands. They come to believe that they have abandoned their children, so much so that some mothers stay in England and seldom live overseas with their husbands.

"British adults in empire colonies don't often realize they have missed the opportunity to nurture little ones. During her visits, Gertrude Bell, for instance, loved to play 'make believe' with our children for hours on end. She was starved of the privilege of nurturing and observing little ones. For British children, no Christmas holiday in England with an aunt or uncle or other parental surrogate could make up for not seeing or being with—not bonding with—their own parents. The loss of intimacy all around is very sad. Many of our 'pakka burra imperial sahibs' were raised this way; it is almost a cultural trait of English imperial overseas society. They consider it normal even now that the empire is their pseudo parent, their *ma-baap*[14] as it were." John paused reflectively.

"The Ottoman governor's interest in babies surprises me a little," said John, after a silence. "They're much more matter of fact about these things in Arab society. When a baby is born, there is usually one of two announcements. The first, if it's a boy, is: 'Praise God, you have a son.' And for a baby girl, they say: 'Praise God, the mother is well.'"[15]

"There are also unpleasant outcomes regarding the birthing of children and the care of their mothers—but let's not dwell on them," said Wells. "In the difficult cases, a doctor may be called. Otherwise, a midwife handles the delivery as best she can."

"Of course, of course. Let me return to my original point. Your father was an activist. When he and your mother were here in Basrah, they got to know the American consul and his wife, both Americans. Consuls in those days did not need to be citizens of the country they served; they could be citizens of any country. For a time, during the pre-World War I days, I handled British consular matters here in Basrah.

---

[14] Mother and father.
[15] Van Ess, *Pioneers in the Arab World*, 101.

Hills Bros. date packing, Basrah, Iraq, 1900 (SJT)

For the American consul at that time, it was mostly a ceremonial office with nothing to do most of the time; much of his correspondence with Washington was in the form of letters begging to be paid. There were a few Americans in Basrah because of the date trade over on the Shatt al-Arab. In fact, the trade continues today through Hills Bros. Inc. This American couple was returning to the United States. The consul must have suggested to Sharon, your father, that he might apply to become consul. Sharon did, and was appointed American consul by the State Department but without the mission's approval.[16] It ruffled feathers at the board. In later years, we missionaries were informed by 'New York' that we could not serve 'God and mammon' simultaneously. Sharon was definitely a change maker, and such folks trigger new policies by their actions. You know, I think Sharon becoming the American consul may have accelerated his move to Bahrain. That, and the fact that he had not been able to get Ottoman accreditation of his University of Michigan medical degree when he visited Constantinople in 1898."[17]

---

[16] Lorimer, *Gazetteer of the Persian Gulf*. Lorimer identifies the consuls of world nations resident in the Gulf. For a time, Sharon Thoms was the designated consul in Basrah. Lorimer's work remained a classified British Empire document until 1955.

[17] Mission policy subsequently accommodated "mammon." The mission approved of Edwin Calverley consulting regularly with Aramco in the 1930s, and John Van Ess was approved as US consul in Basrah during World War II.

"My understanding is that my father could get his medical degree recognized only if he took the Constantinople certification exam, offered in French and Turkish," responded Wells. "My father didn't know French or Turkish, and he thought it would take too long to learn French well enough to pass the exam. There was no accreditation of non-Turkish medical schools then. The Flexner Report on accreditation of American medical schools came out in 1908, and it was the very first effort to evaluate and standardize the quality of medical education programs in America.[18] By moving to Bahrain, my father was beyond the reach of the Ottoman Empire, so he could practice medicine there without an Ottoman medical license. In fact, the University of Michigan had one of the leading US medical schools of the time." In recounting his father's experience, Wells' own loyalty to the University of Michigan and its professional schools came welling up, surprising him. He had not realized that he was such a loyal alumnus.

Imperial interest in petroleum

"When your father and mother and James Cantine originally came to the Gulf," began John Van Ess one evening, "it wasn't really clear why the Great Powers were so interested in this part of the world. The British under Lord Curzon, viceroy of India, wanted to declare the Gulf an 'English Lake.' The French wanted to block British efforts and did this by assisting every little shaykhdom in the trade of slaves and arms, which the British strongly opposed. The Germans wanted the Berlin-to-Baghdad railroad extended to the Kuwait area in order to access Gulf ports. Imperialism was in the air then. The Arabian Mission was not immune to this expansionist motif. Some of our mission founders used militaristic language to further Christianity in the Gulf. I've never approved of that, and I think James Cantine and your father would have agreed with me.[19]

"A few years after I arrived in Basrah, British businessmen became interested in the possibility that petroleum existed here in fairly large quantities. Until then, the only part of the British Empire with petroleum was Burma. The Burmah Oil Company was one of the movers in this area too. Around 1908 a group of their geologists arrived to sniff around. They may have known their rocks, but they had precious little knowledge of the customs and language of this area."

---

[18] Flexner, *Medical Education in the United States and Canada.*
[19] See Cantine's argument in "The Nearest Way to the Moslem Heart."

"How did they ever get it in their heads that there was oil in the Gulf?"

"In the nineteenth century, it became clear that there weren't enough whales in all the oceans to provide enough whale oil for lighting. Coal gas is tricky to work with and requires a central organization to manufacture and distribute it. Coal was not a viable alternative. Then oil was discovered in Pennsylvania just before the Civil War, and that became a possible alternative. Kerosene, produced from the oil, could be put into five-gallon tins and distributed worldwide. Kerosene lamps are a great improvement over candles in light output, durability, and cost. My life changed enormously when it became possible to read and grade lessons by kerosene lamp in the evening here in Basrah. The real boom in demand for petroleum began about the time your parents and I came to the Gulf. The internal combustion engine had the potential to be used in ships, trains, and automobiles. It soon became clear the British Empire was going to need huge supplies of petroleum.

"It was only a question of time before people would come looking. You may not have thought about it, but the Bible suggests one ought to look for oil hereabouts. After all, what do you think the story of Daniel and the fiery furnace was all about?[20] That story comes out of ancient Mesopotamia. Did you know there is at least one 'furnace' here that has been burning continuously for centuries? Natural gas leaking to the surface somehow exploded into flames, and it has never been snuffed out. It's up north near Kirkuk. Another possible allusion to oil flows in the Bible is the 'pillar of flame by night.' This was easier to understand because of the Jewish Exilic period in Mesopotamia, even though the 'flame' episode does not refer to Mesopotamia explicitly.

"There is a good deal of local lore about oil and gas bubbling to the surface in Iraq. Even if those Bible stories don't refer specifically to oil and gas flames, they may have referred to the many kilns that Mesopotamian society fired to make bricks for building. This may also account for why there is not much tree cover left in Mesopotamia today, the timber supply having been ravaged for charcoal and brick making centuries ago. In the middle of this huge plain, there are no boulders and rocks to use for building materials, so the early Mesopotamians fired bricks from clay instead.

"When the oil prospectors showed up, they didn't know how to organize an expedition. When they learned I spoke Arabic, I couldn't

---

[20] See Daniel 3:1-30 for the story of King Nebuchadnezzar and the fiery furnace. See Exodus 13:21-22 for the cloud by day and pillar of fire by night.

get rid of them. I organized their expedition. I hired forty mules with mule skinners, got the supplies they needed, and sent them off toward Mohammerah with introductions to the shaykh there. The rest is history. That became the Anglo-Persian Oil Company, and it is making lots of money. In fact, the British government is a part owner.[21]

"This was all accelerated because Winston Churchill, as First Sea Lord of the Admiralty, decided the Royal Navy should be fueled by oil rather than by coal. By hindsight, oil-fired ships don't give a navy any significant advantage unless, of course, another navy still uses coal-fired ships. Coal-fired ships give off much more black smoke and can be seen much farther away than oil-fired ships—and coal smoke dissipates slowly into the air. This means coal-fired naval vessels cannot easily sneak up on enemy ships. Countries with imperial pretensions have to have oil-fired navies today.[22]

"Even the civilian BI Company in the Gulf does not yet have oil-fired ships on its Bombay-Basrah route. Their ships all date from before World War I. Stoking the boilers on a coal burner is a 'killer job' because of the heat, doubly so because of the high temperature and humidity of weather in the Gulf."

"You can draw some satisfaction in having had a hand in launching the oil industry here in the Gulf," Wells observed.

"Satisfaction is the sum total of what we received. You know, you'd think Anglo-Persian oil might have been grateful enough to give us one share of preferred stock for each mule I arranged for those prospectors. The dividends on forty shares would have supported scholarships far beyond those we have been able to give at the School of High Hope. I expect the Gulf region is going to become geopolitically even more central in the future because of oil."

Seconded to Bahrain

Dorothy called upstairs to Wells, "A telegram just arrived from Bahrain. Louis Dame, our mission doctor there, has just been called to Ta'if in Sa'udi Arabia to treat one of Amir[23] Abdal Aziz bin Sa'ud's family. He needs a replacement as soon as possible. Would you consider replacing him?"

Wells jumped at the chance. "Of course. I can have my bags packed and ready to go on the next Bahrain-bound steamer."

---

21   Van Ess, *Meet the Arab*, 137.
22   Colamaria, "The United States Navy." See also, Dahl, "Naval Innovation."
23   *Amir*: title of ruler; precursor to the title "king."

Arabic language study with the Van Esses had turned into a first-rate education not just about Arabic but also about life and history in the Gulf. Wells had not been practicing medicine regularly now for nearly two years. He had grown increasingly impatient to begin the work he was trained to do, and this was the perfect opportunity. He was headed to Bahrain.

CHAPTER 5

Land of "Two Seas"

> I'd recommend Bumpus & Co. in London
> for reading materials.
> They supply books to colonials
> the world around.

Setting sail 1932

Wells kissed Beth and Nancy tenderly, bade the Van Esses farewell, took his luggage by the mission's bellum down the Ashar Creek onto the Shatt al-Arab, and boarded the BI's SS *Barala* anchored in midstream. Watercraft abuzz with vendors, passengers, outbound cargo, and well-wishers surrounded the ship like flies drawn to a juicy pineapple. The morning was still relatively cool, and a faint breeze stirred across the water. One had to be gullible to think so many people were actually going to travel on this ship. Wells drank in the spectacle as they approached. Whatever happened, he was contented, for he was on the last leg of the long journey to his new vocation.

Luggage was being manhandled up the gangway from river level to the deck. Passengers shouted to each other and to relatives, friends, and boatmen in the bellums below. Babies squalled at the uproar and at the strangeness of the towering black ship belching acrid smoke. Loading high-value freight onboard, the crew operated steam winches that emitted an eerie, mechanical mantra, "pocketa-pocketa-pocketa-

Ashar Creek and the Shatt al-Arab, Basrah, 1920s (MTC)

fssss." Much of the cargo was being forwarded from Europe for minor ports down the Gulf. There was a large wicker basket with a hinged door on the side for ease of entry and exit, like those attached to hot air balloons. This ungainly contraption was for pakka ladies and invalids traveling first class; they were lifted aboard, elevator-like, by steam winch.

Wells clambered up the gangway while a ship's steward supervised his luggage being stowed in his stateroom, making sure no light-fingered stevedore made off with any of the ship's fittings. The remainder of his luggage was to be secured in the "Not wanted on voyage" baggage room below deck. After inspecting his cabin, Wells locked it and returned to watch order emerge from the chaos and acrimony of the Basrah port stopover. On the main deck, many passengers had marked out personal living space with their belongings. Apparently, they were going to stay out in the open air. Part of the British India Steam Navigation (BISN) Company's business plan was to accommodate passengers traveling "unbunked," and this ship could billet more than one thousand passengers sleeping on deck. This was anything but a luxury cruise ship.

That evening everyone noticed the poised young man entering the ship's dining room. Unconscious of his effect, Wells wandered in

SS Barala, *ca. 1914* (PD)

looking for a place to sit. The captain stood and proffered his hand, "Dr. Thoms, I think? My name is Smethers, and I am master of the *Barala*. Delighted to have you aboard. Please sit with me at the captain's table."[1] Smethers pronounced Wells' name as "Toms." Wells let the mispronunciation go.[2]

"Happy to be traveling with you, Captain Smethers. As a boy, I traveled by British India Steam Navigation vessels. This is my first experience on a BI ship since before World War I."

"You may well have traveled on the *Barala* back then," Capt. Smethers replied. "She was the latest in nautical design when they launched her twenty years ago, and she has served the BISN well." Over the evening meal and drawing on his British imperial and unabashedly commercial perspectives, the captain educated Wells about the realities of life on the open seas. Smethers was proud of the role he, his ship, and his company played in maintaining trade and communications between the far-flung colonies and Britain.

"The BISN has been a constant in the Gulf and the Indian Ocean for decades," he narrated. "We are one of the most important extensions of the British Empire. It is really a maritime empire, you know, stretching around the world. The BISN is part of the civilian navy,

---

[1] Captain Smethers is an entirely fictional synthesis of British imperial views of his time—an intelligent, hard-working, ethnocentric British male, proud of the British Empire. He provides an orientation to the Gulf as understood by knowledgeable foreigners in his time. Wells acquired this knowledge from many, including mission colleagues. See also, endnote 5:1, p. 378.

[2] Wells' surname, "Thoms," is pronounced like "tomes" (i.e., books).

the empire's arteries and veins. Without us, it would be impossible for the British Empire to operate as a unified whole. Our merchant vessels link the colonies with Britain. Of course, the Gulf is a more important seaway than any highway on land. We keep the Gulf in touch with India. We haul nearly all of the high-value merchandise and almost all of the most valuable cargo—people. We are the postal service of the Gulf. Local post offices operate in each British consulate at the larger ports, and our weekly services deliver mail to each shaykhdom.[3]

"Our ships stop at any harbor that generates traffic, so our port calls might have 'iffy' schedules. We also run a more regular express service—our 'fast boats'—that touch just a few ports between Bombay and Basrah. At many of the out-of-the-way places, because there are few proper docks or quays, we anchor offshore and wait for lighters[4] to ferry cargo and people to and from us. Most harbors have not been dredged either. That's how it is at this edge of the empire. Bahrain's facilities are slightly improved since World War I, but we still usually anchor offshore, and local sailboats transfer people and freight.

"Most passengers travel deck class." Captain Smethers was animated by his tale. "They eat and sleep in the open air. We offer toilets and washing facilities indoors, of course. Deck passengers often bring their own food, but they can also buy food from our kitchens. We have our own *halal* butchers on board and Hindu vegetarian and Muslim nonvegetarian cooks too. You undoubtedly saw some animals being loaded. The cattle, sheep, goats, and chickens stored at the stern of the vessel will be slaughtered for our meat supply at sea. Refrigeration is expensive. Until World War I, when I was a cadet, refrigerators on board could explode.[5]

"The last thing one wants on board ship is a fire, so deck passengers are not allowed to cook their own food. After we load all the cargo and leave port, we stretch tarpaulins to shade the deck passengers from the sun as much as possible. The breeze and the shade make traveling by deck class tolerable, except in winter, when the wind can be very cold and the weather stormy and wet. Of course, the heat is constant the rest of the year.

[3] See Blake, *B. I. Centenary*.
[4] Light barges or other watercraft.
[5] When Wells and Beth, in later years, served in more remote ports of the Gulf, they would periodically go out to visiting BI vessels to purchase butter and freshly slaughtered meat because local markets offered little besides either fresh or dried fish.

"*Barala*'s doctor oversees the boarding of passengers. Because of the close quarters in deck class, any passenger who appears to be seriously sick and likely contagious is turned back. It can be a very real problem if contagion were to spread among our travelers, because of the minimal quarantine facilities at each port. If a disease spreads aboard the ship, the entire vessel could be quarantined for ten days, until the epidemic subsides. That would be a black mark on my record if it ever were to happen. Of course, we can't examine everyone; there are always voyagers with colds or influenza. What we have to be on the watch for are cholera, smallpox, and the plague. You, of course, Doctor Thoms, understand all this as plain as the nose on your face." Wells nodded his assent.

"After we leave Kuwait, perhaps you'd like to come for a drink and chat in my quarters topside behind the bridge? We don't generally invite passengers on the bridge since it is the ship's control center. Officers and crew up there pay full attention to running the ship."

"Thanks," Wells replied, "I'd like that very much. Getting a taste of life on board ship would be enjoyable. I don't want to be a nuisance, so I'll fit into whatever the ship schedule allows. In the meantime, if there is any way I can be of assistance, I am available."

Not to be distracted from his train of thought, Smethers returned to his narrative. "In fact, we run a secure ship because so many in the Gulf insist on carrying arms and gunpowder. Doubtless you may have noticed Arabs or Afghans carry *jezails*[6] or more modern rifles, and they want to bring them onboard too. It seems to be a part of Arab male identity. We insist they check their arms when they sail with us.

"Many years ago, the BI learned its lesson the hard way when some men among the deck passengers took over the ship. That was on the old SS *Cashmere*. They lifted the treasure the ship was carrying. It was recovered through the good offices of Shaykh Khaza'al of Mohammerah. You would have thought the Royal Navy would have caught them, but no. The shaykh's men nabbed the pirates and hanged them. The shaykh was a friend of progress and of law and order. For as many years as he lived, every BI ship passing his palace near Mohammerah would fire a salute in his honor. You'll see.

"When I was a cadet, a story was passed down to all cadets about this obligatory ceremonial cannon salute. Apparently, a young officer on one of our ships had dropped a cricket ball down the cannon barrel on top of the blank powder charge. The gun went off, and the cricket

[6] Long-barreled muskets.

ball flew directly at the shaykh's palace guards. Since the shaykh's sentinels didn't know they were 'at bat' there was consternation when they received a shot across the bow. That young officer was lucky not to be put ashore permanently. He wouldn't have had such good luck in the Royal Navy. Fortunately, no one was hurt."

Wells was intrigued by this bizarre incident. He mused about the distance of the cannon shot from ship to shore. He remembered the channel was still relatively narrow at that point. A cricket ball, with its sewn leather cover that sported a different stitch pattern than an American baseball, might be nearly as lethal as a four-pound cannon ball, even though it weighed much less.

Smethers turned from cricket balls to resume his monologue. "The shallowness of the Gulf means low tides can expose banks or coral reefs. Our charts could be more accurate, but we have to make do with what we have. Reading the sea is still important, of course. During the daytime, a bosun casts the lead regularly to verify the depths of the water in comparison to our charts."

Smethers concluded his speech. "If you come up to the bridge in the evening, you'll be struck by the beauty of the ocean. It is one of the great pleasures I see nightly. The varying weather conditions, phases of the moon, and states of the sea make each nocturnal passage different. The view from topside is unmatched—it is the most impressive vantage point of the vessel, and it's always ghostly quiet. As shipmaster, I sleep in snatches of four hours or less, and I rise to make sure all is well. So, I know whereof I speak."

Although it was small by the standards of ocean-going freighters of its day, the *Barala* seemed like a giant Gulliver of a ship. As it made its way down the river, it was escorted by all sorts of Lilliputian sailing craft. Wells judged most of them to be no more than forty tons in size. All had lateen sails, an Arab innovation introduced to the West only in recent centuries. Some of the larger ships seemed anchored in midstream and did not move as the *Barala* approached. Wells asked his Indian cabin steward if he knew why they were anchored in the middle of the river.

"Oh, yes Sahib, I am knowing. These fellows do this way. Take pani[7] from river and put in boat. They sell in Kuwait. Kuwait. Very dry place. Need drinking water. *Pani-jahazzis*[8] *pakka*[9] business."

---

[7] Water.
[8] Water-sailing vessels, i.e., water tankers.
[9] Very good.

Wells was amazed to learn of this innovative way of supplying Kuwait with fresh water. The Shatt al-Arab's great volume of fresh water flowing to the sea was a lifeline for people on its desert margins. Wells supposed that water harvested in midstream was about as clean as it was going to get, some of it having been filtered through the northern marshes. The Kuwaiti craft would open their stopcocks, sinking low into the water as they filled with water. Then they would shut their valves, regain some buoyancy, and sail for Kuwait's water market. *Barala*'s steersman threaded out to sea through this slalom course of anchored sailing vessels.

As the *Barala* was negotiating the Shatt al-Arab, a passenger accosted Wells. Ralph "Dusty" Rhoades was an American geologist hired by Gulf Oil to search for prospecting spots in the Gulf region. Wells and he spent hours together en route to Bahrain. From him, Wells learned that a crew was already at work in Bahrain drilling for oil and that they were using an old-style wildcatter's rig, like those used for sinking water wells.

They had drilled almost to the maximum depth that Gulf Oil had authorized. Unless they hit a gusher soon, they would be going home. Rhoades' job was to find other promising sites they could explore before Gulf Oil turned off the money spigot. He suspected oil could be found in Bahrain because they had found a water well in the central part of the island coated with an oily sheen. Wells remembered that his father, Sharon, had observed an oily sheen on a water well in 1909 near Jabal Dukhan,[10] Bahrain's highest peak. Back then, nobody thought to ask Sharon what he knew about the oil slick.

Rhoades' optimism resurfaced as the ship slipped down the Shatt al-Arab and passed Mohammerah, where the obligatory salute was tooted out. When the flares and smokestacks of the Anglo-Persian oil refinery at Abadan slipped by, Rhoades opined that the same type of thing might soon develop in Bahrain.[11]

As the *Barala* rounded the Fao Peninsula and headed toward Kuwait Bay, Wells took in the sleepy little town of adobe buildings in the distance. A clutch of puffy white sails headed into the bay, each vessel optimizing its speed relative to wind, load, and stability. Wells remembered from reading Zwemer's *Arabia*[12] that there were estimated to be nine hundred pearl-fishing boats in Kuwait. The shoreline was

---

[10] *Jabal* means "mountain" or "hill."
[11] Twitchell, *Saudi Arabia*.
[12] Zwemer, *Arabia: The Cradle of Islam*.

also littered with long-distance sailing traders, the Kuwaiti double-ended *booms* and *baghalas*,[13] with their distinctive sterns and poop decks squared off in the European style. These mighty sailing vessels roamed as far as South India and Ceylon to the east and Zanzibar and Pemba on the African coast. Wells had heard that there were from 100 to 150 of these large vessels, although he saw only a fraction of them in Kuwait's harbor.

To complete the seascape, scores of fishing and other small boats scooted around the larger vessels. As their canvas sails billowed gracefully, the late afternoon light played on them and then dimmed quickly as the sun dropped below the horizon. This visual benediction to the day echoed in Wells' mind with the words of the lovely bugle call, "Taps": "Day is done, gone the sun, from the lake, from the hill, from the sky. All is well, safely rest, God is nigh."

Approaching Bahrain

"Ah, Dr. Thoms," began Captain Smethers over the midday meal. "We are entering a very special part of the Gulf called by the Arabs, 'Bahrain,' which means, 'two seas.' The island of Bahrain carries this name, but the term refers to the area of the Gulf around the island as well.

"Although some think the name refers to two different geographical sections of the Gulf, I think it more reasonably refers to the Gulf being both fresh and salt water simultaneously. Of course, it is much more salt than fresh. The fresh water comes from natural springs or artesian wells on the sea floor. On still nights, close to shore, where it is shallow, you can see the up-welling fresh water roiling the surface. There are several of these natural springs right in the roadstead of Bahrain Island near Manama, one of them very close to the quarantine station at the tip of Muhharaq Island. Of course, Bahrain Island is distinguished from many other Gulf islands because it has its own fresh-water springs that supply gardens, homes, and farms. This has made Bahrain Island a magnet for human settlement for centuries. The offshore freshwater springs have been a great boon to seafarers as well since they can resupply their water at sea."[14]

Wells replied, "I expect such springs are also quite pure, as long as they are not contaminated with refuse and waste. It may, however, be a two-edged sword for health. The better the water supplies are, the

---

[13] Deep-sea sailing vessels.
[14] See endnote 5:14, p. 378.

more likely many people will be drawn to the area. The more people, the more waste. Between the higher population density and waste generation, there is also greater likelihood for communicable diseases to spread. This 'two seas' phenomenon might be a mixed blessing. Thanks for the insight, Captain. Since I am the newcomer, I'll see what my physician colleagues have to say."

As he rose from the dining table, Capt. Smethers said, "Perhaps you'd like to have a chat and drinks in my quarters before dinner—say 6 p.m.? I'll tell the officer of the watch you are expected."

"I'll come, thank you."

As he thought about his pending time in Bahrain, Wells recalled that his father had written about an epidemic of cholera that had hit Bahrain just after he arrived in 1900. Although not widely understood at the time by locals, the disease spread through water and food supplies that were contaminated by cholera victims' waste. Although Sharon was a skilled surgeon relative to the standard of his day, surgery was no cure for cholera. He had no capacity to control its spread. Even so, he treated many cholera cases. Some came to his clinic even when the disease was well advanced. There were no organized hospitals that could handle cholera patients, so Sharon did what little he could.

Bahrainis were naturally suspicious of Sharon since the new, foreign medico used mysterious methods beyond their ken. His success in treating some victims was offset by those he could not help. Not surprisingly, rumors spread that this outsider, the new *kafir*,[15] was "causing" the epidemic because so many flocked to his service with mixed results. Without a wonder treatment to rely on, Sharon was helpless. His had not had an auspicious start in Bahrain, and he soon left in hopes of a more promising practice in Kuwait.[16]

Eager to begin with more promise in Bahrain, Wells prayed that no major epidemic was lying in wait. Like his father, he carried few "miracle" drugs. He had only vaccines to either prevent or minimize the effects of smallpox, typhoid, and cholera, and he knew vaccination worked only with advance warning of infection, and although they were a good preventive strategy, they were not curative. He would have to keep his wits if he was not to be overtaken by outbreaks of contagious diseases.

---

[15] Unbeliever in Islam.
[16] Sharon had received his "baptism by fire" with a cholera epidemic in 1903, one year after opening the new Mason Memorial Hospital in Bahrain.

At six o'clock, the officer of the watch escorted Wells to the captain's quarters abaft the eerily quiet bridge where the officer, the steersman, and a crew member stood. The steersman deftly read the ocean swells and compensated for their effect to minimize the roll and pitch of the ship. The man was a seamless extension of the vessel; his slight, continuous adjustments of the ship's wheel anticipated the time necessary for the rudder to respond. This was something like playing hymns on a tracker organ for a sleepy church congregation, Wells thought; a seasoned organist had to anticipate the time lag between depressing the keys and the resulting melody leading congregational vocalization. And so it was for the steersman.[17]

"Dr. Thoms, good of you to come. Welcome to my aerie topside, my abode for ten or more months every year. It is comfortable compared to my officers' and crew's quarters, and it affords me twenty-four-hour access to the bridge, chart room, and radio. As master of the ship, one becomes obsessive. My apologies for using psychological terms that I am really not qualified to use. Being away from England and my family for most of each year, I read a great deal. My mail comes via Bombay, much of it magazines and books. I try to read fairly widely because the world is changing so rapidly—but I don't read politics. I'm for 'King and Country.' I like science, engineering, and biography. What about you, Dr. Thoms?"

Wells replied, "I love to read, although in recent years, I've read mostly medical books and journals. My wife and I like to read biographies and histories. True stories—interpretations of things that have actually occurred—seem so much more interesting than any novel, except for Dickens, whose books we love. We grew to enjoy longwave radio in the States, but shortwave radio is so sporadic in this part of the world that we don't expect to tune into it much."

"We get ship call signals in Morse code mostly," offered Smethers. "Other shortwave signals come and go as if from another planet or jammed by the X-rays of the universe. In case you don't know of them, I'd recommend Bumpus & Co. in London for reading materials.[18] They supply books to colonials the world over. Just tell them what you like, and they will send you a selection. When you return the books, tell them what you liked and disliked, and they will adjust future selections as

---

[17] See endnote 5:17, p. 379.
[18] Bumpus & Co. became an intellectual lifeline for Wells and Beth for at least three decades. They developed a habit of reading aloud to each other at the end of the day, just before nodding off to sleep. For both, this was a complete switch from the pressures of the workday.

they understand your tastes. That's what I do. Bumpus serves everyone in the colonies right up to the viceroy—although he has more than enough money to ship his entire library to India and back.

"Please understand that nobody much cares what a lowly captain in the merchant navy thinks. I did not have the option to go to university, although I loved my studies and received high marks. My father was a riveter in a Liverpool shipyard, and I knew enough not to hope for a position higher than I could reasonably expect. Nobody would have selected me to go to Oxford or Cambridge before World War I.

"Ah, well," he said with a sigh, "what will you have? I live by the ship's clock. As a young man in the Royal Navy, I liked my daily tot of grog. I still do. Every evening I ration myself to one drink at specifically this hour. No exceptions. If you make exceptions, everyone knows, and the ship's crew becomes lax and lazy. I am not paid to be lax and lazy. I have no intention of allowing the nightmarish stories by Joseph Conrad[19] to become remotely possible on my ship. I am going to have just one G&T [gin and tonic]. I also have whiskey and orange crush cordial, which my steward can top up with soda water. What will you have? Please understand that drinks are to be consumed in my quarters only. We do not go on the bridge with drinks in hand."

Wells thought a moment. He was reminded of Peter's vision of a sheet let down from heaven, laden with many animals for eating. It seemed to imply to Peter that no fauna were off limits for believers to eat.[20] Did that inclusiveness carry over to drink? Of course, Jesus turned water into wine at Cana.[21] Not quite sure of what his new status as missionary might entail, Wells was reluctant to imbibe. Yet he was a relational person who wanted to know and understand others. He said, "I'll have a G&T too, but could you make it very light on the gin? I've not been one to consume alcohol much. A light G&T, however, would be refreshing; besides, tonic water—made with quinine—is an antimalarial therapy."

After his Luso-Indian steward distributed drinks, the captain continued, "Cheers! Health to all at home and to all who roam the seas. God save the king!" In this way, a brotherhood of sorts was launched at the captain's self-limited happy hour.

---

[19] Among his writings, Conrad had several tales of misadventure on the high seas.
[20] Acts 10:10-16.
[21] The story of the wedding at Cana, John 2:1-12, refers to Jesus turning water into wine.

After his initial appreciative sip, Smethers unfastened the top collar button of his uniform. "Doctor, I suspect you may know this already. If you don't, permit me to tell you that the Persian Gulf is not only the major highway of this region but also its lifeblood. The Gulf provides food and employment for most of the workers on its shores.

"According to Lorimer's *Gazetteer of the Persian Gulf*, whose six volumes I have as my bedside companion, this entire coast focuses on one major activity—pearling. Many who live near the Gulf shorelines—from Kuwait to Bahrain, Abu Dhabi to Dubai and the other emirates, as well as communities on the Persian side—engage in pearl 'fishing.'

"The only seafaring province that does not benefit significantly from pearling is Muscat." Smethers paused, shifting his train of thought. "Omanis have engaged in the coastal East African trade for hundreds of years. They travel as far as Zanzibar in their magnificent, lateen-rigged sailing vessels. Zanzibar, you may know, has been under Omani control from much of the nineteenth century until now.[22] My understanding is that the Americans in the early nineteenth century negotiated a treaty of peace and friendship with Oman, largely because they wanted to do business in copal and other commodities in Zanzibar.[23]

"Let's not talk much about the slave trade," he cautioned, as he nevertheless launched into the topic. "Even though the United States stopped its slave trade after the Civil War, slavers continued to ply the Gulf waters until recently, as they have for centuries. Although transportation of slaves on the high seas is now illegal by international convention, slavery itself is not illegal in many of these countries.[24] Most black-skinned people in the Arab world are descended from slaves. Indeed, they may still be slaves themselves. As far as I know, even the free ones are not very high up the rungs of the social ladder. Not all slaves in this area are of African origin; the trade in humans has engulfed unfortunate victims from around the Indian Ocean."[25]

---

[22] The lateen (Latin) rig was really developed by Arabs. It allows ships to sail much closer to the wind than the old, square-rigged ships. Zanzibar shed its Arab Omani overlordship in the 1960s.

[23] The treaty with the US was signed in 1834. Morison, *Maritime History of Massachusetts*. The main object of American traders was copal—an essential ingredient for varnish—from East Africa. They also traded for cloves from Zanzibari plantations.

[24] The 1930s.

[25] The oceanic slave trade was outlawed on the Arabian Sea in the 1870s by the British. It was not made illegal on land, however, until the 1960s, or even until 1970, in the case of Oman. Slaves could be smuggled into some Arab countries until relatively recent times.

The captain was warming to his subject. Clearly, he was a man who did not often have opportunities for recreational conversation, and his conversation was more soliloquy than dialogue. Wells listened intently, not only because the topics interested him but also because this man—an imperialist to his bone marrow—had a perspective that supplemented Wells' book learning. Wells was receiving a lesson on the state of Gulf societies from a Western, outsider's viewpoint. He was determined to test the validity of this information in the years to come.

"Yes, Doctor, slavery is a sad business," Smethers concluded with a sigh and shake of his head. "But let's get back to the gentler topic, pearling in these parts. On second thought, it may not be much gentler. The pearling trade is avaricious and loaded against the poor devil hoping to work his way out of debt and penury. In effect, it is very much a casino where roulette is the only game. If you have any knowledge of gambling, you will know roulette is not a reliable road to wealth—quite the opposite. Look outside now, or later from the bridge. You may see fleets of Arab sailing vessels on the horizon with their sails raised. This means they are actively pearling, and others should not intrude. It is a very tough business. Perhaps half the able-bodied men on Arab shores are employed in the nautical life, one way or another, including ship building, repairing, and chandlering. Most of them work in pearl diving and in the support of pearl diving.[26]

"You must understand that, since the Great Crash of 1929, the Persian Gulf economy has been thrown into as much disarray as the rest of the world. To complicate matters, the Japanese have now perfected raising 'cultured pearls.' The result is that there is at present a surplus of pearls beyond any world demand. Prices have tumbled. Until a few years ago, this was unheard of. Pearl buyers came to the Gulf to acquire their product. Now Gulf pearl merchants go to London and Paris as supplicants in search of buyers. I carry them to Bombay to connect with ships heading for Europe. It is not only the merchants who suffer. It goes right down to those unfortunates bringing oyster shells up on deck in search of pearls within them.

"Dr. Thoms," said Capt. Smethers, still pronouncing it "Toms," "I hope you have a heart for the plight of pearl fishermen. These men come from all over—even from deep within Arabia—in hopes of discharging their debts. Each one is grateful to be hired. He is given an advance payment to meet his family's expenses for the pearling season. He perhaps does not realize he is obligated to repay his entire debt whether

---

[26] Carter, "The History and Prehistory of Pearling in the Persian Gulf."

or not he finds enough pearls to make his payments. Effectively, these men and their families for generations to come can become perpetual 'slaves in bondage.' We can only be grateful that British common law does not allow this evil in some parts of the Gulf.[27]

"The job of a pearl diver is a precarious one. They are tethered to the sailboat when they go over the side and have absolutely no equipment except for the clips on their noses and leather 'thimbles' for their fingertips. They have barely a minute to scoop oyster shells into bags around their necks before they are hauled back to the surface. There they gasp for air and hand over the contents of their bags. When they have recovered their breath, they dive again, all day long. The more times they dive, the more chances they have to bring up a large, perfect pearl, one that will set them on easy street. It is the ultimate lottery, with very few winning tickets."

"What you are telling me, Captain, is that this business on the high seas has been very lucrative and probably very dangerous. I remember my father writing that his first surgery in Bahrain was performed on a pearl diver who had been attacked by a shark. My father had to perform the surgery outside his clinic in broad daylight in order to have enough light to operate. He amputated the arm of the diver at the shoulder. My father had no choice but to do this major operation as an outpatient surgery, after which the poor wretch was taken home by his relatives. Miraculously, the diver survived. His father returned several days later most grateful for my father's services. My father was deeply affected by the father's tears of gratitude and his kneeling and kissing my father's hands. I would expect divers have many health problems. I'll just have to see when my patients come to the clinic."

"Just one other thing before we go down to dinner, Doctor," said Smethers. "This watery highway to wealth is very different today because of 'us.' The British Empire has brought law and order to the high seas. In the nineteenth century, there were many slave ships navigating these waters, and arms smugglers and pirates too. Raiders could run ashore and kidnap children, as well as men and women, and carry them into slavery up and down the Gulf—quite aside from the trade in African slaves. Pearling vessels had to be able to defend themselves from marauders intent on stealing their pearls. Trucial Oman, with the shaykhdoms of Abu Dhabi, Dubai, and the others, were closest to the

---

[27] Sir C. Dalrymple Belgrave, *wazir* (chief advisor) to the *hakim* (ruler) of Bahrain for thirty years, was instrumental in imposing a system of fair contracts for pearl divers that excluded the possibility of debts being transferred from father to son.

rich pearling banks. Offshore islands could be occupied by raiders with ulterior motives. No one was safe. It is no wonder that this region was known as the 'Pirate Coast.' It was the Bombay Marine, the East India Company's navy, and then later the Royal Navy that imposed order on these waters, and it was not easy. The ocean is huge, and the slave trade, the illegal arms trade, and piracy all offered prospects of quick returns. This is why we Brits take pride that the Gulf is sometimes called 'an English Lake.'" Smethers paused to let the message sink in.

"Now, let's go down to dinner," invited Smethers, feeling he had provided sufficient insight for this American novitiate to digest about the British Empire's Persian Gulf presence.

The next day, the SS *Barala* nosed into Bahrain's roadstead, ringed by coral reefs. BI ships had anchored there for decades. Having waved a final salutation to the captain on the bridge, Wells and the *coolies*[28] carrying his baggage eased down the gangway into a sailboat and then headed for shore.

Bahrain had changed since Wells' father and mother had first landed there at the beginning of the twentieth century. Like Wells, they, too, had taken a sailboat ashore—his mother having been lowered over the side in a basket dangling from the steam winch's cable, much like the one Wells had seen in Basrah. But his parents could not reach the tiny pier by boat since the water was much too shallow at low tide. As they wondered what to do, men with large white donkeys came splashing out through the gentle surf. Amid stifled giggles and raucous laughter, passengers climbed atop the braying donkeys for the rest of the trip ashore, their baggage following on similar conveyances.

This time, Wells rode in the sailboat right up to Bahrain's new pier that extended to deep water at high tide. Mission personnel expected him and were on the pier waiting with hearty greetings and warm embraces.

"Welcome, welcome," they pealed. "Thrice welcome. You'll put up with us at the hospital for the time being. We are, however, looking for a house where you and your family can reside. We are building more housing, but nothing is finished yet. Not to worry—all will sort itself out in the next days. Ahlan wa sahlan. Beitna beitkum."[29]

---

[28] Day laborers.
[29] Welcome! Our home is your home.

CHAPTER 6

Manama Memories

At the time, no Bahraini believed such a grand hospital building was going to be used for patients.

Arrival in Bahrain

"Dr. Thoms—Wells—I'm Gerrit," announced Rev. Gerrit Pennings, chaplain of the Bahrain hospital. They shook hands on the Bahrain pier as Wells scanned the port area, taking a moment to stretch his sea legs. "We're very glad you decided to suspend your Arabic training and come so quickly. Dr. Louis Dame has gone to Ta'if in Sa'udi Arabia because of an emergency call from King Abdal Aziz.[1] The king's mother is ill. When Dame returns, you can continue prepping for your language exams. In the meantime, you are the only one on duty at the hospital. We hope you are going to be comfortable. We are especially pressed just now because our Indian doctor, Dr. Lakra, went to India to get married and has not returned. Goodness knows, your family has ties to Bahrain." All this information tumbled out as Pennings, a self-

---

[1] Abdal Aziz bin Sa'ud had several titles during his ascendence. The term "king" is used because that was his final title. He was also known as Ibn Sa'ud, the son of Sa'ud. He ruled from his stronghold in Riyadh, the capital of present-day Sa'udi Arabia. See also, endnote 6:1, p. 379.

confident person, tried to make Wells feel comfortable. Wells' welcome to Bahrain was their first meeting. Gerrit and Gertrude Pennings and Louis and Elizabeth Dame were veteran missionaries, commissioned at the close of World War I.

"We prefer to have several doctors here in Bahrain for situations such as this. When an emergency call comes from King Abdal Aziz bin Sa'ud or one of the other shaykhs on the Trucial Coast or Qatar, one of our doctors can respond quickly. That way, the hospital does not have to close because it has no physician. You will stay with us for the time being since no mission-owned houses or apartments are available. We have started looking for a place for your family. In the meantime, *beitna beitkum*. Dinner will be at eight; Mrs. Dame and Dr. Tiffany are coming after Neoskelita finishes her rounds in the Women's Hospital and you check Louis Dame's patients."

"Thanks for meeting me at the pier with this warm welcome. I am pleased to have a break from language study and to be able to dig in. I have not done surgery since we were in Jerusalem more than a year ago. I'll settle in and see you at dinner."

Over supper the conversation turned to medical matters. Dr. Mary Tiffany asked with a smile, "Dr. Thoms, may I call you Wells? You may call me Mary, but please," she glared good humoredly at Gerrit, "don't call me by my middle name, Neoskelita."

"Your middle name is definitely an attention getter. It's the first time I've known anyone with it. There must be a story behind it."

"Yes, but it's too long to go into now, someday maybe," said Mary. "I expect you will soon be responsible for the patients in the Dr. Marion Wells Thoms Women's Hospital, too, since I am getting married and will soon be leaving Bahrain.[2] This will be tricky for you because Bahraini men and others from the mainland are reluctant to have a male doctor examine their wives and daughters. You will have an advantage over other male doctors, though. The hospital is named for your mother, and we can tell patients coming to the clinic and the hospital of 'Umm Wells' that you are her son and will be treating them until another woman doctor takes my place."[3]

[2] The Marion Wells Thoms Memorial Hospital opened in Bahrain in 1926. Whether Bahrainis remembered her twenty-one years after her death is not known, but Marion's death had so deeply affected the community of the Arabian Mission that it named the new Women's Hospital in her honor.
[3] In 1935 Dr. Esther Barny took on the duties of the Women's Hospital. As the daughter of Fred and Margaret Barny, Esther was the second child of Arabian missionaries to become a missionary in the Gulf (after Wells).

Clinic prior to the new hospital, Bahrain, ca. 1901 (SJT)

"Without question, I'll adhere to local custom while I serve women patients. Perhaps I can come over to the hospital periodically before you leave, and we could examine clinic patients and do hospital rounds together. That way folks can get used to my presence. I am under no illusions. I am not a long-term substitute for a woman doctor, and I will definitely consult the husbands and male relatives who come to hospital with their womenfolk."

Beginnings of Western medicine in Bahrain

Cautiously broaching a delicate subject, "Ma" Dame, nicknamed for her maternal bearing, remarked, "Your parents were in Bahrain almost from the start of the mission work here. Your mother died here, didn't she? She was the first woman doctor in Bahrain. We opened the Women's Hospital named after her just six years ago."

Wells replied, "She and my father were among the first Western physicians to practice in Bahrain—at least they were the first doctor couple. It wasn't easy getting started, even though Uncle Sam Zwemer had established Bahrain as a mission station before 1900."[4] He paused reflectively.

"That was well before our time," Mrs. Dame mumbled, as Wells seemed lost in reverie.

---

[4] It was common for children to refer to adults in the mission as "Aunt" or "Uncle." Over time, missionary colleagues became closer than relatives in the States.

American Mission Hospital's original building, 1903 (SJT)

Dr. Tiffany interrupted the awkward silence. "I don't think I know that story, Wells. Do you mind recounting it?"

With her prompting and the look of anticipation on the others' faces, Wells reluctantly launched into his family story. "Uncle Sam did first aid and rough dentistry here in the 1890s. First aid was a good conversation starter with Arabs. The need for better medical care made Zwemer ask for a doctor, and the need for a hospital was not far behind. Samuel and Amy Zwemer, James Moerdyk, and my father and mother designed and erected the hospital. There were no other buildings in Bahrain like it at the time."

Wells continued, "My father, being the only surgeon, had the most input on the original hospital's design, but James Moerdyk, a detail person, was instrumental in the final plans. No Bahraini believed such a grand building was going to be used exclusively for patients. They assumed that the missionaries would live in such a mansion. There was no air-conditioning in 1902 when the hospital opened, so the rooms were intentionally designed to be airy, with large windows, high ceilings, and wide verandas for shade.[5]

"My mother's medical degree was in homeopathy, which is out of vogue now.[6] Back then, allopathy and surgery, both established

---

[5] See endnote 6:5, p. 379.

[6] In America, homeopathic principles put forward by German physician Christian Friedrich Samuel Hahnemann had flourished in the last quarter century of the 1800s, in close association with Christian Science.

Sharon John Thoms and hospital staff, 1904 (SJT)

Western medicine, did not have very good tools—or reputations, for that matter. As you well know, even now, our tools are far from perfect. Most of our equipment and pharmacy can still fit into a doctor's bag. The University of Michigan, where my mother studied, closed its homeopathic medical school some years ago.[7] My mother was such a promising student that she took half her courses with the regular med-school students, but none of her courses included either dissection or surgery. Homeopathy did not cover those subjects. Nor did Marion's father, a bitter and wounded survivor of Civil War battles, allow her to become what he called a 'butcher doctor.'

"My mother and nurse Amy Zwemer provided the best care they could. They attended many women in childbirth and with complications. They ran clinics for women, but only the most courageous local women came. I was told mother's first clinic patient was so frightened she fled in panic as mother prepared to clean her infection. Most women felt comfortable only in their own homes, as probably they do even now. My mother and Amy mostly made house calls, and they and the rest of the medical staff would ride big white al-Hasa donkeys to visit their patients. Each donkey was led by its owner,

---

[7] See endnote 6:7, p. 379.

running alongside it. My mother knew enough allopathic medicine to serve her patients, but she consulted my father in other more difficult cases. She was an excellent care provider, and since Bahraini homes at that time were far from antiseptic, cleanliness was the first treatment of choice." Wells stopped to catch his breath.

A typhoid death

After a silence, he continued, "I never really knew my mother. When she died, I was just sixteen months old. My memory of her is quite hazy. The hospital and mission house were then on the southern edge of Manama. The Shi'ah Muslim cemetery was just beyond the hospital. There had been no land reclamation then, so the hospital was not far from the sea at high tide.[8] There was no public water supply or sewage treatment, as there is now. Water was either transported on the backs of camels and donkeys or carried by porters from natural springs. Most people used the intertidal zone as their toilet—what choice did they have—and hygiene was not the priority it is now.[9] Along with so many others in Bahrain, my mother contracted typhoid fever and died in 1905. Presumably, bacteria had migrated into the water we used, and it is possible our cooks did not properly boil our drinking water, since practically no Bahraini accepted the germ theory of disease in those days. Typhoid may also have spread because flies, breeding in human feces, infected our food.[10]

"My father nearly went crazy with grief. As a doctor, he diagnosed my mother's illness as typhoid fever, but he could not do a thing to cure her. She was completely lucid throughout and agreed with his diagnosis. Finally, her intestines ruptured, and peritonitis set in. The relatively primitive state of surgery and pharmaceutical research at that time meant that Father could only attend her in hopes she would weather the crisis.

"After she died, he raged. It was as if half of him had been amputated. His soul mate and partner in mission was gone—taken against his will. Everything they had dreamed and planned during

---

[8] The horizontal expansion of Bahrain onto the shallow tidal flats beyond its coral platform had not yet begun.

[9] The modern age, in which water supplies are segregated from human sewage by water and sewage treatment facilities, in Bahrain had to wait for the substantial revenues from petroleum and natural gas extraction.

[10] The ever-curious Dr. Paul Harrison of the Arabian Mission corroborated the association of fly reproduction with exposed human feces and the probable cross contamination by flies of uncovered, cooked foods.

Marion Wells Thoms and Frances, ca. 1900 (SJT)

their six-year marriage had turned to ashes. Very bitter, bitter tears. To make it worse, we three children needed care. I was just sixteen months old and did not understand any of this. Although we did have a young American governess, Father wondered how he was going to care for my sisters and me and continue as a mission doctor. He even had to move into the hospital to stop the gossip that he was living in the house with the governess, a single woman.

"The one treatment they did not try that might have helped my mother was cooling her fevered body with ice. My father's exasperation was that ice was available just over the horizon. A British gunboat, the HMS *Redwing*, had an ice-making machine on it and was anchored in Bahrain's roadstead.[11] But the weather was so hot, the ice would have melted before the sailors could carry it ashore, and there was no room on the gunboat for a deathly ill person.

"Father vowed something like this should never, ever occur again in Bahrain. In desperation, he ordered an ice machine from the United States. He informed the mission board he would pay for it himself. The

---

[11] The history of natural ice in Asia and the replacement of naturally frozen ice from New England with artificially manufactured ice is told in Dickason, "The Nineteenth-Century, Indo-American Ice Trade." A portion of ice imported to India from the US was always reserved for medical use to reduce high fevers.

HMS Redwing, *ca. 1909* (SJT)

machine was not cheap, and another person in Bahrain volunteered to go shares in a business partnership to make ice available to everyone who needed or wanted it. The mission board, however, did not like a missionary being a businessman on the side, even if for a good cause. They feared prattle about mixing the affairs of God and mammon, even if the business did fulfill God's redeeming purpose. The ice machine finally arrived, but only after another missionary, Mrs. Jessie Bennett, had died, also from typhoid. The machine languished in an *ambar*[12] because its use had not been approved. It remained a festering reminder of Father's frustration at his own helplessness and the lack of understanding that persisted between his American and Gulf colleagues. Years later, Dr. Stanley Mylrea told the Thoms family that the ice machine had come to an inglorious end when it exploded after Father insisted it be started up—as if in a sign from On High.[13]

"Father grieved my mother's death deeply. When Dr. Mylrea was first posted to Bahrain, Father insisted that the mission purchase brass insect screens to keep flies and insects away from the food and water in their houses. In addition to protecting the food, these screens would reduce the possibility of mosquitoes transmitting malaria. Although they were expensive, Mylrea concurred with Father's proposal, and they imported and installed the screening together.[14]

"Those were truly tragic times, but our family was not the only missionary family to suffer. The Zwemers lost two of their

---

[12] Storeroom.
[13] The Bahrain ice machine saga can be found in letters to the Arabian Mission headquarters in New York and in the early minutes of the Arabian Mission annual meetings in which the main "action" was to table (i.e., delay) action on the ice machine. Then the record goes silent. Only after Dr. C. S. G. Mylrea retired to Kodaikanal (India) in the 1940s was the story revealed over dinner at the Thoms cottage, "Dar-Es-Salaam."
[14] The mission experienced no further loss of life for many years among Bahrain missionaries after fly screens were installed.

Arabian Mission annual meeting, Bahrain, 1907 (SJT)

three children, Fatimah and Ruth, in a single month the year before my mother died. Mrs. Bennett passed away in 1906. My father was frustrated not to be present to help the Zwemers and to be powerless without the ice machine to relieve Mrs. Bennett.[15] As you know, they are all buried in the Christian cemetery beyond the Shi'ah cemetery, around the corner from the British cemetery.

"My mother's death was a contributing factor to opening the medical mission in Oman. My father was in such a state that his colleagues thought he needed a new challenge and a change of locale. They worried that he could not stop grieving my mother's death. At the annual mission meeting in 1907, it was decided he should open a new medical practice and hospital in Muscat, Oman. Father brightened at the idea of pioneer medical work, and in due course, our family went to Matrah, the commercial twin town to Muscat, the sultan's capital.

"I'll visit my mother's grave, of course," concluded Wells. "From all accounts and her letters, she was quite amazing. It is a tribute that the mission named the Women's Hospital in her memory." Glancing at his watch, he said, "Sorry to have run on so long about my parents. If

---

[15] See endnote 6:15, p. 380.

you need my help at any time, Dr. Tiffany—Mary—please don't hesitate to call on me."

With that, Wells thanked the Pennings for dinner on his first day in Bahrain and departed to prepare for the busy days to come. He was not sure what to expect, in part, because the Great Depression and the loss of the pearl trade had hit Bahrain's economy with devastating force. He suspected some Bahrainis' living conditions would be little better than in his parents' time. One thing he was sure of, his capabilities as a physician were going to be tested.

CHAPTER 7

Bitter, Bitter Tears

*What you did was unconscionable!
I should have realized what an unwise
and risky path Marion was following.
You should be horsewhipped!*

More painful memories

    The evening's dinner conversation with the Pennings and Mary Tiffany dredged up memories Wells had long buried. He thrashed restlessly in bed as sleep evaded him, and in his reverie, he wandered again through imperfect images of earlier times. He tried to make sense of them, to arrange them in a semblance of order.

    After Mother's funeral, Father moved out of the mission house to live in his hospital office. We—Frances, Lois, and I—continued living in the house supervised by our governess, May DePree. She had joined us after the previous furlough when it became clear Mother could not perform her medical tasks while parenting three young children. Father felt obliged to move out of the house because a prudish mission colleague said it was improper for him to sleep under the same roof as his single, female governess. In this way, Mother's death stung Father triply—having lost the one he loved most, having lost intimacy with us children, and having his moral standards impugned. Did his fellow missionaries understand how deeply he had been wounded by Mother's loss?

As if his life had not become difficult enough, Father knew he was obliged to inform Mother's parents, Grandpa Seth and Grandma Etta Wells, of her tragic passing. Father knew they would also be devastated by the news of their eldest child's death. Father's relationship with Grandma Etta was open and warm, in sharp contrast to his rapport with his father-in-law. Grandma Etta would be more understanding because she had encouraged her daughter to go to medical school and to pursue her passion to become a missionary doctor at Father's side.

Grandpa Seth, on the other hand, posed a real challenge. He had only grudgingly accepted his daughter's desire to become a doctor. He specified that Mother could enroll at the University of Michigan but only to become a homeopath. Homeopathy specifically excluded surgery from its tool kit.

Grandpa Seth's opinion of doctors was scarred by his experience in the American Civil War. In his mind, battlefield surgery was akin to butchery, combining primitive training with the crude tools and minimal anesthesia of the Civil War era. My grandfather had fought in the battles of Manassas and Gettysburg and in the rout of the Union Army at Chambersburg. He had been wounded but was one of the lucky ones to have survived mostly intact. On the other hand, Grandpa Seth's brother, Will, died in an explosion when he was transferring artillery shells for use against the Confederacy. I suspect that Grandpa may have had survivor's guilt because he had lived, and his brother and so many friends had not. Grandpa seemed to suffer from shell shock brought on by his Civil War experiences.

Wells' trancelike recollection continued.

Uncle Will was engaged to Grandma Etta before he enlisted. When he did not return, it seemed natural that his surviving brother would marry the loving fiancé who had waited in vain for her beau to return. There was more than a touch of sadness in this marriage of convenience that may have made Grandpa Seth feel endlessly in his brother's shadow. Pain and grief frequently turned Seth the peaceable farmer and talented barn builder into an emotionally volatile presence.[1] In those moments, Mother

---

[1] See endnote 7:1, p. 380.

was one of the very few who could console him. Mindful of these bitter memories, Father did not know how Grandpa Seth would take the news of Mother's death. The text of the letter Father sent is seared into my memory. I have read it countless times.[2]

> Bahrein, Persian Gulf (Arabia)
> April 28, 1905
> (via Bombay)
>
> My Dear Mother and All:[3]
>
> May the Lord direct my pen and be with you all when you receive this, for God in His wisdom has seen best to take from us our precious one. It seems so hard to believe how it can possibly be so, but her answer when I told her the end was near has greatly strengthened and helped us, and may it also help you. She said: "We all know how we would like it to be, but God knows best, and He never makes a mistake."
>
> She seemed better on Sunday, and we thought the crisis past; but Monday her temperature went up to 105.3, and after remaining there about three hours, in spite of cold sponging, it suddenly dropped to 100, there being profuse perspiration meanwhile (and I feared a perforation had occurred); shortly symptoms of peritonitis set in, and she passed away at 10:50 Tuesday night (with her arms clasped around my neck) conscious to the last. She said, "Tell the home people how I loved them," and if ever a girl loved her home and her home people, it was she; it was only because she loved her Master more that she felt she must obey His call. From 6:30 p.m. until she died at 10:50 p.m., her head was on my arm, and she was arranging things, giving me advice, and messages for all. She even had a message for the helpers, and Philip and the cook, who is a converted Mohamedan [sic].
>
> Miss Lutton has offered to write to you this week and tell you more about the last precious minutes, and Miss DePree will

---

[2] Sharon was an eager adopter of new technology and was one of a few missionaries who absolutely required a "new-fangled" typewriter on the mission field; he was also an avid dry-plate photographer and velocipede racer. In Bahrain, he raced his high wheel velocipede against the best of the large Al-Hasa white donkeys—and won.

[3] Sharon seems unsure if addressing Seth by name in this letter would enrage him. He had always felt uneasy with Seth. The letter is in the family collection.

write next week and will tell you especially about the children. They are so sweet about it all, and Frances seems to understand what we tell her so well; she asks a great many questions and seems so glad that Mama will not be sick any more in heaven. She says she is Papa's little comforter, and when she sees tears in my eyes she comes and pats me on the back and wipes my eyes. Little Lois does not seem to wonder or think very much, she is so young; but we will show them Marion's picture often and tell them much about her, so their memory of her will grow, and include all her sweet qualities. She was so patient and loving through her sickness, as she has always been through her life.

She told Miss DePree about her funeral clothes, household things, and the children and asked that certain of her dresses be sent home when the next missionary went home. She gave her watch to Frances and her cloverleaf pin (green enamel and pearl in center) to Lois.

Mr. Moerdyk had the coffin made and covered with black cashmere, and the funeral was held at 11 a.m. the twenty-sixth, Mr. Moerdyk reading the fifteenth chapter of I Corinthians in Arabic in the chapel.[4] The native helpers were the pallbearers, and at the grave, he had a brief English service; she was buried next to Katherine Zwemer.[5] She wore her new white silk mull dress, with the Woman's Board pin at her neck, and she looked so sweet and happy. She wore the wedding ring that has not been off her finger since I put it on that happy night at Garbutt, six years and seven months ago. Mr. Zwemer gave me his large American flag when he went home, and she asked to have it draped about the coffin, for next to her God and her home, she loved her country—in this she was her father's daughter.

Throughout her illness the weather was so cool, except one day, and she felt so thankful for this. The day of the funeral was rather hot, 93 degrees in the shade, and as the coffin could not be finished before, we had to have the funeral in the heat of the day. Frances walked with me to the cemetery, about a quarter of a mile away, and Lois and the baby stayed at home with one of the colporteur's daughters.

---

[4] See endnote 7:4, p. 381.
[5] When Samuel and Elizabeth Zwemer lost two of their three children in one month, Sharon Thoms was in the US on furlough. Sharon often wondered if he could have prevented those deaths.

I think Marion told you about the beautiful nasturtiums we succeeded in having in the garden. The coffin was trimmed very prettily with almond leaves, nasturtiums, and sweet alyssum.

The boat is in sight so I must close. I shall be praying for you much during the month before you receive this, that you may be as resigned to the Father's will as she was.

With much love from the children and your loving son and brother,

S. J. Thoms

Our governess, May DePree, was the sweet and loving sister-in-law of Rev. James Cantine, one of the Arabian Mission's cofounders. She was not a "regular" missionary appointed by the mission board. Instead, a generous parishioner[6] had paid for May to become our governess. I was just a toddler, and we quickly became very close. My sisters, Frances and Lois, however, were old enough to remember Mother and feel her loss more acutely, so although they were always respectful of May, their relationship with her, albeit proper, was more distant.

Fifteen months after Mother's death, Father married May DePree. To some extent, this must have been a marriage of convenience since there were no other eligible Western women in Bahrain.[7] In many ways, it was not unlike other arranged marriages in the Gulf and India where weddings sealed family alliances, and therefore were a bond of expediency. Gradually, mutual affection bloomed between Mother May and Father, and a warm and tender home life resumed.[8] Of course, it could never erase Father's bittersweet memories, but from the depths of his despair, Father resolved to continue in mission service with renewed zeal.

---

[6] Mrs. Eben Erskine Olcott, whose husband owned the Hudson River Day Line of cruise ships.

[7] This was an age when disease and accident carried off young adults relatively frequently. Not everyone survived from birth to ripe old age. Widow or widower remarriage was common in the US and Arabia at this time.

[8] As token of his troth to May, Sharon bought a cottage in Kodaikanal (South India) and named it after her—May Villa. It stands to this day. May Villa was to signify the place they would celebrate their family's solidarity while receiving respite from the incredibly hot summers of Oman. The children attended Kodaikanal School nearby.

Sorrow compounded

For Wells tossing restlessly on his cot, the grim images tumbled forth one after another. His mental picture jumped to 1910, when the entire family was on furlough in the United States.

> It had been seven years since Father had seen his own and Mother's families. We children had grown considerably. I was almost eight years old and distinctly remember Father saying we needed to visit Mother's parents. I think Father was hoping to reconcile with his in-laws after Mother's tragic death, but he strongly suspected the visit would be difficult. Father had not received any conciliatory letter of understanding or encouragement since Mother had died.
>
> Father decided it would be better to visit my grandparents in Garbutt, New York, soon after our boat landed in New York City. We would take the New York Central train directly there, and then, after our visit, we would continue west to Detroit. In Detroit we would change to the Michigan Central Railroad and travel on to Kalamazoo. From Kalamazoo we would take the last leg of our trip by interurban trolley to Father's family home near Three Rivers.[9] It all sounded so exciting the day we set out.
>
> Father sent a letter to his in-laws announcing our planned visit. As the reunion approached, a growing tension replaced Father's normal serenity. When the train chuffed westward from Syracuse, Mother May, too, seemed increasingly apprehensive, wanting us to be absolutely neat, clean, and ready to meet the Wells clan. A neighbor, Tom Pullings, met us at the train station with a horse and carriage. Except for the horse's clopping hooves, all was silence on that ride. It was as if time itself hung suspended. Once there, Grandma Etta and our cousins welcomed us with warm hugs and kisses.
>
> Soon we were ushered into the drawing room to meet Grandpa Seth.
>
> Father started out awkwardly and said something like: "Brother, I would like you to meet again your grandchildren, Marion's—our—beautiful children. This is Frances, then Lois, and that's Wells. They have grown so much since last you saw them. I am so proud of them and am very happy to present them to you. Children, give your grandfather curtseys and hugs."

---

[9] See endnote 7:9, p. 381.

Grandpa Seth, however, would have no social niceties nor warm family embraces. He turned around raising his arm toward Father with an accusatory finger extending from gnarled knuckles and shouted, "Murderer! You murdered Marion! I told you this in my letter. You took her on your ill-advised escapade, and she paid for your foolishness with her life!"

We children were petrified. After what seemed like an endless black silence, Father demurred quietly saying he would gladly have exchanged his own life for Mother's. He was beginning to say that the two of them had fully agreed before they were married to go into Christian mission work together regardless of the risks, but he was interrupted.

"No excuses for Marion's death are acceptable!" Grandpa Seth roared. "What you did was unconscionable! I should have realized what an unwise and risky path Marion was following to become a doctor. I should never have approved her going to Ann Arbor in the first place. I thoroughly regret allowing Marion to marry you and of her going on this fruitless and dangerous missionary experiment. You should be horsewhipped!"

Grandpa Seth fulminated some more in this vein. Painful as it was to hear, I came to understand later that this grizzle-bearded Civil War veteran was a survivor broken by two of the bloodiest battles of that conflict, grieving again those many deaths and that of his firstborn child. Overcome by tears and rage at the uselessness of it all, he sat and wept. He understood bravery and devotion to country. Unflinchingly, he had answered his own call to duty. That his daughter had responded to a similar call to a higher spiritual cause, he just could not comprehend. A loving, gentle man overpowered by his own scarred past, he could not rise above the tides of recurring grief. He could not embrace us children to reassemble the pieces of his family's broken life.

Father turned and said quietly, "Children, let us go to the other room. Your grandfather needs to be alone." Overawed and wide-eyed at the intensity of the exchange between Grandpa Seth and Father, we filed silently out of the room.

Grandma Etta materialized suddenly to normalize the situation. Cookies and milk helped even more. The rich milk from Grandma's "American" cows was nothing like we were used to in Bahrain or Oman. Even though we were still smarting from the former exchange, we could not help smiling at our images in the kitchen mirror, complete with creamy white lactic mustaches. The sweet, crisp-yet-moist butter cookies with a whisper of cinnamon on top entranced us. Grandma Etta did not have difficulty persuading us to "test out" another cookie or two.

Grandma Etta, in a voice intended only for Father and Mother, murmured that Grandpa Seth had not been so emotionally wrought up for years. She reminded Father that it was at such times in the past that only his daughter Marion could comfort him.

"What should we do now, S. J.?" whispered Mother May timorously.

Father was perplexed. He turned to Grandma Etta and asked, "How soon do you think Seth will recover a semblance of self-control and hospitality? Would it appear we are waiting to engage further in the fray if we stayed another day or two? Will Marion's death always stand as an unforgivable block between Seth and me? Would it be better if we go on to Michigan, and if so, when?"

It was quickly decided that it would better if we set out for Michigan immediately. Grandma Etta promised she would write if Grandpa Seth ever expressed regret or interest in reconciliation. We reloaded the carriage. Father and I sat up with the driver, Tom Pullings, who returned us to the station in time for the evening train to Michigan. During their lifetimes, however, we never returned to the Wells farm in Garbutt, New York.

Wells thought it unnecessary and inappropriate to share these most intimate family remembrances with the other mission personnel. Whether or not they could imagine the family dynamic behind the tragic death of his mother, Dr. Marion Wells Thoms, he did not know, and he was not going to try to find out.

CHAPTER 8

Of Beards and Brains

You can't be the doctor.
You have no beard! You're just a boy.
Everybody knows that when
a man's beard appears,
then his brain also matures.

Learning the ropes

Wells eagerly threw himself into the Bahrain Mission Hospital's flow of work.[1] In later years, he recalled his first day of mission duty. "When I landed in Bahrain on a bright spring morning and walked from the mission house to the hospital to start my first day of medical missionary service in Arabia, I experienced a feeling of exultation I cannot describe. My fondest dreams were realized that day as I sat to treat patients in the same office my father had used for consultations, and then later in the day, I operated in the splendid operating room in the Marion Wells Thoms Hospital for Women."

By the end of the day, Wells' head was spinning from all the demands being thrust his way. At the same time, he was ecstatic about the medical opportunities that had presented themselves. "There is every kind of malady here a young doctor could hope to see," he

---

[1] Originally named Mason Memorial Hospital but now called the American Mission Hospital. See also, endnote 8:1, p. 381.

crowed. He was, of course, not reflecting on the hospital's short-staffed situation and the heavy load on the doctor's shoulders.

Wells began with hospital rounds of inpatients who had either received treatment or undergone operations. The hospital employed several competent young South Indian nurses, and they gave brief descriptions of their patients' histories, so far as they knew them. The nurses did not speak Arabic or any other Gulf patois, so they were sometimes hampered in obtaining the requisite facts from their patients. Wells elicited further information from patients using his limited command of Arabic medical terms.

Many recovering patients said gratefully, *"Barakat el Messiya."*[2] This surprised Wells since he had not yet learned that Jesus of Nazareth is highly revered in the Q'uran.[3] Whether or not they intended this to be a sign of openness to religious conversion, these responses indicated patients were aware that they were being treated in a Christian hospital.

To others, he said, *"Akhui,"*[4] we will do everything in our power to help you. We know that the Great Physician, God personified in Jesus Christ, will help you to get well. Rest comfortably." After breakfast and morning devotions led by Rev. Pennings, Wells prepared to open his clinic for outpatients.

Wells asked one of the Shi'ah Muslim nursing staffers, "How many will come to clinic?"

"Many, for they want to see the new doctor. Many others arrive each day from all over the Gulf and from deep inside Arabia."

"Do we have an emergency room for the people who are seriously ill and need immediate attention? If so, who makes that decision?"

"Anyone in the queue could be an emergency case. There is no choice. Of Bahrain's seven doctors, four are here at Mason Memorial." Wells did a quick mental tally: two mission doctors were away, and the third would leave after her impending wedding. He was the fourth.

His Shi'ah assistant added, "People are good at waiting their turn. When we go on tour into Arabia or to the shaykhdoms in the Gulf, nobody wants to wait. Everybody wants to be treated first, but here at the hospital, they have learned to wait for their turn."

Wells understood that the clinic would involve a combination of triage and on-the-spot diagnosis and prescription writing. He would have to develop a soothing, confidence-building clinical manner,

---

[2] My progress is a blessing from Jesus.
[3] Book of Islam.
[4] My brother.

emulating an Arab shaykh. There was no time for rescheduled appointments or for referrals to medical specialists. He would have to do it all.

"Do we maintain medical records on our patients?"

"We don't have space for such records. The weather is so hot and humid that paper records quickly mildew or are eaten by insects. In any case, it would take much effort and time to organize them for use later."

"Hmm. Basically, our medical records are stored in our memories, the memories of our patients, and their families."

"Yes sir."

Wells suspected that the British advisers to the Bahrain government did not require careful record keeping. There was certainly no government agency or insurance company reimbursing the hospital for patient care. He realized many patients might never have visited an allopathic doctor or clinic before, and likely they would not be able to describe their symptoms in a meaningful way to a Western doctor.

"Do we know whether our patients have received treatment before coming to us?"

"Most people have already received their preferred treatment. They consult an indigenous doctor, a religious preceptor, or a spiritualist to exorcise an evil spirit. Only if the other cures have not worked will patients come to us. We get the hard cases, often too late for proper treatment."

So, Wells thought uncharitably, these quacks and shamans are the first responders. People are going to come to us as last responders and then only if everything else has failed. This makes everything more difficult.

"You will know if patients have consulted others by the signs on their bodies, Sir," his nurse assistant continued. "Often they will receive clinical cauterization. They may be burned by a hot, metal poker. After a woman gives birth, a midwife may pack the birth canal with salt to stem the bleeding. Only in neighborhoods around the hospital do the people have confidence in us and come for early treatment. We expect the people coming from far away to have sicknesses that they believe are nearly incurable. Their suffering is so severe that it forces them to travel far from home."

"If I write a prescription, where does it go?" Wells asked.

"It goes to the hospital's compounder-pharmacist," replied his nurse assistant with a straight face. "We have our own pharmacy here at the hospital because there are no local pharmacies with the needed drugs. We order these drugs from India or Britain. Our compounder is very good; he is a Shi'ah colleague. He is very reliable, exacting in his work, and very well respected in Bahrain."[5]

"If I order a lab test, what happens?"

"You give it to the patient, who gives it to me. Then, when the clinic is over, I will have all the lab test requests ready for you." This was said with a hint of a smile.

"You mean the doctor does all his own lab tests?"

"Oh, yes. It has always been so. Our people do not know how to do the test or to interpret the results."

Looking at the crowd outside his office, Wells thought, "I am going to have to dial up my antennae to their most sensitive reading or I could spend days in the lab doing the tests I ordered on a single day. I also need time for operations and patient care. This is definitely not Gorgas Memorial Hospital with a lab and a lab tech for each ward."

"Now, if I decide an operation is needed, what happens?"

"You schedule when the operation should occur, and you do it with help from our operating room staff."

"If I order an X-ray, what happens?"

"Nothing. We don't have an X-ray machine."

"Great," thought Wells. "Basically, I am 'flying blind.' Many surgeries will be exploratory, but I will have to confirm or change my diagnosis while the patient is on the table. I do not want to open up any patient twice, and besides, I will not have time to do that because of the long patient queue."

"Do we have an anesthetist to manage the patient during an operation?"

"Well, yes and no. No, there is no doctor anesthetist. You are the doctor and will have to decide about what anesthetic is to be used and how much. Yes, we have two assistants who have learned to give anesthetics like chloroform and ether."

Wells realized that speed would be of the essence. The rapidity with which operations could be concluded successfully was going to be very important. Long, slow operations would mean increased risk to the patient.[6]

---

[5] See endnote 8:5, p. 381.
[6] Wells met only a few surgeons that operated more rapidly and accurately than he. He admired Dr. Somerville, a mission doctor in Neyoor near Nagercoil, Kerala (India), who was the fastest, most accurate surgeon he had ever observed. Somerville made surgery a choreographed "ballet," pacing the operation itself as

"We always do operations in the afternoons, sir. The weather gets so hot that people go indoors after *namaz salah*.[7] Then there are hospital rounds in the afternoon or evening, and depending on the day, there may also be house calls to people who are so ill they cannot come to the hospital."

"Is there is an ambulance service in Bahrain?"

"What is an ambulance service, sir?"

"What happens in the evenings? How do we handle medical issues at night?"

"At night," said the nurse, "one of us or a knowledgeable orderly is on duty, as well as the night watchman. If a patient's condition changes, we see if a new bag of saline solution is needed or a dressing should be changed, and we administer any prescriptions listed on the chart. For anything else, we are calling the doctor. Also, we are calling you if somebody comes to the hospital gate requiring the doctor."

To complicate matters further, Wells learned that he had to fit in time for consultations with the patients in the Marion Wells Thoms Hospital for Women. Dr. Tiffany was excellent with general obstetrics and gynecology, but she was not a surgeon. For Caesarean and other procedures, he expected to be called.

"Thank you for orienting me to the hospital and our routine, Nurse. Now, let's get on with our morning clinic."

Chastened out of his naive euphoria, Wells walked resolutely into the doctor's office in the Mason Memorial Hospital, Bahrain. This was the same hospital, with the same teakwood furniture, that his parents and their colleagues had built[8] and equipped in 1902.

Wells sat at his father's desk in his father's swivel chair and experienced a rare sense of serenity when his first patient came in. He was a Bedouin from the Nejd desert in Sa'udi Arabia, and this initial encounter shattered the romance of the moment:

"Where is the doctor?"

"I am the doctor."

"You can't be. I have come a long distance for my operation, and I want to see the doctor—not the doctor's boy."

"I am the doctor. There is my diploma." Wells pointed to the framed document on the wall.

---

if it were in an Olympic 200-meter dash, and he showed amazingly successful patient outcomes. Dr. Somerville was originally a Himalayan mountaineer.

[7] Prayers.
[8] With James Moerdyk and Samuel Zwemer.

"That paper doesn't impress me; you don't have a beard."

"What has a beard got to do with it?"

"Don't you know that when a man's beard appears, then his brain also matures?"[9]

Sulayman, his experienced Bahraini Shi'ah hospital assistant, strode purposefully into the office. "See here," he explained, "you are really speaking to the doctor. If you want treatment, there are no other doctors available. Many people are waiting. Either tell him your problem or leave in peace. The doctor is very busy." Sulayman ushered the Arab onto the verandah to think things over. The Arab later returned and, in time, became a grateful patient—even though his doctor was still "only a boy." Strange were the ways of these Nasranis,[10] he thought, with boys doing men's work.

Never enamored of facial hair, Wells ever after wore a narrow, carefully trimmed mustache. Only on medical tours into Oman, Sa'udi Arabia, Qatar, or the Emirates did he sprout a beard to demonstrate his standing and age. On return to the mission hospital, he once again became nearly clean shaven. A beard was uncomfortable in the operating room where temperatures soared.

Wells discovered that Rev. Pennings, left in charge of the hospital, was a good adviser and an excellent interpreter. Pennings sat in on many medical cases, and together he and Wells diagnosed patient symptoms. Wells believed Pennings was acutely observant and had developed intuitive knowledge of a great deal of medicine. His recommendations were helpful. His main advantage was that he knew Bahraini Arabic.

Wells reflected that he felt in his first few years rather like the farmer in the *Saturday Review* cartoon. Standing in his barn looking at his sick Holstein cow with a black pattern on her white hide that was strikingly reminiscent of a map of North America, the farmer said, "Larry, I don't think so. I'd say her problem is closer to Cincinnati."

The chief medical officer (CMO) of the mission hospital and the senior physician-in-residence in Bahrain was Dr. Louis P. Dame. Wells came to admire Dame as a paragon of what a contemporary physician should be and how he should function. Dame was a fine surgeon, an empathetic practitioner, and handsome, with a magnetic manner. Perhaps because he and his wife had no children of their own, he threw himself totally into the practice of medicine.

---

[9] Thoms, "Forty Years of Remembering."
[10] Meaning "Nazarenes," followers of Jesus of Nazareth, i.e., all Christians.

Dame said his call was to serve God by serving Arabs in Sa'udi Arabia, so he took it upon himself to discover Sa'udi Arabia firsthand. On several occasions King Abdal Aziz bin Sa'ud had invited him as a trusted medical confidant to come to Riyadh and treat the royal family and himself. The king had first met mission doctors in Kuwait. In 1914 Dr. C. S. G. Mylrea had treated the Ikhwaan, the Muslim militia Abdal Aziz used to consolidate the multiple principalities of Arabia into a single country. So impressed had the king been with Mylrea that he depended on Dame to be his "on-call" physician.

When Abdal Aziz contracted a severe cellulitis infection of his face and eyes, he sent an SOS for Dr. Dame who, as it happened, was already en route to Riyadh intending to look after Abdal Aziz's father. Now the trip took on greater urgency. For almost three days, a camel trotted across the barren wasteland carrying Dame to the capital city. Dame was warned not to stop, stretch, sleep, or—of all things—fall off his camel, for he would not be rescued. The riders carried a minimum of baggage and water for this express trip to Riyadh.

Dame found the king seriously ill. One eye had swollen nearly to baseball size, and his face was unrecognizably swollen. Dame knew the infection was far advanced, and it could easily spread to the king's brain, inducing meningitis with a likely lethal outcome.

"Oh, my friend, I was afraid you wouldn't come in time. I surrender myself into your hands; whatever you want to do, do," mumbled Abdal Aziz fuzzily.[11]

Abdal Aziz was then a relatively young man. He had probably contracted his skin infection by insect bite. Dame focused intently on draining the infection and keeping the patient and sick room scrupulously clean. He monitored the king three times a day, leaving instructions that he should be called if the king's condition changed in any way. Dame's treatment produced almost miraculous results. The king rallied,[12] and he was deeply grateful. Henceforth, Abdal Aziz invited mission doctors to visit Riyadh frequently.[13] In the first few years, Dame went on these expeditions across the desert, while other

---

[11] Dame, "Touring Inland Arabia," 3.
[12] It is likely that Abdal Aziz's lifelong impaired vision in one eye originated with this illness.
[13] Abdal Aziz had other doctors on his personal staff. Muhammad Khaled Kashoggi (a distant cousin of Jamal Kashoggi, the ill-fated *Washington Post* correspondent) was a Turkish doctor, and there were Syrian doctors on retainer, too. Perhaps the in-house medical staff in Riyadh was pleased to hand off the major risk of adverse patient outcomes to the missionary medical "interlopers."

medical personnel kept the hospital running in Bahrain. He also made visits by sailing vessel to the emirates—to Qatar, Abu Dhabi, Dubai, Sharjah, Umm al Quwain, and Fujairah.

When he returned from Ta'if, Dame discussed the mission's medical agenda with Wells. He said, "I was delighted to go to Ta'if. I was able to treat many more Arabs than just those in the royal household, and I traveled deeper into Sa'udi Arabia than I had expected to go, and that was very satisfying. I would give my right arm to be able to provide medical care to the whole population because no one there has access to modern medical diagnoses and cures. There is a world of difference between being here in Bahrain and being on the mainland. Here we are recognized for the work we have done, and the people are much more aware of the health options we offer. Of course, we cannot do everything, but we do so much more now than your parents were able to do a generation ago. Medicine has made big strides."

"Yes, I can imagine" responded Wells. "When my parents came to Bahrain, they were confronted by the ancient communicable killer diseases—cholera, plague, malaria, typhoid, smallpox, and dysentery. Bilharzia was also found routinely among date farmers around Basrah. All were endemic. If smallpox or cholera or the plague erupted into an epidemic, it could carry away a quarter or more of the population." He was in a reflective mood now that he was dealing with a fellow medico.

"My father used the latest, most up-to-date surgical techniques," Wells continued. "He discovered a revolution in surgery had occurred during the ten years after he had graduated from medical school. Adhering to the norms of his day, he scrubbed his hands in tincture of carbolic acid before operating with his bare, ungloved hands. This practice soon changed. Paul Harrison of our mission was one of the Johns Hopkins team that proved surgery carried out with gloved hands was much more effective than bare-handed surgery. With that simple, hygienic adaptation, patients contracted far fewer dangerous infections. That meant more successful surgical outcomes. My father went back to school at the University of Michigan in 1910 to learn the new gloved methods, and he went on to even greater success in Oman afterward."

"A wider range of maladies than just the historically endemic diseases exists now," warned Dame. "You may be confronted by a raging epidemic from time to time, I suspect. There are also numerous health problems of congenital origin. You will see more of them in time. Often, we are not given a chance to work with birth deformities,

Bahrain hospital staff, 1935 (PD)

although I think we see a higher-than-random incidence of cleft lips and palates. I suspect this is associated with cross-cousin marriages among Arabs.[14] There are variations on these craniofacial anomalies, but unfortunately, we do not have time to research or document them carefully, and we do not have any specialists. As an eye surgeon, you are our first true specialist in the Gulf. But, sufficient to the day are the challenges thereof," Dame concluded.

"Perhaps it will be possible to establish a medical society in Bahrain when more doctors practice medicine here."

"*Insha'Allah*. The world is changing, and Bahrain is going to change, too."

Bahrain's centrality on the Arab side of the Gulf, with its plentiful supply of fresh water, meant that mission personnel, beginning with Samuel Zwemer and James Cantine at the start of the twentieth century, concluded that Bahrain should be the staging point from which the mission would launch its efforts to spread Christianity into the Arabian Peninsula.

Wells found that Bahrain's hospital staff was educable, and many among the Shi'ah and Sunni Muslim employees quickly got the hang of Western medical methods. The doctors were so busy, they did not have time to train their Bahraini staff in more than the most essential care practices, and this training occurred amidst their work with sick patients. Schools in Bahrain were *kuttab*[15] schools, focusing

---

[14] The marriage of first cousins, to this day, is not unusual in the Arab world.
[15] Book.

on the Q'uran and related texts. As a result, they taught little or no modern science, so it was unreasonable to expect that job applicants would have even intuitive comprehension of such notions as the "germ theory" of disease. The hospital was dependent upon local staff because of costs. It could hire only a handful of trained nurses from India to help with patient care, because the hospital had to be self-financing in every respect beyond the small salaries the mission doctors and nurses received from the RCA.

Wells brought resourcefulness and his excellent medical training to bear in his service to the Mason Memorial Hospital. He wanted to raise Bahraini medical practice to the highest standard of Western allopathic medicine, but there were major constraints. The hospital was now thirty years old and had not received preventive maintenance; the facilities were showing their age.

The mission was eventually able to rent a house for the Thoms family, and Beth and Nancy joined him in Bahrain. Their arrival made it possible for Wells to modify his daily hospital regimen. Beth, the lab technician, started training hospital staff to carry out more routine lab tests. When the doctors no longer had to do their own lab tests, a huge efficiency leap occurred. Because of this rudimental specialization, the number of patients who could be treated every day increased significantly.

Beth happily returned to Kodaikanal, South India, for her second baby's birth. Her parents still lived in Ranipet, where she had grown up. She had lived in Kodaikanal as both a schoolgirl and as a young woman, and her fluency in the Tamil language was still strong. Kodaikanal would provide an excellent retreat from the heat of Bahrain since this hill station was perched at nearly seven thousand feet above sea level in the Palani Hills just north of Madurai. Beth's mother and others from the RCA's Arcot Mission could host Beth in the Cotswold-like stone cottages owned by members of the mission. She could move across the road to the Van Allen hospital when the baby's time came.

Peter Scudder Thoms arrived April 15, 1933. A telegram from Beth to Wells told of Peter's birth. Wells proudly proclaimed to all of Bahrain, "Praise God, I have a son." In keeping with established tradition in the mission community, Peter was given an Arabic name, Ameen.[16]

Eighteen months later, Norman Wells Thoms was born to the Thoms family on November 5, 1934, in Bahrain. Bahrain's weather was

---

[16] Trustworthy.

cooler at this season, so birthing a child in the Marion Wells Thoms Hospital was not as arduous as it would have been in midsummer. Moreover, Beth could avoid the stress and logistics of taking two children and an *ayah*[17] on the eight-day, Bahrain-Kodaikanal trip. Wells was again able to tell all Bahrain, "Praise God, I have another son." Norman's Arabic name was Sa'eed.[18] Young Norman grew quickly.[19] In later years, the two boys seemed almost as if they were twins, despite their age difference, and that similarity triggered their paired names as "Pete and Repeat."

Because there was no room for the Thoms family in the mission homes near the Bahrain hospital, they rented a two-story house nearby. Wells took advantage of the municipal garden with its artesian well and unlimited supply of fresh water. The house had an interior courtyard that could be made into an ideal garden and give expression to one of Wells' hobbies. Wells applied to C. D. Belgrave, the shaykh's wazir,[20] and received permission to use some of the artesian water from the garden.[21] Not only was there water for plants, but there was also enough water for a splash pool for the children, and this made the hot summer weather far more bearable. They had become a lively family of five: Wells, Beth, Nancy, Peter, and Norman.

---

[17] Nanny, nursemaid.
[18] Happy.
[19] Norman was a colicky child. This was interpreted at the time to mean he was always hungry, and he was fed regularly and frequently. As a result, he also grew rapidly, and before too many years was about the same size as his older brother.
[20] *Wazir*: a ruler's principal advisor, often British.
[21] Belgrave and Wells had strikingly similar interests and characteristics. Not tall men, both were energetic. Both loved painting. Both loved plants, particularly flowering ones, and each had an acute sensitivity to the colors of flowers and landscapes.

CHAPTER 9

The Story of a Book: The Eleventh Century Speaks to the Twentieth Century

In treating cases of malignant anemia with a diet of geese livers, I found my patients were restored to health within a period of a few weeks.

Bahrain 1934[1]

While doing rounds at the Mason Memorial Hospital on a steamy September morning, Wells stopped at the bed of his Muslim Indian merchant patient from Karachi to write his discharge order. The man had received a hernia repair under local anesthetic eight days before, and since his wound was well healed, there was nothing more he needed except a few words of advice.

Wells said, "Don't lift heavy boxes; don't get constipated; no jumping off a camel's back."

The patient assured Wells that he would not overexert himself and then said apologetically, "I promised to pay you twenty-five rupees[2] for my operation and hospital care, but I am ashamed to say

---

[1] Thoms, "Story of a Book." This section, slightly modified from Wells' own words, is abbreviated from the above publication and focuses on the *Qanun* of Abu Sina (Avicenna). Pronouns are modified to maintain the narrative style of other chapters and to clarify who is speaking or writing.

[2] About five dollars, a considerable sum in the Depression years

I cannot. You see I am a towwash[3] but not a big one owning my own fleet of pearling ships. I just buy and sell a few pearls on the side. Since Japanese cultured pearls have flooded the market, the price of pearls has dropped, and I am bankrupt." He quickly followed this admission with a reassurance.

"I do, however, have some medical books which were highly prized by my father and grandfather who practiced Unani[4] medicine in Karachi. Please take your pick of them in exchange for your fee." He leaned over and drew a teakwood box from under his bed and took out several books wrapped in cloth. The largest one he reverently handed to Wells, "This is the prize of them all. My father used to say, 'If one knows the *Qanun* by heart, one has all the knowledge of medicine and philosophy that there is to know.' It was written hundreds of years ago by that peerless teacher, the hakeem,[5] Abu 'Ali ibn Sina."[6]

It was a big book of almost a thousand pages of finely printed Arabic in a red Morocco leather binding. Wells opened it to the title page, which confirmed the owner's statement. It was the complete five volumes of the *Canon of Medicine*, plus the *Kitaab an-Nejat*, the *Book of Salvation*,[7] by Avicenna. Printed in Latin on the title page of the *Kitaab an-Nejat*, toward the back cover of the book (in keeping with Arabic's movement from right to left), was the name of its publisher and the date and place of printing—Romae, Typographia Medicea, MDXCIII—printed in Rome by the Medici publishing house in 1593. Wells remembered enough of his course in the history of medicine to know that he had in his hands a rare book. He assured the patient that he would gladly accept the book in exchange for his fee.

Wells recalled that no single work had influenced the thinking of the medical world over such a long period of time as had the *Canon of Medicine*.[8] That evening, he scanned the book and was amazed at some of its passages. In the third book, which dealt with pathology, he found this: "In treating cases of malignant anemia with a diet of geese livers, I found my patients were restored to health within a period of a few

---

[3] *Towwash*: a pearl merchant.
[4] Ionian, i.e., Greek medicine practiced by Muslim practitioners.
[5] *Hakeem*: wise man, physician, philosopher, a title accorded to a distinguished member of the community.
[6] Better known in Western medicine as Avicenna, or Abu Sina (980-1037 CE). He was widely known in the ancient world as the "Second Teacher," Aristotle being the "First Teacher."
[7] *Kitaab an-Nejat* or *De Viribus Cordis*.
[8] See endnote 9:8, p. 382.

weeks." This was especially startling, for Wells had thought the notion that a liver diet might be used to treat pernicious anemia originated in the 1930s, with Minot and Murphy.[9] Yet here before his eyes was a statement showing that more than nine hundred years earlier, a Persian doctor had recorded his observation that liver was useful for the treatment of severe primary anemia.

In another part of the *Qanun* appeared the theory that sometimes one disease counteracts the harmful effects of another: "One disease becomes the medicament for curing another. Thus, quartan malaria often cures insanity." At the time Wells read this, the new treatment for general paresis[10] at the University Hospital in Ann Arbor was hyperthermy, inducing high fever in patients by infecting them with malaria. In the section on skin disease, Wells found scabies, ringworm, and athlete's foot well described and sulfur ointment rubs and hot sulfur baths recommended as treatments. Wells' experience in treating scabies with sulfur ointment made him feel that Avicenna's enthusiasm for sulfur might be justified.

By midnight, when he reluctantly put the book away, Wells was convinced that it contained much information that was still considered new and original in 1934. On his first free afternoon, Wells looked up his former patient. He found him in his little cupboard of a shop in the "*souk at-towwash.*"[11]

"Business is bad," the merchant said, so he had time to tell Wells all he knew about the book. His story took an hour in the telling, but Wells boiled it down to this single paragraph:

> I was the black sheep of the family. All the eldest sons of our ancestral tree were doctors as far back as we have any record. The *Qanun* was the main textbook used by my father and grandfather and great-grandfather. They not only read it but practically memorized it. I am not endowed with a good memory, nor am I a scholar at heart; still, I would have taxed my brains and attempted to comprehend the gist of the book to please my father. One day, he told me to open the temporal vein of one of his patients who was suffering from migraine. This I did, but so much blood ran out of the vein that the patient and I fainted, and my father had to revive us both. Soon after that, my father died. I inherited his

---

[9] In 1934 George P. Murphy and George R. Minot received the Nobel Prize in medicine for developing liver therapy to treat pernicious anemia.
[10] Inflammation of the brain can cause dementia and paralysis.
[11] The pearl merchants' market.

> books and his practice. I decided I was not cut out to be a doctor, so I sold his practice and some of his medical books written in the colloquial languages of Sind and of Hind and came to Bahrain to deal in pearls. If those satanic inventors, the Japanese, had not meddled in the business, I would be rich today.

If this volume could talk, thought Wells, it would give us an exciting story of travel from Rome, perhaps in the hands of a Persian or Indian medical student who, after completing his medical studies at Salerno or Padua, was returning to practice medicine in Isfahan or Hyderabad. There, his son and his son's son, each in his turn, would practice the system of medicine as taught by the Mu'allim at-Thani[12] Avicenna in the *Canon*. This system became known throughout the Orient as Unani medicine because it was widely acknowledged that much of it came originally from the Greeks ("Ionians"). When Karachi became a large and flourishing seaport in the latter part of the nineteenth century, many Persian and Indian doctors went there to practice, as did the ancestor of the pearl merchant.

A letter Wells received from Lt. Col. M. H. Shah, a medical officer in the Royal Pakistan Army Medical Corps in Karachi, confirmed Wells' assumption about the Pakistani medical environment in times past and present:

> In Pakistan there are still many hakeems—practitioners of Unani medicine. Most of them have, however, only a smattering of the knowledge from Avicenna. A few have studied in Unani schools—of which there are three in Pakistan. These hakeems have also a "hotchpotch" knowledge of modern medicine and use sulfa and antibiotics.

Wells was fascinated[13] to read in the sixth section of the second book of the *Kitaab an-Nejat* that Avicenna discusses the five senses—sight, hearing, smell, taste, and touch—and says:

> But concerning sight, a different view has been maintained, for some people have thought that something issues from the eye, meets the object of sight, takes its form from without and that this constitutes the act of seeing. They often call the thing, which according to them issues from the eye, "light." But

---

[12] The Second Teacher.
[13] See endnote 9:13, p. 383.

true philosophers hold the view that when we see an actually transparent body—i.e., a body with no color intervening between the eye and the object of sight—the exterior form of the colored body on which light is falling is transmitted to the pupil of the eye, and so the eye perceives.

Wells was in the right spot at the right time to receive from this son of a lineage of Persian doctors the rare and treasured book that had been for many generations his family's "medical Bible."[14]

---

[14] See endnote 9:14, p. 384.

CHAPTER 10

The Ins and Outs of Bahrain

Oil! We struck oil! Number One well is a gusher!
We've tried to cap it, but we just can't do it.
We need help! Now!

Chasing pearls

Wells learned quickly from Louis Dame's extensive medical knowledge. Having only assisted surgeries in Michigan, Wells needed to develop self-reliant skills for the time when he would be either the lead or the only surgeon on the island. The most common operations involved repairing hernias, removing hemorrhoids, and excising benign tumors. Soon, these were Wells' exclusive domain, in addition to all the eye operations that he had been doing as resident ophthalmologist. When no other doctors were available, he would handle all surgeries.

Dame and he consulted on difficult cases, the most frustrating of which were intestinal obstruction cases. The overriding questions were: What had caused the obstruction? And could it be relieved without surgery? Dame's philosophy was to use the most conservative, safe methods first, a view with which Wells concurred.

Dame reminded Wells, "Remember, a bowel obstruction can be caused by a big ball of round worms[1] in the small intestine that has

---

[1] Ascaris worms can form an obstructive "ball," causing ascariasis.

become so large that it actually obstructs the small gut. Worms are a very common problem, particularly in children, and are associated with malnutrition. The worms take much of the food supply in the intestine and then move on to infest other parts of the body." Total bowel obstruction caused by round worms was statistically rare, but there were so many cases of worm infestation that Wells learned to extract these large balls, often with hundreds of worms knotted together.

The doctors caught many other maladies in the clinic before surgery was needed. A common ailment was "runny ears,"[2] or chronic otitis media. When this progressed into an acute state, there was no choice but surgery. The only method to keep the infection from progressing to fatal meningitis was to dig into the inner ear to clean out the infected mess. Ear infections were common because of pearl diving. Pearl divers would descend from thirty to sixty feet, where the pressure on their eardrums was tremendous. Then their eardrums could puncture, and their ears could become infected.

Because of the hazards of their occupation, pearl divers and their families frequented the hospital with severe health problems. Because the pearl market was so depressed, the pearlers could rarely pay for the services. Wells found that the hospital was becoming one very big charity ward. How could they be expected to pay? They often did not have enough to eat. Inevitably, this caused a financial problem for the hospital because it was only partly sustained by donations from Christians in the United States. The American churches and their members provided funds for the buildings and equipment and for the meager salaries of the American Mission medical staff.[3] Everything else had to be paid from the revenue the hospital generated. Drugs, local staff, locally contracted doctors and nurses, supplies, and cost of services and infrastructure all had to be covered by patient fees. Wells was grateful that this was the CMO's nightmare. At least for now, that made it Louis Dame's problem.

Shortly after he had arrived in Bahrain, Wells decided to visit the Bahraini pearling fleet at work in Gulf waters to know better what could be done for the divers. Captain Smethers had shared many anecdotes and even called on him to "have a heart for the plight of

---

[2] Chronic otitis media, in its most acute form, was known as chronic mastoiditis.
[3] The Arabian Mission never received financial support from the US government, which offered minimal social services to its citizens. The same was true of the shaykhdoms of the Gulf.

pearl fishermen." In response, Wells wanted a firsthand understanding of their life. In particular, he wondered if the medical staff might treat divers while out on the pearling boats rather than waiting for them to come to the hospital after returning to port. Hospital personnel already visited villages outside Bahrain to treat those who could not travel; why couldn't the same approach apply for pearlers? Accordingly, Wells went and lived on board a pearling boat.

The sailing ships were generally *sambuqs*, vessels no more than fifty feet long with two masts sporting lateen sails and square sterns. To his surprise, given the size of the *sambuqs*, Wells realized they were an elegant design that incorporated both Eastern and Western features. Wells found as many as one hundred men on board each boat, of whom from fifty to sixty were pearl *ghawwas*.[4] They worked in two shifts, from twenty-five to thirty men at a time, following a well-established rhythm. Each diver was attended by a *saif*[5] who managed his diver's descent to the ocean floor and back. The *saif* dropped a heavy cannonball-like stone that pulled the diver down with it. From one-and-a-half to two minutes later, he hauled the ball back up to the surface, the diver with it. The diver came up slowly to avoid the bends. The myriad medical implications of this slow-motion pageant tumbled through Wells' mind.

Wells found the divers generally made five dives and then huddled on deck around a fire to warm up. Although the surface temperatures of the Gulf were very warm, the deep waters were much cooler. As one shift of divers warmed themselves, another shift was diving. In this way, diving continued all day without a break.

On rare occasions, a shark would attack a diver. At other times, an eel, its thick body anchored in a coral crevasse, would wrap itself around a diver's arm. Divers who could not get away from their attackers drowned. All divers accepted these occupational hazards without noticeable emotion. Wells was struck by their fatalism. If a tragedy happened, it had been "written on their foreheads," foreordained by Allah.

When not under sail, Wells observed that crews rowed their vessels galley style, chanting to synchronize their efforts. The oars were used to row the vessel in ever-greater concentric circles around a central buoy marking the territory where each pearling boat harvested oyster shells. Periodically, a pearling boat would lift its buoy, move to another

---

[4] Pearl divers.
[5] Pearl diver's rope tender.

site, drop the buoy, and begin again, tracing ever-increasing spiral arcs in its hunt for oysters. When not moving, the oars would be extended outward over the gunwales. A raised sail in total calm indicated that a pearling boat was standing still or drifting slowly and could not evade traffic.

There was even a man on board for religious duty. He was supposed to pray in place of those who were diving at prayer time. On occasion, he would relieve a ropeman so the latter could offer his own prayer.

After morning prayers and breakfast came the ritual of opening the previous day's oyster catch. When a diver found even a small pearl in the pile of oysters he had harvested, he would extract it with his knife and place it on the top of his big toe; the pearl would usually be sticky with oyster flesh, so it would adhere to his toe. The captain and first mate would circulate among the divers, picking up these "toe gems." Occasionally, there would be a shout as someone discovered a large pearl, and a chatter of congratulations would echo up and down the ship. Most were small seed pearls. A diver's eternal and elusive wish was for a large, lustrous pearl that would bring as much as fifty thousand rupees.

Accounts were not kept for each diver. The revenue from all harvested pearls was divided by shares among everyone on the boat. If there were one hundred men on the boat, the ship owner would get five shares, the *nakhoda*[6] three shares, the first mate two shares, the divers one share each, and their tenders a half share. All other costs of the pearling season—food, fuel, and ship repair and maintenance—also had to come out of the revenue stream. As long as the price of pearls increased, as it had during the nineteenth century, income prospects were good for everyone. Pearling, however, had fallen on hard times when Wells had visited because Japanese cultured pearls, combined with the Great Depression, had slashed the price of natural pearls.[7] This reality was reflected in the wilting morale of those aboard the pearling boat Wells had boarded.

Just before the divers had completed their shell shucking, an eager towwash, intent on beating the Bahrain auction prices, clambered aboard the diving boat from a smaller craft that had arrived from shore.

---

[6] Captain.
[7] Some pearl merchants mixed Japanese cultured pearls in among the more valued natural Bahraini pearls. When European dealers discovered they had been duped, prices for Bahraini pearls fell even further, and bad economic times became worse.

He hoped to make a deal for the day's pearls without having to contend with the pandemonium of competition in the port. It immediately struck Wells that such a preemptive visit to the pearling fleet might be combined with a floating clinic. By joining such a visiting towwash, he could tend to the injured and sick divers before they returned to the mainland.

As he watched the unfolding scene, Wells quickly realized this would never work. The negotiations for the pearls created such tension that the ship's crew was totally distracted. As the *nakhoda* and the towwash haggled over the price for the day's haul, all other activity stopped. If, in the divers' view, the final price seemed too low, they would call out to the *nakhoda*, "No. No sale, Captain. Keep our pearls and get a better price later." Everyone was on edge. This was clearly not a good time to treat pearling crews, even if they were very sick. Moreover, it was definitely not a good time to talk about the Great Physician.

As his stay lengthened in Bahrain, Wells came to understand how difficult it is for a Muslim to convert to Christianity. In leaving Islam, people risked being disowned and shunned by the family, friends, and community they depended on in these difficult economic times. Speaking about the Gospel was possible, and many Bahrainis responded favorably up to a point, but going beyond that point was rare and formed a continuing conundrum for Wells and the rest of the mission. He wrestled with it continually. Religious conversion was a particularly tough problem because it had economic as well as social and cultural ramifications. Furthermore, Wells soon realized that there was another more seductive competitor for the hearts and minds of Bahrainis.

The gospel of petroleum

When Wells arrived in Bahrain, he discovered that fellow mission physician Mary Tiffany was about to wed Walter Hinge, an oil company engineer. Walter took Wells out to the drill site near Jabal Dukhan in the middle of what looked like a crater. When they drove to the interior of Bahrain, they gradually ascended to the rim known as Rifa'a,[8] from which the road dipped down sharply, zigzagging to the floor of the crater. Wells learned this was a typical oil dome.

Most of the European and American residents in Bahrain attended the wedding of Mary and Walter on June 1, 1932. A reception followed at the Dames' house, where a somewhat smaller group

---

[8] Raised place.

attended, including the omnipresent C. D. Belgrave (wazir to the ruler) and his wife Marjorie, the head of the BI shipping agency, the head of the Eastern Bank, the Englishman in charge of Bahrain's electricity supply, and other American missionaries and oil company representatives.

During the reception, a car roared up outside, its horn honking wildly. In ran a driller dripping with crude oil, "Oil! We struck oil! Number one well is a gusher! We tried to cap it, but we just can't do it. We need help! Now!" Everyone, including the bride and groom and Wells, raced to the well site.

Wells discovered drillers struggling to cap the well and fighting to keep it from catching fire. They wanted to prevent the oil from flowing into the crater's valley, fouling everything in its path. Others filled burlap gunnysacks with dirt and sand to make a dam in the nearby ravine so the oil would not flow into Shaykh Isa's water wells. Shaykh Isa was more concerned about the oil polluting his precious water supply than he was about his newfound petroleum wealth. Just one month after Wells had arrived in Bahrain, this first solid evidence of oil in the lower Gulf promised to revolutionize Bahrain.

For Wells and the other missionaries, the oil-driven changes that began to sweep through Bahrain were hard to fathom. The Anglo-Persian Oil Company had functioned for decades in the northern Gulf region, but it had had little impact on daily life either in Iraq or the other Gulf principalities. This time, however, the impact on life in Bahrain was more visible and transformational as the implications of the "gusher" developed.

First, oil brought strange bedfellows to the shores of Bahrain. Through Walter and his other new friends in the oil business, Wells came to realize that wildcatters were a motley crew. He watched as the Bahrain Petroleum Company (BAPCO) built an oil camp outside Manama in Awali. Awali was a rough-and-tumble oil camp, filled with an assorted mix of expatriate workers reveling in behavioral excesses, not the least of which was alcohol abuse.

Ever alert to medical needs—and financial opportunities—the mission doctors realized the discovery of oil might provide them with an unexpected windfall. The Great Depression had so depleted the income of loyal RCA churchgoers that world missions funding had also declined. Wells knew dwindling financial resources had been a nightmare for Dr. Dame. The Arabian Mission was receiving one-third less financial support than before the Depression. A reduced budget meant the hospital was forced to cut its services and charity work. The needs of poverty-stricken Gulf residents had grown, but the mission's capacity to meet the needs of the poor had sharply plummeted. The government of Bahrain had never provided a subsidy for the mission's medical services, and it certainly could not do so during the Depression years. Bahrain's ruler had been more than happy to accept the benefits of free health care for the bulk of his people.

BAPCO soon discovered it had medical needs and asked the mission to provide medical services until the company could build its own hospital and clinic. Wells and Dame quickly assented—not only because of the mission's need for income but also because BAPCO did require genuine medical assistance. Dame and Wells together proposed a contract to BAPCO for as much money as they could imagine—two thousand rupees per month. It seemed like a king's ransom relative to the hospital's revenue that had nearly dried up. BAPCO accepted their offer eagerly and offered to supplement it further if the mission would provide an American nurse to staff a ward of the hospital in Awali. BAPCO agreed to construct and maintain the Awali ward and pay for a ward at the hospital in Manama as well. This welcome decision arrived just before the worst of the Great Depression years.[9]

Wells and the rest of the medical staff soon learned that the discovery of oil ushered in unique medical problems. Automobile accidents of every kind multiplied as Bahrainis switched from donkey power to (mechanical) horsepower. Industrial jobs differed sharply from those of earlier times, and the resulting accidents were often medically challenging. The oil camp attracted workers with an array of bad habits from malingering and invented maladies to psychological disorders contracted during World War I to alcohol and drug dependence.

Bahrainis were accustomed to saying, "*Allah kareem.*"[10] As novice drivers of trucks and buses, however, they discovered Allah did not generously protect them from the law of momentum when rounding sharp curves. The resulting calamities sent carloads to the hospital with fractures and internal injuries. Accidents formed a much larger share of the hospital's inpatient demands. Severe burns, too, were new. Bahrainis had learned to smoke, but they had not learned that they should not smoke in garages where autos and trucks were being repaired. Lighted matches sent numerous repair shops up in flames.

---

[9] This agreement had an unexpected consequence for the Arabian Mission. A train of single, female mission medical personnel—both nurses and doctors—found spouses among the oil company executives. It became a rueful joke when yet another woman left the mission community in this way. See also, endnote 10:9, p. 384.

[10] God is generous!

Some young men burned to death, and others came into the hospital with extensive third-degree burns. Burns were always the most difficult cases, requiring more staff time than any other injury.

One day a tall Somali was brought to the hospital. He had been a pearl diver. He was exceptionally thin, but otherwise healthy. BAPCO gave him a job as a painter. He painted the large oil tanks where oil was stored before it was transferred to tankers. One day he had to paint the top of a tank, but he became drowsy and fell asleep. He dreamed he was back on the deck of his pearl diving *sambuq* and that the *nakhoda* roused him and told him to get back into the water and dive for pearls. Without opening his eyes, he flipped over the edge of the tank as if into the water and fell to the ground below. It was a wonder he was not killed. He was brought into the hospital paralyzed from his waist down with a compression fracture of the upper lumbar vertebrae. Wells and Louis Dame operated immediately to remove pressure on his spinal cord. When the operation was over, they put the Somali in a plaster cast and hoped for the best, even though they thought his spinal cord had been irreparably injured.

Six weeks later, Wells walked past the Somali's hospital room. Wells thought he heard him say, "*Al hamdullilah! Al hamdullilah!*"[11] Wells wanted to know what he had to praise God for, so he entered the room. There he saw the Somali's big toe sticking out from under the sheet, and the Somali staring intensely at it. Wells looked too. Suddenly, his big toe moved just slightly. The Somali understood that if his big toe could move; his spinal cord had not been completely damaged.

"Keep moving your toe as often as you can. See if you can move other toes and your foot," said Wells excitedly.[12] As the days passed, a tingling sensation returned to the Somali's feet and legs. Slowly, he was able to get onto his feet and learn to walk again; in time, he was able to resume work. He solemnly promised to do no more back flips from the tops of oil tanks. The entire hospital staff joined in the refrain, "Al hamdullilah!" They offered praise to the Almighty for the Somali's miraculous recovery.

---

[11] Praise God! Praise God!
[12] At this time, there were very few physio/physical therapists, and rehabilitation therapy was almost unknown in Western countries and nonexistent in Gulf countries.

CHAPTER 11

Fast Dhow to Doha, Qatar

*The shaykh gave me in marriage
to one of his old geezer slaves.
But I'm in love with one of the shaykh's
younger slaves; he still has all his teeth!*

Qatar 1934[1]

One morning, a *chit*[2] arrived in Wells' mail from Bahrain's political resident, Sir Cumford Fowle. The note was written on behalf of Shaykh Abdallah bin Jassim al Thani, the ruler of Qatar, to invite Wells to travel to Doha, his capital. Shaykh Abdallah had learned of Wells' presence in Bahrain through his brother, Shaykh Mohammed bin Jassim al Thani. The latter, when visiting Bahrain in 1914, had been treated at the mission hospital by Wells' father, S. J. Thoms, and was favorably disposed toward the missionaries.

The note said to Wells, "You come. I know my people need eye treatment. Our family retainers and the people in town, as well as the Bedu nomads, all have eye problems." Wells welcomed the invitation. Following the advice of Dame and others, he usually waited for

---

[1] This chapter is based on the tape recordings Wells Thoms made during the last year of his life.
[2] Handwritten note.

invitations before making trips outside Bahrain. Arab hospitality is famously warm and welcoming, but Wells had learned from John Van Ess not to test its limits when he was uninvited. This, however, was an invitation he eagerly accepted. Accordingly, Wells jumped on the first dhow[3] to Doha before a countermanding order could change his plans.

When he came ashore at Doha's customs pier, the town was strangely quiet. Few people were on the street. A local official met him.

"Where is everybody?"

"They are in the middle of Doha, in front of the shaykh's castle. Shaykh Abdallah's eldest son, Shaykh Hamad, is having an eye doctor whipped."

"Bad news," thought Wells. "Perhaps I should not have come."

To the customs official, he said, "I've been summoned here by Shaykh Abdallah to treat people with eye diseases, and I would like to talk with him immediately."

As he emerged from the customs shed, Wells observed that Doha was a very small town, baking in the glaring sunlight. As far as he could see, Qatar seemed flat and desolate, even barren. Wells hoped the brilliant light would not trigger one of his nauseating and immobilizing migraine headaches.

Wells was taken to the town square where Shaykh Hamad sat in the shade of the castle wall and dispensed justice. A noisy crowd had assembled around a man stripped to the waist and tied to a pole, a sight that immediately repelled Wells. Wells repeated his announcement that he had been summoned by Shaykh Hamad's father to tend to Qataris' eye infections. Shaykh Hamad nodded in acknowledgment.

In the next breath, however, Wells declared, "I want the ship that brought me to Doha to take me back to Bahrain immediately."

Shaykh Hamad was incredulous. "Why? You've only just arrived."

"That is true. I hear, however, that you are going to have an eye doctor whipped. I am an eye doctor. I have come here at the request of your father to treat people with eye diseases. I do not like the idea of giving whippings because some patients are not happy with their medical treatment." A kangaroo court is a terrible way to handle a malpractice suit thought Wells.

Shaykh Hamad smiled and replied, "Oh, that wouldn't apply to you. You are my father's guest and we've heard you do good work in Bahrain. You studied in America, and you know what you're doing."

---

[3] *Dhow*: an Arab sailing ship.

After a moment's reflection, Wells responded, "I will stay on one condition. It is this. You let me examine the man with the complaint against this doctor, and I will find out what this situation is all about."

The old man who had brought the complaint came forward at Shaykh Hamad's beckoning. Wells took out his ophthalmoscope and noted the man's cataract had fused to the lens in one of his eyes. He could also see the retina of that eye and the optic nerve. He noted the pallor of the optic nerve and realized the old man had chronic, advanced glaucoma. He could not possibly have seen anything prior to the operation.

"Your Persian doctor here did a cataract operation all right. He removed it. I, however, can see the interior of the eye, and I know the patient could not see anything before the operation because his sight had already been killed by glaucoma. I'm sure you know this disease, *mai aswad*,[4] since it is not uncommon." The old man confirmed this, saying he had lost all vision in his bad eye years before the recent operation.

Wells turned to the doctor about to be whipped, "You are wrongfully accused of failing to restore this man's sight. If the old man had been able to see well before the operation and afterward saw nothing, then he might have grounds for complaint. He, however, could not have seen anything before you did the operation, so he has lost nothing except the few rupees he paid you. You made him believe you could help him. That was fraudulent."

The gathered townsfolk listened in rapt silence. Wells' calm, magnetic, commanding manner was convincing. There was no debate or argument about his resolution of the issue.

Shaykh Hamad declared, "Untie the man, and let him get dressed. Young man, you must repay this old man what he paid you. You should have warned him before recommending the operation that, because his eye did not see any light, he would not benefit from the operation." The young Persian doctor, grateful for Wells' intervention, made restitution and immediately headed back to Iran by the first outbound dhow.

Shaykh Hamad took Wells to his father's country house in Ar Rayyan that afternoon, a pleasant ride not very far away. The "country house" was a large Arab mansion built like a fort with four walls and central front doorway, a veritable *qasr*.[5] The *qasr* was built on elevated ground, and Shaykh Abdallah was standing out in front of

---

[4] Black water.
[5] Castle, mansion.

his big wooden entry gate just as they drove up, observing his camels, donkeys, cows, goats, and sheep filing through the big gateway into the courtyard. They had pastured all day on the plains surrounding the house. Wells thought Shaykh Abdallah looked like a contemporary version of Job, the Old Testament prophet who also had many sons and daughters, in addition to camels, donkeys, goats, and sheep.

Below the house was an extensive garden of date, lime, and banana trees, with alfalfa and other crops growing under the arboreal canopy. There were wells from which water was being lifted to irrigate the garden. The pulleys through which the ropes passed had not been oiled and gave out a high, piercing screech as each full leather water bag was raised. The sound may have been a bucolic symphony, soothing to the experienced ear, but to Wells, it was a fingernails-on-the-blackboard grating, not at all calming to his migraine-prone ear.

Entering through the grand gateway, Wells found that the interior looked out on a square courtyard with two stories. As was the case in many homes in Bahrain, the lower floor and courtyard were used for the servants, slaves, and animals. The herds that had just been driven in filled the courtyard with noise and pungent odors. Upstairs were rather elaborate and extensive family quarters. Shaykh Abdallah explained proudly that each son had a cluster of rooms for himself and his family; these were arrayed along a balcony that ran around the entire second floor.

Over the big evening meal, Shaykh Abdallah told Wells about his life in Qatar. He was especially pleased that his young men hunted gazelle. With their falcons, they also hunted *habara*.[6] The shaykh loved gazelle and bustard meat, and he relished the fact that they were plentiful in the surrounding desert. He reminded Wells that Louis Dame had been coming to see him for years and that he liked Dame very much. Now he was glad Wells had come. Many people needed eye care, and Wells would be welcome to stay in Ar Rayyan for as long as was necessary to treat himself and his relatives. If Wells could stay even longer, he would find him a house where he could also treat the people of Qatar.

After these pleasantries had been exchanged, Shaykh Abdallah pointed to one of his knees and said, "This knee is giving me a lot of trouble. Dame gave me medicine for it, but my knee doesn't get better."

Wells examined the offending joint. "It seems to me," he said, "you have gout. What medicine did Dr. Dame give you?" A servant quickly

---

[6] Bustard, a large game bird.

retrieved a prescription to take orally and a liniment to massage into the knee. "Well, that is about the only known treatment for what you have. The only additional thing I can advise you to do is to stop eating meat for a while; at the very least, you should give up eating venison and game birds."

When he heard this, the shaykh replied grimly, "You have told me the same thing Dame told me, and I am going to tell you the same thing I told him. I would rather have the pain and eventually die from it than give up the pleasure of eating venison and *habara*." The shaykh was hoping Wells had a special injection that would take the swelling down and make the pain disappear. Wells told him medical science had not yet discovered such a cure.

Shaykhs Hamad and Abdullah then took Wells to the quarters of Shaykh Hamad's mother, Shaykh Abdallah's first wife. Wells could tell both men had great affection for the old lady. She was still a handsome woman with a very gracious manner. She was in great pain though. Wells gathered she had an abscess on one of her buttocks, not far from the anus. The pain never eased and was getting worse each day. Since it was quite dark, and there were only a few lighted candles in the room, no inspection of the abscess was possible. Wells gave her aspirin with codeine to reduce her pain for the night and a plaster of ichthyol on lint that her maid could apply to the site of the pain to draw the infection out.

The next morning, she reported that she had had a better night, but her pain was even more intense in the one spot. Wells told her the pain could be relieved very quickly if she allowed him to operate. This was embarrassing to her because of the location of the problem, but given the intensity of the pain, she agreed to treatment.

Wells said, "Don't worry, Mother, I have to see only the tiny spot of your problem to fix it. The rest will be covered. Only the knife will touch you, and after that, your maid will do what is necessary upon my instructions. Mother, you must understand, there must be pain to get rid of the pain." This made sense to the old lady because traditional Arab medicine averred if a treatment was painless, it was also probably worthless. The old lady was draped appropriately, exposing only the offending boil.[7] With a quick scalpel incision, the abscess opened, and

---

[7] Fortunately, boils are a skin infection associated with past times. Men more frequently contracted them than women. They occurred on the neck, armpits, groin, and back. They could also occur around the nose and eye, this latter in the form of a sty. Today, the decline of poverty and the availability of good, purified water and antibacterial soap have sent boils into the history books. A more

foul-smelling pus spurted out. Her female attendants recoiled, shocked by the smell, expostulating over the volume of pus that flowed. Wells instructed the handmaid that at first "Mother" should sit a long time in a tub of hot water to draw the infection out. Then sulfa powder and a gauze bandage should be applied. This should be repeated every day, and eventually, the wound of the abscess would heal.

Shaykh Abdallah's brother, Shaykh Mohammed, lent the medical team his big house in Doha so Wells and his Bahraini assistants, Sulayman and Sourir, could treat Qatar's people. The residence had a large courtyard surrounded by rooms set directly off it. These rooms were ideal for an office, an examination room, and if necessary, an operating room. There were even small rooms with high slit windows, probably granaries, which could be used to house patients that needed to stay overnight. On the second floor were rooms perfect to billet Wells' little team.

On the very morning the clinic opened, the team was overwhelmed with the throng of people who came for treatment. Wells recommended that serious cases should come to Bahrain where surgery would be more successful. Unfortunately, many patients were too poor and too sick to make the trip, so Wells had to operate then and there. As the days passed, Wells was amazed at the efficacy of his surgery in Doha—the results were remarkably successful.[8] Each day was filled with work, and the team fell gratefully into their beds every night after the evening meal.

As Wells was readying for sleep one night, he was stopped by an electrifying sound. A woman was groaning and then shrieking in great pain. He called to his male coworkers to see if they could locate the source of the sound.

The moans came from one of the rooms in the house that Shaykh Mohammed had reserved for his private use. The team called inside to see if anyone would answer and asked what was wrong. The moaning stopped, but after a few moments, a woman's anguished voice responded. She said she was being punished and had been hanging suspended by her wrists a few inches off the ground. Her wrists and shoulder joints hurt so much that she could not help screaming.

---

extreme form was the carbuncle, a series of boils that fused together under the skin.

[8] The mission doctors elsewhere in the Gulf reported similar results. They observed very little cross infection of patients, despite lack of a sterile environment for treatment. They attributed to the patients themselves a high degree of immunity to infection.

Wells did not know what to do. He and his team were guests in a foreign country that had its own laws. In Qatar a master could do anything he wanted to a slave. Anything was legal, even the most inhumane deeds. Wells did not have any idea what the woman had done to deserve her treatment. He also knew it was going to be impossible to sleep with her shrieking in excruciating pain. What could he do that would not deeply offend the shaykh but at the same time relieve her pain and allow his team to sleep? It was a dilemma, and he had to do something.

Finally, he decided he should do as his heart dictated. They jimmied the crude lock on the door, found a stool for the woman to stand on, and then untied her wrists. Wells told her that he and his team had no right to untie her or to let her out. She would have to stay right there.

The woman told them she feared for her life. In answer to Wells' questioning, she said, "I am a slave. The shaykh gave me in marriage to one of his elderly slaves, an old geezer who already has several wives. But I am in love with one of the shaykh's younger, more handsome slaves; he still has all his teeth. When I rejected that old geezer—my new, so-called husband—the old goat complained to the shaykh." She had then been punished this way to teach her a lesson. She did not know what would happen now.

When Shaykh Mohammed arrived the next day, Wells told him about her. He said, "She is still in there. We did not let her out, but we just could not stand hearing her screaming and pleading that she had been punished enough for her crime." The shaykh was angry that anyone dared intervene in his household affairs and had stopped her torture without his specific command.

"You have a right to be angry. If, however, you cannot accept what we did, you may have your house back. We will leave you and your house in peace. We ask your permission to take our leave. We just cannot stand needless cruelty." It was a pivotal moment. Wells realized he might be closing Qatar's door to his ministrations and even to future mission work.

At the same time, Shaykh Mohammed was also in a difficult situation. He realized that he and other Qataris needed the medical help of the mission. Silence ensued. Flies buzzed languidly. Subdued courtyard noise filtered into the room as if from afar. After some length, the shaykh said, "No, don't go. Stay. I should have left instructions to let her down at sunset, but I left the house and forgot to say anything about her."

Wells said quietly, "You know what happened, don't you? She is a young woman, and she is in love with one of your younger slaves. You gave her to this old man, who already had several wives. Naturally, she fought him off. She's not in love with him."

The shaykh may have been tempted to ask, "What's love got to do with it?" but he held his tongue. He made no reply, and soon the woman was led out of the house.

Wells learned a significant lesson with that encounter. He realized that these honest, even confrontational, exchanges between principled men of different cultures did not bring an end to their relationship. Instead, it created a deeper friendship of mutual respect and understanding.[9]

When Wells took his leave from Qatar, "Mother," the wife of Shaykh Abdallah, now fully recovered from her painful boil, took from her own box a pretty gold necklace with complicated filigree and semiprecious stones in it, put it in a fancy box, and said graciously, "Here is a present for your wife, Jauhara.[10] I wish I could meet her."

"Perhaps you will," said Wells. "For now, though, she is at home in Bahrain. She is the mother of three little children. You know what three children mean because you have raised children of your own. She is a busy lady."

It's a bird, isn't it?

Back in his clinic in Bahrain, Wells was detained one morning by the royal retinue of a minor shaykh. They arrived suddenly, filling his office. Dressed in resplendent clothing and armed with rifles and swords, the shaykh and his men jammed into Wells' clinic, leaving no room to sit. The shaykh had just returned from visiting King Abdal Aziz in Riyadh, he explained, and was now being entertained by the *hakim* of Bahrain. In a short time, he was sailing to Doha to see Shaykh

---

[9] Indeed, Wells was invited back to Qatar four times—each time to the discomfiture of the British political resident in Bahrain who wondered whether this "American" (a term of disdain) was stealing a march on the British push for oil concessions up and down the Gulf.

[10] Jauhara, "Gem Lady," was the Arabic name given by the women in Bahrain to Beth Thoms, which she retained in later postings. It was a famous name. King Abdal Aziz's much-beloved first wife was also Jauhara. It was a name reserved for those who had a particular sparkle, cool, charm, and poise.

Abdallah and then on to other shaykhdoms before returning home. He was well known as one who liked to be entertained.

Drawing up to his full height, the shaykh asked if Wells would look at his eye.

Upon examination, Wells declared, "You have a true cataract, a *mai abyadh*.[11] It is possible to operate and successfully remove this cataract. We have a private room upstairs in the hospital, and we can take care of you tomorrow or the day after that."

The shaykh eyed Wells sharply and began bargaining. "How much will you charge?"

"One hundred rupees."

"No. I'll give you fifty rupees only. No more than fifty."

Wells, knowing the shaykh was not a poor man, having certainly received many gifts in his recent travels, and knowing full well the hospital's need for revenue could only be relieved by its wealthier clients, held firm. "A hundred rupees. No more, no less. *Bas*.[12] I am not going to bargain about this because you are not poor. You will need a room. You will probably have to be in the hospital for ten days. A hundred rupees will be your whole bill, including food."

The shaykh responded, "I'll do it on one condition—that you do the operation on my boat out in the harbor." Wells replied that he thought the suggestion was ridiculous. Undertaking such a delicate operation on a boat, bobbing at anchor, and rocking from all kinds of wind and waves, might torpedo the operation's success. After discovering Wells would not budge, the shaykh said, "All right. I'll get it done somewhere else," and he and his retinue marched out.

When Wells' assistant came in, Wells told him about this strange conversation. Why would anyone want to have an operation done on a boat in the harbor instead of in the hospital? Sulayman chuckled and said, "It's obvious. He is stingy—a skinflint. As a shaykh and a wealthy man, he is obliged to serve his visitors coffee and halwa[13] or other refreshments when they visit. If he were in the hospital, all kinds of people could stop in, but on a boat in the outer harbor very few people will visit him. So, it is better from his point of view."

As Wells later learned, the shaykh chose to have his operation done in Bombay. He knew that the shipping company gave free passage to Gulf shaykhs just to keep in their good graces so the company could

---

[11] Literally "white water," referring to cataracts of the eye.
[12] That is final. Enough.
[13] *Halwa*: a sticky, sweet form of candy, perhaps a variant of Turkish delight.

maintain its Gulf shipping business. In Bombay, the shaykh went to see Abdur Rahman Qasebi, one of Hofuf's big merchants from the Al-Hasa Oasis of Sa'udi Arabia. Abdur Rahman, one of Wells' closest friends from the mainland, had gone to Bombay with pearls to sell and other business to transact.

The shaykh said to Abdur Rahman, "I don't know any eye doctors here in Bombay. Please introduce me to one you have confidence in so he will take good care of me."

Abdur Rahman took him to Dr. Banerji, an able eye surgeon. In due time, the shaykh left Bombay and returned to the Gulf. When the doctor's clerk asked him to pay up, he said, "Oh, no. Didn't Abdur Rahman Qasebi bring me here? I've been his guest and of course he'll take care of the bill."

Sometime later, Wells had another occasion to travel to Qatar. Shaykh Abdalluh's chief falconer had developed cataracts. He was marvelous at training falcons and hawks, and he had unsurpassed hunting skills and superb eyesight; his cataract-encrusted eyes, however, had "ripened" and needed excision to prevent him from going blind. Wells removed the cataracts in the Bahrain hospital. Concerned, lest the operation's outcome would be indifferent, Wells equipped the falconer with dark glasses saying, "When I next visit Qatar, I will test you for distance glasses and for reading glasses, too."

When he arrived in Qatar, Wells went to visit his friend, Shaykh Abdallah. One afternoon, Wells, the falconer, and the shaykh were sitting outside the latter's Ar Rayyan *qasr*. Wells had picked out glasses for the falconer, who was delighted at his newly restored vision—one pair of distance glasses and another pair for reading and seeing objects close-up. Shaykh Abdallah looked into the distance and said, "That's Shaykh so-and-so coming. He's here for a visit; he's very *bakheel*.[14] He went to Bombay and had an operation on one of his eyes and left Abdur Rahman Qasebi to pay the bill."

"Doesn't surprise me," said Wells. "He came to me and asked me to do the operation, but he wanted it done on board a boat in Bahrain harbor. I refused to operate recklessly on his eyes."

The visiting shaykh came into their circle, and they all exchanged greetings and pleasantries. Shaykh Abdallah said, "Well, you went all the way to Bombay for your operation, I understand. You could have had it done by Dr. Thoms in Bahrain, but I suppose you preferred the big city and the doctor there. Did you get a good result?"

---

[14] Stingy, tightfisted.

"Yes, yes," said the shaykh, "an excellent result."

"Well," said Shaykh Abdallah, "Let's test you out. Put on your distance glasses." The visiting shaykh did so. "Now," said Shaykh Abdallah, "Do you see that bird flying over there? That bird? What kind of a bird is it?"

The visitor said, "Oh, yes. Oh, yes. There's a bird over there. It's not a hawk. It must be a crow."

Shaykh Abdallah told his newly cataract-free falconer to put on his distance glasses. "Now," he said to him, "Look over in that direction. Do you see a bird over there?" His falconer squinted, adjusted his glasses, and looked very carefully again in that direction. "No, I don't see any bird," came the answer.

Shaykh Abdallah said to Wells, "Do you see any bird over there?" Wells said, "No. No, I don't."

"You know," Shaykh Abdallah said, "I don't see any bird either. I don't think anyone but shaykh so-and-so sees a bird. He's gotten such a good result from his cataract surgery that he sees things we don't see." Everyone but the visiting shaykh had a chuckle at his expense. Wells understood from this exchange that there are as many variations in Arab personality styles as there are among Americans.

Oil concessions

Concessions to drill for oil were essential in order for developers to gain access to potential Arabian oil fields.[15] Sir Cumford Fowle, Bahrain's political resident and agent of the British government, visited Qatar repeatedly to encourage the shaykh to sign a concession with the partly British-owned Anglo-Persian Oil Company. Shaykh Abdallah played "hard to get" with the British. He was not pleased to have only one bidder for Qatar's hydrocarbons. The realist in him knew he would get a much higher bid if at least two companies were in competition, so he stalled when the British came calling.

One day, when the British were preparing to present a new automobile to the shaykh as *cumshaw*,[16] Wells was just taking leave from the shaykh's palace to return to Bahrain. After a pleasant conversation, coffee, and refreshments in the royal mejlis, Wells stood: "I'd better go now."

---

[15] Qatar's petrochemical reserves, some of the largest in the world, are in the form of natural gas. The wealth of the country in the age of liquefied natural gas (LNG) has grown immensely, so Qatar, with its small population, is inordinately important on the international scene today.

[16] Inducement or bribe.

"Why?" asked the shaykh. "What's the hurry?"

Wells said, "I have other things to do. I am leaving for Bahrain tomorrow. Besides, the Rais al Khalij[17] is waiting outside to see you."

The shaykh replied, "Don't worry. He won't run away. He's too anxious to get his contract signed." Wells realized he was being used as a foil to prolong the anxiety of the Brits.

As the shaykh and Wells left the mejlis, Fowle and company were standing outside waiting quietly but impatiently. The shaykh bade farewell serenely to Wells, climbed into his new car together with his sons, and drove off. Wells heard him calling back to Fowle: "Please join us for dinner tonight at my place in the country." The shaykh had successfully delayed negotiations for yet another day. Fowle was left clucking and scratching his head disconsolately, knowing he would have to sort out transportation appropriate to his imperial status in a land without taxis.

Wells was thoroughly amused at this British comeuppance from the shaykh of Qatar, yet Wells had to be cautiously diplomatic and not show his amusement. The British, as the imperial go-betweens with treaties ostensibly protecting the shaykhdoms of Bahrain and Qatar, were also the gatekeepers that insisted on preapproving the visits to Qatar of Wells and others of the mission. The British were prickly about this approval power. Wells was not hostile to the colonial reality, but he was nobody's pushover. Besides, he worked too hard to play political games.

---

[17] Fowle, the Bahrain resident.

CHAPTER 12

Bahrain Blues

> *We must first know the Moslem heart.*
> *We cannot know, understand,*
> *and appreciate, without first loving.*
> *We have to touch his heart with our hearts.*

Daily demands

By 1936 Wells' honeymoon as a missionary doctor in Bahrain had long ended. The hard work was all consuming, and the outlook was for much more of the same. Even though he continued to experience great satisfaction in treating his patients, stress and disappointment rained down on all sides.

Wells had learned a great deal since arriving in Bahrain. He had not abandoned his core beliefs, but it was difficult for him to express exactly what had changed. He endured a growing malaise—partly spiritual, partly psychological, and partly motivational—that had come from all the negative forces he faced: the unrelenting poverty and privation of the Gulf peoples, decreased charitable giving by home churches in the United States due to the Great Depression, diminished fees collected from patients, a steadily increasing patient load with increasingly complex cases, constant staff shortages, very few Christian converts, and unproductive, niggling relationships with self-important British imperial bureaucrats and overweening oil company executives.

A just God would have sorted all these things out. Wells knew it was wishful thinking to expect God to do all the heavy lifting, but the weight of it all pressed down upon him. He believed that people needed to do their own creative problem solving, supported and inspired by the Holy Spirit. Where was the Holy Spirit when he needed him? It was always darkest before dawn, he assured himself. But when, if ever, would dawn come?

Beth noticed the change in Wells, too. She saw that her partner was qualitatively different in his workaday habits from his normally upbeat self. Finally, she said, "Wells, something is bothering you. I am not sure what it is because I have never seen you this way. You need to do something about it. It is more important than your daily routine because it affects your whole life. Perhaps you are working too hard. I know work is consuming you; we hardly see you at home. Is working harder the solution? How much more can you possibly give to your work, to the hospital, to your patients, to God?"

Wells replied after a brief silence and several deep sighs, "You're right. Thanks for putting into words what I have grown increasingly aware of. I do not really know what is wrong. Nothing I have done to solve the problem has helped so far. I have to work out of this funk one step at a time. It is not fair to you and the children for me to continue in this way."

A new chapter in his private life began, one in which Wells searched for a new balance that did not come easily or quickly.[1] He questioned everything he knew and believed as a missionary doctor. It was his personal equivalent of Christ's forty days in the wilderness. He searched Scripture. He prayed. He meditated.

On the surface, little appeared different. Wells was running and managing the hospital. He continued to see patients in clinic every day. He responded to calls from the Women's Hospital. He operated on patients with problems reparable only by surgery. He made house calls in the middle of the night to deliver babies and attend to the dying in their last hours. He traveled to places like Qatar. He was a loving father of three children, insofar as he was home when they were awake. The children were a great satisfaction but also a concern. They were growing rapidly and had all the curiosity and energy he could have hoped for, but they were subject to a full range of childhood diseases.

---

[1] The same malaise often occurs in the lives of deeply committed pastors, rabbis, mullahs, and imams. In truth, these crises occur in the lives of many people who follow a deep calling that is more than just a job.

He had a loving wife and constant partner who provided sympathy, moral support, and serenity of spirit.[2]

Wells' first step toward wholeness was to look inward. He had decided on Christian service in Arabia because of the indelible memory of his parents and their vision. The missionaries that had triggered his decision were the estimable Dr. Paul Harrison and the revered Rev. Samuel Zwemer. Harrison was an early advocate of Arabian Mission work for Wells. Indeed, he was central in pushing the "Plan B" that had emerged at the end of Wells' medical training. Zwemer, the Arabian Mission's cofounder, was a close family friend. In childhood, Wells called him "Uncle Sam." Zwemer was one of the great Protestant churchmen whose inspiration stemmed from the nineteenth-century foreign-mission movement. Zwemer presented "Christianity triumphant" in a confrontational style, consistent with the prevailing Western cultural notions of the "white man's burden," making a case for the undoubted superiority of Christianity in the face of Islam's shortcomings. A commanding and charismatic speaker, Zwemer inspired countless Americans to go into Christian service, and Wells was one of them.

As Wells served in Bahrain, he began to see a dissonance between the supposed superiority of Christian thought and the presumed superiority of the Western Enlightenment over non-European cultures. He came to realize that Christianity had become so wrapped up in Western—especially American—cultural trappings that it was difficult to distinguish between Christian religious thinking and Western secular bias. Moreover, he sensed, empathetically, that "winning" an argument with a man was not the way to convert him to the religious views of the one who outscored him. Likewise, "losing" a religious argument did not make a man abandon his beliefs. Converting Muslims to Christianity was not like selling Hoover vacuum cleaners or the *Pictorial Review* magazine.

What was Wells' alternative to the Christian imperialism of Samuel Zwemer? He had hardly to look closer than home, where he had discovered Rev. James Cantine's views. Cantine, a cofounder with Zwemer of the Arabian Mission and a relative by marriage,[3] was someone Wells had always deeply respected. Cantine had wrestled with the militant notion of mission and come to a different conclusion than Zwemer. Cantine, an irenic pastor-counselor, believed that "like

---

[2] See endnote 12:2, p. 384.
[3] Elizabeth Cantine was Wells' step-mother's sister.

attracts like. The nearest way to the Moslem heart is to use that which appeals to the heart rather than the intellect."[4]

Written in 1912, Cantine's words sounded old fashioned in the 1930s. Wells read and reread Cantine's essay to absorb it. He reviewed Zwemer's writings, too, in light of his own conversations with Arab Muslims. Wells was no theologian, nor did he relish Christian doctrinal debate. His solution had to come from his own heart; he had to be true to himself. He did not have much time to devote to study and meditation. By 1938 he had recomposed his religious commitments, and the "Bahrain blues" receded.

Although Wells never summarized his theological thinking in writing, he affirmed and reaffirmed some basic tenets in conversations with family and friends, tenets that were worked out during his Bahrain blues. He held firmly to the great commandment of Jesus to love God above all and to love one's "neighbors" as oneself.[5] This commandment, he believed, lay at Christianity's core. The challenge, therefore, for every Christian, was to adhere to it completely, and it set the stage for his own medical mission work. Understanding the God of love more deeply in this life was central to Christian living. All Christians needed to do was to remain God's faithful disciples one day at a time.

Wells resolutely believed that God was essentially a loving being—although God possessed all attributes imaginable to humans, and more. A God of love transcended all previous monotheistic human conceptions. Therefore, since God was essentially loving, then all believers should model God's love, too. A truly loving person was most able to carry out the spirit of God's great commandment.

Wells held steadfastly to the Trinitarian idea of One God in three Persons—Father, Son, and Holy Spirit.[6] These were not separate gods. Anyone who thought so, as some Muslims maintained that Christians did, reduced God to the limits of human imagination. God, far above anything mere mortals could ever imagine or invent, was a mystery beyond human comprehension. Wells could not envision a God of love without the example of Jesus Christ, the earthly expression of God's love. Wells firmly believed that the Holy Spirit intervened in daily life. In fact, he believed the Holy Spirit inhabited his operating

---

[4] See endnote 12:4, p. 385.
[5] Matthew 22:35-40 and Mark 12:28-34. These are thought to be paraphrases of Deuteronomy 6:4-5 and Leviticus 19:17-18.
[6] See endnote 12:6, p. 387.

room, facilitated each operation, and aided in each patient's recovery.[7] Because of this, Wells always prayed before each operation, asking for God's grace and for the Holy Spirit to restore the patient to health.

God as judge, God as sacred church doctrine, or God as remote and terrible had little place in Wells' theological views. Wells did not believe in deterministic predestination, either as expressed by his Calvinist ancestors or as found in the fatalism of his Muslim neighbors. How could everything be "written on people's foreheads"? If it were, then what would be the point of missionary life or of sharing the Gospel with everyone? Was not salvation offered to all, and did it not depend on people's free will to accept it? Wells came to understand evangelism in this way. He did not waste time on catechism-like formulae. These lists were not products of faith, he decided. They were the byproducts of church bureaucracy, jurisprudence, and contentious Christian church history and politics. Notably, these byproducts were mirrored also in Islam's *madhabs*[8] and *Shari'a*[9] analogs. He was convinced that anyone could be redeemed, no matter what they had done or thought. Moreover, redemption was not a matter of the hereafter. The promise of heaven after life on earth was not of central importance to him. What was key was how people lived here and now as an expression of their faith. Wells could not know the nature of the afterlife and therefore put little stock in deliberating about it.

These principles, Wells discovered, were sufficient for his full spiritual revival. They synthesized and modified Cantine's, Zwemer's, and Calvin's views.[10] In order to carry on his mission calling, he did not need to find fault with Islamic society and its people—either in the shaykhs, imams, *muftis*, and *maulvis*[11] or in individual Muslims. He did not need to find fault with his Christian colleagues. He did not need to find fault with church traditions and church leaders. Nor did he need to find fault with nominally Christian, British Empire officials. He just needed to persist each day as a faithful disciple of God. He chose to look inward, and in so doing, he progressively regained his spiritual balance, his natural ebullience, and his zest for living.

There remained, of course, the stress of being overworked. Wells had hoped—perhaps unrealistically—to make Mason Memorial

---

[7] See endnote 12:7, p. 387.
[8] Islamic school of jurisprudence.
[9] Islamic law based on the Q'uran.
[10] See endnote 12:10, p. 387.
[11] An *imam* is a prayer leader in a mosque; it is also the title of a Muslim leader of a high order. *Mufti* is a Muslim legal expert. *Maulvi* is a teacher of Islamic law.

Hospital and Marion Wells Thoms Hospital for Women into shining examples, beacons of Western medical modernity. This realization would be a tribute to his parents, who had started the hospitals, an offering to God, and a source of personal satisfaction. On top of that, Wells had proposed to Louis Dame that they should start a professional medical society in Bahrain, even though there were only seven Western-trained physicians practicing there at that time. Having honed his surgical skills in Bahrain under Dame's tutelage, Wells aimed to become a fellow of the American College of Surgeons when he returned to the United States on furlough.[12]

Wells realized that the extra-heavy load of running the oil company's hospital wards exacted an unwanted toll, and that was in addition to the usual challenges of medical work. He was their principal physician-in-residence in Bahrain, but because the oil company wards were a critical revenue pipeline that allowed the hospital to continue to function as a charity hospital, he had no option but to keep the enterprise going.

The Arab employees of BAPCO presented the biggest challenge. From time to time, they came to the hospital with severe burns, injuries from bad accidents, and compound fractures. Burns were the most difficult, in large part because burn patients required intensive care, and patient recovery was slow—if indeed they recovered at all. Wells' concern for these patients nearly consumed him. His ethic of Christian service, his perfectionism as a doctor, and his compassion and empathy for his patients meant he was a deeply committed Good Samaritan, going beyond the call of duty.

This sometimes led to confrontations. One day, an Arab employee of BAPCO, who had suffered in an accident, came to the clinic. A brass object had punctured his inner eyeball, and Wells was unable to extract it. There was no option but to remove the man's eye and replace it with a glass eye. Wells gave the man a note to BAPCO's business manager asking compensation from BAPCO. A loss like this to any European or American worker of the oil company would have brought substantial payment.

---

[12] Paul Harrison, Wells Thoms, and Harold Storm were all accredited by the American College of Surgeons. They had the highest approval of their surgical skills and were justly proud of their accomplishments. As further testimony to their accomplishments, Harrison had been offered a position with Harvey Cushing at Massachusetts General Hospital and Wells a position at the University of Michigan Medical School.

Wells received a reply saying it was none of his business how BAPCO compensated an Arab employee, implying that no compensation would be given. The unfairness triggered Wells' anger. In a flurry of letters, he let BAPCO know it should be as concerned for its Arab workers as for its expatriate employees. Moreover, Arab workers were not wealthy and had few resources to cover heavy medical costs. If BAPCO persisted in treating its Arab employees in this way, he would prefer not to work on retainer for the company.

BAPCO badly needed the mission hospital and its personnel, so the management responded to Wells' salvo by saying it was developing a compensation policy for Arab employees, and Wells could rest assured that details would be worked out. Wells concluded that his letters had triggered talks between BAPCO and the government of Bahrain about workmen's compensation. His vitriolic response in this case illustrates how tense he had become, and why he needed relief from the stress of his work.

The most common ways to relieve work stress elsewhere were not available to him, and he searched within for spiritual relief. Maybe he could not fix these problems, but perhaps he could modify the way he reacted to them. In this search, Beth accompanied him. Together they studied the New Testament for insight and inspiration, landing upon the third chapter of the Acts of the Apostles. This passage recounts the incident in which the apostles John and Peter, after having seen the risen Christ, met a beggar as they were entering the temple to pray. When the beggar, paralyzed since birth, asked for alms, Peter said, "Silver and gold have I none; but such as I have, give I thee. In the name of Jesus Christ of Nazareth rise up and walk."[13]

A miracle then occurred, and the man began to walk, so the account goes. The man and the crowd then wanted to make heroes out of Peter and John. Instead, the apostles credited Jesus Christ for the cure. Wells saw something in this passage that he had not previously noticed. He could begin to think of Jesus Christ as the Great Physician and the head of the Bahrain hospital. Wells was *his* resident physician. Wells was expected only to do his best, leaving his concerns in the able hands of the Great Physician, and with him in charge, said Wells: "I could relax after realizing that. I was able to sleep and wake up refreshed to do my work the next day." Ever after, Wells thought of the Great Physician as being the hospital's CMO. By submitting his anxieties to Him, Wells was no longer alone or responsible for everything. He was

[13] Acts 3:6-16.

part of a team. He could work with renewed vigor and decreased stress, even though his actual workload demands had not otherwise changed.

Wells also found another way to lighten his load. He slowly relinquished his perfectionist mentality, which when stressed could magnify into unproductive micromanagement and worry. By thinking of himself as part of a team, his personal standards of medical perfection no longer had to apply. He was initially concerned that a lower medical standard might adversely affect the quality of patient care. But in submitting to the Holy Spirit's partnership, he came to believe that there was no significant difference in successful outcomes. In fact, because of his newfound "partnership," hospital morale seemed to improve, which in turn improved the overall success of patient results. The entire hospital staff was, after all, God's team. To actually "let go" of personal and organizational control was difficult for Wells, but with time, he gained confidence in this approach to patient care.

It was as if—like a steel blade tempered in hot coals to become more flexible—Wells had gained adaptability and resilience. He was stronger for this transformation and could more effectively surmount his daily challenges. He came to realize, "It's not about medicine or about me, the doctor. It's about the people."[14] People—his patients, friends, and acquaintances—now became the focus of his attention. He referred to his patients as "brother," "sister," "mother," and "father," as well as by name.[15] In this communication style, he was reflecting the best in Arab culture: he treated others as his equals, deserving his best effort. His bedside manner was impeccably professional but also warmly intimate. He spoke to patients as if he was with an old friend and member of the clan. Without plan or self-consciousness, Wells had been transformed into a compassionate and knowledgeable hakeem.

---

[14] This is from a letter to Harvey Doorenbos, who first came as a missionary surgeon to Oman and then went to Ethiopia for the remainder of his career. See Heusinkveld, *Margaret's Mission*.

[15] Col. H. Dickson noted this tendency by medical missionaries to refer to patients by familial forms of address, forms used by townspeople. He noted that Bedu men—nomads—did not refer to their fathers as *Abui*, "my father." Rather they referred to their fathers in the third person as *Abuna*, "the progenitor." Dickson perhaps did not realize the deliberately egalitarian nature of the doctors. Of course, among hospital patients, townsmen far outnumbered nomads.

CHAPTER 13

Road to Riyadh: Oases of Al-Hasa and Katif, 1934-35

"Salaam alaikum, ya tawil al 'amer."
Suddenly, the old man
barked harshly, "Gahwa!"
Bin Jiluwi's command came so suddenly...
Wells felt he had jumped seven inches.

Invitation from the interior[1]

The road to Riyadh had rumble strips that made the trip rough going. The obstructions came not just in terms of terrain but also in terms of travel logistics. Just because Wells was a well-respected Arabian Mission doctor did not mean he could go to Sa'udi Arabia whenever he pleased. The Sa'udi state carefully controlled the visits of foreigners, and a foreigner had to prove his worth to gain entry. Travel to Riyadh came only with an invitation from King Abdal Aziz bin Sa'ud.[2]

Wells' first trip into Sa'udi Arabia occurred in 1933, when the shaykh of Dareen, on the Arabian Peninsula, across the water from Bahrain and up the coast, asked for a doctor to treat his sick wife. Gerrit Van Peursem, the mission padre, knew the shaykh well and introduced Wells to him. Under Wells' care, the shaykh's wife recovered

---

[1] This chapter is based on the tape-recorded oral memoir that Wells made in the last year of his life.
[2] Sa'udi Arabia is even today a country that controls traveler access. It is not a tourist destination.

within a few days, and Wells' attention shifted to the people in Sanabis, adjacent to Dareen. As was the mission's longstanding practice, service to local villagers took place in the home the shaykh had lent. When he came to know his new patients, Wells was surprised to note that the shaykh and ruling clan were Sunni Muslims, whereas most of the village people were Shi'ah Muslims.

Situated on a promontory, Dareen juts into the Persian Gulf near Qatif Bay. At low tide, Dareen is connected to the mainland by a sandy spit. This location was presumably more healthful than the secluded villages on the mainland because of its airiness and drainage. But even though there were both hot and cold springs along the coast, Wells was surprised at the general state of uncleanliness among the people. Something was wrong. They had a "hangdog" look, listless in their movements. As he examined the people who came for treatment, he saw signs of public health concerns that he had not observed in Bahrain.

First, almost everyone suffered from chronic malaria. Wells had observed that, generally, malaria did not kill people outright. It debilitated them, so that a person might suffer from malaria for thousands of days before they died. Usually, other maladies combined with malaria to cause death.

Second, Wells discovered that many villagers had contracted tuberculosis, and it accounted for their weak constitutions, reduced stamina, and shortened life spans.

Third, he uncovered a widespread malady similar to syphilis[3] and yaws but not either. It was a nonvenereal, communicable disease caused by a spirochete. Locals had their own names for it, depending on the community and their dialect of Arabic. Dr. Ellis Hudson[4] had identified and researched it along the Euphrates River in Syria. Hudson was able to show it was a disease of poor, unhygienic people. The people around Sanabis and Dareen called it *najis*.[5] This, Wells thought, was appropriate because *najis* means literally "dirty" or "filthy" in Arabic. *Najis* had syphilis-like symptoms and consequences, but it appeared that small children could contract it first and spread it to their mothers while they were still being carried around on their mothers' hips.

---

[3] Syphilis also occurred in the port towns of eastern Arabia and was called by another name (*fremzy*). It was found more often among men, who were ashamed of having contracted it—presumably from having consorted with prostitutes.
[4] Hudson and Young, "Medical and Surgical Practice on the Euphrates River."
[5] This same disease was known by other names in other regions: *bejel, barash, bajal,* and *tao*.

The people of Sanabis and Dareen were so chronically ill from this mix of diseases that they were very inefficient workers, careless of their dress, cleanliness, and demeanor. Their hangdog look visibly portrayed this blend of diseases. Treatments available to Wells were limited to a narrow arsenal of drugs.

When the shaykh realized that Wells and the hospital team were treating villagers at the house he had lent them, he was appalled. He found these poor people to be repulsive; they fouled and insulted his abode just by their presence. After four days of busy clinics, the shaykh could no longer tolerate these dirty, smelly people; he lost his temper and sent them scurrying—shouting all sorts of names at them.

Wells tried to explain that it was natural to be prejudiced against people who looked and smelled as these villagers did. He explained that he and his hospital team would persist in treating the villagers because the medical team was following Christ's loving example of healing similar people in New Testament times. Jesus touched and healed lepers when no others would come near.[6] The shaykh calmed down somewhat and expressed interest in hearing scriptural references to Jesus' healing and teaching. On the other hand, his patience had been pushed to its limit, and his warm Arab hospitality could no longer be assumed. Wells indicated the medical team would return at another time when they could make different arrangements to treat those who needed care. On this promising note, Wells and his colleagues returned to Bahrain having assisted only a handful of patients. Thus ended Wells' first foray into Sa'udi Arabia.

Al-Hasa Oasis

A year later, Wells was approached by his Sa'udi friend Abdur Rahman Qasebi, the man who had been so badly treated by the stingy shaykh in Bombay. The wealthy merchant informed Wells that he was needed to treat one of the sons of Abdallah bin Jiluwi in Hofuf, the capital of the al-Hasa province.[7] Abdallah bin Jiluwi bin Turki al Sa'ud was the governor of Al-Hasa in eastern Sa'udi Arabia. An older, distant cousin of Amir Abdal Aziz, bin Jiluwi was one of the compatriots who had successfully stormed the fort in Riyadh in 1902 and brought the

---

[6] His hospital team was comprised mostly of Muslim assistants.
[7] Hofuf is the city that dominates the Al-Hasa Oasis, Sa'udi Arabia's most productive farming region.

city under Amir Abdal Aziz's control.[8] In fact, bin Jiluwi had saved the amir's life in that sortie and had also killed the governor who lived in the fort. Bin Jiluwi was one of Amir Abdal Aziz's most loyal supporters and given the responsibility of bringing the eastern region of the country under unified political control. Abdallah bin Jiluwi was famous for his incorruptibility and rigid adherence to Sharia law. He was a ferocious man, and everyone was wary of his stern judgments. Qasebi relayed that Wells was to travel to Al-Hasa and present himself to Abdallah bin Jiluwi.

This would be a major undertaking. First, Wells and his assistants had to get from Bahrain to Hofuf. In 1934 no causeway linked Bahrain to the mainland of Sa'udi Arabia, nor were there paved roads in Sa'udi Arabia or Bahrain. The first leg of travel would be in a sailboat from Manama, Bahrain, to Ojeir, the Sa'udi customs port closest to Hofuf. Then a V-8 Ford touring car with nine-inch sand tires deflated to low pressure would carry Wells and his team fifty or sixty miles across huge, shifting sand dunes. The car would roar up the big dunes, keeping to the convex curving side of the dune, and come very close to the dune's apex, revealing a terrifying view of the precipitous drop of fifty to seventy feet to the hard desert floor below. Then the car would plummet down the steep side of the dune and race up the next one—dune after dune. Wells said it was like a grand "shoot the chutes" ride, better than at any theme park, county fair, or "dune schooner"—and far more terrifying. All the while, the driver whipped the steering wheel back and forth in a weaving motion to keep the tires from bogging down in the sand.

After roughly forty miles as the crow flies, and many more miles zigzagging over the dunes, the desert flattened out until the rumpled passengers arrived safely at the rim of the Al-Hasa Oasis. The view from the rim was breathtaking—beautiful, emerald green date palms as far as the eye could see. What a contrast with the dry browns and parched tans of the desert. The bright sea of green was a visual delight for the travelers as they exited the blazing desert. It was like going from an ocean of desolation to an island of plenty, as if they had passed from hell into Paradise.

On high ground, in the middle of the oasis, is the city of Hofuf. Most of its main buildings at that time were made of mud and stone,

---

[8] Paul Harrison, of the Arabian Mission, dedicated his first book, *The Arab at Home*, to Amir Abdal Aziz, Shaykh Abdallah bin Jiluwi, and Abdur Rahman bin Sualim, whom Harrison identified as three of his "best friends."

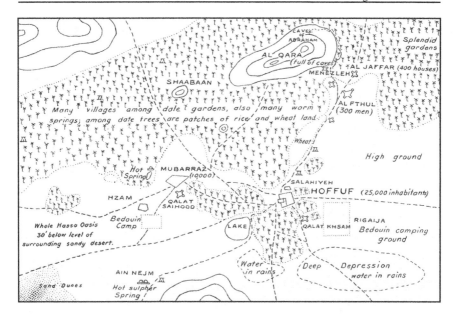

Al-Hasa Oasis, 1937 (HD)

and minor *barastis*[9] were built of date stick mats and thatched pallets attached to central timbers for rigidity. As Wells and his assistants ascended the final elevation to the city, they learned that Hofuf was fortified. It was here that they were to meet Abdallah bin Jiluwi.

Bin Jiluwi's mejlis inside the fort was dimly lit. Narrow shafts of sunlight shot through what looked like arrow slits in the walls. Mud benches lined three sides of the room and were occupied by guards and troops armed with all manner of weaponry from antiquated muzzle-loading *jezails* to modern rifles. Coming from the bright sun of the desert into the gloom of the semidark mejlis, Wells could not see clearly. He stumbled forward to the far end of the room, ushered by his guide. There he found a wizened, bearded man sitting hunched over, clothed in a brown, woven camel-hair *bisht*.[10] On his head was a white kaffiya,[11] and he was gazing at the ground.

Wells saluted the old man, "Salaam alaikum, ya tawil al 'amer."[12]

The old man's only acknowledgment was a wave of the hand to gesture Wells to sit down next to him. Suddenly, the old man barked, "*Gahwa!*" Bin Jiluwi's command came so suddenly out of the darkness

[9] Houses or hovels.
[10] Cloak or outer garment.
[11] *Kaffiya*: head cloth.
[12] Peace be upon you, oh Long of Life.

and silence that Wells felt he had jumped seven inches. He saw some of the men nearby were amused, but they disguised their amusement quickly. When bin Jiluwi spoke, not only did visitors jump, but his staff also leapt into action. The *"Gahwa!"* order was yelped repeatedly down the mejlis line and out the door to the kitchen where the coffee was prepared.

The servants knew, of course, that coffee would be required in the mejlis, and they soon appeared with freshly brewed, strong, cardamom-spiked coffee in tall brass stylized coffee pots. In their hands were finjans[13] that they filled for each visitor, as well as for bin Jiluwi. The coffee steamed. Wells drank it in the traditional way, taking in small amounts while sucking audibly to cool the coffee as he drank. The superheated coffee, with its moisture and caffeine, quickly restored him.

After the third ceremonial refill, Wells wig-wagged his cup to indicate that he had had enough. He expected that now polite conversation would start, but silence weighed heavily in the room. Then Sa'ad bin Jiluwi, Abdallah's son, motioned Wells to follow him out of the mejlis.[14]

Sa'ad bin Abdallah bin Jiluwi was young and friendly. He wore his hair in the Bedu-nomad style, long and flowing. He was a son of the desert and open country; he did not like town life. He loved to hunt but no longer had the eyesight to shoot well. He had asked his father to send for Wells because he could no longer ignore his deteriorating vision. Wells discovered that Sa'ad had a very acute form of trachoma. His upper eyelids were rough with sand-like trachomatous granules, and his eyes watered constantly. He could hardly keep his eyes open in sunlight, so he kept his head down, shaded by his kaffiya. Wells told him both the good news and the bad news. He could be helped, but the treatment would be painful, and it could not be known in advance how successful or permanent the treatment would be.

Sa'ad wanted to know, "How painful?"

Wells replied, "I will inject Novocain under your eyelids so you will not feel anything. Then we will drop cocaine, also something that kills the pain, onto these granules. Then we will scrape them off. There could be pain during and after the operation. I will put soothing

---

[13] *Finjans*: small cups for coffee.
[14] This was the first and last time Wells saw Shaykh Abdallah bin Jiluwi, one of the great Arabian warriors of the century. He died later that year, an honored and revered personage, without whose courageous acts Sa'udi Arabia might never have come fully into existence.

Abdulla bin Jiluwi (r), son Sa'ad (c), Mohammed Ajaji, early 1930s (LD)

ointment and a disinfectant in your eyes, and we will treat you with eye drops every day."

Sa'ad said, "Anything is better than what I am experiencing. If you can save my eyesight, I would be very grateful." So Wells carried out the procedure on Sa'ad, bandaged him up, and on the third day took off the bandages and put ointment and zinc oxide in his eyes. Now all that remained was to see how well he recovered.

In the meantime, Wells decided to use his temporary residence, the municipality's *beladiyya*,[15] as a clinic. Once again, the downstairs rooms would be ideal for outpatient treatment, and the upstairs would remain the medical team's private quarters.

The king's purchasing agents

Wells' friend Abdur Rahman Qasebi and his family were wealthy merchants, acting as King Abdal Aziz's purchasing agents in Bahrain. Abdur Rahman was cultured and well versed in Arab history and poetry. He was a man who knew how to spend his leisure hours enjoyably. One evening, after a hearty meal, coffee, and a long talk at his house, Abdur Rahman asked Wells if he would like to see more of the oasis. He ordered up two of Al-Hasa's famous white donkeys, almost as big as mules, and they explored the territory. One of their first calls was on Mohammed al Ajaji, a rival merchant. Engaging in noncompeting trade with the Qasebis, the Ajajis were among the largest landowners in the oasis. Mohammed al Ajaji was a country gentleman, reputed to be extremely truthful and righteous. Indeed, he exuded trustworthiness.

Mohammed gave Wells a short course in the kinds and quality of dates produced in Hasa, the best and most famous being *khalas*. Wells found them to be delicious, melt-in-your-mouth fresh dates, rivaling the *barhi* date of Basrah for succulence.[16]

---

[15] Two-story building.
[16] *Ratbs*, fresh young dates, can be had only at certain times of the year in Middle

Sa'ud bin Jiluwi (PD)

The next day, in the midst of a busy morning clinic flooded by local residents, a grandly dressed man broke into the line and commanded, "*Tabib, cum! Ta'al!*"[17] He was a slave of Sa'ud bin Jiluwi, another son of the amir of Al-Hasa and the effective ruler of that region. Wells looked up and was reminded of Dame's advice. Dame had said, "Slaves of VIP's often put on airs. They can be far more demanding and insolent than the big men themselves. This is particularly true of the slaves of King Abdal Aziz, who is a very polite man. Slaves often take on the reflected glory of their masters. They seem to relish their self-importance in public life this way. God knows they don't get much positive reinforcement otherwise. Don't let them push you around. You need to control your schedule, or you will never get anything done if you are at the constant beck and call of every self-important person."

Wells looked the slave in the eye and said, "Who are you?" The reply, "I'm Sa'ud bin Jiluwi's servant and you are needed right now at the palace."

Wells responded, "I know Sa'ud bin Jiluwi well enough to know he is a gentleman. If he wanted me right away, he would have sent a note written in polite Arabic. Rest assured, I am planning to come to the palace when I have finished seeing these very sick people." The slave was abashed, for he did not know that Sa'ud bin Jiluwi had already asked Wells to come to the palace in the afternoon to test his eyes and refract him for glasses.

Upon arriving at the amir's residence that afternoon, Wells was escorted to Sa'ud's private, upper-story living chamber, with many servants in attendance. Wells set up his equipment on a table, including a vision chart and test lenses to correct to 20/20 eyesight. Wells

---

Eastern groceries and only in the season when they ripen. They do not store or travel well.

[17] Doctor, get up! Come!

discovered that Sa'ud had trachoma and that no combination of lenses would give him perfect vision. He also discovered Sa'ud needed reading glasses. Despite his disappointment about the overall prognosis, Sa'ud was delighted with the corrected vision that his new glasses would give.

After the test, Wells asked, "Did you call for me this morning? Did you send one of your servants to tell me I was needed in the palace?"

"No."

"Well, I didn't think so. One of your servants present here now came to me and rudely commanded me, '*Qum, ta'al!*' I asked, 'What do you want?' and he said, 'You're needed in the palace right now.' I replied, 'If Sa'ud bin Jiluwi needed me in haste, he would have sent a message written in polite Arabic. I refused to come then."

Sa'ud bin Jiluwi glared, "Which man was that? I'll have him whipped."

"I won't tell you. If it doesn't happen again, we'll just forget it."

The news coursed rapidly throughout the palace that Wells did not panic when he was given a so-called order on behalf of the amir's son, nor was he vengeful in asking for retribution when someone got out of line. It also became known that the governor's household could not be treated sooner than local townspeople just because of their affiliation with the VIP visitor.

Later that same day, Wells treated the miscreant slave and his womenfolk and children, again showing no partiality or vengeance. By the end of the stay, Wells had developed an excellent personal relationship with the slave. Wells clearly did not approve of slavery, but there was also nothing he could do to intervene when the system was functioning normally. He was the outsider, the foreigner, with absolutely no legal standing.

Hajj holiday in Al-Hasa

The month of the Hajj arrived while Wells was still in Al-Hasa, so he was a personal witness to the rituals that unfolded during this religious period. The tenth day of the lunar month was Eid al-Adha, the most sacred holiday in the Islamic calendar. Pilgrims to Makkah walked between the hills of Safa and Marwaha, threw stones to commemorate driving off the devil, and sacrificed either a goat, a sheep, an ox, or another animal. On the plain, they sacrificed either a goat, a sheep, an ox, or another animal. Once these ceremonies were complete, the Hajj was over, and pilgrims were officially declared to be

"Hajjis." In recognition of this distinction, the men dyed their beards henna red. People went around in their best clothes, shooting off guns, dancing and having a merry time. With all this celebration going on, Wells closed the clinic and gave his assistants the day off. Wells was exhausted. He had contracted a bad cold and desperately wanted sleep and rest.

When Abdur Rahman received word that Wells was under the weather, he came to his residence and announced, "We're going to have a picnic out at Ain Nijm."

Wells said, "Please let me rest just today. I have a bad cold, and I want to take a day off, sleep, and get the cold over with."

Abdur Rahman said, "If you go with me to Ain Nijm, I guarantee you'll get over your cold quickly. There's an old Turkish bath at Ain Nijm with a hot spring and a cold spring under the same roof. If you come there with me and get the hot spring treatment, a rub down, and the 'sweats,' then you'll eat heartily and sleep peacefully. I guarantee you'll get better."

He was so eager to show Wells the local cure that Wells gave in. When he arrived at Ain Nijm, Wells submitted to the full treatment. It began in a hot room where he took his turn in hot water and then in sweat-hot steam. Next, he received a rubdown with a big towel from one of the male attendants, and then he lay down briefly before going into the cold-water spring. This was followed by a return to the steam room to sweat some more, then another rubdown, and finally a normal temperature bathing room.

With all these ministrations completed, Wells tucked into a roast mutton pilaf made just for him. He ate heartily and chased the food with good Arab coffee. He then fell asleep for two or three hours, absolutely exhausted from this treatment. By the time Wells went home at sundown, he felt much better. To his delight, he found that the next day his cold had fizzled out.

Meeting King Abdal Aziz bin Sa'ud

Not long after the Eid holiday in honor of the Hajj, Wells was told that King Abdal Aziz would be spending a few days in Hofuf. Wells hoped to meet him. In due time, a note came from Sa'ud bin Jiluwi saying that the king would like to have his eyes tested. Could Wells come that afternoon? Wells replied he was happy to do so. This was Wells' first meeting with the formidable monarch.

Wells' first impression upon meeting King Abdal Aziz was that he was very tall. He came across as a dignified yet friendly and crisply intelligent man in his midfifties. Indeed, he appeared every foot a king. He told Wells that one of his eyes had been partially blind for many years but that the other one had good vision. He was still a good rifleman and could shoot accurately at a distance. The problem now was that he could not read his watch very well and had difficulty reading letters. Could Wells help? Wells confirmed the king's strong distance vision and lesser near vision. He would require corrective lenses for reading.

Abdal Aziz was pleased to see the fine print of the test card when his test lenses were in place, and he exclaimed, "Yes, that is quite satisfactory." Would Wells give him a prescription for glasses?

Wells said, "I don't actually have those glasses here. I will measure your face and the distance between your pupils, then I'll order the glasses from Bombay."

Abdal Aziz was impatient. He wanted them immediately.

Wells said, "I can't get your new spectacles right away. I can only test your vision. I don't make them. I will send the prescription by airmail and ask them to hurry your order. I'll ask them to send the glasses back to Bahrain by airmail, then the Qasebis will send them to you. What kind of frames do you want? Gold? Rolled gold? Silver? Platinum?"

Abdal Aziz now looked displeased. "Isn't there anything plainer?"

"Well, yes. There are simple plastic frames."

"You know, Wahhabis don't go for gold decoration, so I'd like my glasses to be as plain as possible. While you are ordering them, please order me a dozen." Wells looked up, surprised. "You know how it is. I have a big palace, and many wives and children. Then I have my car, of course, and I'm apt to leave my spectacles here or there. That way, if I have a dozen, I'll have at least one at hand wherever I am."

That sounded reasonable, and Wells sent to Bombay an order for a dozen of their cheapest spectacles to be sent to the King of Sa'udi Arabia.

Hofuf hospitality

Before Eid al-Adha, Wells was called out for a house call to a very sick patient. As he walked through the streets of Hofuf that rainy cold night, he passed a fascinating shop, a jeweler's place of business. An old man was sitting amid a group of artisans, most probably his sons and relatives. They were concentrating intently, making gold scabbards for swords and *khanjars*[18] with precious inlaid stones. They worked as if under pressure. The old man was courteous, but he apologized for not stopping to talk or have coffee.

He said, "Eid al-Adha is near. I have to get these things done to send to Riyadh so they arrive before the Eid. This is a consignment ordered by the king. He wants to give these out to his sons and to his favorites on the Eid day. When the Eid has passed, I'll send for you, and we can talk in the way I would like." Wells agreed and continued on his way to his outpatient's home.

The day after the *Eid* celebration, as good as his word, the jeweler sent a man to invite Wells to join him at his father's house. Wells was ushered into a well-built, three-story home. As was usually the case, the ground level was for servants and storage rooms. The second story was the main level for family quarters. On the third level was the old man's special mejlis, complete with a hearth. Coals were glowing in the grate, and one of his younger sons was making fresh coffee. Wells watched in silence, fascinated by the process unfolding before him.

The lad first put some coffee beans into a shallow skillet over the fire. Then with an iron poker, he moved the beans around so that they roasted without burning. The roasted beans went into a metal mortar, where they were crushed with a rhythmic mortar-and-pestle staccato. The pounding ended in an explosive flourish, the sound carrying downstairs into the street. Finally, the crushed beans were put into a coffee pot with a stylized, oversized spout and brought to a boil several times. The coffee was poured into another pot and back again to make sure it was well brewed. The young man waited patiently as Wells sipped down several finjans of coffee and then wig-wagged his cup to say he was finished. With a bow, the young man withdrew, leaving Wells and the old man to talk.

"We Hassawis, we Shi'ahs, are second-rate citizens in Sa'udi Arabia," began the old man. "The Sunnis feel so superior. This goes way back because, in a sense, we are a conquered people. Our forefathers were forced to adopt Islam, and we were Shi'ahs before our conquerors were Sunni. Most of the artisans in Hofuf and neighboring Katif are Hassawis, like me. We are the ones who know how to make things. We're the ones who make leather sandals and camel hair *abbas* or *bishts*.[19] We're the ones who know how to embroider *abbas* with gold thread, to

---

[18] Daggers with sheaths.
[19] Outer cloaks that men wear.

make them fit for a king. Others of us make pottery, and many others are gardeners."

The old man sipped his coffee before it cooled entirely, sucking it down with an audible "sssp" sound. "We are taxed to the limit. The Bedu nomads aren't taxed nearly as much. When the Bedu see a tax collector coming, they send somebody out into the desert with most of their flocks of sheep and goats so only a few remain behind. This is what the tax gatherer sees and bases his tax on. Besides, King Abdal Aziz favors the Bedu. They are his regular fighting force. Even though they are very independent, he has used them many times to keep his kingdom together." He paused to swallow his coffee again and let his message percolate.

"I'm an artist. You're a doctor," the old man's lament continued. "You know you can do only what your conscience tells you to do because you have pride in your art and science of medicine, and you couldn't do it so well under pressure and force. The king knows I and my family are the best jewelers in the kingdom, and so he sends us his orders. He provides us with the gold he expects us to use on the scabbards of swords and *khanjars*. The gold is all weighed out, and we have to show that the items we make contain all the gold he provides. Generally, he believes we give good value and are honest, but his underlings cause us endless trouble with their accusations."

"You and your sons are real artists," Wells replied. "I stood in the front of your shop admiring the work you did on those scabbards."

"Yes," said the old jeweler, "my ancestors were sword and dagger makers going back to the time of Carmuti.[20] In those days, Al-Hasa was as famous for its excellent steel as Damascus. Steel of that quality took a long time to make. They had the art of refining it and knew how to make a steel sword that would not shatter in combat. The steel had resilience; it could bend but not break. Then, at the time of Carmuti the third or fourth—I've forgotten which—my forefather of that time lost pride in making swords and took shortcuts. He must have just wanted to sell more of them. His swords looked good but were poor products. That forefather of mine, right here in Hofuf, was as responsible as anyone for the downfall of our nation. In those days, the king was the champion of his side. When an opposing army came, a single swordsman from each side would call out in challenge.[21] The two men would fight a decisive duel. In the middle of that duel, at the

---

[20] The Carmathians were subjugated in the tenth century CE.
[21] This reflects the story of David and Goliath as told in I Samuel 17.

very peak of it, Carmuti's sword snapped—the very sword my forefather had made. It did not stand the test, and we were conquered and have been under the heel of despots ever since."[22] Wells silently vowed to look up the history of the early Shi'ah communities, including the Carmathians.

"My private quarrel with the king is that, although I have served him well and faithfully as his chief armorer, I want to go to Bahrain for an operation. I need a hernia operation, and I know Dr. Dame would do it. I've asked permission to leave from King Abdal Aziz. I would especially like to go during Muharram, because at that time the Shi'ah in Bahrain are allowed to celebrate the ten-day memorial of the Battle of Kerbela and the deaths of Hassan and Hussein. Here in Hofuf, we can't do that celebration. Every time I request to go to Bahrain, I am told I can't go. Now you are here in Hofuf, you could do the operation here."

Wells responded that, yes, he could do the operation in Hofuf, but he would prefer to do it in Bahrain, where the operating room was better, and the chance of success much greater. He was concerned about the advanced age of the old armorer, and the matter was left unresolved at this precarious juncture.

As Wells returned to his house in Hofuf, his mind drifted to the famous painting by Rembrandt, *The Man with a Golden Helmet*. The colors and shadows in the jeweler's mejlis, and the jeweler himself, made an equally striking scene as that of Rembrandt's wizened warrior. The wonderful light and shadow in the mejlis had almost taken Wells' breath away. If only he had time to paint that scene.

The king's request

King Abdal Aziz stayed in Hofuf several more days, and Wells visited his mejlis one evening. There were many people there, particularly al Rashid tribesmen, from whom Abdal Aziz had wrested control of Riyadh and the surrounding region. Abdal Aziz had deliberately adopted a policy of lenience toward his former enemies, but to err on the side of caution, he kept some Al Rashidis close to him as virtual hostages. As long as these "guests" were carefully supervised, his former enemies were not a risk either to him or his state. He also

---

[22] King Abdal Aziz gave Wells a gift of antique armor and an antique sword (without scabbard) of amazing flexibility that came from this armorer's collection. The sword is in the author's possession.

contracted marriages with women of conquered tribes so that they became further unified through descendants with mutual blood ties.[23]

On the evening Wells was in attendance, King Abdal Aziz commented nonchalantly, "Maybe some of you have noticed that I'm not wearing my good, faithful, and familiar kaffiya. Today, I was up on that mountain nearby," he said, pointing to the nearby Jabal Gharra.[24] "It was hot, so I took my kaffiya off and left it there. It doesn't have much monetary value, but it has sentimental value to me. I would like it back. I'd like one of you to volunteer to go up and retrieve my kaffiya tonight, lest it get lost. Tomorrow night, I'll reward well the one who recovers my kaffiya."

Then he turned to one of the hostages from the al Rashid family—Wells thought perhaps it was Mohammed, the head of the group—and said, "You come from a renowned family. I challenge you to go up and bring my kaffiya down for me. If you do, I will give you a bag of gold pounds." At this challenge, the man could do nothing but accept. He left the tent as if to go up the mountain immediately. The night was dark, and between the encampment and the mountain was a dark valley that had to be crossed. There were many superstitions about that valley; one was that it was inhabited by djinns.[25]

The next evening, when everyone was sitting in the king's tented mejlis, Abdal Aziz announced, "Look. I have my kaffiya back. It was returned to me, and now I'm going to wear my good old familiar worn kaffiya. I'm going to reward the one who has brought it back to me."

Then he looked at Mohammed al Rashid and seemed about to toss him the bag of gold pounds. Abruptly, he stopped and said, "No, no. It wasn't you who retrieved my kaffiya. It was a black man, because I had a spy up there to see who would come. The black man who brought my kaffiya back looked very much like your servant, Musa." He beckoned Musa forward and gave him the bag of gold. Thus did Abdal Aziz reward loyal performance and chasten obfuscation and posturing among his subjects.

---

[23] Only later would the counterintuitive nature of this wise, short-term decision become apparent—when there were a huge number of his progeny to reckon with. At this writing, the last of his 144 sons from these marriages sits on the throne.

[24] By tradition, the Prophet Abraham was thought to have brought his animal herds into the sandstone caves of Jabal Gharra for safety.

[25] *Djinn*: evil spirits.

CHAPTER 14

Riyadh

*All of a sudden, the boy stopped breathing.
Wells thought the boy's heart
had stopped too. Crisis!
He ducked his head down
to listen for the heartbeat. Nothing!*

The interior

In 1937 King Abdal Aziz bin Sa'ud invited Wells to Riyadh, the capital of his kingdom, to treat vision defects in the royal family. If time remained, Wells was told, he could treat commoners. Upon his arrival, the king's chamberlain told Wells he would be assigned the house of the renowned British explorer and author, Harry St. John Bridger Philby,[1] who was not then in Riyadh. This comfortable and well-furnished guesthouse had been assigned to Philby by the king. Visiting it gave Wells access to Philby's library and favorite reading materials.

The king wanted Wells to tend to his daughter and granddaughter first. They were both about fourteen or fifteen years old and were soon coming into their marriageable years. They might become beautiful

---

[1] Philby was famous as an Arabist, explorer, intelligence officer, adviser to King Abdal Aziz, consultant to SoCal (precursor of Sa'udi Aramco), convert to Islam (who reverted to Christianity in later life), and father of Kim Philby, one of the post-World War II spies in the British intelligence service.

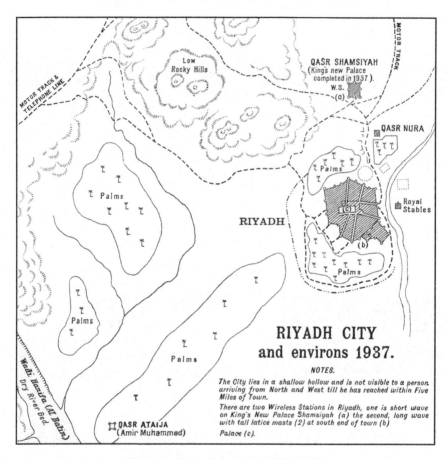

Riyadh, Sa'udi Arabia, 1937 (HD)

young women, but each had a prominent blemish, a defective eye that protruded from its socket. Neither teenager had vision in her bad eye. Never having seen either child before, Wells had no sense of the disease that caused their blindness. He could only speculate that this was an anterior staphyloma, probably caused by ulceration of the cornea. He thought the girls' condition could have resulted from any of three likely sources: gonorrheal conjunctivitis, trachoma, or smallpox.

After examining the girls, Wells realized that there was really nothing he could do to restore their vision. The main medical procedure available was to make sure the infection was controlled so that it would be less likely the girls' good eyes would become infected. This meant removing the bad eye and, after the socket healed, replacing it with a prosthetic eye. Wells knew that successfully removing an eye would be an heroic measure given the primitive field hospital conditions in Riyadh. Nevertheless, he set to the task with his considerable skills, and both operations were successful.

Upon recovery after her operation, the king's daughter asked to try a prosthetic eye. After the misery her bad eye had caused, she was excited that a glass eye might make her look normal, even beautiful again. Wells had a variety of glass eyes for her to select from.

Her good eye lit up when she saw the assortment of eyes available. As if picking out a piece of jewelry, she said, "Hmm. Let me try this one."

Wells was dubious about her selection, but what harm could it do to humor the young lady? He showed her how to put it in and how to remove it, and he explained the care she would need to give a glass eye for long-term use. She looked at herself in the mirror and was delighted.

"This is it," she said aloud, "I'll take it. I want it."

Wells hesitated, "You must get your father's approval first. He said he wanted to be consulted, and we should wait to decide until he comes home."

The king was absent on an extended hunting expedition. Upon return, he learned his girls had healed from their operations, and that he could see for himself the extent of their recovery. Abdal Aziz announced he would visit the women's quarters the next day.

Before the appointed hour, Wells came to see the girls and make sure all was well. The king's daughter told him, "I want to wear the glass eye that I like so my father can see how nice I look." In went the eye. When the king entered, she said, "*Abui*,[2] see how well I have recovered. The doctor did his work well."

The king stopped in his tracks, shocked. Seldom did anything shock him so visibly.

"*W'Allah!*"[3] he exclaimed. "No, no. I cannot allow it. It is not right." He turned to Wells and directed him to take back the offending glass eye. Did he have a more acceptable substitute? Wells had anticipated the king's reaction and was ready with other choices.

"This one," said the king, pointing. The young lady was crestfallen. Alas, the prized glass eye she thought made her look so beautiful was not to be hers. The king had been thoroughly spooked when his daughter had batted her eyes—her one pretty brown eye and the fake

---

[2] Father Dear.
[3] By God!

brilliant blue one. Not only was it unnatural, the king thought, but it was also far too decorative for Wahhabi social standards of the day. How could she even think of it? No, no, a thousand times no.

On the prophet, Isa bin Miriam

As the days passed, Wells learned more about King Abdal Aziz, specifically, that he was a thoughtful man. The mission's minister-evangelist, Rev. Gerrit Van Peursem, had also been invited to Riyadh but was unable to come.[4] The king knew Van Peursem as the padre Jerjous, or George, as close as Arabic could get to "Gerrit." Van Peursem had asked Wells to give the king a book, an Arabic translation of Paterson-Smythe's *The Life of Christ*, a chronological account of the life of Jesus.[5] The king thanked Wells and promised to read it. He was interested in the life of the Great Prophet Isa bin Miriam, whom Muslims revere in the Q'uran.

One night, rather late, Wells entered the king's mejlis during a heated discussion. As soon as the king saw him, he called out, *"Tome-iss, ta'al. Ijlus hina."*[6] The king said, "I've been reading this book, this history of the life of Jesus, the Prophet Isa bin Miriam. It's a fascinating and moving story. I've come to the part where he was crucified, that he was tried by the Jews first. He was slapped and spat upon and insulted in terrible ways and then killed on the cross. This is what *your* book says about him, though *our* book says he was not crucified. Now, my question is: Why don't you Christians hate the Jews like the Germans do and like we Arabs do, for what they did to the Prophet Isa?" The king was clearly wrought up about this point of theological and historical injustice. Wells sat thinking quietly for several moments. He knew this was an important question. He prayed silently for deep wisdom in answering the king.

After an uncomfortable silence, Wells said, "Since you have asked me a very important question, I will answer you as best I can. You understand that Jesus, Isa bin Miriam, is our King. We American Christians have no king. We have a president who is the leader of our nation. Yet, the One to whom we are truly loyal is Jesus, our spiritual

---

[4] Mrs. Van Peursem, a nurse, was a favorite of the ladies in the king's *hareem*. She had been to Riyadh several times but was not part of the group on this trip.
[5] This was probably Paterson-Smythe, *A People's Life of Christ*. It is not known whether this book was translated into Arabic, but it seems likely given the context. If there exists a translation, it is undoubtedly an abbreviated version of the original.
[6] Thoms, come and sit next to me.

King. He is the one who sent us to Arabia, for we believe he is living and gives orders to his servants.

"Oh, King, you remember His words on the cross as He was dying. In this record, you have read that Jesus said to God, 'Father, forgive them, for they know not what they do.'[7] He, Our Master, forgave them. If somebody in your kingdom committed a great crime against you, and yet, in your mercy and compassion, you forgave him, that would be a wonderful act. I know, in the past, you have been generous to your enemies. Suppose this person, who was forgiven by you, would pass outside your front door and was attacked by your servants. What would you do to those people who attacked and injured or even killed the person you had pardoned?"

The king replied, "I'd have them executed, for that would have been a great insult to me as the ruler of this country."

Wells responded, "Exactly, Sir. Our Master forgave the Jews at that time for what they had done, and we, His followers, must indeed forgive also.

"In addition, ya Taweel al Amr,[8] this happened a long time ago—almost two thousand years ago. Should we blame today the descendants of people that lived two thousand years ago for what they did at that time? When this happened, your ancestors were worshiping idols, which is well-known throughout the world. Before Islam, Makkah had many gods, and your ancestors gathered there from all over Arabia to worship tribal gods. They were idolaters, according to your creed; this is a terrible sin, almost unforgivable. You recognize that. Are you responsible, and should you be punished, for what your forefathers did in their ignorance in the time of the Jahiliyya?"[9]

"No," said Abdal Aziz, "Of course not. That was the era before Islam, and we are bound by the tenets of Islam that we believe in now."

"Well," responded Wells, "that, I think, is a second answer to your question. Because what happened occurred a long time ago, Jews living today should not be held responsible for the crimes of their ancestors.

"Finally, O King, we believe the strongest thing in the world is love. You can bind men together by iron fetters, and they will do their utmost to break those chains and cut them apart. They will leave each other when they can if they are bound only by chains. On the other hand, if they are bound by love, there is nothing in the world that can

---

[7] Luke 23:34.
[8] Oh, Long of Life.
[9] This term refers to the "Age of Ignorance" before Islam arrived.

separate them, because love is the strongest bond in the world."

After pondering this point for a few moments, King Abdal Aziz responded, "That is true. Recently, we had a war with our neighbor, Imam Yahya of Yemen. My son Sa'ud marched down the wadi to the east of Sa'na and attacked the capital from the east, while my son Faisal marched down the coast to Buraida from the west. They surrounded Sa'na, and Imam Yahya had to surrender. The terms were thus: Because we were both Muslim countries, we would not demand reparations. The old borders would remain, and we would each keep the peace within our borders as we had for many years previously. This has been a real boon to me because I don't have to keep an army there, and we are now friends as a result of our generous terms."

Restoring sight

After Wells had finished treating the royal family's eye ailments, carried out tests, and done the scheduled operations, Abdal Aziz said to him, "Now, Riyadh is yours. I and my family are going out to the plateau country for a long picnic. There we will hunt, and our animals will feast on the fresh growth of the range grasses. I want you to treat the rest of my people because so many of them are ill. I will give you whatever space you need for your clinic and for operations. Please treat everyone who comes to you. I will pay your bill when it comes time for you to leave."[10]

When the clinic opened, Wells was mobbed by patients eager for treatment, including the seriously ill, the somewhat sick, those with sniffles, and the hypochondriacs. His team formed the prospective patients into a line to pass Wells' makeshift examination room at the rate of about one per minute. In each morning's clinic, he saw from 175 to 200 patients. Wells could examine each one only perfunctorily, identifying only the most apparent disease or condition they manifested. This procedure was not at all satisfactory, but there was no other way to deal with the endless throng of people queued up. Those who were suffering the most were scheduled for operations as soon as possible. Because of the primitive conditions available to him in Riyadh, Wells recommended that those requiring major surgery should come to the Bahrain hospital, even though making such a difficult trip might well spell their end.

The most frequent operation was for trichiasis, a complication

---

[10] Wells noted later in life that this was the only time in his career he practiced "socialized medicine," his bill being paid by the government of King Abdal Aziz.

of trachoma. Wells did hundreds of these operations in Riyadh to keep the eyelashes from turning inward, and he devised a method so he could operate in an almost mass-production style. Three side-by-side beds (really doors or broad planks set up on sawhorses) served three patients at a time. Each patient would receive a local anesthetic for the affected eyelids at about the same time, and then Wells would race from one plank to the next. As one procedure was completed, a new patient would be brought in, while Wells moved to the next plank bed. Wells was normally able to do a complete surgery in fifteen minutes per eye, but using this mass production mode would take less time. In effect, the three planks became, "pre-op," "op," and "post-op" surgical stages.

Almost all surgery was on an outpatient basis, after which the patients were released to their families with instructions about post-operative care. In this way, Wells carried out about thirty eye surgeries in an afternoon and might still have had some time for another, more demanding, surgery or two. Using the light of a single Petromax pressure lantern, he often continued to operate until as late as nine o'clock at night.

Although the trichiasis operation posed little risk of complication, it was hugely important. Saving patients' sight meant they could continue to work at home or in oasis fields or outdoors with their animals. Without sight, a person was almost totally handicapped; there were few jobs they could qualify for. One job some blind men could undertake was to recite the Q'uran passages already committed to memory, but these opportunities were few and paid little. Having many blind people in a family was impoverishing and drew heavily on their resources. More grimly, it was deemed to be God's punishment for some familial evil.

Wells avoided doing cataract operations in his makeshift operating theater. The only cataract surgeries he did were on patients with "clean" eyes—that is, if there was no complication from trachoma. He did not want to risk infecting a good eye, because such reinfections meant almost surely that the patient would lose vision totally.[11] As Wells' stay continued from days to weeks, a routine was established. His workday was split into two parts: clinic in the morning and operations in the afternoon. He and his team of two assistants kept busy throughout the entire day, taking a short break for lunch. The

---

[11] Wells received his first antibiotics (penicillin) from his friend and medical school classmate, Gifford Upjohn, in 1948. Before then, he was operating without such an important antibiotic.

crowds would not leave them alone except at prayer times. At noon, the *muezzin* would climb up on the balcony of a nearby mosque and call the faithful to prayer, sonorously intoning: "La Allah il Allah wa Muhammad rasul Allah."[12] As soon as patients heard the beginning of the prayer call, many would start toward the mosque. Others with toothaches, high fevers, or excruciating pain would not leave. On such occasions, the patrolling *muttawiyun* would come into the clinic area and whip the remaining people with their canes, ordering them to leave. This was prayer time—no exceptions. It was only during the noon prayer hour that there was relief for the medical team; they could get their lunch and organize for the afternoon surgeries.

Dangers of surgery

Surgery was often of an emergency nature, and major surgery was undertaken only when the patient could not survive being transported to the hospital in Bahrain.

One major operation involved a patient brought in by camel from a town about fifty miles from Riyadh. A man presented his eleven-year-old nephew, Hamid, a child with a strangulated hernia. No food could move through his intestines. Hamid was vomiting, and his abdomen was badly distended. Wells was not sure what he could do because the boy was so far gone, but he said he would try to save the lad. Wells knew there was great risk in operating, but Hamid was certain to die if Wells did not attempt the operation immediately. Wells spoke with Hamid's uncle, told him about the gravity of the situation and the great risks, and asked permission to operate on the boy.

Wells said, "If I do not operate on him, he will die. If I do operate on him, there is no guarantee he will be cured. Hamid is such a promising lad; I believe we should try to save his life." Wells had only a minute or two to consult with the uncle, but he suspected the uncle understood the situation was serious and that extreme measures were called for.

The uncle said, "If you take him inside, I go too. I promised his father I would be with him every minute no matter what, and I must keep my promise." Wells agreed to his request.

Hamid was prepped. Wells also made the uncle prepare for the operating room by taking off his grimy outer garments, fumigating him for bugs and bacteria, dressing him in a hospital gown, fixing

---

[12] There is no God but Allah, and Muhammad is his prophet.

a cap over his long, unkempt hair, and putting a mask over his face and bushy beard. Wells told him to sit in the corner of the dimly lit operating room, which he obediently did.

The operation had to be done under local anesthetic because the boy's condition was so perilous. Wells just could not risk administering a general anesthetic. Local anesthetic also gave him a better reading of the patient's status as the operation progressed. As he always did, Wells prayed before he began the procedure. He then opened up the boy's abdomen and readily found the piece of intestine that had been pinched off. That's when complications set in. The affected section had become gangrenous because the circulation of the artery and veins had also been pinched off. Three or four inches of intestine had to be cut out and then the boy's internal plumbing sewn back together again. This took more time than Wells had expected. It was definitely not an operation he would ever have contemplated doing in the equivalent of somebody's garage or a barn in the United States. Once he started, however, he had no choice but to make the best of a terrible situation.

Growing impatient, the uncle rose and stood behind Wells, pushing forward to see what was going on. He was no longer willing to sit in the corner as instructed. He was curious and pressed even closer to look over Wells' shoulder. Wells kicked him in the shins every now and then and stepped on his toes to keep him back, all the while remaining focused on the operation. After a seemingly interminable period, the uncle finally got tired and bored, not understanding what was going on, and sat back down in the corner.

All of a sudden, the boy stopped breathing. Wells thought the boy's heart had stopped, too. Wells ducked his head down to listen for the heartbeat. Nothing.

The elderly uncle immediately realized something had gone wrong. He tried to get up and interfere, but he could not. He seemed immobilized and could not rise. The color of the boy's face was the giveaway that he was, to all intents and purposes, dead. His face had turned dark blue-gray from a lack of oxygen. Wells grew very concerned because he knew the custom in Arabia was to bury a person immediately after death. There were no undertakers or morticians, no ceremonies, no flowers, no receptions, no memorial services, no music, no condolence books, and no sermons of comfort. Visitation with mourners came after the body was buried. Wells was afraid this man, believing his nephew to be dead, would prevent any effort to resuscitate him. He feared that the uncle would grab the boy and rush out to bury him. The uncle, however, seemed restrained by a power stronger than himself, and Wells and his team continued doing what they had to do.

"Boys and girls," Wells thought, "this is worse than being between a rock and a hard place." He prayed fervently for God to help him remain cool and focused, to help him do what he needed to do, and by all means to keep the uncle sitting in the corner. Wells did not need more interference. He took an adrenaline solution and injected it directly into the boy's heart. Immediately it started beating again, and Wells undertook artificial respiration to restore the child's breathing. Just as suddenly as he left, the boy re-entered the land of the living. His blue-gray countenance lightened to a warm brown tone. Wells finished the operation without further crisis and put Hamid to bed. This was one patient that Wells would monitor closely.

Wells was inordinately thankful that night as he rolled into bed because he had felt that the Lord, the Great Physician, had really saved that boy. What happened on that operating table was entirely beyond Wells' expectation or experience. He was one-person deep with no backup and minimal resources. He knew only too well what was not available to him in that rustic clinic. Yet he felt compelled to try. Wells was filled with gratitude for the reassuring presence of the Holy Spirit that he felt even as he operated.

A few days later, the uncle prepared to take the boy back to his father. As he gently placed the child on the camel, he said, "You know, this boy was dead for a little while. I do not know what you did to him, but he came back to life. That boy up there was dead," he repeated, pointing to Hamid, now sitting on the camel's back. "Very fortunate for you he did not die. I vowed to his father, my brother, that if the boy died, I would have your life in revenge." Then the old man uncovered the dagger concealed under his clothes. With that visual display and without a further word of thanks or acknowledgment, the uncle mounted his camel, and Hamid and he returned whence they came.

That night, Wells was doubly thankful for the deliverance of the boy and was astonished at the uncle's viewpoint. Why would anyone wish to slay a Good Samaritan who had gone beyond any call of duty?[13] It did not make sense. Did not this man know that Wells was trying to help him and his nephew and that Wells was his nephew's only hope? What crazy logic was the uncle using? Had he taken his nephew to a

---

[13] Very likely, the old man had never heard of the Good Samaritan story told in Luke 10: 25-37.

native healer first and gotten no satisfaction? That would have put the boy's life at greater risk, but Wells knew that intense grief makes some people irrational. There was, however, no time for contemplation; other people were in the never-ending queue for Wells' assistance, clamoring for his expertise.

The learned mullah

One of Wells' patients in Riyadh was a religious divine, a learned mullah.[14] He had a cataract uncomplicated by trachoma or any other eye disease, so he was an ideal candidate for surgery in Riyadh instead of Bahrain. He was one of the Wahhabist Ikhwaan warriors that Abdal Aziz had called upon to help consolidate Sa'udi Arabia into a single state. The mullah was a teacher and priest of this sect and had seen almost nothing of any other group. Wells thought he probably classified everyone except Wahhabi Muslims as *kafirs*, unworthy of God's compassion, even though Jews and Christians had always been considered Ahl I Kitaab,[15] and, therefore, not total infidels.

This mullah was in desperate straits. He could not see anything other than large objects with either eye. His greatest pleasure was to read the Q'uran, and he wanted to do so again. He had heard that Wells performed seemingly miraculous operations, so he came asking for an operation. After giving him an examination, Wells successfully performed the cataract removal.

Ten days after the procedure, Wells invited the mullah to his house on a Sunday afternoon to test the mullah for spectacles. It appeared that one set of lenses would give the mullah useful distance vision and that another set would be good for reading. These were such common prescriptions that Wells had several such lenses with him, so the mullah could get his new spectacles immediately.

With the close-distance spectacles on the mullah's nose, Wells opened the Gospel of John to the ninth chapter and asked the mullah to read. This is the chapter about the young man who was born blind and healed by Jesus. Wells frequently used this passage to test reading vision for patients recovering from cataract surgery. After a moment, the mullah realized he was not reading the Q'uran, and he dropped the Bible. Wells caught it before it landed on the floor, annoyed by the way he had treated the Christian holy book. He told the mullah how annoyed he was and that he would never have handled the Q'uran

---

[14] *Mullah*: theologian or religious leader.
[15] People of the Book, that is, Christians and Jews.

that way. He explained that he had come from Bahrain to Riyadh to treat people like the mullah. Wells said that what he had in his hand was the holy book of Christians, the Injeel, and the holy book of the Jews, the Torah. Both are mentioned in the Q'uran. The mullah was confused and partly apologized, saying he had never read anything except the Q'uran, and it had shocked him to know he was reading something else.

"Have you never read the Injeel?"

"No," came the answer. "Nothing like that. There is no knowledge in the world worth reading that's not in the Q'uran or the Hadith."[16]

Puzzled at this, Wells asked, "Don't you ever read magazines or newspapers?"

"Never."

Wells had been surprised to learn there were no newspapers or magazines published in Sa'udi Arabia. Perhaps a few periodicals from outside the country were read secretly by clerks of the king. People from Jeddah and Makkah had some Egyptian newspapers. No radios played music or broadcast the news in public, although the king listened in his mejlis to radio news programs and commented on them to assembled shaykhs. The king also listened to readings of the Q'uran.

A few nights after this encounter with the mullah, Wells wrote his sister, Frances, then living in Greenwich, New York. He was still upset about his experience. The stress of more than a month working both day and night was beginning to take its toll. He wrote to Frances, "I came to Arabia to make converts to Christianity. What is happening, though, is that all my eye surgery accomplishes is to allow Muslims to read the Q'uran again and become better Muslims." Wells was learning that he was just one of many on the Great Physician's team. In the midst of his misgivings, however, the Holy Spirit protected, energized, and inspired Wells when he reflected on the strangulated hernia operation, and he came to the realization that it was not his responsibility to judge what came of his ministrations.

Conversation with a king[17]

One evening, shortly after this episode with the mullah, Wells closed the outer door of the mud house that served as his home and

---

[16] The Traditions of Muhammad.
[17] This section follows an unpublished account by Beth Scudder Thoms, completed 22 June 1973. She was an excellent writer, fluent in Arabic, and a confidante of Wells. It was always hoped by her family that she would recount his biography because of the authenticity of this story. Unfortunately, it was too painful for her to revisit their precious years together.

hospital and once again wearily found his way through the dusty lanes to the mejlis of King Abdal Aziz. As he did every evening, the king was sitting in audience, available to all who wished to see him.

Wells enjoyed people watching in the king's mejlis, and these visits filled up an empty evening with little else to do. He entered at one end of a long, mud-walled reception room spread with grass-matting rugs, bare of all accessories. At the other end, the king sat on a pallet. Each person, upon entering, found a place in line with others seated on the floor, backs to the walls, heads covered by red checkered kaffiyas and black-roped *agals*. All sandals or shoes had been left at the entrance. Bare feet were either firmly planted with soles on the floor or covered for modesty, to avoid offending anyone.

As was usually the case, silence prevailed as Wells entered the mejlis. There was no small talk. No one minded, and no one, but no one, spoke, except the king and those to whom he addressed his remarks. From time to time, the king ordered "*Gahwa!*" and like pistol shots, the word was taken up and passed down a line of attendants to a Stygian area from which emerged several Nubians in flowing orange *gelebiyas* (robes), each bearing a brass coffee pot in his left hand and a nest of five or six china finjans in his right. Beginning with the king, they poured steaming bitter black coffee, a couple of tablespoons at a time, into a finjan and passed the steaming cup with their right hands to each guest. When the cups were emptied, they were collected, with the server backtracking to the first one he had served, picking up the finjan, and serving the next waiting guest with the now-used cup. There was a cheerful clinking of cups and a sense of belonging in the still atmosphere of the mejlis. The Nubians obviously enjoyed their role and poured the coffee with a flourish.

On this evening, Wells entered the mejlis, and the king motioned him to sit in a space near him.

"Et Tome-iss," he began, making "Thoms" into two syllables. "Do you know," and he jabbed his finjan in Wells' direction for emphasis, "why I gave our oil rights to the Americans?" Without waiting for a reply, he continued, "I will tell you."

Now he paused for effect, looking around the room to make sure he had everyone's attention. The king's pronouncements in these public forums served as news headlines for a country where news media were nonexistent. With attention secured, he focused on Wells again.

"I'll tell you why. It's the same reason why you are here among us today. We trust you. We invited you to come even as we asked Dr.

Harrison and Dr. Dame to come from the American Mission Hospital before you. Our trust has not been misplaced.

"Now, there is oil under our sands. To whom should we give our concessions? Many countries want them—the Russians, for instance, and the Japanese have offered us more money than anyone else. The Italians want the oil and also the British, as well as the Americans.

"Who would best vindicate our trust? The Russians? But the Russians say there is no God. We cannot trust people who say there is no God. The Japanese? But the Japanese worship their Emperor. They say he is God. That is blasphemy. We want no dealings with them. The Italians? They are already in Yemen and Ethiopia and say they love the Arabs, but Mussolini loves the Arabs like a wolf loves a lamb. The British? *W'allah*! They are men—but when they get close, they take over, and we don't want that here. So, Tome-iss, since you Americans have worked only for our good, it's to you I have given our oil concessions." Then he added, "When you go back to your country and call on your shaykh, please give him my salaams."

The audience then turned to other matters, but Wells kept thinking with amusement of bin Sa'ud's concept of America. "When you call on your shaykh," indeed. Wells knew that he could not explain the social structure of the United States to the king in one sentence, nor did he want to upset so pleasant a picture. In musing about his assignment, he wondered how he could ever carry it out.[18]

In 1973 Beth recounted how Wells did, indeed, carry the king's greetings to the highest ranks of American society through his friend, the world traveler and radio commentator, Lowell Thomas. Beth recalled the relevant incident:

> Lowell Thomas and Wells knew each other, and Lowell had printed some of Wells' writing in his magazine. When Wells [was] on furlough in the United States in 1938, Lowell invited Wells to a luncheon and radio broadcast at the Waldorf Astoria Hotel in New York City.
>
> "Come," said Lowell, "relax, enjoy yourself. There will be interesting people there. The program is made up. You won't have to speak." Wells accepted.
>
> Seated next to one of the speakers at the luncheon, Wells noticed a man nervously pecking at his food. Wells started to kid him.

---

[18] See endnote 14:18, p. 388.

"You should worry," said the man. "You don't have to face the mike [*sic*] with this gang at your elbow."

"Quite true," thought Wells as he savored his steak. After the meal, the broadcast began on schedule.

When the last speaker sat down, Lowell Thomas looked at his watch and said, "We have three more minutes. I'll call one of my guests at random. We have here with us Dr. Wells Thoms just returned from Arabia. I'll call on him. Dr. Wells Thoms, the mike [*sic*] is yours."

"Dirty trick," the words flashed in Wells' mind, followed by, "Three minutes. What can I say?" Then he recalled his conversations with King Abdal Aziz about the new-formed petroleum alliance between Arabia and the United States. Wells told the radio audience of his oil concession conversation with Abdal Aziz and closed by saying, "I hope my 'shaykh,' the president of the United States, is listening—or perhaps his deputy—for I now fulfill the assignment given to me by Abdal Aziz bin Sa'ud, king of Sa'udi Arabia. I bring my shaykh the king's greetings: 'Salaam alaikum,' and may our two countries always remain friends."

CHAPTER 15

The Little Fort: Kuwait

*"Of your goodness, Khatoun,
a tiny drink of water!"
The desperate cry of the Bedu nomad
woman with children in tow
pierced even the hardest heart.*

On the move again, 1937

Wells and Beth and their three children boarded the gently bobbing dhow that navigated the rising tide out to the venerable SS *Barpeta*, tugging at anchor in Bahrain's roadstead. The *Barpeta* was a British India Company "slow mail" boat that threaded its way among Persian Gulf ports and eventually on to distant Bombay. The Thoms family was headed to a new home, the little fort town of Kuwait. All their worldly goods were on board.

Once the children had eaten dinner, been bathed, and put to bed, Wells and Beth sat on the lower bunk in their cabin and reflected on all that was transpiring in their lives.

"Hopefully, it's just for a year," Wells reminded Beth for the umpteenth time. "Just while Stanley and Bess Mylrea are on furlough. Stanley has done amazing work in Kuwait, where he has improved people's health tremendously. He's become a legendary figure these last thirty years but can't do much surgery anymore; he's sixty and has a back problem. He needs relief." Wells paused in his reflections and then admitted what was gnawing at both of them. "There's a chance we might replace them when they retire." Beth nodded. She had thought the same.

"My father tried to start a medical practice in Kuwait in 1903 when Shaykh Mubarak 'the Great' was in power." Wells mused aloud, launching into an account of his parents' rapid retreat from Bahrain that had taken them to Kuwait. "A cholera epidemic had broken out in Bahrain. Bahrainis knew nothing of epidemics or the germ theory of disease. They thought Father had caused the epidemic by building the hospital. Because the Bahrain hospital treated so many cholera victims, people were afraid to come to the clinic or stay in the hospital. Father, therefore, thought it was time to start again elsewhere, perhaps Kuwait.

"It, however, wasn't to be. Shaykh Mubarak's men bundled Father back onto the dhow he arrived on for fear that the British would disapprove of this American presence. Kuwait had signed a treaty with the British in 1899, but no Crown representative had lived in Kuwait until 1903. The shaykh had promised the British that, in return for British protection from the Ottomans next door in Iraq, he would not traffic with other nations. He didn't want to jeopardize that protection, so he refused entry for my parents."

After a brief pause, Wells continued. "Kuwait has changed a lot since Father's day. In 1910 Shaykh Khaza'al of Mohammerah convinced Shaykh Mubarak of Kuwait to let the mission set up a hospital in Kuwait. Shaykh Khaza'al's daughter had been cured by Dr. Arthur Bennett, an Arabian Mission physician from Basrah. Shaykh Khaza'al thought it would help Mubarak and Kuwait if the town had a mission hospital. As a result, Shaykh Mubarak ultimately donated the land for the mission hospital.

"Of course," Wells concluded, "Kuwait will change. Oil has been discovered. Bahrain, Sa'udi Arabia, and Kuwait as we know them will all change. Our concern must be for Kuwaitis. Dr. Mylrea will introduce us to the local dignitaries. The rest of the mission staff is warm and gracious. Mary Van Pelt is an excellent nurse-midwife, and Dr. Mary Allison will handle the Women's Hospital. Mary Allison's a GP, so I'll only be called in for emergencies. I can teach her the simpler eye surgery procedures. Rev. Fred and Margaret Barny will be there, too; they were colleagues of my parents way back when."

Wells noticed Beth's eyes were shut, her breathing regular. He whispered to her sleeping frame, "Time for bed and rest, My Love. You've had busy days packing all of our stuff and caring for the children without an *ayah*. You mustn't get too tired with our new babe on the way." As Wells climbed into the upper berth of the four-berth cabin, he said, "I'll get up if the kids wake. Sweet dreams."

"Mm-hmm," responded Beth.

Welcome to Kuwait

Dr. C. S. G. Mylrea,[1] Kuwait's only mission doctor, stood on the customs pier to greet Wells and Beth. "Welcome to Kuwait," said Dr. Mylrea in a resonant voice. He shook hands with the two Americans. As they left the customs shed, he announced rather formally in sonorous Arabic, "Let me introduce you to one of our more distinguished citizens. This is Abdullah bin Hijji. *Salaam alaikum*, my friend. How is your health?" Abdullah, seemingly in his sixties, was sitting on a rickety chair in the shade of the shed. He hardly had the appearance of a "distinguished citizen."

Abdullah replied equally formally, "Alaikum salaam. Unfortunately, I am feeling quite unwell. That is why I am not at the al Shaab Gate.[2] I've had fever and weakness. *Insha'Allah*, I shall feel better tomorrow."

"Let me see," said Dr. Mylrea. "Hmm," he said, turning to Wells and commenting in English. "He has a pretty high fever but a steady pulse." To the shaykh he said, "Are you eating well and drinking coffee and water? Do you have other things wrong besides your fever? How are your bowels?" The shaykh had not noticed anything seriously amiss and indicated so noncommittally.

"If you do not feel better in a few days, please come see me. If you feel very unwell, send one of your men, and I will come to you." Abdullah grunted and nodded his assent. Mylrea then swept his hand toward Wells. "Let me introduce Hakeem Thoms. He is taking my place for a little while. Hakeem Thoms is an excellent doctor. His father was a doctor before him and opened the first hospital in Bahrain. His mother was the first lady doctor for Bahraini women. Hakeem Thoms lived in Bahrain as a boy and speaks Arabic well. Of course, his Arabic

---

[1] Kuwaitis thought Mylrea had almost mystical powers. His keen diagnostic eye and his knowledge of the community gave him exceptional insight into their lives and ailments. His hospital had no lab technician, so he did all his own tests. The hospital had no X-ray machine either. Mylrea had barely the resources of a good first-aid station. Yet, his situation was no better or worse than Wells' had been in Bahrain. Practicing medicine in these parts was not for the faint of heart. See also, endnote 15:1, p. 388.
[2] Al Shaab Gate was Kuwait's second-most-important gate through the city wall, the Sur.

is not the beautiful Najdi Arabic you speak, but he understands Arab ways. He has been in Bahrain for five years and has treated everyone from Qatar to Riyadh, from Katif to Sharjah. He knows all the shaykhs and has treated them. He replaces me only temporarily. Now I must take the new hakeem and the mother of their children to the mission hospital. You must rest and sleep, my friend. *Fi man Allah*."[3]

As he led the Thoms family away from the port, Mylrea explained: "He's one of Shaykh Ahmad's key supporters. He knows everyone. That's why he is gatekeeper of the al Shaab Gate, Kuwait's main entry point. He's a good friend to have if issues arise," Mylrea confided in Wells. "His symptoms are nonspecific. It could be malaria, but that is unlikely. He may have food poisoning or even tuberculosis. Could be enteric fever. By the time we could complete a Widal Test to confirm it, however, he might be dead. The only thing, for now, is to keep an eye on him and hope for the best." Wells made a mental note to inquire after Abdullah bin Hijji.

A touring car pulled up beside them. "Who have we here?" Mylrea exclaimed as a distinguished, colonial official clambered out. "Ah, Col. Harold Dickson, let me introduce Dr. Wells Thoms, my replacement while Bess and I are away. Wells' father was Dr. S. J. Thoms, who started the first hospital in Bahrain and the first hospital in Oman."

Turning to the new arrivals, Mylrea continued in his proper manner. "Wells, Col. Dickson is a Kuwait institution. As political agent here for many years, he was the British Empire personified." Dickson extended a hand to Wells and stood a bit more stiffly. Mylrea resumed, "He advised the shaykh and expressed official British views. Now he represents the Kuwait Oil Company. He can answer all questions about the history of the place. Dickson has the additional advantage of knowing Arab nomadic culture, having been wet nursed by a Bedu woman. He is virtually a member of the Anaiza tribe. It is always a pleasure to go into the desert with Harold and Violet to see Arabia through a totally different lens."

"Col. Dickson," said Wells. "It is a pleasure to meet you. I hope we will become well acquainted. For now, we'll say goodbye, so that we can get the children and Beth to the house on the mission compound." As the touring car hastened away, the Thoms family clambered into the mission car, with Mylrea taking the driver's seat.

"Let me orient you a bit. The customs pier and the suq are about in the middle of the town buffered by shipyards at the waterside. The

---

[3] God go with you.

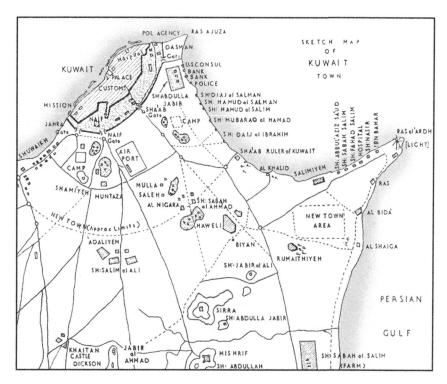

Kuwait, 1947

al Shaab Gate is over there, to the southeast. We will drive half the length of Kuwait's seafront to the hospital, which is to the southwest. Back there, at the other end of town from the hospital are the political agent's house and the shaykh's residence, Dasman Palace. Our hospital faces Kuwait Bay and is nearest to the desert frequented by caravans. At our end of town are the cemeteries. So far," he said with a wink, "we haven't had a problem with djinns, even though cemeteries are not places to be after sundown."

"Belief in djinn and in the 'evil eye' are probably like the belief in voodoo I encountered in Panama," Wells responded. "I had a patient there about to curl up and die because he believed he had been cursed by a voodoo shaman. We took him to confront the man who had cursed him. When the voodoo maker saw the sick man, he suddenly believed the patient possessed a greater power because he had survived his hex. Will we see patients who believe in spirit possession?"[4]

---

[4] Maloney, *The Evil Eye*.

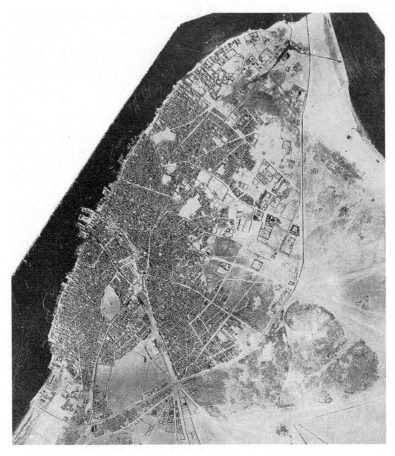

Kuwait from the air, ca. 1940 (PD)

"Indeed. Spirits can possess people alone at night outside their houses and villages. This seems to happen mostly to men, although women and children can contract the evil eye, too. Many Africans, both slaves and ex-slaves, believe in *zar*.[5] You'll hear drumming coming from slave and ex-slave neighborhoods at night, often associated with *zar* exorcisms.

"Look beyond the hospital to Kuwait's outer wall," said Mylrea, pointing through the windshield to the distant wall. "The wall was built in 1920, when Kuwait feared invasion by King Abdal Aziz's Ikhwaan. Building it was a sign of weakness on the part of Shaykh Salim al-Mubarak. His father, Shaykh Mubarak the Great, always proclaimed fearlessly, "I AM THE WALL," and dared Abdal Aziz and his followers to

---

[5] Spirit possession.

invade. Such an invasion would have been a tragic betrayal. In earlier times, Mubarak had protected the exiled and countryless Abdal Aziz and his compatriots inside Kuwait. What a violation of trust it would have been for the Sa'udis to 'bite the hand' that extended them dakhil if they invaded Kuwait. Salim bin Mubarak was not as fearless as his father, nor as confident that Abdal Aziz would honor dakhil for another generation, so he ordered the wall built. We are fortunate the hospital is inside the wall.

"The mission has been accepted, albeit grudgingly, as an integral part of Kuwait. The turning point was the Battle of Jahra in 1920, when the Sa'udis really did try to invade. Of the Kuwaiti men injured in that battle, around 120, I treated them all," said Mylrea. "Only four died. We did not have any of the new drugs, like sulfa, or the very promising penicillin discovered so recently. As a result of caring for wounded Kuwaitis, we are much more accepted today than in the early years when Paul Harrison, Eleanor Calverley, and I had just arrived in Kuwait.

"Shaykh Mubarak 'the Great' supervised the survey of the mission hospital property himself and announced to all Kuwaitis that he was granting this land in perpetuity to the mission for a hospital. I remember the day he came to the site. He was the only one authorized to ride in an open coach with a team of horses. There was a crowd following him. He personally oversaw placing the property markers and told all Kuwaitis what he was doing in a public ceremony. He wanted no confusion. The mission was to be part of Kuwait forever."

Wells and Beth had grown used to Bahrain's copious artesian water in the midst of its arid environment. Upon arriving in Kuwait, they realized the lack of a ready water supply made Kuwait completely different.[6] In Kuwait, everything was parched, dusty, and dry baked. As they scanned the landscape on their way from the pier to the mission compound, Wells saw fewer than two dozen scraggly tamarisk trees. Mylrea mentioned that he had planted most of them on the mission hospital grounds, but because of their thin conifer-like needles, they

---

[6] This meant that Kuwait had no sewage disposal either. Medical equipment, bed pans, and "thunder mugs" had to be washed out with salty water pumped up to hospital tanks by a windmill. All utensils would be sterilized for reuse, but sewage was not treated in more than a cursory way through septic tanks. As in the rest of the town of Kuwait, sewage overflows, water breakdowns, and effluence of privy tanks went directly to the beach and the bay. Kuwait's modern municipal infrastructure was not envisioned by the most futuristic Kuwaiti in the age before oil.

cast almost no shade. Their advantage was that they did not need much water.

Kuwait's water wells had such a high salt content that most plants could not survive, even if they were watered by attentive owners.[7] Local water came from "gray water" wells and was undrinkable. Drinkable water was delivered to households every day in goatskin bags. As Wells had learned during his voyage from Basrah to Bahrain years before, wooden tanker sailing ships brought water eighty miles from the Shatt al-Arab in Iraq. Donkey men came to the tankers and filled their goatskin bags by gravity flow to deliver fresh water to their customers. Poor people carried their own water. Without imported water, Kuwait would have been a ghost town. The price of water increased to a penny a gallon when few water tankers were in the harbor.

"Of your goodness, Khatoun, a tiny drink of water!" The desperate cry of a Bedu nomad woman with children in tow pierced even the hardest heart. To give a near-fainting, dehydrated passerby a drink of water was an act of real compassion. The heat radiating back from the tawny walls of buildings and from the sandy streets parched even the imagination. No wonder Arabs perceived Paradise to be a garden with canals and fountains splashing and gurgling with sweet water. How could this resuscitating elixir not be associated with life eternal?

Teeth of Abdullah bin Hijji

Several weeks after Wells and his family had settled into their Kuwait home, a rough-hewn stranger called at the clinic. "Doctor, come please! Abdullah bin Hijji needs you. He is sick." Just as I expected, thought Wells. No sooner has Mylrea left town than Abdullah takes a turn for the worse.

"Can you describe your master's illness?" asked Wells.

"He is very hot and weak," came the answer. "His face is big and red. Also, his head hurts."

"Does he have a stomach ache?"

"Only God knows"

"Probably not enteric fever," thought Wells, "although it's hard to tell what it might be. I'll take along dental instruments in my bag, just in case. If his facial inflammation is not referred from elsewhere in his

---

[7] This suggests a sodium chloride (NaCl) content of more than 250 ppm in Kuwait's well water. The water was so salty, it even tasted salty and was to be avoided by all who tended toward hypertension. But these wells may also have been too salty to allow malaria-transmitting mosquitoes to breed, for Kuwait was malaria free.

body and seems to originate in his head, the problem could well be his teeth. I did not notice anything unusual about his eyes. Tooth, gum, and eye problems are the most common maladies associated with the head."

Wells walked briskly across town in the moonlight and entered al Hijji's doorway. He was shown into a room lit dimly by a kerosene flame. "Do you have a Petromax lantern? I need bright light," said Wells as he began to check al Hijji's symptoms. "You have fever, but your pulse is regular even though it is weak. Let me look at your shoulders and listen to your chest and back." Then he palpated the old man's abdomen and listened to his heart. Ascertaining nothing beyond general weakness and fever, Wells examined the shaykh's face and head. "Your face is swollen. Do you have pain? Open your mouth, please, and say aaaah." The shaykh pointed to his upper facial area in response to the pain query. He had previously lost several teeth. Not unusual, thought Wells, for people to become snaggle-toothed. He examined as best he could al Hijji's gums and teeth.

"Have you had fever at all since I met you weeks ago?"

Abdullah nodded slightly.

"Brother," Wells said, "I suggest we do something soon. Your fever is very high. You are weak. If we don't do something before long, you may meet your father and your father's father face to face. You have an infection in your head. Probably it is in your jaw under one of your teeth. It is impossible to know by looking. This is my suggestion. Your remaining teeth must be removed. They must come out because the infection is somewhere in your mouth. More than one tooth could be infected. It is called an abscess. If your teeth come out, the infection can drain. In time, *insha'Allah*, your gums will heal, and you will get well. With false teeth, you will be able to eat solid food. If, however, your teeth do not come out, the infection will not drain. It could travel to your brain, and then there is nothing to do except pray." Wells waited for this grim news to sink in. Quietly, he said to Abdullah bin Hijji, "What do you want me to do, Brother?"

Abdulla thought for a minute or two and then said, "Take them. What is written is written. *Insha'Allah*, I will recover." Abdullah's remaining rotting teeth easily slid out of his spongy gums. Wells gave him careful instructions about follow-up care.

Several weeks later, during his daily horseback ride, Col. Dickson visited Abdullah at the al Shaab Gate. Dickson had heard Abdullah was ill and asked after his health.

Abdullah replied, "Yes, yes, I was very ill. Hakeem Tome-iss pulled out all my teeth."

"What!" Col. Dickson expostulated. To a nonmedical man, this seemed truly an unnecessary, excessive measure.

"Thanks be to God," Abdullah continued, "I am well again. The infection is gone."

"Yes, but you have no teeth!" said Col. Dickson.

"Oh, those are only teeth," said Abdullah. "I will buy a set of false teeth for twenty-five rupees. The doctor gave good advice. Because of him, I am speaking with you." Then Abdullah conversed happily, albeit toothlessly, of other matters.

Col. Dickson, however, the medically unschooled, ex-political agent, still felt Dr. Wells Thoms had been an impulsive medic straight out of the Wild West. "Those Americans!"[8] he muttered disapprovingly.

Lois "Lowey" Ethel Thoms

On February 10, 1938, Lois Ethel Thoms was born to Beth and Wells in the house of Mary Van Pelt. Van Pelt was the nurse-midwife of the Olcott Women's Hospital. "Lowey"[9] was the first child of the mission to be born within the city walls of Kuwait.[10] The Thoms family was now complete, with two daughters and two sons.

"Praise God, the mother is well," said many well-wishers in reaction to the happy news.

Not long after Lowey's birth, Kuwait ushered in its first gusher oil well. February 22, 1938, marked the arrival of Kuwait on the doorstep of unimaginable wealth. The well, however, was capped almost immediately to deny oil to the Germans or Italians if war spread to the Gulf.

Wells and Beth settled into the routine of life in Kuwait. Besides the constant activity of the hospital and its clinics, they enjoyed picnics in the desert with mission colleagues. They went to afternoon teas and evening dinners at notables' homes, including the Dicksons and Shaykh Ahmad of Kuwait. The European expatriate community was a small one, and Wells and Beth came to know most of its members.

---

[8] An extended version of this story, "Abdullah bin Hijji's Teeth," is in Dickson's *Kuwait and Her Neighbours*.

[9] Wells and Beth's daughter Lois was nicknamed "Lowey" to distinguish her from the other Loises in the family, including her aunt, Wells' sister, after whom she was named.

[10] In later years, being born within the walls of Kuwait ascribed citizenship to the newborn.

Learning the local ways

In the meantime, Wells had learned that the Kuwaitis were suffering—as were the Bahrainis—from the encircling Great Depression and the shift of pearl harvesting from the Gulf to Japan. And there was no demand for Kuwaiti-built wooden ships or for overland camel caravans to cruise deep into the hinterland of Sa'udi Arabia. Kuwait's elite knew that within a decade major changes were likely to come. For the time being, however, they sat in the "lee" of the old Kuwaiti economy while being squeezed in the vise of the Great Depression.

Despite these privations, Wells noted that small entertainments still continued. On sacred Eid days, everyone visited everyone else to bid each other Eid Mubarak[11] in the traditional style. This included visiting the mission personnel. The town was big enough for greetings to carry into a second day. On the first Eid day, those who lived on the west side of town visited those on the east side; on the second day, the reverse would happen. In such a way, all the residents would pay their respects to the shaykh and the Kuwaiti political elite. To the delight of the Thoms children, the same exchange of visits occurred on Christian holidays when the shaykh and Arab dignitaries would visit the houses of the mission. In this way, the town maintained its tradition as a civilized community.

Wells and Beth adapted to the rhythms of British colonial life, too. Among Western expatriates, social calls centered around the most British of institutions—afternoon high tea. Teatime was a safe compromise for alcohol-tippling Europeans on the one hand and teetotaling mission personnel and abstemious Arab Muslims on the other. On one of these occasions, the mission held a tea to which Col. and Mrs. Dickson were invited. Harold Dickson loved to do sleight-of-hand parlor tricks at children's parties. On this occasion, the Thoms children were present, and Harold launched into his "Gully-Gully-Man"[12] act. Coins, spoons, and sweets disappeared and reappeared in unlikely places, with Harold instructing the children not to try this for themselves because it was "magic." Peter and Norman (ages three and four) were entranced as his hands moved more quickly than their eyes.

Harold then queried, "How would you two like to exchange places? How would you, Peter, like to become Norman, and you, Norman, like to become Peter?" It sounded like fun, and their heads

---

[11] Happy Eid.
[12] This is a term used to indicate magicians and card sharks who would accompany their tricks with "gully-gully-gully" rather than "abracadabra."

Thoms Family, 1939 (WWT)

nodded vigorously. Yes, this would be lots better than playing "make believe." Col. Dickson officiously waved his hands and arms amid a blizzard of words and—presto!

"Peter is now Norman, and Norman is now Peter. You are switched. See how you play together now." Off the boys went, chattering in their new identities.

As the social occasion drew to a close and visitors were taking their leave, Peter and Norman ran up to Col. Dickson anxiously. Pulling on the diplomat's sleeve, Peter asked plaintively, "Col. Dickson, could you please change us back again?"

Vi Dickson clucked reproachfully, "Oh, Harold!"

Col. Dickson said, "Oh my goodness! How could I have overlooked changing you back into your real selves?! Yes. Yes. We must do something about it. Now, Norman, or Peter, or whoever you are, please stand up straight in front of me with your eyes closed. Stiffen your shoulders, bend your arms at the elbow, and make fists with your hands, like this. Are you ready? Alright, then here we go, one at a time. Keep your eyes closed until I say you can open them." With that, he lifted each boy up one at a time, his hands under their crooked elbows, and twirled them around in a graceful circle saying that the real Norman was returning into what looked to all the assembly like Norman, and the real Peter was returning into what looked like Peter. "You can open your eyes now. See? Peter is Peter again, and Norman is Norman again! Do you feel like you? Yes? Yes? Pinch yourselves to make sure."

They did so and nodded in relief. He rubbed his hands together and pronounced, "Good! Excellent! All's well that ends well." To his wife he said, "Perhaps it's time for us to go. We've had enough excitement for one afternoon." With thank you's and greetings all around, they were off.

Hospital ship

One afternoon, a group of men ran into the hospital carrying a compatriot on a shoulder-high litter. The man groaned in pain from the jostling. Wells broke loose immediately from his other duties.

"How did this happen?"

One of the workmen said, "We were in A.'s[13] shipyard preparing to build a Kuwaiti *boom*. We were selecting timbers for the inside—the ribs—of the ship. These timbers are always naturally curved. He was picking the ones we should use.[14] Suddenly, one of the curved logs flipped over as we tried to move it. The log hit A. in his upper leg, so we have brought him." Wells' examination showed A. had broken his femur above the knee.

Wells shared the news with his patient, "You will need to stay here for some time, perhaps two months. In that time, your leg will become as strong as it was before the log broke it."

"Two months! That is half the time necessary to build a new ship. I don't have that much time."

"Perhaps you don't understand. Allah requires you to take two months out of your schedule. There is no way you can be on your feet and build a ship with a completely snapped femur. If God wills, *insha'Allah*, your leg will heal fully. Only then can you go back to work."

Resigned to his fate, the patient was taken into the operating room where his leg was aligned and stretched lengthwise and put into traction, so the two sections of the femur joined cleanly. This entailed

---

[13] A.'s name is thought to be Ahmad bin Salman, one of the last of the great Kuwaiti ship builders, but this has not been verified. Wells used only his nickname in his dictated memoir.

[14] Kuwaiti ship builders, like their New England nineteenth-century counterparts, did not use paper plans. The design of each ship was visualized in the builder's mind.

searing, stabbing pain that A. bore stoically. In time, the patient was wheeled to one of the hospital's rooms for a long stay, and he went to sleep.

In a few days, A. grew restless at his forced inactivity despite the visits of family, friends, and shipyard colleagues who sipped coffee; shared choice, ripe dates; and conversed about all manner of things. He was not used to such inactivity. One of Kuwait's last great ship builders, he had his professional pride and creative drive to build ships.

If A. could not go to the mountain, the mountain might just come to him. He toyed with the idea of building a *boom* or *baghala* at his home where he could recline on the roof and direct its construction from a rooftop cot. Then the completed wooden hull would "only" have to be hauled out through the broken wall of his courtyard and dragged hundreds of meters to the bay. Even A. had to admit the idea was grossly unrealistic. The patience of his workers, to say nothing of their strength, would be taxed to the limit if he tried to do this.

"Brother," said Wells stopping to see A. one evening during hospital rounds, "I want to place an order for a wooden ship. Will you build me a *sambuq*, a pearling boat?"

"I would be happy to build you a boat," said A., "but not now while I'm stuck in bed. What did you have in mind, a yacht like Shaykh Ahmad has or a working boat?"

Wells said, "I'd like it to be a little bit of both. I want it to be like a real pearling boat in every detail, and I also want it to be pretty and look something like Shaykh Ahmad's boat and something like a storybook boat. Perhaps it can look like the one that Sinbad had. It should have big sails."

"You don't want to use the sails then or the ship will capsize. Do you want this vessel to be equipped with a motor? This is possible, but in my view, it spoils the sailing quality of the ship. The noise is awful. The beauty of a *hawa-i-jahazz*[15] is its complete harmony with nature on the water. That is why I build ships."

"Oh, no, I don't want a motor in it. I want the traditional design."

"Well, how can this be done since it won't be able to sail safely?" asked A.

"I want the ship to be small, so small that you can build it right here at the hospital. It should be so small that you and your men can build it in this room. It does not need to be big, just a couple of cubits in length but with all the features of a real *sambuq*. The small size will

---

[15] Literally, a "ship of the air" (or wind), a sailing vessel.

Sambuq ship model, 1939 (WWT)

make it easy to transport. I will pay you for it so your hospital stay will not be so expensive. Will you do it?"

A. wrinkled his brow and thought for a minute or two, and then said, "Yes, I and my men will do this. We will make it like a full-sized ship but with fairy-tale sails. I shall think on this, and we will begin soon, *insha'Allah*."

To seal the deal, the two shook hands. Thus began a unique shipbuilding venture. In addition to the normal sounds of coffee preparation and muted conversations, the hospital soon resonated with the less-than-discreet sounds of hammering and sawing and the smell of sawdust and wood finish. Over the next few weeks, a beautiful pearling boat came into being, with sails bound by cordage, just as real sails were, complete with carefully crafted rigging and handmade block and tackle. It sported carvings at the bow, below the railings, and on the stern, with cooking pots and a firebox kitchen on deck. At the side of the vessel were fish traps; on deck was a working steering wheel that controlled the rudder, and on one side hung a small *jalbut*, a skiff in davits. A. and his men were consumed with making this vessel. It was perfect occupational therapy for shipbuilders.

A.'s femur healed in two months. Slowly, he resumed walking on crutches, and finally, the day came for him to leave the hospital.

Wells saw him off and said, "You have made a good recovery. You have paid your bill. What do I owe you for the *sambuq*?"

A. said, "How about seventy-five rupees?"

"With pleasure. Here are seventy-five rupees. I will move this little ship from your hospital room. I will 'launch' it in my house. It will always remind me of you and your men. Thanks be to God you were willing to build it."

Upon returning home, Wells placed the little ship in a prominent place at the entrance to the mejlis of *beit* Tome-iss. The ship represented not only Wells' medical expertise but also his compassionate care of his patients. A. and his men received respect for their craftsmanship and expertise, and the not-insignificant price of the ship symbolized the reciprocity of equals embodied in the handshake of a business deal.[16]

Entertaining Shaykh Ahmad

Later, Wells and Beth entertained Shaykh Ahmad, the ruler of Kuwait. The shaykh had previously invited the Thomses to a feast, so now Wells and Beth would reciprocate. As the senior doctor in the mission hospital, Wells wielded soft diplomacy, so it would be unthinkable to invite the shaykh without also inviting the British political agent, Gerald Simpson de Gaury. Simpson de Gaury, however, was temporarily absent from Kuwait, so Col. and Mrs. Dickson were invited in his place. Wells knew very well that the political agent was supposed to vet every interaction the shaykh had with non-British expatriates. Other visitors from the agency and oil company had also been invited to the Thomses' table. The mission pooled dishes, silverware, and kitchen and dining room help in order to accommodate all the guests.

The evening proved a culinary and conversational success. The shaykh was familiar with Western cuisine, but Beth had made sure that it had touches of the Middle East, with meat and vegetable dishes lightly garnished with spices used in Arab dishes and with a pudding and fresh fruit for dessert. Conversation seesawed from the gloomy state of European affairs to more rosy matters in Gulf countries. The guests reflected on how things used to be and how they were likely to change.

Wells was able to trade stories with Dickson and Shaykh Ahmad, as well as with the oil company personnel. He had met leading shaykhs and rulers in the Gulf, so he could talk knowledgeably about King

---

[16] See endnote 15:16, p. 389.

Abdal Aziz, Sultans Faisal and Taymur of Muscat, Shaykh Abdallah of Qatar, and Hakim/Shaykh Isa of Bahrain. He also knew about current affairs in Iraq because of letters he had received from his mother in Baghdad and his uncle James Cantine in Basrah. In addition, he knew many prominent merchants up and down the Gulf. Oil was on everyone's mind.

Wells said, "I may be the lucky mascot for the whole Gulf area."

"Lucky mascot, what is that?" queried His Highness.

"It is a pet or symbol that brings good fortune," answered Wells. "I was just suggesting that perhaps I am a harbinger of change for the better in the Gulf. After all, Bahrain's first oil well came in during my first month there. Sa'udi Arabia also struck oil shortly after I was in Riyadh visiting the king. Now in Kuwait, the same has happened. Who knows what will occur in Qatar, Oman, Abu Dhabi, and Dubai, as well as in other emirates on the Trucial Coast? The people of the Gulf need relief from bad economic times. Maybe I will bring them good luck, too."

Col. Dickson was feeling expansive and recollected stories of Kuwait's past, including stories about the mission's history in Kuwait. "Yes," he said, "Kuwait is fortunate to have the Arabian Mission here. It has made a world of difference, particularly because of the talented doctors and staff. Back in the early 1900s, it was Drs. Paul Harrison and Eleanor Calverley. Men and women could each see a doctor of their own gender. Dr. Stanley Mylrea, who has been here for decades now, replaced Dr. Harrison. Mylrea has been so good that people complain about him. Some think he is too influential and knows too much about Kuwaiti society. From my point of view, Mylrea is one of the great Englishmen of the twentieth century. He introduced modern medicine here, and he has proven extremely valuable in keeping Kuwait strong. He was remarkable when he treated the casualties of King Abdal Aziz's Ikhwaan in the desert when relations between Kuwait and Sa'udi Arabia were not cordial. Then later, after the Battle of Jahra, he heroically patched up Kuwait's wounded. More than that, Mylrea never gave up on Kuwaitis, even in the early days when there was hostility toward a foreign Christian doctor. The townspeople were very independent and did not approve of the welcome that Shaykh Mubarak extended him. Mylrea did not have any gunboat to back him up like the political agent did."

"Yes," agreed Wells, "Stanley Mylrea has made my job much easier. People trust me because of him and the other doctors that have served here before me. People know he is peppery, though; he speaks his mind, and this is not totally in the Arab style. They also know he cares about them and about Kuwait, and he would do anything for a Kuwaiti in need." Wells turned to look at the shaykh. "I don't know if you know that Mylrea was a colleague of my father, Your Highness. Mylrea had originally come to Bahrain and only later to Kuwait."

Dickson interrupted Wells' overture to the shaykh. "Mylrea was English, of course." This seemed to strike a note that was bothering Dickson. "Your Arabian Mission people seem to come from everywhere. You Americans have origins in all kinds of places. Many of your people were born in different parts of Europe and still speak those languages. It is very confusing. How do you know they are loyal Americans? They could be spies or enemy agents," said Dickson.

"We can tell," said Beth gently. "Our people are all Protestant dissenters, except for Dr. Mylrea, whose wife is American. Except for him, they were not part of the state churches in Europe like the Church of England, and they came to the United States to practice their religion without government interference. They love America because of this. They have never looked back or wondered why they came to America. It is reassuring to know you can pick the religious group of your preference in America and worship God the way you prefer.

"We are here, not because our government has told us to come, but because we have been instructed by our prophet to reach out to all peoples of the world to let them know that God loves them, regardless of who they are or how deserving or undeserving they think they are."

Dickson interrupted again, "I know the mission has also operated schools. Rev. Edwin Calverley started the first modern school in Kuwait. It taught everything including modern geography, science, and mathematics. When Calverley displayed a globe representing the earth, it was thought to be heretical. Most Kuwaitis then believed in a flat, earth-centric universe. Nevertheless, Calverley persisted, and his students became leaders here in Kuwait. Today, they head departments of Your Highness's government. What would Kuwait do without them? Old-fashioned Kuwaitis wanted to open their own traditional schools to counter the mission. That was fine; they were responding to Calverley's school. But they could not turn the clock back. The mission brought Kuwait into the twentieth century. Moreover, the missionaries made no money from it."

"Did you know, Your Highness, that there are several sides to Dr. Mylrea?" asked Wells. "He has a wonderful memory, better than nine of ten people. He has memorized large portions of our Scriptures, and these are much longer than the Q'uran. Islam has a wonderful tradition of people reciting scriptural passages from memory in very polished ways. I know there are competitions for doing this in many Muslim countries. Dr. Mylrea not only has memorized the Holy Bible, but he also recites Scripture beautifully and meaningfully. He makes the New Testament Gospels, the Injil, seem as if they were written yesterday. They become fresh when he recites them from memory. They are poetry written on his heart. Of course, he would not be here if he did not also believe he needed to share with everyone the words and the understanding that have fallen from heaven to people here on earth. He is, very simply, a man of God."

"Quite so, quite so," said Dickson, wanting to propel the conversation in a more secular, imperial direction. "Your Highness probably remembers that Dr. Mylrea received the King George V Silver Jubilee Medal in 1935, the same year you received it. You, of course, also received the King George VI Coronation Medal just last year and other medals from the British government. Likewise, Dr. Mylrea has been recognized by the British government with the Order of the British Empire and the Kaisar-i-Hind medals. Who knows? His career is not over yet. He may be recognized in other ways before he retires, and I would entirely approve of his receiving further honors. He is an extraordinary person." No one at the dinner table demurred.

"Well, Dr. Thoms," said Dickson, "your fame, like that of Dr. Mylrea, has also spread rapidly up and down the Gulf. That is what you get for being an eye surgeon. There is so much here in the way of vision problems. I'm told you get tremendously good results in the eye department." Then, smiling wryly, Dickson looked at Wells and continued, "But you seem to be quick off the mark in the tooth department. At least, Abdullah bin Hijji no longer has his teeth, thanks to you."

Wells was not to be put off by this gentle rebuke, even if it did come from the august Col. Dickson. "It may seem that way to the casual observer," he remarked with a smile, "but when a person as important as Abdullah bin Hijji has had an infection for weeks, one suspects the malaise resides in his head. There were no signs of infection in his ears or eyes, nor in his brain. By a process of elimination, I was directed to his teeth, which were in poor condition, I am sorry to say. I could not have known, of course, that a dental abscess was at the root of his problems. But because I ruled out every other alternative, it seemed we either had to do something about his teeth or release our friend to the mercy of God. We could not have known which teeth were involved, but we had to solve the problem immediately. It was better to pull all his remaining teeth and have him return to health than not to pull the infected tooth and have him die. A difficult choice, I know, but I did what I did in Abdullah's interest and for his wellbeing. Praise God and the Holy Spirit, he is with us today, a healthy man, once again able to serve His Highness."

At length, His Highness Shaykh Ahmad said, "Dickson, it is ten o'clock. You never stay anywhere after ten at night. I am enjoying our conversation greatly, and I wish to continue it. You may bid everyone goodnight and go home to bed. Don't wait for me to leave." With a wave of his hand, he dismissed Col. and Mrs. Dickson, who were taken aback to be so summarily dispatched.

Wells thought he saw Col. Dickson's eyes narrow ever so slightly. What did it matter that Dickson was suspicious that missionaries of the RCA were undercover intelligence agents? It was laughable. It should have been clear years ago that missionaries had no designs on Middle Eastern oil. Nevertheless, Wells realized, suspicion springs eternal.[17]

Once Dickson had retired, Shaykh Ahmad looked around and saw the *sambuq*, the model of the pearling ship, sitting on a Kuwaiti sea chest near the front door. "That is a beautiful ship model you have, Doctor. Where did you get it?" Wells explained its Kuwaiti origin. His Highness was very interested in its finish and detail and that Wells had thought to have it built as occupational therapy for A.

"Beautiful or not," said His Highness, "you should know that your ship is not in compliance with Kuwaiti law. The oars on this ship are extended outward with ropes dangling down so the divers can hold on to them when they come up for air. The sails are up, too. Together this means the pearling ship is not, in fact, moving. It signals it is stationary and other ships should avoid it. There is one thing as owner of this ship you have missed. On deck the rule is that there should be one man assisting each diver. It is always very hot on deck. Our rules say that a canvas tarpaulin must be spread overhead so the men on deck do not get heat or sun stroke because they cannot cool off in the water. This tarpaulin is missing. There is a fine of 200 rupees for this omission." Wells raised his eyebrows wondering what was coming next.

---

[17] See endnote 15:17, p. 389.

His Highness concluded with a twinkle in his eye, "I think I can expect that by the next time I visit you will have remedied this problem. Let it just be a warning to you this time."

Wells and Beth soon left Kuwait and took the little ship with them, still in un-tarped violation of the Kuwaiti pearling rule of its day.

Part II: Hope

"Nothing that is worth doing can be achieved in a lifetime; therefore, we must be saved by hope."*

---

* Niebuhr, *The Irony of American History*, 63.

CHAPTER 16

Glimpsing the Sultanate

> *The careworn woman climbed on the streetcar with 10 children trailing behind her. The conductor said, "Are these all your'n or are you going to a picnic?" The woman said emphatically, "They're all mine—and 'tain't no picnic!"*

Anticipating new adventures

The Thoms family boarded the SS *Excambion* in New York City on September 21, 1939, bound for Bombay, India.[1] The year's furlough in the United States had come and gone remarkably rapidly, and it was now time to return to the field.

Wells, Beth, and the four Thoms children sailed for Arabia with Wells' stepmother, May DePree Thoms, who was returning to her position in Baghdad. They could not have otherwise afforded such a lengthy family reunion with her, and now there would be time on board to talk, write letters, plan, and reflect—especially thanks to the ship's daycare staff helping with the children. Although the terrible specter of war beclouded Europe, the voyage itself was peaceful. The 1938 announcement by the British prime minister, Neville Chamberlin, of "Peace for our time" dissolved when Germany invaded Poland just three weeks before the *Excambion* set sail. As a US-flagged ship,

---

[1] Bombay is today known as Mumbai. The *Excambion* was an American Export Line ship. See also, endnote 16:1, p. 390.

the *Excambion* was officially a neutral one, so it sailed with presumed impunity. Tensions, however, were still high because the new prime minister of Great Britain, Winston Churchill, had formally declared war on Germany on September 3.

As the ship left the New York harbor, Wells stood on deck, watching reflectively as they passed Ellis Island and the Statue of Liberty. A man at the rail turned and addressed him. "I hate to leave New York. I love this city. I live on Manhattan's west side not far from the Empire State Building. I'm lucky to have a job. Hopefully, I'll be back soon enough, and with a fistful of contracts if this new war doesn't wreck Europe. What line of business are you in, Friend?"

"I'm a doctor. I work in the Persian Gulf and am taking up a post in the Sultanate of Muscat," replied Wells. "I'll be gone for seven years, so I'm taking my family with me. The Reformed Church in America funds us. We're fortunate for their support in these difficult times."

The man nodded, uncomprehending, and decided to change the course of the discussion. "We are lucky to travel on this ship. The American Export Line (AEL) scored a real coup after the Great Crash of 1929. The United States Shipping Board built lots of new ships in the twenties and offered them for sale or lease to American shipping companies. Well, the Depression caught up with that program. The AEL bought four of them for $1 million each, even though they had cost $30 million apiece to build. They were designed as luxury liners, with a limited number of exclusive, first-class cabins. No other liners are better, not even Cunard. That's how AEL can set our ticket prices so low. It was a good deal for them and a great deal for us."

"Yes, it is luxurious. I don't think I've ever been on a nicer ship. When I picked up the tickets, they said we were going on one of the '4 Aces.' I didn't know what that meant, but I guess it refers to these four ships?"

"I expect so," replied his companion. "I dunno how they got that moniker. It could just signify they trump all other passenger ships. Or it might refer to AEL itself. The '4 Aces' label reminds me of Mark Twain talking about the riverboat gambler who had 'the calm confidence of a Christian with four aces up his sleeve.' If anything is a guaranteed money maker, it has to be these ships."

The *Excambion* gracefully slipped through the Verrazzano Narrows. Shortly thereafter, the port pilot clambered down the ladder at the Ambrose Light Station, and the ship nosed eastward into the deep ocean swells. They were aiming for the "Pillars of Hercules," as the Strait of Gibraltar was called in Homer's time. Once through the strait, they plunged into the Mediterranean and made port calls at Marseilles, Beirut, Alexandria, and Port Said and then proceeded through the Suez Canal to Bombay.

"This is my last trip to Baghdad," May announced softly from the comfort of her deck chair as she sat with Wells and Beth one brisk morning as they rocked gently on the Red Sea. She was in a reflective mood, her eyes closed. "It's not just the war. I've worked in the Arab world for a long time. I came with your parents, Wells, to settle in Bahrain in 1904. Who could have imagined what was to come?" She shook her head. "I really came to Bahrain because my sister, Elizabeth, was there. She had married Jim Cantine, one of the gentlest persons imaginable. I was to be governess for the Zwemer and Thoms children. By the time I had arrived, the Zwemer girls had died. Then your mother died just after we landed in Bahrain. What a shock.

"Before long, the Zwemers left Bahrain; they returned to the States and then relocated to Cairo. It was just too much for them, burying two children in a month's time. I took responsibility for you and your sisters," she nodded to Wells. "We went to Quetta[2] in the hills on Afghanistan's border with British India to get a break from the heat of Bahrain. This gave your father time to think because he had been so busy in the hospital. In the evenings and at night, he could mull his alternatives without worrying which of you children would next come down with whooping cough or some other malady."

"Didn't you find it daunting to take charge of the three of us?"

"Yes, it was. But what could I do? I just had to keep on and stay calm as best I could. Your father, too. He and I were a 'high wire act with no safety net,' as they say in the circus."

"Not long after you returned to Bahrain, Father asked you to marry him, didn't he?"

"Yes, he did. In some ways, it was a matter of convenience. I had not come to the Persian Gulf to find a husband. It was never like India where the annual 'fishing fleet' of young women arrived from Britain in the cool season hoping to find husbands among respectable British Raj *sahibs*. I could have married in America, but I wasn't ready for marriage. I felt good about coming to the Gulf because my sister was there. Sharon and I were not simply taken with infatuation. He had lost Marion, the polestar of his life. How could I possibly replace her? I loved her too. She had a beauty and serenity very few possess. Slowly, Sharon

---

[2] Now in Pakistan, but at that time in British India.

and I came to understand that we saw the world similarly. I loved his honesty, candor, and easygoing style. He was so calm, confident, and friendly; people liked him almost the minute they laid eyes on him. I liked him too from the start. I never met a better, truer gentleman." With that, she lapsed into silence.

"I'm excited about going to the Sultanate of Muscat," Wells interjected into the silence. "At the same time, I do have some concern about how I'll feel after being away for so long. Maybe it's just bittersweet memory."

After a further musing, filled with the shushing white noise sound of the open sea, Wells resumed. "You have been a wonderful mother to me all these years. In fact, you have been both a father and a mother to me. I have depended on you for love, advice, and support, and you never, ever disappointed me." He reached over and took her hand gently from the deckchair's arm, kissed it, and murmured, "I love you."

May looked him in the eyes and whispered, "I love you too, Sonny Boy."[3] She had much to ponder, realizing that, in loving and raising Wells and his siblings, she had blossomed unexpectedly into motherhood. What more could they have done for each other, she wondered?

"Do you remember the letter I wrote you as a teenager?" Wells queried gently. "I wrote that I didn't want either of us to look back, grieving for 'what might have been.' I decided, even as I was writing that letter, that I wanted to look forward to the opportunities of life."

"Yes, I remember your letter very well. I saved it. You are a good writer, Sonny Boy; your letters have always given me a lift. You *should* look forward to Muscat. Your father was happiest there of any place he served, and the Omanis loved him." Again, she paused before speaking further.

"The first Western medicine in Muscat was brought by my sister, Elizabeth, when she came with Uncle Jim. Aunt Elizabeth was treating women even before your father and I landed in Oman. Aunt Elizabeth's clinic set the stage for the opening of the Women's Hospital when Dr. Sarah Hosmon arrived. Remember Mary Balasundram, the Indian midwife? She and Sarah were the heart of medical work among women in Oman for a long time."

Wells broke into the story, "It's too bad that Dr. Hosmon left Muscat last year. The Women's Hospital had to close. To top that off,

---

[3] This was May's own name of endearment for Wells.

Rev. James Cantine and freed slave boys (SJT)

when Dr. Harrison and his wife, Monty,[4] went on furlough recently, the men's hospital in Matrah had to shut its doors, too. Because of those departures, it is a question whether our medical services survive at all in Oman. We'll see what has been done in their absence."

Slaves, Muscat (Oman), and the Brits

May resumed her narrative: "My sister, Elizabeth, lived in Muscat for several years with Jim. Before they were married, Jim had come to Muscat several times. In the 1890s, he rushed to Muscat to take over the Freed Slave Boys School after the tragic illness and death of Sam Zwemer's younger brother, Peter, who had died of typhoid, probably contracted from the slave boys. The poor wretches—eighteen of them—had been captured with their families in Africa, but their parents all died en route to a life of slavery. A terrible tragedy! An Arab slave ship brought them from Zanzibar to the Gulf, where they were about to be sold in Sur. A British frigate intercepted their ship and brought them to Oman, where Peter took them in. Thus was founded the Freed Slave Boys School. Tragically, their stay was not without challenge, as you can imagine.

---

[4] The Harrisons had both lost their spouses in tragic circumstances before they found each other. Regina, Paul's first wife, disappeared overboard from their BI ship quite mysteriously one night as they returned to the US for furlough. Rev. Henry Bilkert, Monty's first husband, was shot by an Ikhwaan tribesman. Bilkert was escorting the industrialist C. C. Crane to Kuwait from Basrah when he was killed. The shooting was the only event of its kind experienced in the Arabian Mission before World War II.

Muscat seafront, 1909 (SJT)

"The British had outlawed slave shipping on the high seas because they controlled the Indian Ocean, the Red Sea, and the Gulf, but they could not outlaw slavery itself. The French tried to drive a wedge between Britain and their dependent, Arab, slave-selling shaykhs. They authorized Arab slavers to fly the French flag, which meant that the British Navy would not stop or board their ships for fear of international reprisal. A Msr. Ottavi cooked up the whole stratagem. He was a real conniver who sequestered himself in the French consulate in Muscat.

"When Uncle Jim went to Oman after Peter's death, he and a British official, Sir Percy Cox, were the only other Westerners besides Ottavi in Muscat. Jim and Percy would have afternoon tea together periodically. They felt comfortable in each other's company and liked having someone convivial to converse with in English. One summer afternoon, Jim and Percy were sitting on a shaded British consulate verandah next to the sultan's palace. They hoped for a puff or two of sea air to fend off the nearly unbearable heat.

"Over a scalding cup of tea, Jim said to Percy, 'Colonel, what is somebody of your talent doing in a place like Muscat?'

"Percy savored his tea languidly, and finally responded: 'I work for the king and I go where he sends me.' Silence ensued, broken only by the sound of wavelets lapping on the nearby shore. After a time, Percy said, 'And what is somebody of your talent, Rev. Cantine, doing in a place like Muscat?'

"Jim sipped his tea, thought a little, and said, 'I work for the King of Kings, and I go where He sends me.' Silence reigned as the hot tea relieved the worst of their heat stress.

"Percy shook off his lassitude after a bit and declared, 'The sultan is going to evict you from your house presently. Actually, I instructed him to do so. Please don't take it personally. I have no choice. The French are trying to drive a wedge between the British Crown and the sultan. I cannot allow that. I want the French consulate to be located inside Muscat's walls where we can know everyone who comes and goes, and your house is the only one available for lease. It's the only proper house for a foreigner, other than the American consul's residence, and I can't evict him. The French are pressing the sultan for a coaling station down the coast. We totally oppose it, but I cannot prohibit Sultan Faisal from dealing with the French. That would be bad form. I've suggested a concession to the sultan. They may have their coaling station, provided it's placed on the far side of Muscat's harbor. That way, I can train my telescope from here to see what they are up to. I also offered them your house.'

"After a weighty silence, Percy said to Jim, 'To make it up to you, I'll ask the sultan to grant you a piece of land up the hill outside the wall, beyond Muscat's main gate. It is a desirable location, even if it's not within the wall. Muscat's best water comes from the aquifer under it. For centuries, its water has trickled down to the harbor below the guns of Fort Mirani where passing ships could rewater. You'll have a good garden and more space for your school and church than you would ever have had inside the walls. Moreover, you'll be far away from that pestilential, stinking cesspool of a pond on the low ground behind Muscat's wall. That scummy pool really has to be filled in.'[5]

"Knowing full well that he could not fight the eviction order, Jim merely nodded his assent to Col. Cox's proposal. Besides, it was more than fair treatment under the circumstances," said May. "After all, there were no realtors in Muscat, and it took a ruling by the sultan for anyone to obtain a piece of land, including the mission." May paused to catch her breath.

"I remember Jim recalling that at the end of one of those afternoon teas with Percy Cox, just as he was about to leave, he heard a terrible screeching sound and loud, angry voices shouting on the landward side of the consulate. Percy rolled his eyes, sighed, and said, 'Not again!'

"Jim asked what the disturbance was. Cox replied it must be a female slave who had come into the consulate compound, was hugging the flagstaff where the Union Jack flew, and was screaming she couldn't

---

[5] See the reference in Zwemer and Cantine, *The Golden Milestone*, to Cox's role in getting the property for the mission house outside the walls of Muscat.

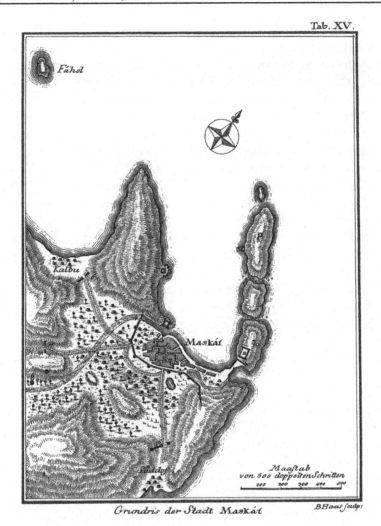

*Muscat, 1765 (*Niebuhr, Travels through Arabia, *[PD])*

stand being a slave anymore. She wanted her manumission papers. Cox explained that only he, the British consul, could issue such papers. British policy did not outlaw slavery in any colonial jurisdiction but admitted the right of slaves to claim their freedom when on British territory. In Muscat, the only way they could claim freedom was to force their way into the consular grounds and hug the flagstaff. On this day, Cox indicated he would have to see how it played out, for often slaveowner family members would come to the consulate promising to make amends if only their slave would come home. Cox noted papers

Cantines, Thoms, and staff, 1909 (*SJT*)
L-r: James Cantine, Elizabeth Cantine, Frances Thoms, unidentified local woman, Lois Thoms, May DePree Thoms, Wells Thoms, Sharon Thoms. Most likely, the three male native workers (*in back*) were not Omani Arabs since they are wearing the Ottoman fez, and this photo dates from before the demise of the Ottoman Empire.

of freedom were all very fine, but once a slave became a free person, how was he or she to live? Where could they find a job? Would they not live in abject poverty the rest of their lives? He could only offer any slave the choice of either precarious freedom or continued subjugation."

As an afterthought, May added, "Aside from its fundamental inhumanity, slavery is very inefficient. It has probably held back Arabia just as it held back the American South before the Civil War. I think St. Paul understood just how pernicious a system it was in his time when he recommended that people be kind to their slaves.[6] Slavery brings out the least attractive features of the slaveowner."

May then returned to her initial story about the slave boys under Peter and Jim's care. "After the little slave boys grew up and went either into the British Navy or to India or the United States, the church board in New York disapproved taking in more slave children, even though Jim thought it a good idea. Many of them had become Christians. I always wondered what might have happened if our Arabian Mission had focused more on slaves. After all, Christian converts grew rapidly under the occupation of Rome, and many converts came from among the slaves and the lower classes of society then."

Beth, who had grown up in India, was learning a great deal about their new home, and she anticipated learning much more. The full implications of life in Oman broke on her when Wells said, "It is going to be a challenge to get the hospitals going again. Unless we can find a qualified woman, we won't be able to open the Women's Hospital.

---

[6] Colossians 4:1.

The two hospitals are too far apart for one doctor to handle both, and husbands will generally not consent to their wives being examined by a male doctor. Perhaps we can find out what has happened to Nurse Mary when we stop in India."

"It could be almost as challenging to reopen the men's hospital. I hope the four or five workers Paul Harrison recruited are still there. Where would they go in these Depression times? If they are doing just fine not working for the mission, it could be a problem. I'm banking on their loyalty to Harrison to keep them tied to the mission. I hope to persuade them to become a team again. I will be so thankful if they are acting as the hospital's guardians."

Beth responded, "You'll have new challenges, but they will be challenges exclusively in Oman. You worked so hard during our first term in Bahrain and Kuwait, what with language study; medical tours to Qatar, Dubai, Abu Dhabi, Sharjah, and Sa'udi Arabia; working with the oil company personnel in Bahrain; and doing your research and applying for accreditation by the American College of Surgeons. To face the challenges of only one location will be so much more manageable."[7]

Wells was not going to minimize all that Beth had done, either. "In the meantime, you've been busy yourself," he responded. "You've had four children, and the responsibilities of raising them have fallen mainly on you, Sugar. You've kept our home humming during my busyness." Leaning over from his deck chair to hers, he planted a noisy kiss on her cheek.

Political undercurrents

"I was really pleased with the letter saying that I'd been elected a fellow of the American College of Surgeons," Wells began, shifting the conversation. "It's not that I intend to hang my shingle in the United States or open a clinic in Harley Street in London, but it is gratifying to know I could. I also think Arabs should be confident, knowing they could not get a better surgeon anywhere else. I have always believed patients deserve nothing but my best. And although I have trained in eye surgery and done many other exacting surgeries, I need to stay current in medicine and general surgery. I can pursue continuing education when we go to India each year on vacation. Also, I can go back to the University of Michigan during every furlough to update

---

[7] Neither Wells nor Beth initially realized how much larger and more difficult of access Oman was when compared to the other RCA mission sites in the Gulf. They were to understand this later.

Wells Thoms, 1908 (SJT)

myself on recent medical advances. From here on, I want to concentrate on the people, while practicing the highest level of medicine."

"Did you know your father did much the same thing, Wells?" asked May. "Medicine was much more primitive then, of course, but when we returned to the United States in 1910, Sharon was shocked by the surgical advances since his graduation. He spent a lot of time at the University of Michigan learning new practices to use in Matrah." Wells nodded, recalling the many days his father was absent from home while they sojourned in Ann Arbor.

"Speaking of practicing medicine in Matrah," said May, "did you know there was official resistance to Sharon setting up a practice, even though missionaries had been here for years?"

"What was the problem? His medical degree? That was the case when Father first went to Basrah. I recall the Ottomans insisted he take a certification exam in French. Father said he did not have time to learn French well enough to pass the exam, so he moved to Bahrain because it was beyond Ottoman control."

"No, it was when you were just a little boy. Sultan Sayyid Faisal bin Turki raised the objection, saying that he did not need a Western doctor. Fred Barny and your father went to the sultan to plead their cause; they said there were no other Western physicians and that local healers could not handle difficult cases beyond minor surgery. Besides, the country was growing rapidly, and medical cases were growing along with the whole population. There was certainly a need.

"They soon learned it wasn't the sultan who was objecting. It was the British. The sultan was a puppet of the British and had been so for a long time. They treated him like an Indian maharajah, even though Muscat was an independent kingdom that had signed treaties with both the United States and France, as well as with Britain. The sultan told

Fred and your father that the British consul, Robert Erskine Holland, and the 'British doctor' told him there was no need for an American doctor. Erskine Holland was clearly unfriendly, and the doctor's name I forget. The British 'doctor' was the agency doctor. He was allowed to treat only British subjects, including Indians from British India. He was not allowed to treat Arabs or locals. He did not do surgery either. The agency 'hospital' was just a clinic."

"How did it work out?" asked Beth. "Sharon and Marion stayed on, so permission must have been granted. I don't remember anything about this history in *Neglected Arabia*."[8]

"No," responded May. "The editor deleted everything Sharon had written about this incident, so it didn't get into *Neglected Arabia*, which gives only the public image of the Arabian Mission, and as a result, does not print the juiciest stories. Yet, I know it was like this." May settled into her deck chair, clearly relishing the extraordinary tale. Beth leaned closer so as not to miss a word.

"Uncle Jim Cantine was in America on furlough. Your father-in-law had written him, so Jim conferred with the RCA Mission Board in New York. The consensus was that Jim should write the secretary of state in Washington and lodge a request for the United States government to insist on the terms of their treaty with Muscat. The treaty dated pre-Civil War, and it guaranteed citizens of the sultanate could practice their trade in the United States and, likewise, that Americans could settle and practice their trade in Muscat and Zanzibar. Subsequently, Jim contacted our congressman from Holland, Michigan. Congressman G. J. Diekema was a committed churchman and knew the Reformed Church's mission work. He wrote the State Department, which readily agreed to help. It placed its views directly with the Court of St. James in London, asking the British government to send instructions to the British consul in Muscat through its colonial agents in British India. Ultimately, the British relented, and they did not interfere further. Sharon and Marion were able to set up shop there. Although they did not object to missionaries, the British seemed to be opposed to medical doctors. Perhaps the British feared that Americans would become popular with Omanis because of the hospitals, and the Brits would lose control." May chuckled to think of the political intrigue that played out on both the personal and international levels.

---

[8] *Neglected Arabia* (later, *Arabia Calling*) recorded significant events in the lives of the Arabian Mission missionaries. It also included essays of narrative and theological stripes.

Sayyid Sa'eed's first birthday, with Lois and Wells (SJT)

"Now that I think of it, the British may also have been concerned because we were starting something new in Matrah, around the corner and out of sight of the Muscat consulate. Sharon wanted to purchase three houses in Matrah that Dr. Jayakar had owned—oh, I just remembered that Jayakar was the British Agency's Indian doctor. He wasn't even British. He wanted to retire and go back to India. These homes were out of sight of the British consulate. The British stoutly opposed our purchasing those houses, perhaps for the same reason they opposed the French coaling station down the coast. In the end, we rented another residence.

"In the long run," said May, "Sultan Sayyid Faisal became a friend. He and the rest of the royal family were Sharon's patients. Sharon even took their photographs. One of the nicest ones was of Sultan Sayyid Faisal bin Turki, his son Sayyid Taymur bin Faisal, and his grandson Sayyid Sa'eed bin Taymur, who was just a toddler. He was a sweet boy."

"Yes," Wells chimed in. "I had forgotten Father photographed the sultan. Father took me along that day. I met Sultan Sayyid Faisal, Sayyid Taymur, and Sayyid Sa'eed, all three. I remember the sultan asking my Arabic name and Father responding that it was 'Ameen,' which pleased the sultan very much. I'm not sure I'll remind Sayyid Sa'eed that I knew him when he was 'knee-high to a grasshopper.'"[9]

---

[9] Very young.

L-r: *Taymur bin Faisal, Sa'eed bin Taymur (in front), Sultan Faisal bin Turki, Nadir bin Faisal, 1912 (SJT)*

May resumed her political narrative. "The sultan was hemmed in by the British. He or his father had been forced to decree that slavery would be illegal. As a consequence, the sultan's revenues plummeted. To complicate matters further, the British were having a great deal of trouble with arms being smuggled into Afghanistan at the start of the twentieth century, much of it transiting through Oman. They pressured the sultan to outlaw the arms trade, too, so the sultan lost even more revenue. The final straw was when Lord Curzon, the British viceroy of India, an imperious man, visited Muscat for just one day. He never left his ship and instead forced the sultan to come on board to be humiliated as if he was a two-gun maharajah. Sultan Faisal did not like it one bit, and he let Sharon know his frustration; it really affected his health.

"We didn't realize it when we were in Muscat because we were still relatively new, but the tribes beyond Muscat did not like the sultan's edicts either. The decrees cut into their income, and they blamed the sultan rather than the British. While Jim Cantine was here in 1905, there was an attempt to dislodge the sultan, a coup that failed. Then after we left, there was another insurrection in 1913. During the latter uprising, the tribesmen took control of Matrah and Muscat. The sultan and his family, servants, and guards escaped over the rooftops to Jalali Fort overlooking Muscat. Finally, the British sent in a contingent of the Indian Army to eject the tribesmen, indebting the sultan to the British. An Indian Army unit has been in the country ever since.

"But the discontent did not end with the sultan's restoration. Up and down the coast, it was not just that tribes didn't salute the sultan's flag, other local leaders refused to pay their *zakat* tax.[10] As a result, his revenues dropped even more. It was not a happy situation, to say the least. Consequently, some tribes, like the Bani Bu Ali, created their own seaports and customs posts on the south side of Sur at the village of al 'Ayqa.[11] At these renegade ports, slaves were imported and auctioned, and arms were for sale.

"When we moved to Muscat from Bahrain, we had to pack up not only the household but also Sharon's medical equipment and all the supplies and drugs he would use in his clinic and for surgeries. At the time, there were no pharmacies or medical supplies available in all of Oman. Whatever we needed would take months to arrive by ship and might be broken or pilfered on the way. We had two hundred packages of different sizes, weights, and shapes. None of them could be heavier than what one or two men could lift, and they had to be small enough to be portaged in small boats from ship to shore. There were no quays or cranes for ships at Bahrain or at Matrah. Packing was a nightmare.

"Your father would just shake his head. He said it made him feel like he was living the joke about the careworn woman getting on the streetcar with ten children trailing behind her. The conductor, after helping her and the children board the trolley, said in a friendly way, 'Are these all your'n or are you going to a picnic?' The woman said emphatically, 'They're all mine—and 'tain't no picnic!'"[12]

After a chuckle, Beth said, "What has happened in Muscat since the old Sultan Sayyid Faisal bin Turki died in 1913? And who is in charge now, and what should we expect?"

May answered, "His son, Sayyid Taymur bin Faisal, became sultan. Sultan Taymur really did not want to rule. It was a constant battle to

---

[10] The *zakat* tax is known as a religious tax, but politics plays a role. To whom one pays the tax indicates who is recognized as being in power. Whoever received the tax could also decide its uses, within broad limits.

[11] Now there is a bridge that links Sur with al 'Ayqa, a dramatic reminder that today all of Oman is a single, unified, modern state.

[12] The "'tain't no picnic" punch line of this joke was used by Wells and the Thoms family as a shorthand way of gaining perspective on themselves and the situations they experienced.

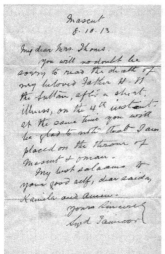

Sultan Sayyid Taymur's letter and envelope, 1913 (MdPT)

sustain his kingdom on limited revenue. He took prohibitive loans from Indian merchants so the state could pay its bills. That meant he had to pay high interest rates, so he actually had less than he thought. I do not know how he did it, but Sultan Taymur is a friendly, generous man and was Sharon's close friend. He sent me a letter immediately after his elevation to the sultan's throne."[13]

May paused, reflecting on the passing of time and people. "Perhaps Taymur's friendliness and generosity were personality flaws. I know he did not like to wield power, and his very weakness made him a pawn in the British Gulf game. They did not let him abdicate for almost twenty years. In 1932 he finally got his wish and moved abroad. He liked living outside Arabia and had a place in India, where he was born, and also one in Japan. His son, Sayyid Sa'eed bin Taymur, became sultan after that and remains on the throne today.

"The toddler in Sharon's portraits is now the sultan and doing quite a good job by all accounts. He personally has handled some tough issues and has largely hauled his kingdom out of debt. He has been a decisive ruler so far. Of course, he has not resolved all his country's challenges, but he has done pretty well with the resources at his command. I am not sure his British advisers like his independence, but it is his country, isn't it? It's not as if his British advisers were really protecting his interests."

---

[13] See endnote 16:13, p. 390, for a transcription of the letter.

CHAPTER 17

Muscat and Matrah Matriculation

Sahib, some of the Prophet Muhammad's followers wanted him to be recognized as imam of all Muslims, and others did not. The Prophet Muhammad said it was not necessary. Why, if the Prophet Muhammad did not need to be recognized as the imam of all Muslims, does the imam in Nizwa need to be recognized as such?

Where matters stood

Rev. Dirk and Minnie Dykstra, passengers on the BI's slow mail steamer from Bahrain, were returning with Beth and Wells to Muscat from the mission's annual conference in the fall of 1939. The Thoms family had bid farewell to Mother May in Bombay and then made their way to Bahrain for the mission gathering. Now they were bound to their new homes in Muscat and Matrah. Sitting on deck with the Dykstras, Beth and Wells basked in the balmy ocean breeze.

Their conversation inevitably turned from reflections on the recent mission meeting to the work that Wells and Beth would take up when they arrived at their new post.

Dirk said, "I told the al Mas brothers you were coming. They will be your welcoming committee. They have done a good job keeping a first-aid clinic going at the hospital in the absence of Dr. Harrison. Yet, who knows what condition the clinic will be in or what supplies remain?"

Dirk continued, musing aloud, "Harrison left six months ago, and Dr. Hosmon up and quit the mission a year ago after twenty-one years. Her main assistant, nurse-midwife Mary Balasundram, returned to India. The Women's Hospital closed when they left, since we were not authorized to keep it running without a woman medico. Dr. Harrison's assistants, Mubarak, Mohammed, and Qumber—the al Mas brothers—are good men and were instrumental in making the hospital work. They were very loyal to Paul, and I think you will find them loyal to you, too. At the very least, they will welcome a steady income. There are very few jobs in Muscat because the sultan is reluctant to start new projects. We in Muscat are caught in a time warp where very little changes. We have no electricity, no sanitary sewers, and practically no roads. The locals think the sultan is stingy compared to his father, Sayyid Taymur; he even shut down a government-funded elementary school to save money. It is not just that he is *bakheel*; he just does not have much revenue to fund his government.

"Your challenge is to get the hospital up and running. Do not expect the sultan to provide a subsidy. In some ways, it is a relief that Paul Harrison did not have more than four or five hospital employees. You will need relatively little revenue to finance the hospital, but that also means you cannot treat very many patients. The challenge will be to grow the hospital's clientele and its revenue, which will allow you to increase the hospital's staff and services. Then there's the women's hospital in Muscat. Minnie and I live next door, so we can help you there. It will be a challenge to get that going, to say the least. Unless the mission board provides a female nurse, it will be nearly impossible to reopen women's medical work. Sarah Hosmon was here for almost the whole time since your father's death; she will be difficult to replace." Dirk paused to let this loss sink in.

"Fanny Lutton was here for a long time, too," he resumed. "She was an evangelist-social worker and did she ever work. She knew everyone in Muscat on a first-name basis, from the women in the royal family right down to the poorest of the poor. The women loved her, and she loved them. She was a key link to Sarah in the Women's Hospital. Now we have lost them both, so the women's work needs rebuilding. It's going to take time before your plumb line returns to vertical." Wells noticed that Dirk liked to use construction metaphors. Although he was the mission's pastor-evangelist in Muscat, he was particularly good at brick-and-mortar projects. He had laid out and supervised construction of the hospital and the doctor's house in Matrah.¹ Wells and Beth remarked to each other that his keen sense of humor sharply contrasted with the serious, if not dour, demeanor of his wife, Minnie.

The Agreement of Seeb

"This country has a 'split personality,'" Dirk remarked, shifting topics once again.

"How so?"

"Well, the only part open to the outside world extends along the coast, called the Batinah. It runs as far south as Muscat and is in the sphere of influence of the sultan. The interior of the country the Muscatis call 'Oman,' and it has been shut off from the coast for almost twenty years, ever since 1920. The accessible coast, the Batinah, and the inaccessible interior, the Dakhiliya, seem to be almost two different worlds. Harold Storm and Paul Harrison went into the interior once or twice but only briefly. They were not warmly welcomed. There are very few people from the interior who come to the coast either for treatment or for any other reason. The interior is ruled by an imam, almost like a separate Islamic state. Behind the imam are two very powerful paramount shaykhs called *tamimas*, leaders of the main factions opposing the sultan in Muscat. As long as the two of them agree, the imam will handle matters smoothly. According to Ibadhi Muslim convention, the imam must be continually available to his tribal constituencies.² He opposes all forms of modernization, so there are no cars or trucks in the interior. Omanis in the interior believe the sultan in Muscat has sold out to modernization, Westernization, and foreign ways of thinking. He does business with all sorts of non-Muslims, and therefore cannot be a good Muslim.

"In the coastal cities of Muscat and Matrah, the sultan rules. We can move, preach, and treat people up and down the coast. Most of your life as a mission doctor will be spent at the hospitals in these twin towns that make up the sultan's capital and clearly inside his zone of

---

[1] Dykstra also installed electricity (including a generator) in the mission's Kuwait hospital. Shaykh Ahmad of Kuwait asked him to also install a similar system in his Dasman Palace. See also, endnote 17:1, p. 390.
[2] The Ibadhi are an early offshoot of the root of Islam. They are called "Dissenters" (Khawarij) by some. Ibadhis came very early in Islam's history and are rather democratic and less respectful of external religious authority, although their jurisprudence is broadly similar to that of Sunni Islam of Arabia. In modern times, they think of themselves as corresponding to the Protestants of Christianity, although the Protestants came late in Christian history.

influence. Paul Harrison drove his car up along the coast to Birkah on Thursdays, treated people, and came back the same night. He could do this as long as he timed his travel with the tide. He had to drive on the wet shoreline sand at low tide because there are no roads between Muscat and Birkah. The wet sand is packed firmly, thereby keeping the car from sinking in and allowing speedy driving. Once on soft, dry sand, though, the tires must be deflated to get across the dunes. Then, of course, they must be pumped up again to drive across rocky desert trails. As you can imagine, all this pumping must be done by hand. There are no filling stations here and no automobile road services. In fact, there is only one place to refuel in the entire country—between Muscat and Matrah. They sell only five-gallon cans of gasoline, and nobody checks your oil and coolant or cleans your windshield." Dirk chuckled at the thought.

He added parenthetically, "Paul's car was a crazy hybrid. It was a Ford convertible. His friend, Dr. Harvey Cushing of the Massachusetts General Hospital, gave it to him and arranged with Henry Ford for it to be juiced up. A customizer added a second rear axle, so that it looked a bit like one of those German staff cars pictured in *Life* magazine, with three pairs of wheels. Well, that modified Ford did not work very well because its standard clutch engaged the drive wheels of both rear axles. The clutch burned out again and again in soft sand and rocky terrain. It just made sense to revert to a regular car, and the hospital got a ragtop Model T to replace it.

"We have a great advantage over most local people, though," said Dirk. "We can access the coast by car and go farther by car in a day than Batinah residents can travel in the same amount of time. They are stuck in place near their homes because they must either walk, ride a donkey or camel, or take a boat along the coast. It is a twenty-mile trip from Matrah to Seeb on the coast.[3] That would be a good day's trip by donkey. To go from Muscat to Nizwa in the interior is at least a three- or four-day camel trip with stopovers under the stars or in friendly towns each night."[4]

Wells interrupted; his imagination was piqued by Dirk's earlier narrative. "I don't remember anything about a 'split personality' for the country hereabouts when I was a boy. I recall that the shaykhs of the interior opposed the sultan, had had their own imams periodically,

---

[3] Seeb is the location today of the international airport serving Oman's capital cities complex and is readily reached by car on high-speed highways.
[4] Today, the drive from Matrah to Nizwa takes less than three hours.

and almost displaced the sultan several times. Why do you say its 'personality' is 'split'?"

"I don't know if I'll get it entirely correct. What I know I learned from the Van Peursems, who learned it from Fanny Lutton, who learned it from the women in the *hareems*. The women always seem to get the inside scoop from their husbands, brothers, or sons. At any rate, after the insurrection by the interior tribes was put down in 1913, the rebel shaykhs still wanted control of the interior and separation from the sultan and the British. Sort of an 'Oman for the Omanis,' I guess you would say. That is why they resurrected the institution of the imamate that had been largely forgotten, hoping it could be used against the 'infidel' British. In Oman's Ibadhi view, the position of imam does not need to be hereditary. The first step was to select an imam that tribes in the interior could agree on. The lot fell to Muhammad bin 'Abd Allah al-Khalili, who was agreed to by the two *tamimas* of the Ghafiri and Hinawi factions.

"Now here's where it gets convoluted. Ghafiri and Hinawi are supposed to be clear categories, but so much history has transpired since those tribal groupings originated that some of the tribes no longer adhere to their original faction, having switched sides. The two paramount shaykhs are Salih bin Isa of the Hirth tribe and Sulaiman bin Hamyar of the Bani Riyam tribe. They and their allies agreed on Muhammad bin 'Abd Allah al-Khalili becoming the imam and set him up in Nizwa. With their agreement, a de facto state was set up in the interior during the reign of Sultan Sayyid Taymur bin Faisal, although the imam did not have a formal government in our sense of the word.

"This was definitely a problem for Sultan Taymur, but it was just one of many problems he had to deal with at the time. The British also wanted the sultan to dominate the interior, so they came up with the idea in 1919 to have the sultan decree a new customs tariff on produce from the interior—a 20 percent tax. Previously, it had been just 5 percent. Merchants in the interior were incensed because they could not make money exporting dates, dried limes, wheat, and such through the coastal ports of Muscat, Matrah, and the Batinah without paying the prohibitive tax. They were being driven backward into poverty.

"The tax was a major headache for the new imam, who was not yet firmly ensconced in his position. A confab was called in the town of Seeb on the coast at the mouth of the Wadi Sama'il, the main river valley leading from Nizwa to the coast. About forty shaykhs from the interior came to Seeb, led by Shaykh Isa bin Salih of the Hirth tribe. It was understood that the imam would agree to whatever the shaykhs accepted, so he did not need to be present or to sign the ultimate agreement.

"They met with R. E. L. Wingate, the British political agent that represented the sultan, a telling sign. Palaver went on for days, and lots of coffee was brewed and sipped. Finally, the parties neared a four-part agreement, but there was a problem. The shaykhs wanted the agreement to acknowledge Imam Muhammad bin 'Abd Allah al-Khalili' as 'Imam of all Muslims.' Wingate would never accede to that title because it would set a precedent in Britain's dealings with Arabs throughout the Middle East. He firmly resisted; it appeared as if the conference would fail on this point. Nobody would compromise. At the last minute, an idea came from Wingate's Kashmiri Muslim butler. He had been serving coffee and dates and listening to the debate. The ladies of the *hareem* tell us his name was Etisham.

"Etisham mentioned quietly to his patron, 'Sahib, you know the Prophet Muhammad also had this problem. Some of the Prophet Muhammad's followers wanted him to be recognized as imam of all Muslims, and others did not. The Prophet Muhammad said it was not necessary. Why, if the Prophet Muhammad did not need to be recognized as the imam of all Muslims, does the imam in Nizwa need to be recognized as such?'[5]

"Wingate liked that argument and introduced it into the discussion. The shaykhs were flummoxed and had to admit the truth of the story and its relevance to their negotiations. With further discussion, the problem was surmounted, and the so-called 'Agreement of Seeb' was signed without any phrase alluding to the 'imam of all the Muslims.'

"The Agreement of Seeb recognized two spheres of influence—the coast under the sultan and the interior under the imam. It also established peace between the two and reduced the customs duties back to 5 percent. The two jurisdictions could even exchange criminals on their 'wanted' lists.[6] The imam allowed the sultan to issue passports to all 'Omanis' from the interior and to equip them with photographic

---

[5] The Agreement of Seeb is also described in Townsend, *Oman*, 49-50, and in Peterson, *Oman in the Twentieth Century*, 172-76. It was a secret agreement, never acknowledged publicly by the British as a "treaty," but it organized the territory into two units, one called "Muscat" and the other "Oman."

[6] The Agreement of Seeb continued throughout the lifetime of Imam Muhammad bin 'Abd Allah al-Khalili to 1954, when the imam died.

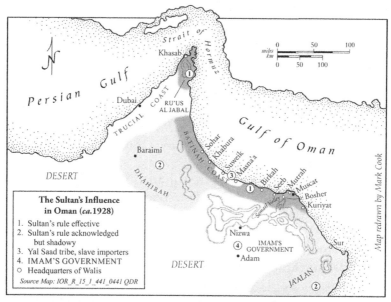

Extent of the sultan's influence, 1928 (QDL)

identification, which was a standard requirement for international travel. Yet he refused to recognize that there was a single, unified country called 'Muscat AND Oman' that included the coast and the interior. The imam did not want any intrusions of modernity in the interior.

"You will get very few visitors from the interior to your hospital, and ever since the Agreement in 1920, it has been next to impossible for Arabian Mission personnel to go beyond the limits of the sultan's coastal domain. The imam is supposedly completely opposed to non-Muslim foreigners entering his territories. It is probably as hard to visit the interior of Oman now as it was to visit Riyadh or elsewhere in Sa'udi Arabia in the past. We just have to work with and through the political realities as we find them, although we ought to try to make a trip into the interior at some point."[7]

Dirk was thoroughly engrossed in his political geography lesson. "I have often thought that our mission station in Muscat and Matrah is related to all of Muscat and Oman just as Bahrain is related to

---

[7] Travelers, such as the explorer Wilfred Thesiger, believed that the interior of Oman was extremely difficult to penetrate after World War II and that Omanis of the interior were anti-Western in the extreme. Thesiger avoided contact with Omanis as he and his comrades went nearly into the Rub al-Khali. See Thesiger, "Across the Empty Quarter."

Sa'udi Arabia, Qatar, Abu Dhabi, Dubai, and the minor emirates. Both Muscat and Bahrain are ideal 'jumping off' points for penetrating the interior of the Gulf nations.

"The interior regions of Oman are so isolated from Muscat-Matrah that their shaykhs and tribes don't think of themselves as part of a nation. They live in tribal *diras* ruled by a shaykh or by a confederation of shaykhs. In the mid-nineteenth century, Oman's most important province was Zanzibar on the coast of East Africa, a long distance from Muscat proper. Many Omanis migrated from the interior to Zanzibar.

"Somewhere along the line, the sultan in Muscat acquired Dhofar next to Yemen, and it is still his personal fiefdom, where very few outsiders have visited. The sultan also claims Sur near the southeastern tip of the peninsula; it has an excellent natural harbor. The Suris have engaged in commerce and slavery for a long time, traveling to Africa and Zanzibar and around the Indian Ocean. Sur is not fully controlled by the sultan, so the slave trade continues there to some extent. The area of the interior of Sur is called Ja'alan, and the route from the coast to the interior has many Sunni Muslims, rather than Ibadhis.

"So, there are a number of regions that have their own cultural and historic identities, and they resist the sultan's efforts to make incursions into their space. At the same time, the sultan wants to expand his influence. It is up to us to wage our own soft diplomacy with each of these independent groups. We cannot afford to offend the sultan since we are allowed to be here as a result of his agreement. Nevertheless, it seems to me that we need to reach into each of these regions and follow up our original contacts as windows of opportunity open up to us."

"That makes sense," replied Wells. "Much food for thought. Thanks for sharing this background with me. I will have to see how I can extend the influence of the hospitals and mission. I am sure it will depend a great deal on the sultan's ongoing relationship with the shaykhs and interior tribes.[8] I will have to see whether my boyhood acquaintance with the sultan makes any difference."

---

[8] After the Agreement of Seeb, it was inconvenient for the British Foreign Office to refer to a separate state, so the sultan was referred to as the "Sultan of Muscat & Oman," even though his administrative jurisdiction did not extend throughout the Oman of the interior. After its split from Zanzibar, the sultan was often referred to as the "Sultan of Muscat." Finally, after the cessation of the incipient civil war following the death of the imam, the sultan became the "Sultan of Oman," and this nomenclature has been concretized in the modern age.

The Daressa *unloading, Muscat Harbor, 1940s (WWT)*

Muscat and Matrah

The flat, nondescript, sandy coast of the Batinah, visible to the voyagers for the last fifty miles as they chatted on deck, ended abruptly in a rocky promontory. The ship slowed and nosed gently between the engulfing arms of natural outcroppings into the twin harbors of Muscat and Matrah. There it dropped anchor and with a blast of its deep, wheezy steam whistle, announced its arrival. Small boats shoved off from their moorings on the shoreline, and the quarantine officer's skiff, with the agency hospital's doctor, rowed briskly from shore to certify the health of passengers and crew.

Wells and Beth gazed with wonder at the forbidding landscape. Muscat harbor was ringed by bare, beetle-dark crags descending sharply into the sea. Neighboring Matrah showed almost the same contours, except for a curling arc of buildings on a sandy shoreline where fishing boats were drawn up on the beach. No trees or greenery softened the view. It was like a high-contrast, black-and-white photograph. The bright reflection from the water, the beach, and the whitewashed, adobe-like buildings almost hurt Wells' eyes. Behind them, dark cliffs were etched against the brilliant sky. Despite these contrasts, both towns presented their best seasonal profiles, which had not changed

Muscat seafront, ca. 1880 (JD)

in decades.⁹ The winter weather was delightful. The temperature was so pleasant it hardly seemed imaginable that the mission insisted that Muscat-Matrah missionaries take annual summer leaves of absence to go to India, Iran, or Lebanon to escape the heat.

A young man bounded up the gangway, enthusiastically shook hands with Dirk and Wells in the Western style and announced himself. *"Ahlan wa sahlan.* I am Qumber al Mas, and I welcome you to Muscat. We are happy to see you. I have arranged for boats, two for the Dykstras and others for the Thomses, to take you to the Muscat customs landing. I will help. We hope no customs duty will be charged on your goods. Usually, that is what happens, thanks be to God. The sultan exempts the mission from customs duties, but I may have to remind the Indian customs director of this," he said, with a wry smile and a knowing twinkle in his eyes.

Thanks to the ebullient Qumber, the transfer of the families and their luggage to shore went smoothly, as did the encounter with the Indian customs official. Soon enough, the Thomses were installed in the doctor's oversized house, with its thick walls of reinforced concrete. Looking around, Beth exclaimed, "This place is so big, it's almost unlivable. It seems as big as the hospital." On the ground level

---

9 Muscat's seafront had not changed significantly from the 1880s as shown in photo, a woodblock engraving by one of Europe's foremost woodblock engravers at the end of the prephotography era.

were *ambars* for construction materials, tools, and spare parts. Above ground level, there was a mejlis room to receive visitors, a large dining room, and a large storeroom for drugs and hospital supplies. The distance from the kitchen to the dining room almost guaranteed that food would be cold by the time it was served. With the exception of the dining room, the family's living space was on the third floor.

Shri Naraindas Toprani

Soon after Wells settled with the porters, an Indian gentleman arrived at the door. He was dressed in traditional Indian garb of *pace kachem dhoti*[10] and an old-fashioned Bania merchant's cap, and he sported an umbrella to ward off the sun. A *coolie* with a loaded basket on his head trailed behind.

"Allow me to introduce myself," the gentleman said in a formal, somewhat staccato, style. "My good name is Shri Naraindas Toprani. I am a trader here. Your father was my customer. It was my privilege to serve him, and it will be my privilege to serve you. I am at your service for any request for foodstuffs or supplies, and I shall have them delivered to you as soon as they are arriving, and also at best price. I have contacts and suppliers throughout the whole of the Arabian Sea region and Oman's interior too. I am bringing food and fruits right now, since I am thinking you might have nothing in stock. This is my gift, a welcome present. You can find me at my shop in the suq. It is open almost every day, except for Eid and Hindu holidays. I live in the tallest building on the Matrah shoreline with my wife and family. You can always find me in one place or the other, even on holidays. I have many things in my shop, but I can also get any other things for you on special order. You have but to ask, and I am doing the needful." He took a breath from this torrent of words and looked around.

"If your good wife is also available, there is one thing more I must do." Wells called Beth to the front entrance. While they waited, the *coolie* gratefully deposited his burden on the steps. When Beth arrived, Mr. Toprani produced two garlands of crimson and gold threads wound intricately together. He said, "I and my wife and family are welcoming you with these garlands. We hope you will be very happy here. We will be doing our utmost to make you comfortable."

Wells said, "Mr. Toprani, it is a pleasure to meet you again. I was just a little boy when my father was here. I remember you very well.

---

[10] Long cotton cloth worn by men, draped as if it had separate legs.

We shall come to you as soon as we set up housekeeping. Thank you for your thoughtfulness and your generous gifts. We look forward to making your acquaintance and that of your family. Do come in. Please take tea."

With a smile Mr. Toprani waved the invitation away with the back of his right hand saying, "No, no, I have already taken *tiffin*. I came to welcome you only. You have many things on your schedule. Another time we shall talk and take tea." With that, Wells and Beth's new, unbidden friend departed.

A house becomes a home

To their immense relief, Wells and Beth learned that, along with their new residence, they had inherited a household staff from Paul and Monty Harrison, the previous occupants. The Thomses were especially grateful for the Arab cook who already knew something of Western cooking and could purchase a few everyday needs in the suq.[11] The staff also came equipped with built-in childcare in the form of Hasseena, an African ex-slave in her forties or fifties. Hasseena looked stern, but the children soon discovered that her bark was worse than her bite. She had lovingly tended many children in the mission, thereby earning the endearing title, "Ma." Not quite a stereotypical nanny, governess, or *ayah*, Ma Hasseena had her own style. When she was displeased with the children's misbehavor, she addressed them with a fierce look and then added a good-humored chuckle.

Many of her injunctions to Lowey, the youngest Thoms child, ended with, "*Sawee, tup-tup.*"[12] When Lowey endured something particularly unpalatable, like a hair wash, Ma Hasseena would reassure her, "Aw dun dolly."[13] Ma Hasseena quickly became a devoted family retainer that the Thomses could depend upon. Her presence made it possible for Beth to undertake her responsibilities in the Matrah hospital, teaching women to read and ministering to community women and families.[14]

---

[11] The suq was a men-only market. Women did not frequent it very often. When they did have to go there, they were covered or wore distinctive facemasks. Beth did not usually venture into the suq, and Wells was too busy with patient care to visit the marketplace regularly. In some parts of Oman today, there are still women's suqs. That is, customers should be exclusively women, even though store personnel may be men.

[12] If you do not do this, you'll get a spank.

[13] All done, darling.

[14] Ma Hasseena lived well into her senior years, working in the Thoms household.

With introductions and the initial stage of unpacking done by nightfall, the Thoms family had a simple dinner and readied beds for the children and themselves. The new day with its promise of adventure and discovery would come soon enough.

The Matrah hospital's rebirth

On Wells' agenda the next morning was meeting Qumber's brothers, whom Paul Harrison had recruited. They had been unswervingly loyal to Harrison, so Wells suspected they might have mixed feelings about having a new supervising doctor dumped on them. Knowing, however, that there were very few other jobs available, Wells assumed they would want to continue as loyal hospital employees. Still, Wells wanted enthusiastic employees, not just begrudging ones.

He began his conversation with them in this way: "I have come to replace Dr. Harrison. My father was Dr. Sharon Thoms, the first mission doctor in Matrah. When he died in an accident, Dr. Harrison came and replaced him. We have the new hospital now, but I know that Dr. Harrison could not have run it by himself. You helped him and were an important part of the hospital. People became well because you worked as a team with him. That is what we wish to continue to do, *insha'Allah*. The people need your help, not just mine alone. I am not the head of the hospital. The head of the hospital is the Great Physician, whom Muslims call the Prophet Isa and Christians call Jesus Christ. As we restart this hospital, we should ask His blessing. I will offer a prayer asking that He bless each one of us as we begin this effort again." Wells then bowed his head and invoked God's blessing, through Jesus Christ and the Holy Spirit, on their enterprise.

Looking up he glanced around at each of them. "I think you should continue in the same jobs you were doing when Dr. Harrison was here and at the pay you were getting then. I do not know if you were receiving provident fund pay. If not, we should start it." When he saw the quizzical look in their eyes, he said, "We'll go into that another day, but it is money that we will set aside each month so that when you are old and can no longer work you will have money to live on." The brothers looked at each other in wonder and with growing smiles on their faces. Such generosity had rarely been heard of. "I hope you will say yes to continue working at the hospital. I know we will work well together." The brothers seemed relieved to know that they were trusted employees with secure positions. They gratefully sealed their agreement over coffee. Once everyone was relaxed, Wells turned to

al Mas brothers, back row, l-r: Mubarak and Qumber; front, Mohammed (TH)

each brother and asked what special training he had received from Dr. Harrison. They readily described their unique skills.

Mubarak, the oldest, had become a good "compounder" or pharmacist. He could mix powders containing the components of different prescribed drugs. The powder would be added to water and either drunk by the patient or taken on the tongue and washed down with water or juice. Often, it had a bitter, unpleasant taste, but that just reassured the patient that the medicine must have power. Mubarak was also good at collecting fees from patients. He could tell rich patients from poor ones. The poor were treated at no cost in this charity hospital.

Mohammed, the middle brother, had mechanical aptitude and was an experienced chauffeur. He was good at keeping the mission automobile running so hospital staff could go up the Batinah coast to treat people in the small towns and villages along the way.

Qumber, the youngest, was an experienced surgical assistant and took great pride in keeping the operating room exceptionally clean. Qumber said that he was eager to learn how to do minor operations. Wells was very pleased that their training and interests so nicely complemented each other.

In the next few days, Wells and the al Mas brothers swept and scrubbed Knox Memorial Hospital clean of the accumulated dust, dirt, and clutter. They also hired additional, unskilled staff to assist in their preparations. The main challenge on day one, however, was to locate the hospital's remaining medical supplies. The hospital clinic rooms that had served as a crude "nursing station" in the absence of the doctors had been stripped bare. In the six months since Harrison had left, the al Mas brothers had dispensed most of the supplies in their effort to maintain a simple first-aid station.

Wells explored the *ambars* on the first floor of his house. He found bandages and gauze pads, tincture of iodine, and little else. The iodine would be good, he thought. Experience had taught him that Arabs liked medicine that stung. Wells was eager to find quinine powder. It had not been important in arid Kuwait because Kuwaitis hardly ever got malaria. In the humidity of Muscat, Matrah, and Oman, however, malaria was endemic. There were mosquitoes in every rural irrigation ditch and in the scattered villages and towns. Wells knew that every patient would have more than one medical complaint, and he expected that malaria would be the common denominator.

To his dismay, Wells was unable to find any quinine powder in the prescription drug supply.[15] He knew it would take quite a while for an order of quinine to arrive—if he could even get it. He soon discovered from Mr. Toprani that quinine was not stocked anywhere locally. What was he going to do? He needed it right away.

As a last resort, Wells thought of the *ambars* in the women's hospital in Muscat. Mohammed cranked up the Model-T, affectionately known as "Zem" for the characteristic rhythmic sound that the cylinders made when idling,[16] and set out for the sister city. They arrived at Dirk and Minnie Dykstra's mission house in Muscat and retrieved the keys to the Women's Hospital *ambar*. There, *mirabile dictu*, was a large supply of quinine hydrochloride.

"Bless Dr. Hosmon," said Wells in a low voice. "But I'm going to have to keep looking to replenish our supply." The cost of quinine, produced in the Dutch East Indies, was rising steadily because of fears of Japanese trade wars in Asia and of Japan's alliance with Germany

---

[15] Synthetic substitutes like chloroquine did not become available in the Gulf until after World War II.
[16] Ford autos had a distinctive rumble that anyone could identify. It was always a surprise to hear all the cylinders fire, i.e, with a "brrm" (English) or "zemm" (Arabic) sound, followed by a silence, and then another "brrm" or "zemm" sound. The name had nothing to do with the famous well of the same name in Makkah.

and Italy.[17] The cache of quinine found in the Women's Hospital *ambar* would have to do for the time being.

[17] With the Japanese invasion of Southeast Asia, this became the Greater East Asia Co-Prosperity Sphere. Quinine supplies entered Western trade only illicitly through smuggling. When Wells would receive word of an Arab sailing ship's arrival in Matrah with quinine on board, he would race out to the ship to purchase the supply at whatever its asking price. That peaked at Rs. 1,500 per kg., an astronomical price increase compared to the mid-1930s.

CHAPTER 18

Home Again

Here were exquisite perfumes, aromas, odors, and stinks intermixed: burning charcoal, roasted coffee, wheat and grains, spices, honey, henna, frankincense, cloves from Zanzibar, clove oil, and all manner of spices from India all blended with dust, chaff, kerosene, animals, garbage, and sandalwood incense sticks—a real suq, a cacophony and symphony of smells.

Unbidden memories

On his third day in Matrah, Wells rose early and headed for the suq. He picked his way through the camel yard, where the camel drivers in the early morning unloaded their kneeling beasts. Foremost on his purchase list were firewood and charcoal. Then came bags of dates and other farm produce from up the coast and deep in the interior. The yard was quiet except for the sound of these masticating brutes, hunched on their haunches and seemingly glad to be rid of their loads. They asserted their relief in a language of intermittent grunts for the benefit of any who would listen.

Wells headed through Matrah's main gate, where community elders and visitors congregated to exchange news and views of the sultanate and the imamate. The air was rife with the fragrance of cardamom-spiced coffee. Joining them, Wells mounted a rugged bench and cheerfully exchanged appropriate greetings and bids of best wishes. Then, in wordless, comfortable companionship, he noisily "inhaled" three finjans of the muddy brew.

A general store in the Matrah suq, 1950s (RB)

How different it was now than in his boyhood when he had seen the lepers congregate on the perimeter of this area. Before World War I, forbiddingly stern men also gathered at the gate, visitors drawn to the coast from the deep interior for reasons known only to them. Their conversations betrayed their insularity and anger about modern ways. One of their driving purposes was to evict the sultan from his Muscat throne and replace him with a leader unsullied by the heathen non-Muslim world. When Wells and his father took late-afternoon walks out beyond Matrah's main gate in those days, there would invariably be a backcountry passerby intoning, *"Astaghfirullah!"*[1] The rural visitor would seek forgiveness for unwittingly being close to a Western nonbeliever. Never would the dour men invite one of them to sit and have coffee.

Having swilled his third finjan, Wells bid the well-mannered men at the city gate a cordial adieu and slipped into the suq. He was immediately stunned by the many aromas he had not inhaled since childhood. Here were exquisite perfumes, aromas, odors, and stinks intermixed. Here were the domestic scents of burning charcoal, roasted coffee, wheat and grains, spices, honey, henna, frankincense (its pungent odor drifting from individual burners in stores), fresh cloves from Zanzibar and clove oil for numbing excruciating toothaches, and

---

[1] I seek the forgiveness of God.

all manner of spices from India, all blended with the less salubrious fragrances of dust, chaff, kerosene, animal sweat and droppings, garbage, and the smoke curling from sandalwood incense sticks in Hindu shops. There was no place like a real suq for such a cacophony and symphony of olfactory stimulation.

After a careful buyer-seller verbal minuet with Mr. Toprani, Wells placed a bulk order for food and medical supplies from India to be delivered to the hospital. Then he passed from the suq's cooler semidarkness into the glaring heat of the seafront just outside another entrance.

Wells was surprised how far the detritus of urban life had pushed the shoreline seaward since his boyhood. He recalled that Mr. Toprani's house was originally built on top of the breaking waves at high tide, but now it was well above all but the highest waves.[2] Indeed, all the houses on the water's edge were comfortably above high tide now. One thing had not changed—the beach was still the principal privy for most townsfolk, although lower-class women preferred to use the empty land outside the city wall close to the hospital. Rich families were served by courtyard conveniences.

Squinting into the sun, Wells turned left past the Sur Lawati, a walled settlement within a settlement that sheltered Shi'ah Muslim Khoja traders from Sindh in western India.[3] Inside its walls, he recalled, was a veritable rabbit's warren of houses containing an amazingly high population density. The Sur Lawati land had been granted long ago to these foreign traders, and the Khojas still controlled it and locked its gates every night.

Baranda (veranda) House

As Wells passed Matrah's beachfront fish market, he unexpectedly caught a glimpse of his childhood home, its tall pillars supporting a second-floor verandah stretching seaward as if to capture a fleeting breeze. He had not anticipated seeing the house, but when it hove into view, he was overcome by indelible memories. "This is where it happened," he mouthed to himself. It was all he could do to keep his knees from buckling as the long-repressed memory welled up.

The story flooded back with unexpected ferocity. When he was just nine years old, Wells and his sisters, Frances and Lowey, had

---

[2] Personal communication with Muneer Toprani, grandson of Mr. Toprani.
[3] Sindh is now in Pakistan.

Baranda House, Matrah

gone by *huri*[4] from their home in Matrah to Esther Barny's birthday party in Muscat, even as their father was operating on a patient in the courtyard. They had a wonderful time on the way, helping to paddle the small water taxi and dipping their hands and arms in the water, even though they were dressed in their very best clothes. Large, silvery fish glided and shimmered in the water below. Mrs. Barny had devised many games for the kids to play, and everyone had gotten into the spirit of the day. It was a perfect Edwardian birthday party.

Because of the long boat ride home, they left Muscat before sunset. The *huri* man was waiting at the pier below the sultan's palace nearby. He dug in his paddle, and they sped past Al Mirani Fort, then past Sultan Faisal's last sailing naval frigate, then around the point past Kalbu and Riyam, and straight on to Matrah, about three miles away. The sea was looking-glass calm, and it was refreshingly cool on the water.

When they landed, Matrah seemed eerily quiet. Puzzled, the children walked up the beach to their home and entered to absolute silence.

"Mama?" Wells half shouted, breaking the stillness.

May appeared from the upper floor and said, "Shhh, children. Leave your shoes below and come up to the parlor. I have something to tell you." Wordlessly they gathered in the sitting room. Something was not right, but what it was, they could not guess.

When May came in, Wells blurted out, "Mama, the party was wonderful. We had so much fun!"

May, deeply distracted, replied, "Father has had an accident. He was tightening a telephone wire to connect our house to the mission hospital in Muscat. Somehow, he lost his balance and fell backward off

---

[4] A canoe with a boatman paddler.

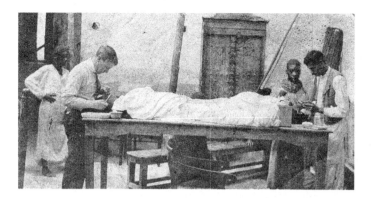

Operating room, Baranda House, ca. 1912 (SJT)

Sultan Faisal's naval frigate, 1909 (SJT)

the ladder. He hit his head on sharp rocks. The men holding the ladder carried him home.[5] He has not opened his eyes or talked since. He is still breathing, so we have faith he will recover," she said, with hope in her voice but doubt in her eyes. "We've bandaged him up. He's resting and sleeping. You may come to the door to look at him, but please don't say anything. Please read books quietly in your room. I'll come when I can for prayers and a good night hug. Pray for Father to recover."

Stunned, the children huddled in their bedroom not knowing what to make of this tragedy in progress. In the morning, they learned their beloved father, Dr. Sharon Thoms, had not survived the night.

---

[5] On his return to Oman, Wells was greeted by the very same men who, smiling and with great pride, informed him they had been holding the ladder when S. J. fell to his death outside Matrah. Lew R. Scudder III wrote later, "Seeing the humor of it, Wells remarked . . . that he didn't know whether the men wanted a tip or congratulations or what." To their great credit, they did not leave S. J. lying on the rocks while running away and muttering, *"Istigfurallah."*

*Cemetery Cove near Muscat
(JK)*

The sad news traveled rapidly. A message from the palace indicated that Sultan Sayyid Faisal bin Turki would provide his steam yacht to carry Sharon to his final resting place in Cemetery Cove. Sayyid Taymur, Sayyid Faisal's son, had become a Mason as a student in India, and Sharon had become a Mason as a young man in Michigan—a unique bond between the American Christian missionary and the Arab Muslim potentate family. The seagoing funeral cortege reflected the ritual bond among Masons that transcended geography, history, culture, and religion.[6] Consistent with multiple religious traditions, the casket was transferred to the sultan's yacht, watched over by scores of women standing silently atop their flat-roofed Matrah homes. The death of an hakeem larger than life was truly sad news.

That very afternoon, Sharon Thoms was buried in a barren cove along the rocky coast beyond Muscat, the one Sultan Sayyid Faisal bin

---

[6] Whether members of the RCA could also simultaneously be Masons was a late nineteenth-century controversy in that denomination. S. J. Thoms was a Methodist Episcopalian, and the double membership controversy seems not to have affected or bothered him. As far as is known, no other RCA missionaries were Masons, and no Arab rulers other than Sayyid Taymur bin Faisal were Masons either.

Turki had reserved years before as a Christian cemetery in perpetuity. The memory of those fateful days came flooding back to Wells as he stood on the shore looking at his former residence.

Things left unsaid

There were so many things Wells wished he could have said to his father. It was as if the accident had sliced Wells' life in half. Once, he was the son of a respected foreign doctor in Matrah, an hakeem. Once, he and his sisters occupied a cozy niche as mission children of a Protestant denomination tracing its origins back to John Calvin. Now everything had changed. Although they had a much-cherished stepmother, within a few short years, they had lost both of their parents. Now they had no income or social standing. They had no choice but to return to the United States, a country they knew only dimly, a country whose realities they knew not at all.

For a month, the family received guests according to Muslim custom. People simply came to sit in silence to be present with the bereaved. Having weathered that ordeal, May stoically packed up the family with three children to face a life of poverty in Indianapolis, Indiana, in a house owned by her brother-in-law. The Thoms family was now remarkably similar to many other single-parent families in that city who struggled with penury.

Wells wore hand me downs, and he looked very different from the other Indianapolis lads since he did not have knickerbockers or knee socks. He spoke strangely accented and peculiar British English. He was picked on at school and had to defend himself from bullies at recess. In the face of these threats, Wells was smart. He allied himself with Ulysses, the biggest boy in class. Ulysses was a slow learner, so Wells traded tutoring for bully protection.

Wells grew up quickly, becoming street smart, self-reliant, and self-confident beyond his years. He was naturally ebullient and full of ideas. He peddled newspapers after school and sold vegetables from the family garden in summer. His earnings helped support the family. When the family moved to Holland, Michigan, Wells entered Hope College's preparatory school. He washed bottles for the DePree Company, did odd jobs on weekends, and was a night cook at Keifer's Restaurant. While May studied at Hartford Seminary in Connecticut, Mrs. Warnshuis,[7] the Thoms family's longtime benefactress, housed

---

[7] Mrs. Warnshuis, a generous supporter of RCA missions, had helped to pay for May DePree's years as nanny.

and fed him and then nursed him through the 1918 Spanish flu. Wells learned the ways of the God-fearing people of Dutch descent in West Michigan. He met Congressman G. J. Diekema,[8] the RCA churchman and lawyer who had helped his father overcome British objections to his practicing medicine in the Sultanate of Muscat.

Following his high school years in Holland, Wells completed his freshman year at Hope College and the next two years at Kalamazoo College. During his junior year, he applied for early entry to the University of Michigan's medical school. On the recommendation of University of Michigan professor, Dr. Huber—for whom Wells' mother, Marion, had worked as an assistant when she was enrolled there—Wells was accepted into the medical program and soon started his medical studies.[9]

To earn his way through medical school, Wells became house manager of the Phi Chi medical fraternity, the very place where he was twice betrothed. With another medical school friend, he sold *Pictorial Review* subscriptions during the summer to the "woman of the house" throughout rural southern Michigan and Indiana.[10] They became *Pictorial Review*'s top salesmen and were treated to a New York City vacation, complete with tickets to a New York Yankees baseball game.

These bittersweet memories flashed through Wells' mind in the few moments he gazed at what they had called Baranda House, his home where his father had died. It was as if the two slices of his life reconnected. He could now function with enthusiasm and renewed purpose to heal the sick and share with them his understanding of a loving God, confident in the knowledge that he was carrying on a remarkable legacy.

Wells circled around and out through Matrah's city gate, walking toward the hospital on the other side of the camel park. Up the wadi, he noticed lonely, ragged people moving listlessly. As he approached them, he saw that little had changed from his boyhood days. Here, a generation later, people with leprosy were still living as outcasts from their villages. They still had no choice but to beg for scraps of food beyond the city gate of the biggest town in the sultanate. As a boy, he had asked his father if nothing could be done for these unfortunate

---

[8] See endnote 18:8, p. 391.
[9] Prof. Huber said, "Because of the high esteem I held for your mother, I'll help you get into medical school, but I won't help you stay in. From now on, you're on your own." Wells thanked the mother he never knew for this boon and resolved to double down on his medical school studies.
[10] See endnote 18:10, p. 391.

people. His father said there was then no treatment, but that perhaps effective treatment would be developed.

Wells now thought, "Perhaps the time for change has come. I'll have to see what can be done to treat these people humanely."

As he reentered his home, he said to Beth, "Let's schedule a family trip to Cemetery Cove where my father and others of the mission are buried."[11]

---

[11] Every year for the next thirty years, the family made a trip by boat to the cemetery in the cove.

CHAPTER 19

Hospital Snapshots: The General (Men's) Hospital, Matrah

A Muslim patient on the operating table stopped Wells from beginning the operation. "You forgot something," said the Omani patient. "What? No, I haven't," replied Wells. "Yes, you did. You were starting the operation, and you didn't pray."

Slow start, 1939

The number of patients coming to morning clinic was not large enough to keep the staff busy. Wells called them together and asked, "Are there not more people in need of medical care? If so, where are they and why do they not come?"

Qumber responded, "Perhaps they don't know the hospital is open. Perhaps they don't know there is a new doctor. Most remember that Khatoun Hosmon left several years ago, and Hakeem Harrison left after that. Hakeem Harrison used to go up the Batinah coast once a week as far as Birkah to treat people. It is difficult for sick people to travel, and perhaps they don't wish to come here if they don't know we are here to help. Perhaps you should ask Padre Dykstra about this. He goes to Birkah frequently. He has a garden house there."

The next Sunday, after worship, when all the missionaries were together from the Muscat and Matrah compounds, Wells took Dirk Dykstra aside. "I'm just double checking. You previously suggested it would be good for us to hold clinics up the Batinah so patients would not have to come to Matrah. Do you still recommend we do this?"

"It would be good for you to meet the coastal people," Dykstra affirmed. "You would see their living conditions, and you would see many more than the ones who are just sick enough, but not too sick, to come to Matrah. You could take Mohammed, he is good with the Model T, and one or two others. You could hold clinics in a date garden. You do not need to go far. You could start at Seeb first. As you become more confident, then take longer day trips. You might go as far as Birkah—Minnie and I have a rural ministry in a date-stick garden hut there. You are welcome to use our *barasti*.

"In time, you could tour farther up the coast. There are no roads, of course, but you can travel along the shoreline. Besides," said Dirk, "if you are like me, you will love spending a day a week outside town in places where Omanis feel most at home."

"Thanks," said Wells. "I'll go soon and take the basics with me, such as aspirin, quinine, vitamins, and smallpox vaccine. We will encourage people to come to Matrah for major surgery. Also, observing how Omanis actually live may clarify what we can do to improve public health."

"Just remember," said Dykstra, "meet with the wali[1] and the shaykh of the community first and get their permission to treat people. They will likely welcome you since everyone on the coast knows about the hospital."

Finding a way

After Wells and Mohammed had made several trips up the Batinah coast, the number of patients coming to the General Hospital[2] still seemed fewer than expected. In another meeting with his medical team, Wells wondered why. "Many from Matrah come to our daily clinics. Of course, they can all walk to the hospital. Unfortunately, we are not seeing many from up the coast whom we have referred here for more complex procedures. What do you think, Qumber?"

"It is not a medical issue, even though few come from outside the capital cities," Qumber replied. "It is difficult to come to the hospital. There are no roads, only tracks. It is very expensive to come to the hospital because patients usually stay more than two weeks. People

---

[1] *Wali*: governor, representative of the sultan.
[2] See endnote 19:2, p. 392.

have to bring all their food and *saaman*³ with them, so they bring family members to cook and care for them. If one is a shaykh, he will have money for camels and for his expenses on the trip and for his stay in the hospital, of course. For others, I am not sure."

"Matrah is at the end of camel caravan routes from up the coast and the interior. No camel caravans come from south of the capital cities; the terrain is too rocky. Camels cannot graze on the basalt hills since they have almost no vegetation. When caravans come, camels are unloaded quickly in the field near the hospital—you can hear them now—and then they go away as soon as they are unloaded because there is no food or water for them here.

"The only other way people come long distances to the hospital is by donkey. It's the same situation, except donkeys can travel from Muscat to Matrah and from the south of Muscat along the rocky coast from as far as Kuriyat. There is no cheap food supply here for donkeys either, so a double trip to Matrah is involved to cart patients who need operations."

"Maybe we could solve part of that problem," said Wells. "Our hospital is located on a large piece of land. We have a windmill and a well. We could irrigate our property like an oasis; we could plant trees, and under them, we could plant other crops, including *jett*⁴ and vegetables. We could grow animal feed. I've seen sweet-smelling *neem* trees, and they have many uses—maybe they would even clear up the halitosis of camels that graze on their branches."⁵

Putting his plan into action, Wells had irrigation canals dug and hired a gardener to tend the property and cultivate the crops. In due time, the General Hospital property became a "green" space, producing food for both the animals and the community of people who came to the hospital for treatment.⁶

Shaykh Isa meets Bob

"Happy un-Birthday, Norman!" said Beth with a hug and a kiss one morning in early 1940. "Guess what! Mrs. Pettyfer says her golden retriever, Jill, had lots of puppies last November 5. She remembered the

---

³ Luggage and supplies.
⁴ Alfalfa.
⁵ Watt, *The Commercial Products of India*, 780. The *neem* tree was also known as the *margosa* tree.
⁶ Personal communication from Wells, October 1965. As Land Rover taxis came into use, they replaced camels and donkeys. By the 1960s, the old garden was largely gone.

fifth was your birthday, too, and she wondered whether you would like to pick out a puppy for a birthday present." Jill was a pedigreed golden retriever that had just produced thirteen pups sired by a pedigreed red setter, more than either Jill or Major or Mrs. Pettyfer were ready to tend. Rather than put them down, they offered their friends choices from the litter.

"Wow!" exclaimed Norman, eyes glistening. "Oh, Mama! Could we have a puppy? Jill is really nice. Yes, yes. Please say yes!"

"I'll talk with your father when he comes back from the hospital. If he agrees, then perhaps we could all visit the Pettyfers for tea one day to see the puppies. The puppies are still too young to leave their mama. For now, a puppy is only a 'maybe.' Somebody has to feed him, wash him, keep him clean, and train him. Who would do that? Do you think you could do that? We'll talk about this with your father first. Only then can we decide about a puppy."

Privately Beth thought a dog would be a very good birthday present, and hers was a significant voice in the household. Matrah and Muscat had no children's toys or games in the suq. Finding suitable presents was always a challenge in an age of handmade, homegrown gifting. A dog would be an ideal gift. Besides, wouldn't caring for a dog teach Norman responsibility? Wells finally agreed that a puppy would be the newest family addition. That is how "Bob" became part of the Thoms household.

Few Arabs owned dogs, and most dogs in Oman were scavengers kept by nomads. Dogs were repugnant to townspeople who thought them bad tempered and untrainable.

Bob, however, was magnificent, with a beautifully plumed tail and legs. He had the color of a red setter and the good nature of a golden retriever. He often rode in the hospital's Ford V-8 touring car and frequently would be let out to run ahead of "Zem-Zem." Bob loved to race the old Ford up the hill over the pass from Riyam to Muscat.

One day, Shaykh Isa bin Salih al Harthi of the Sharqiyya in Oman's interior walked unsteadily into the Matrah hospital. Shaykh Isa was the most important *tamima* of the interior and wielded considerable power. He headed one of the two tribal councils that sustained the imamate.[7] Shaykh Isa had been a major player in Oman's twentieth-century politics and was one of the key personages who

---

[7] Shaykh Isa headed the Hinawi alliance in Oman's interior. His headquarters was in Ibra.

tried to oust Sultan Sayyid Faisal bin Turki in 1913. When the British sent an Indian Army contingent to keep the sultan on his throne, the tribesmen under the shaykh retreated to the interior.

Shaykh Isa bin Salih was dignified, ascetic, about sixty years old, and sick. His white beard flowed down over his immaculate white *dishdasha*. He wore a cartridge belt and a silver *khanjar* at his waist, a white headdress, and sandals. A posse of six bodyguards with rifles accompanied him. He had never used Western medicine before but had been persuaded to visit Wells on his trip to the coast. Native Arab healers had not been able to cure his malaria, anemia, and dysentery.[8] Shaykh Isa was, in fact, so miserable that he came to the hospital as a last resort. Upon examination, Wells sent him to the drug and treatment room of the hospital for medicine and an injection. The shaykh made it clear he would accept an injection only if Wells administered it. Even then, he insisted one of his bodyguards receive the injection first to see if it would kill him.

Wells had not earned his reputation for trustworthiness among the Arabs for nothing. He was used to dealing with suspicion, big egos, and skeptics. Mubarak gave Shaykh Isa bin Salih his first medication in the hospital and then brought him to the doctor's house for the essential coffee ritual and the inoculation.

As they entered the house, Bob bounded into the room waving his plumed tail in happy welcome. Shaykh Isa gathered his garments around him and said faintly but sharply in his sick man's voice, "*Kelb!*" A *kelb* was an unclean Bedu dog, probably infested with fleas, ticks, flies, and who knows what else.

Wells ushered his guest into the mejlis and said soothingly, "No, Shaykh Isa, this is not a *kelb*. He's a dog, and he is a family pet." By this time, they had sat down, and Wells continued, "You know, Shaykh Isa, his name is Bob, and he understands both English and Arabic."

Shaykh Isa bin Salih was now a little more at ease. The coffee being served, he had a finjan in his hand and was audibly sipping that bitter, burning-hot liquid.

"*Ma sh'Allah*,"[9] he said. "I know only Arabic. Show me."

So, Wells put Bob through several commands—first in Arabic, then in English. Sit. Roll over. Play dead. The dog performed beautifully.

---

[8] Peterson, *Oman in the Twentieth Century*, 53, holds that the shaykh was treated for pneumonia as suggested in *IOR/15/3/338: Annual Muscat Administration Report for 1940*.

[9] What hath God wrought?

He was all wiggles and play, his coat gleaming and his eyes alive and eager to please.

Shaykh Isa bin Salih was particularly impressed when he witnessed Bob running ahead of the car when Wells drove the shaykh to Muscat to meet the sultan. "I've never seen anything like him. How much do you want for him?"

"He is very special," said Wells. "He has no price. You see, he is one of the family, and I could not sell one of my family for any price. He belongs to my son Norman. My son loves Bob and won't part with him."

After returning to the Sharqiyya, Shaykh Isa bin Salih must have talked about the wonders of life in Oman's capital, the aromas and variety of produce in Matrah's suq, the automobile ride, the severe beauty of the sultan's antique palace in Muscat, and about Wells and Bob. Truly, this day had held new experiences for the elderly patriarch. Not long afterward, an influx of patients from the Sharqiyya came to the hospital clinic.

One visitor said knowingly to Wells, "I understand you own a very smart animal. It's a *kelb* but you call it a 'dog,' and it speaks both English and Arabic."

Matrah hospital at full capacity

"It's a sparkling new hospital compared to the ones in Bahrain and Kuwait," said Wells to Dirk Dykstra not long after the incident with Bob and the shaykh. "I understand you built it five years ago. Impressive."

"I had good advice from Paul Harrison," said Dykstra, "and we had your father's original pre-World War I plans. The hospital in Kuwait was the first reinforced concrete structure in the Gulf; it has lasted well. I had intended to model it again here. Reinforced concrete runs about double the cost of conventional construction, but conventional buildings deteriorate much more quickly. I hope this hospital will last at least twice as long as any conventional building and be a wise investment."

Dykstra continued, "We padres are the 'utility infielders/outfielders' on the mission team. We double up on our duties and chores as required. So, I preach, teach, help in emergencies at the Women's Hospital, become construction *maistry*[10] when necessary, and I do social work and counseling, too.

---

[10] Manager, construction foreman.

Matrah Hospital from the air, 1936 (PH)

"Supervising the construction of the doctor's house and hospital were more than I wanted to think about. I knew little about reinforced concrete, so I read everything I could lay my hands on. It seemed straightforward enough, except that no builder in this part of Arabia had ever built with reinforced concrete. I ordered, cut, and made the reinforcing rods and cages, and I created the forms to pour the concrete, and we built everything from ground level up.

"I oversaw the construction of the doctor's house as a learning experience. I used more cement than recommended because I was not sure of the quality of our sand and gravel or how effectively we could mix and pour concrete. We poured it one bushel basket at a time; we didn't have a concrete mixer. If the mixture dried too quickly, it would not hold the weight. Because of that, the doctor's house is overdesigned. Better safe than sorry.

"The hospital went up with less worry and more according to plan than the doctor's house. Our workers, however, never felt comfortable with the unfamiliar concrete. Oh, my," Dirk murmured, shaking his head with the memory. "Khaburi, our carpenter, tried to help. When the day came to knock the forms down, he did not show up. I kept asking for him. Finally, someone said he was at the mosque. When he finally arrived, I asked him what had happened. 'I was saying my prayers at the mosque because I thought the building would collapse and crush me when I knocked out the wooden form.' '*Wallah!*' he exclaimed, as he looked at the beautiful building after the wooden forms had been removed."[11]

By 1941 word had spread that the Matrah hospital was open, and the doctor could do wonders for the sick. He could even make blind people see again. Despite difficulties of travel, Wells' end-of-year report showed the medical staff had treated almost thirty thousand people in the main hospital, of whom a quarter were new patients.[12]

Most were outpatients, and with a staff of just six,[13] the hospital could not have accommodated many inpatients. Wells relied on vaccines and injection treatments that were very popular because they "hurt like the dickens." More than four thousand people were treated by hypodermic injections. One-half were treated for gastrointestinal ailments using bismuth and emetine. Malaria, almost universal among the population, as Wells had anticipated, was treated with intravenous or intramuscular quinine injections. Novarsan shots for syphilis made up about a quarter of the injections. Wells gave smallpox vaccinations to nearly twenty-five hundred people during the year.

Inpatients numbered 272 during 1940, and each stayed an average of seventeen days in the hospital. Many patients recovered slowly because they were undernourished, and the array of available drugs was extremely limited. Malnutrition was frequently revealed by large ulcers on patients' legs.

Wells did more than a thousand surgical procedures, of which 10 percent were major surgeries. Of those, one-third were eye surgeries (trichiasis and cataract) and another third were tooth extractions using Novocain. There were no dentists in Oman, and dental care was otherwise unavailable.

Wells made more than five hundred house calls during the year and completed more than five hundred lab tests himself since he had no lab technician. As the sultanate's only trained eye specialist, he refracted countless patients for spectacles. The hospital had a "radiology department," but because X-rays were so expensive, Wells tried to limit most such procedures to fluoroscopic exams.[14]

---

[11] Dykstra, "A Study in Reinforced Concrete."
[12] "Muscat-Mutrah Medical Work, Statistics for 1941." Unpublished typescript.
[13] Along with Wells, there were the Baluchi al-Mas brothers, Mubarak, Mohammed, and Qumber; Nubi (an ex-slave); and Walook—of Baluchi ethnicity. Only later did Arabs apply to work in the hospital.
[14] Ironically, before he had finished installing the X-ray machine, the technician sent by the American company had escaped Matrah on the same BI ship that had brought him. Wells had to figure out how to install and operate the machine on his own.

Wells and Matrah hospital staff, ca. 1942 (WWT)

Every moment commanded Wells' attention. Mindful of his Bahrain season of overload, Wells realized he had to live within the constraints of realistic achievements and his energy reserves. He had no nurse, no anesthetist, and no lab or radiology technicians, and he had to make his small staff into an effective team that would become more medically educated through on-the-job training and experience. He had to keep supplies and drugs ordered. Through it all, he felt satisfied he was doing what he was meant to do, that his patients were real people who experienced very human joys and anxieties, and that they were beloved of God and worthy of Wells' love, care, and concern. Because they were mostly poor, unsophisticated, and good-hearted people, they communicated their concerns openly through words and gestures even within the few moments he had available to diagnose their medical complaints.

Wells was optimistic. Next year would be even better as the medical services gained momentum and as more people came to understand the spiritual reasons that brought him to Matrah.

"Dead, all dead!"

On Saturday morning, May 17, 1941, a taxi stopped outside the women's hospital in Muscat and the driver ran into the clinic. "Dead, all dead!" he shouted at Wells. "Your motor was going up the hill to the pass between Riyam and Muscat. The road is narrow. A lorry was coming the other way, and the car moved over to the edge to make room for it. The road gave way, and all went over the side and crashed down the hill!"

As the resident ER doctor, even when making a regular visit to the women's hospital in Muscat, Wells carried a fully packed doctor's bag with him. The taxi driver drove him to the accident site. At the crest of the pass outside Muscat, he could see the accident debris on the far hillside. The Model-T lay in pieces below the embankment. He also saw Beth sitting up, a good sign. Arriving on the scene, he discovered Lowey to be uninjured beyond bruises and a small cut on her head. Norman had a deep cut in his neck at his jugular vein. Beth was putting pressure on it to minimize bleeding. On closer examination, he discovered Beth herself had a profusely bleeding scalp wound. Mohammed, the driver, had been knocked unconscious and had broken a rib. They carefully loaded Norman, Beth, Mohammed, and Lowey into the taxi and returned to Matrah where they could be examined more completely and treated. Mohammed, who was not bleeding but seemed to have broken ribs, was gently escorted home, as was Lowey. Norman and Beth he stitched up in the operating room.

Word of the calamity spread. The British consul offered to house the family at the consulate for the duration of their recovery. This was indeed a generous birthday gift, for May 17 was Beth's birthday, and it was already dreadfully hot with nighttime temperatures hardly cooler than daytime temperatures. No building in Oman was air-conditioned then, but the British consulate on Muscat's bay, with its airy sleeping verandas, would catch any puff of an ocean breeze and was the coolest place in town. There the family was restored to health, supported generously by the consulate staff who supplied copious amounts of tomato juice and food.[15] Bruised and sore they were, but it is a wonder they were not more seriously injured.[16]

A diverse slate of patients

Wells operated on two Baluchi men whose eyes had been mutilated by a bandit chief. Baluchis came from southern Afghanistan and roamed in the margins of Omani society. The chief discovered the Baluchis spying on his gang and tried to blind them with red-hot branding irons. Wells did plastic surgery to reconstruct the eyelid of one eye on each man, and then did iridectomies on their eyes to give each one enough vision to walk without requiring the help of a sighted person. This was the best he could do to salvage each man's vision to some degree.

Another of Wells' patients, an Arab qadi,[17] came to the hospital with a huge leg ulcer. Wells was foiled by the ulcer's resistance to treatment. He tried every useful medicine he knew. Further treatment

---

[15] The old British consulate no longer exists, having been replaced on the bay front by Sultan Sayyid Qaboos's Muscat palace.
[16] See endnote 19:16, p. 392.
[17] *Qadi*: judge.

would be a placebo at best and definitely a "last ditch" effort. He mixed a triple dye—acriflavine, gentian violet, and aniline green—and a paste of sulphonamide and zinc oxide with shark liver oil. He had no confidence this concoction would make a difference, but it was his last, best "enthusiasm soup" effort.[18] He knew sometimes positive patient outcomes came about psychosomatically.

During the procedure, the qadi worried about his painful and itching leg but then reported to Wells on a dream he had had. "In my sleep, I saw a man in shining white clothes. The man said not to worry. The doctor would bring some dark lotion and white ointment and apply it to my leg ulcer, and it would heal. The man in white spoke so kindly that I knew it was the Prophet Isa.[19] I fell into a deep, restful sleep. Now you are here, and I know I will get well."

Miraculously, the problem ulcer healed in ten days, during which time the qadi read the four Gospels and the Acts of the Apostles while recovering in the hospital. He left praising the name of the Great Physician. The qadi's enthusiasm inspired the hospital medical team who had not placed much store in the effectiveness of placebos. Wells had already seen enough dramatic recoveries to believe in the healing effects of faith.

Too much success?

In the 1942 annual report, Wells pled for improved hospital supervision and for the next stage of hospital construction. He put particular emphasis on the need for kitchen facilities to replace the inadequate and unhygienic accommodations currently in place:

> It is impossible to keep the hospital rooms and verandas clean if they have to be used for storerooms and kitchens. A few patients manage to keep their rooms neat even under such adverse conditions, but the average room contains, besides the patient [and his family members], a sack of charcoal, a water pot which leaks, a coffee pot always simmering on a small charcoal brazier, a skin of dates, and in a corner of the window will be a pile of date stones being collected to take back home to be fed to the family cow.[20]

---

[18] For "enthusiasm soup," Beth's recipe was "throw everything you have into it—including your enthusiasm."
[19] Jesus.
[20] "Annual Report for Muscat Medical Work, 1942." Unpublished typescript in author's possession.

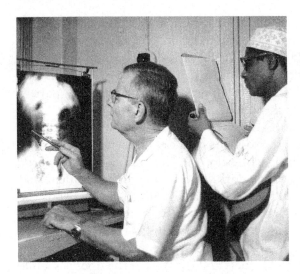

Wells with his lab and X-ray technician, Malallah, 1960s (WWT)

A partial answer to Wells' plea came a year later when he proudly announced that the hospital had a new superintendent—Beth Scudder Thoms. Beth had more free time since the three older Thoms children were in boarding school in India and only Lowey remained at home. As the new superintendent, Beth oversaw the care and keeping of hospital supplies and the maintenance of proper processes.

One of her first steps was to arrange for each hospital room to be whitewashed between patients. This was no simple task because charcoal smoke from cooking fires in the sick rooms blackened the walls and hung in the still air. A laundry service was initiated so that fresh sheets could be spread on beds for each new patient, and sheets were changed frequently. Patients even received periodic baths. All in all, Wells was delighted with the effect of these changes on patient outcomes. In her new role, Beth had expanded the horizon of her duties while maintaining her former tasks, which included overseeing women's sewing, embroidery, and literacy work. Remarkably, having overcome her initial self-doubt about her Arabic language skills, she now taught Arab women and men to read and write Arabic. To lighten Wells' burden, Beth trained Omani staff in laboratory techniques. Her most promising student was Malallah, a quick learner. Wells sent him to India for further training, and he became certified in lab techniques and X-ray technology.

Beth also took on the duties of the hospital business manager, doing all the accounting and payroll transactions so that Wells could concentrate on treating the increasing ranks of men, women, and

Mubarak, patient and pharmacy assistant, 1950s (RB)

children who were coming in for treatment. Her contributions were extremely important for the mission's medical and evangelical work.

Doing the hospital accounts was a "trapeze" act belied by the simple description. Beth had to keep track of income and expenditures, all the while maintaining a provident fund in reserve against the day when workers retired. To complicate matters further, Beth had to work in multiple currencies: (1) Maria Theresa "thalers" (dollars), an Austro-Hungarian currency (called *riyals* in Oman), minted in 1783 and still used in Oman's interior and valued because of their silver purity (some hospital employees, with little faith in Gulf paper currency, insisted they be paid in MT dollars); (2) Gulf rupees, a standard currency invented by the British that could not be circulated outside the Gulf or exchanged at par with the Indian rupee; (3) the British pound sterling, used for drugs and other supplies ordered from England; (4) the Indian rupee, used for supplies and materials purchased from India; and (5) US dollars for drugs and equipment ordered from the United States. Only the US dollar was a decimal currency; the others were all based on other, more complicated systems.[21] And to top it all off, the sultan had minted *baisas*, small coins, to facilitate making change in the suq.[22]

---

[21] Mental gyrations were required to convert Gulf or Indian rupees at different exchange rates (each rupee had 16 annas with 4 pice to the anna, and 4 pies to the pice). British pounds sterling had 20 shillings to the pound, with 12 pence to the shilling—but a guinea was worth 21 shillings. These conversions Beth did either by hand or in her head.

[22] See endnote 19:22, p. 393.

Wartime complications

The Second World War complicated matters, of course. Attendance at the hospital clinic dwindled markedly. Wartime shortages were widespread in the suq, not only in the supply of drugs but also in all commodities, and these shortages affected the quality of community life. Tempers were short under the pressure of wartime hospital demands, and people were further aggravated by the unrelenting heat. Wells discovered one morning that his two most valued employees were arguing over who should get an empty medicine bottle that could be resold in the suq, since empty containers of any kind commanded good prices. As the temperature of their argument heated up, Wells' own temper suddenly snapped. It was time for confrontation.

He stood over them and said firmly, "Give me the bottle!" They did. He did not have the patience—or, perhaps, even the wisdom—of Solomon. Rather, he took the bottle and dropped it on the pavement where it shattered. "Let's clean it up and go back to work," he said unsmilingly. If the disputants could not resolve such a minor issue, then neither would win.

Wells realized from this and other minor fracases that, to keep his little hospital group unified, he would have to cultivate a team spirit for these very stressful days. He reactivated a program of social activity among the hospital employees and their families that Paul Harrison had started. Outside the hospital, it was unheard of for unrelated Arab, Baluchi, and Persian families to interact socially in situations where men and women, boys and girls, teenagers and the elderly mixed freely. With Wells' encouragement, these unlikely playmates found that Friday game nights, with occasional picnics and cookouts at the beach, were prized parts of being in the "hospital family." Wells, most of all, enjoyed these evenings. He did not have to be the "maestro" directing all the fun. He could just enjoy playing musical chairs, Chinese checkers, crokinole, or other games with the family members of his hospital team. The evenings always ended with a hymn after snacks of fruit and coffee. Wells also organized active outdoor sports, like volleyball and tennis, for hospital staff, where healthy competition and sportsmanship could be cultivated. Periodically, hospital teams would play others from the community.[23] Wells liked seeing young people grow and mature in behavior and thought. These times did much to

---

[23] Sayyid Tariq bin Taymur (father of Oman's Sultan Haitham) and Thuwaini bin Taymur were frequent guests and enthusiastic tennis players.

build a community spirit among the Christian and Muslim staff and their patients and guests.[24]

To Wells, one thing was perfectly clear. Personal relationships came first. Medicine, money, and all else came a distant second. His perspective on this was ideal in Oman, for that was how Omani communities and tribes functioned. Sultan Sayyid Sa'eed and his forebears also based their state on personal relationships with shaykhs, amirs, qadis, walis, imams, and tribes. In this way, Wells' natural approach to life fit beautifully with that of his Omani neighbors. Making a medical team out of teenagers and young men with no modern education was a challenge not unlike that of Jesus, forging his disciples into a team from the rough-hewn, simple men He had called to follow Him.

Medical advances come to Oman

While on leave after the war, Wells was impressed (as his father had been a generation earlier) by how far medical practice had advanced since he was last in the United States in 1939. He tried to catch up by visiting colleagues and programs at medical schools and pharmaceutical companies. As he recalled his reaction:

> I didn't realize how empty of new ideas and ignorant . . . I had become. The life of a medical missionary becomes so full of treating the sick that few of us spend enough time reading medical journals. We must set aside a few hours a week for medical reading [just as much] as regular . . . times for Scripture and prayer, so that the hospitals Christ has put us in charge of may not fail to give the best treatment that medical science offers.

He also reflected on the advances that pharmacology had taken during his absence:

> In this connection, since Chloromycetin is both very effective and very expensive, and nowhere is it more needed than in Arabia, a great service would be rendered our patients if church groups would purchase and mail [monthly] to each of our hospitals several hundred capsules of Chloromycetin.
>
> The first outcall I made after returning was to see a boy of ten years who had been running a temperature between 103 and 105 for twenty days. He was emaciated and delirious. The

---

[24] See endnote 19:24, p. 393.

Muscat-Matrah's heat-oven hills (PD)

diagnosis was typhoid, and three days and twelve capsules of Chloromycetin later, his temperature was normal. I was amazed. Before I had used one hundred capsules, I had seen it dramatically cure five other full-blown cases of typhoid.

Back in Oman after his furlough, Wells soon returned to his hectic pace. It took its toll on him physically. As he wrote to May, his stepmother: "I'm holding my weight pretty well at 147 pounds. Beth is holding hers at about 132." Beth, of course, did not have to navigate the operating room every day. Its temperature rose regularly to as high as 125 degrees. In part, this was because Paul Harrison, Wells' predecessor, had equipped the hospital with a small electrical generator, to which he had cobbled together a panel of lights to illuminate the OR, and they added to the seasonal heat. Sadly, there was not enough electrical power to run air-conditioning to cool the OR.

Indeed, with no air-conditioning, the heat was oppressive. Nights were like barbeque grills, with temperatures more than blood hot. Sleepers felt as if they were being steamed on spits as they thrashed on perspiration-soaked beds and pallets. No relief came from sleeping on flat roofs in the open air because the black basalt hills radiated back the intense heat of the daytime sunshine. The first act every morning was to gulp a glass of tepid water to rehydrate after the loss of liquids overnight. Excess poundage slid off the frames of any who tended toward corpulence. Everyone huddled in survival mode. To do anything during the day required a major act of will. No one hankered for food. Prickly heat reminded many how raw and rough were the natural textile fibers of their clothing. Changing clothes several times a day to dry the skin did not help much. Talcum powder provided only minor relief to prickly heat.

By the late 1940s, Wells was feeling the pressure of his untenable pace. In his 1949-50 annual medical report, he remarked on being overwhelmed by the great public demand for medical treatment. At the same time, he noted the amazing benefits of new antibiotic drugs:

> Many [Omanis] have been treated, [but] I know many were treated only as numbers, examined in ten seconds, diagnosed in five, and treated in fifteen. And yet I know that the poorest are given the same treatment as the rich, and much more streptomycin and penicillin was dispensed free of charge than was paid for.[25] Many returned home cured and with thankful hearts, saying in their own words, *"Min barakat al Masih ana shafait."*[26]

Wells increasingly noted the importance of formal training for the Omani staff. Nurses Anne De Young and Jeanette Veldman, together with the doctors on staff, gave ten hours a week of medical and premedical training to the Omani staff. These sessions, however, demanded twenty hours a week of staff time because coeducational classes were not acceptable. The staff who underwent training improved markedly in their service orientation to patients and in delivering quality medical care. They took real pride in their work. Most importantly, Wells was gratified that the staff had learned to place patients and patient care first.

They had come a long way since the hospital had reopened in 1939.

---

[25] Wells was not administering two classes of medicine—an inferior one for the poor and a superior one for the wealthy.
[26] By the blessing of the Messiah, I was healed.

CHAPTER 20

Hospital Snapshots: The Women's Hospital, Muscat

Many girl babies were named "Maryam" after Nurse Mary.

The return of Nurse Mary

"It was a minor miracle that we found Nurse Mary Balasundram at her family home in South India during our annual leave to escape Matrah's blistering heat," said Wells to Beth in the fall of 1940. "To find she was eager to return to Oman with us was a huge relief. Her midwifery mission to the women of Muscat has really become her calling. Nurse Mary will once again be central in that medical work. She will live in the same rooms as she had before, with her next-door neighbors being the Dykstras. I don't know whether Minnie Dykstra or Nurse Mary is the more 'rock-ribbed' conservative Christian, but they will be good support for each other, as they have been for so many years."

"It wasn't always called the Women's Hospital,[1] was it?" asked

---

[1] The Women's Hospital was Wells' primary responsibility, with nurse-midwives staffing it. When, toward the end of his career, a woman obstetrician-gynecologist joined the hospital staff full time, Wells' responsibilities were reduced to surgery only. After 1970 it became known as the As Saada [happiness] Hospital. Having

Beth. "From what I've heard, it was just a clinic at first. I heard that it didn't have inpatients in the days of Dr. Hosmon."

"As you recall, the Women's Hospital was originally a clinic founded by Aunt Elizabeth Cantine, Mother May's sister. Uncle Jim had been sent to Muscat to take over the Freed Slave Boys School. Elizabeth was a nurse and decided a Western medical clinic could be useful for the women in Muscat. With that vision in mind, she staffed it as a volunteer. It was actually called the Women's Hospital very early on," said Wells. "Dr. Sarah Hosmon arrived in 1913, and Nurse Mary came in 1917. Dr. Hosmon was a general practitioner in a 'women-only' practice. After all, would men have asked to be treated by a woman doctor then? There were strong views on the place of women in society, and women doctoring men did not pass muster.

"Dr. Hosmon and Nurse Mary treated most of their female patients at home. Women were either so sick they could not leave their houses and come to the clinic, or their husbands would not allow them to come out in public. Nurse Mary specialized in midwifery and attended women giving birth at home. That is what she will still do because the hospital has beds for only two inpatients.

"The hospital never had an expensive operating room, and the mission board never approved a surgeon missionary to serve that hospital exclusively. When emergency surgery was needed, our pastor—who lived in Muscat—would find transportation to bring the ailing woman to Knox Memorial Hospital in Matrah," Wells explained.

"I wonder how many children Nurse Mary has brought into the world," said Beth.

"I really don't know, but she must have delivered thirty or forty babies a year in the past," said Wells. "She was called on for help many more times than that, of course. She was frequently called to homes nearby, in Muscat and its immediate surroundings. She also held a daily clinic where many women and children came as outpatients.[2] I am assuming she will pick up where she left off.

"Families are large, and women take pride in having many children. Because malnutrition and contagious diseases are common, deliveries can be very challenging for both the mother and the midwife. Nurse Mary must be prepared for health complications of all kinds.

---

functioned as a small clinic, it grew into a very large institution over the years, despite its modest square footage on its constricted site. The hospital was always backstopped by the mission padres, Rev. Dirk Dykstra and Rev. Jay Kapenga.

[2] Boersma, "Nurse Mary of Muscat."

If she has attended the births of a woman's other babies, things are more likely to go smoothly. If, however, Nurse Mary has not attended an earlier birth, it could be catastrophic. This is because native Omani midwives may have employed the methods used for generations that they learned from their mothers or other older midwives."

"What do you mean?"

"Well, to stop the bleeding after birthing, for instance, indigenous midwives often pack the vaginal canal with rock salt. While this impedes the bleeding, the salt may scar the birth canal so badly there's little or no room for the next baby to pass through. The death rate in subsequent pregnancies is probably high, for either the baby or the mother—or both. We don't know how often that occurs because there aren't any statistics.

"When you combine these complications with the challenges to newborn babies in infancy and in their toddler years, it could be that as many as a quarter of them die before their fifth birthday. If a mother gives birth prematurely, especially during the really hot summer months, the preemie may be overly stressed by the heat. Because we do not have air-conditioning, the babies may also not get the fluids they need in hot weather. We do not have well-baby clinics for mothers and babies where families can learn best practices. I haven't any idea how many women die in childbirth. As a male doctor, I am excluded from those procedures. It is very, very tragic. If we had all the resources we would like, we would recruit women doctors and nurses, as well as dietitians and nutritionists. If we could have a proper women's hospital, and if women would be willing to come there to give birth, we could bring many more babies and mothers through the birthing process successfully. It is something to dream about."

"Has Nurse Mary been accepted as a midwife, or is she called only when everyone and everything else had failed?"

"She is much loved. Apparently, women call her first if she is nearby and able to attend the mother. Women see her as a loving midwife who knows what she is doing. Even though she practices midwifery as she learned it during the World War I era, she is still a vast improvement over local midwives. Many baby girls have been named 'Maryam' (Mary) after her. She has learned how to deliver babies in the poorest households with terrible hygiene. Babies have been born in substandard, dirty environments for centuries and have grown up to live long, full lives despite it all. Mary knows how it is in poor South Indian peasant families, as well as here in Muscat. We will give her good support to do a fine job." Wells paused as he and Beth reflected on the challenges awaiting Nurse Mary and themselves.

"As Dirk Dykstra told us, in the 1920s, another single woman missionary, the Australian Fanny Lutton, lived in Muscat with Sarah Hosmon and Nurse Mary. Although not officially tied to the hospital, Fanny was a tireless network builder among the women of Muscat.[3] She was a one-woman 'social services department' and a conveyor of news par excellence in the women's *zenanas*.[4] The women of Muscat had nothing but good to say about Fanny, Nurse Mary, and Dr. Hosmon."

Hospital expansion, 1952-53

In 1950 Beth wrote in her diary: "Sayyid Mahmood al Bu Sa'eed, the oldest living member of the ruling al Bu Sa'eed family, gave the mission a plot of land he owned next to the small Women's Hospital. He was grateful for the successful surgery and recovery of his only daughter."[5]

Over the course of the next two years, Rev. Jay Kapenga—who with his wife, "Midge," followed the Dykstras as pastor and educators in Muscat[6]—enlarged the Women's Hospital. By the time nurse Jeanette Boersma arrived in 1952, the Women's Hospital had seven rooms with four beds each. Four more rooms were added in 1953, with living quarters for nurses.

Meanwhile, the Matrah General Hospital, where Wells spent most of his time, was the destination for more near-term pregnant women from the Batinah than ever before. It was here that operations associated with abnormal deliveries and medical complications of childbirth were handled surgically.

One of these complications was tetanus, which Wells noted was remarkably uncommon, "considering the large number of people who walk barefoot over very dirty ground":

---

[3] The trio of Sarah Hosmon, Fanny Lutton, and Nurse Mary made a major impact on Muscat. See endnote 20:3, p. 393, for more.
[4] The term for "harem" used in India and Persia: a place for women's seclusion.
[5] Thoms, "Forty Years of Remembering." Wells was the only surgeon in Oman at the time, so he must have done her surgery.
[6] Jay and Midge Kapenga became dear friends of Wells and Beth. The Kapengas replaced the Dykstras when the latter retired from mission service. Although Wells and Beth appreciated the Dykstras' orthodox Calvinism, Jay and Midge were very progressive and resonated theologically with the Thomses. Jay had a strong commitment to peace and justice issues. More than for their theology, Jay and Midge were known by Beth and Wells as extremely caring, loving people.

Hospital Snapshots: The Women's Hospital, Muscat 251

Rev. Dirk and Minnie Dykstra (WWT)

Rev. Jay Kapenga (WWT)

Nurse Mary, Jeanette B., and women patients (WWT)

Mother and child in Matrah hospital, 1960s (WWT)

But we saw six [complicated deliveries] last year—three recovered, and three died. Two of the three who died and one of the three that recovered had postpartum tetanus. They were infected during delivery by a blind and ignorant midwife. These cases are, I thought, invariably fatal.

Shahrazad is a living testimony that no case or disease should be considered hopeless, for she had postpartum tetanus of the uterus—and she recovered. She received large amounts of antitoxin, penicillin procaine, and streptomycin by injection and was fed for days by intravenous glucose and saline and was kept quiet with frequent injections of magnesium sulphate intramuscularly, luminal by mouth, and intravenous Pentothal sodium—but so did the others who died.

Several times, she seemed to be going the way of the others, in spite of all we did for her, and the [monetary] cost of the fight amounted to so much that several times we thought we might as well give up and use the time and medicines on other patients. But each time the look of pleading in her eyes, her determination to fight for her life, and most of all the spiritual prodding of the Good Physician kept us trying to save her life.

Large doses of Coramine injected intravenously when her breathing became labored and shallow helped, and so did several ampoules of terramycin. It was wonderful to see our prayers answered and our efforts vindicated when, after twenty days of being tormented by spastic convulsions, she relaxed in natural sleep and after a month was able to walk out of the hospital and return to her home and children. Because Shahrazad recovered, I will never [again] consider postpartum tetanus hopeless.

When telephone connection was finally established between Muscat and Matrah in the early 1950s, Wells noted that he could now be "in both places at the same time," rather than driving to Muscat at odd times of day and night in response to the night watchman's hand-carried message, or when Jay drove a stricken woman to Matrah for surgery. Forty years after Dr. Sharon Thoms fell to his death while stringing a telephone line to connect Muscat to Matrah, the benefits of telephony were finally realized.

Until the mid-1950s, when Nurse Mary retired after forty years of service, few deliveries were carried out in the Women's Hospital. Almost all babies arrived at home assisted by Nurse Mary. In the 1940s, the number of babies born each year was usually fewer than forty.

By 1951 the age of the Land Rover was in full swing, and it had a dramatic impact on Nurse Mary-assisted births. Seventy-five babies were born in 1951, a majority in homes. By 1958, 478 babies were born—all in the Women's Hospital. In 1961, 815 babies were born in the hospital. In 1965 more than twelve hundred kicking and squalling babies greeted their mothers in the hospital. Babies were definitely a "growth industry," and the Women's Hospital was in full swing.

By the late 1960s, Wells noted in one of his medical reports that the Women's Hospital was experiencing more than two hundred live births per month (or 2,400 per year). At the same time, there were many more women and children who came to the Women's Hospital for prenatal and postnatal care. The hospital had developed a huge following, and Khatoun Naeema (Jeanette Boersma) was key to much of it.[7]

For nearly ten years, beginning in 1952, Jeanette Boersma was the only foreign nurse in all the Oman hospitals. Most of her time was needed in the women's hospital in Muscat, but once a week, she assisted Wells at the main hospital in Matrah.

A single woman and effusive about her conservative religious views, Jeanette was inordinately focused on her nursing responsibilities. It was easy for her to overlook or minimize her own needs. Wells

---

[7] The trend continued. In 1971 there were more than four thousand babies delivered, and in 1972 more than five thousand. *Oman Reports* 2 (1973), 3.

became aware of this when Jeanette arrived one Friday afternoon to assist in the operating room; she was listless and fatigued. A quick check verified that she was anemic. A doctor's lecture really does not solve many medical difficulties, but he gave it to her anyway.

"Jeanette," he said, "you are new and have yet to get into the rhythm of Muscat life. You must pay attention to what your body tells you. You are working how many hours, I don't know. You have to pace yourself. I'm going to give you a couple of vitamin shots. Then take these One-a-Day vitamin and iron pills regularly at home.[8] You have to take care of yourself better.

"Look at you. You are as thin as a rail. Make sure you eat properly. We can have you eat with the Kapengas some of the time, so that you don't have to cook for yourself. Or just hire someone to cook for you." Wells was fully into lecture mode now.

"On Fridays, you'll have lunch with Beth and me. As you know, we take a short nap after lunch, and then you can assist me while I operate in the afternoon. Having a proper nurse in the OR will free me from many distractions; it will be so much better. Then we'll quit and have *mai lumi*[9] and a snack.

"Every few weeks, we'll go for a picnic and swim at Qurm Beach with the 'Kappies,' you, Beth, and me. Today is not a day for you to be in the OR. You rest, and I'll take you home after the operations and dinner."

That evening, after supper, he said to Jeanette, "Now, I'm going to drive you back home. After I see you to your door, I'm going to drop letters in the mail because tomorrow the BI mail ship arrives." Wells looked around the room and asked Beth, "Do we have matches and the kerosene lantern?" He then turned to the relative newcomer, Jeanette, to explain further. "The evening gun went off some time ago, so the city gate of Muscat will be closed. I'll have to park the Land Rover at the main gate, light the lantern, step through *al khokha*,[10] and walk to the mailbox at the British consulate. We can't use flashlights because the night watchmen are instructed that anyone who uses a flashlight is up to no good. They regularly arrest flashlight carriers and throw them

---

[8] The Upjohn Company of Kalamazoo, Michigan, had recently sent a sizeable batch of One-a-Day vitamins.
[9] Limeade.
[10] This was the little gate for pedestrians set within the larger door, also known as the "eye of the needle."

into a fort dungeon until morning. All of which is to say, if you have letters to send, I'll take and mail them before returning to Matrah."[11]

"Why do they think flashlight carriers are up to no good?"

"I'm not totally sure," said Wells. "But I think this tradition may go way back, perhaps to the time when the Portuguese controlled Muscat and Matrah in the seventeenth century. Back then, there was no alternative but to have an open flame as nighttime illumination. The practice has never changed. Besides, Sultan Sayyid Sa'eed is opposed to modernization because he thinks it will cost him a pretty penny. Take the postal service, for instance. The sultan has discovered that the British will do it for free, so he has no incentive to set up his own service."

In the mid-1960s, Dr. Alice Vander Zwaag, a Dutch obstetrician-gynecologist, joined the Women's Hospital team. The hospital staff was then enlarged to about a dozen women. These intelligent and hard-working professional women took most of the additional workload associated with the Women's Hospital.[12] It was a tribute to these caring professionals that the hospital had become known as the As Saada Hospital.

---

[11] The evening gun in Oman towns meant that the city gates at the walls surrounding the towns were closed and traffic could not enter until morning. The flame-lit lamp requirement also continued until Sultan Sayyid Qaboos came to the throne in 1970.

[12] Jeanette Boersma recounts much of this section in her memoir, *Grace in the Gulf*, 100-150.

CHAPTER 21

The Interior of "Old Oman" and Points South

"If we had gone by camel the 100-mile round trip, it would have taken us five days. We left after asr prayers yesterday afternoon, and here we are back again before the fejer'athan prayer this morning! I used to be opposed to allowing automobiles in my dira. Now I'm going to ask the Ingleez to give me one." The door had just slammed shut on the "Camel Age."

Nizwa, the imam, and the interior

Wells was first invited into the interior region of Dakhiliyya in 1941, after he had reopened the main hospital and restarted the Women's Hospital. One day, he received a letter in Arabic from the interior. It said grandiosely that Sulayman bin Hamyar, lord of the Jabal Akhdhar[1] and king of the Nabahina, was inviting Wells to answer a medical emergency to treat a shaykh who had been gored by a bull in Menah. Wells knew Shaykh Sulayman was one of two dominant *tamimas* of the interior. Shaykh Isa bin Salih, whom he had already met, was the other. Wells responded that he would come with his spiritual adviser Dirk Dykstra. This was the first trip Wells had made into the interior while the Agreement of Seeb divided the two halves of Oman.

Wells considered the trip to be nothing out of the ordinary. Others, however, such as the redoubtable explorer Wilfred Thesiger, testified that the Agreement of Seeb had so cut off Oman's interior from

---

[1] The Green Mountains.

Wells and Beth at Bedu under-the-tree home, 1950s (RB)

the coast that traveling to the interior was more difficult in 1941 than it had been for centuries. Thesiger believed that Lt. James Raymond Wellsted, surveyor and adventurer from the East India Company, had experienced an easier time traveling into Oman's interior in the 1830s than any modern traveler ever could. Indeed, Thesiger himself avoided direct contact with the imam and his armed guards because foreigners, whom they suspected were Nasranis, were entirely unwelcome in the imam's domain.

Wells was undaunted. He understood the consequences of grinding poverty and saw nothing sacred or romantic in the struggle of the nomad to survive. Harrison and Thesiger both loved the nobility of spirit that Bedus showed, even during times of extreme privation. Unlike Thesiger, however, Wells and Harrison believed in a better future for the impoverished Bedu. The doctors were modernists and agents of change who foresaw a time—a time as yet unimagined in Arabia—that would offer new opportunities for physical, economic, and spiritual health. It was with this optimism that Wells ventured into the forbidding interior.

Wells and Dykstra left Matrah in the mission's Ford and drove to Rostaq at the end of the rough, barely passable, track. From there, they journeyed by donkey on a narrow trail that led steeply upward to the village of Bilad Sait, an Abriyin village, and thence by a zigzagged donkey path up the steep rock face to almost eight thousand feet. They came down the other side to Tanuf, Shaykh Sulayman bin Hamyar's capital, only to find him absent. He was reported to be at his imposing Birkat al Moz Fort, which commanded the head of the Wadi Sama'il. That fort sat atop a steady flow of stream water gurgling into the *felej*, feeding lush date palm groves and gardens downstream. Much of Shaykh Sulayman's power and influence derived from his control over these well-watered tracts draining the Jabal Akhdhar.

Wells was surprised after their tough ascent to be greeted with no ceremonious welcome and to be served a simple, watery, onion-gruel supper with a little rice. What sort of reception to Tanuf was this? Even prisoners were treated better. He surmised that either the shaykh had not left instructions, or if he had, someone thought to economize on these outsiders who probably did not know Arab customs.

Rather than try to find the shaykh at his fort—which would have required a major detour—Wells and Dirk Dykstra continued by donkey toward Nizwa, the home of the imam. Wells thought he should meet with the imam to ensure safe passage, but he also wanted to meet the imam. En route, armed guards on horseback intercepted Wells and Dykstra. The boys on donkey back that had been escorting them fled when the guards arrived. The boys later said they were sure these foreigners would be killed. As it turned out, the imam's armed retainers politely escorted them to the great round tower of Nizwa Fort where the imam resided and awaited their arrival.

Wells recalled what transpired then. "We were led past crowds of people standing outside the fort, through a large outer gate and a smaller inner gate, and then up two long flights of stairs to the mejlis or audience chamber of the imam. When our eyes became adjusted to the dim light of the interior, we saw a thin old man wearing a large white turban on his head and sitting on a rug at the far end of a rather long room. On his right were a couple of other old men similarly attired, and on either side of him were seated his bodyguard of armed men.

"When we entered the mejlis, he rose to shake our hands, and then his frailness was even more apparent, for he seemed to sway a bit when he was in the upright position and his hand clasp was not strong. He indicated by waving his hand that he wanted me to sit next to him. I protested and said that Rev. Dykstra was my elder and also my spiritual adviser. Then he gestured for Mr. Dykstra to sit on his right and me on his left. Coffee and halwa were next passed and then rose water was sprinkled over us. While this was going on, the imam asked

Possibly Imam Nizwa's mejlis (see endnote 21:1, p. 394)
(*Nizwa, undated,* WWT)

us numerous questions about our purpose in leaving our country to live and work in Muscat.

"When we answered him that Jesus, the Anointed One, whose followers we were, ordered his disciples to go to all nations to teach men his doctrines, heal the sick, and share with all men the good news of the Injil, the imam asked, 'Do you believe that God is One?'

"We said, 'Yes.'

"You are not idolaters or *kafirs*. You are 'People of the Book,'" he concluded. "We believe you are mistaken in some of your doctrines, but we respect you because you fear God, the Praised and Exalted One; therefore, you may proceed in safety in our land. May God give you skill and wisdom to heal the sick man. I will send another guide to take you to your patient."

Thus began a long and happy acquaintance between Wells and this most unusual Muslim spiritual ruler. He lived simply. He and his only wife and daughter lived in two or three rooms in part of the great round tower fort of Nizwa. His only visible possessions were a few worn rugs, two score books, a few mattresses, pillows and blankets, a rifle, a dagger, and a few changes of raiment. He was known to be a just and strict disciplinarian. Murderers and thieves were usually tracked down and punished. Murderers were turned over to the relatives of the murdered person to be dealt with, the means of retribution being modeled in the fashion of the murder.[2] Thieves were usually punished by imprisonment. On more than one occasion, Wells saw prisoners with shackles around their ankles, each fastened by three-foot-long chains to heavy iron balls, sitting with the soldiers at the entrance of the fort, drinking coffee and conversing quite cheerfully.[3]

The imam was kind and sympathetic to the poor, as well as to orphans and widows. During his lifetime, most of the income from the sale of dates from palm gardens belonging to the *awqaf*, or department of religious endowments, was given to the poor and needy. He, himself, was incorruptible and remained a poor man until the day of his death.

To the Sharqiyya and back

On another occasion, Wells and Qumber toured briefly into the interior region of the Sharqiyya, where he had previously treated its elderly paramount shaykh, Isa bin Ali. Wells discovered this region, and its peoples were not as openly hospitable to outsiders as those who lived farther north and in the Jabal Akhdhar. Having treated a number of patients in the town of Adam, Wells said to the shaykh that they would be leaving soon.

To which the shaykh responded, "You will leave when I say you can leave."

Given that he had come on a mission of mercy, it shocked Wells to be under the village equivalent of house arrest. He was being repaid with arrogance. He and Qumber continued to treat patients in clinics in the next days. Among his many patients was the mother of the shaykh. She recovered rapidly and was most grateful to Wells for her care and cure, at which point the shaykh's attitude became more cordial. He then exercised traditional Arab hospitality toward his visitors. Wells concluded that he had been anxious about his mother's health. When she recovered, the shaykh's biggest worry was lifted, and

---

[2] See endnote 21:2, p. 395.
[3] Although there were judges (qadis), most legal issues were decided by tribal shaykhs at this time. Both the interior of Oman and the coast were administered based on a tribally decentralized system. This meant that a person was imprisoned at the command of the sultan, the imam, or a tribal shaykh. Prison terms were indefinitely long, but prisoners were released when leaders agreed the prisoner had "paid his dues," providing his shaykh would vouch for him (akin to serving as probation officer).

he could function normally again. This incident reminded Wells that mothers are very important in Arab society, regardless of the status of women generally.

Wells and Qumber bid the Sharqiyya farewell and returned to the coast via the Wadi Dhayka, where Wells wanted to visit other communities. The donkey trip was arduous. Having stayed over in Mazara, where its shaykh was always hospitable, they ventured the last leg down the wadi through a deep canyon. The Wadi Dhayka was one of a few in Oman where a stream of water flowed year round. They picked their way slowly around larger and larger boulders that had been carried downstream by flash floods over the centuries. Traveling by donkey was difficult as they had to surmount boulders as large as army trucks. It would have been impossible to drive a vehicle up this wadi. It was difficult to believe these huge boulders had been washed down the canyon, but how else could they have gotten there?

As the day progressed, Wells noticed the sky toward the interior showed a heavy gray color, changing to nearly black clouds. Their steeds were struggling slowly through the last great canyon defile known as the "Devil's Gap," which had sheer rock walls rising about one thousand feet on each side.

Wells turned and asked their donkey-boy guide, "What happens when it rains in the mountains?"

"The stream rises," was the nonchalant reply.

"How high does it rise?"

"See that crevice up there?" said the speaker, pointing forty feet upward to a crack in the wall face where the bole of a lonely date palm tree jutted out crazily. "The water often goes that high." Wells noticed that below this ledge all plants had been scoured away by earlier floods.

In the time they had stopped to converse, the stream seemed to have risen an inch or two.

"Where can we go to get out of reach above an oncoming flood?" asked Wells with some urgency in his tone of voice.

"A little farther down the canyon, there is a place the donkeys and we can climb the wall pretty high," came the answer.

"Let's hurry, Qumber!" said Wells.

They reached the spot known to the donkey boy and climbed and dragged their donkeys upward until they could climb no higher, perhaps fifty feet above the canyon floor.

The flood began slowly. Then a surge looking like a syrup of oily water snaked over the flat rocks on the canyon floor. More water gushed

Wadi Dhayka, ca. 1960 (WWT)

by with plants, twigs, and vegetal debris. Soon the water brought big branches and whole trees. Besides sand and gravel, the water was pushing small rocks downstream. Then with a sudden roar, the full tsunami-like flood hit. The noise of the floodwaters drowned out everything else. Large boulders bounced downstream grinding against each other unseen below the surface.

Wells, Qumber, their companion, and donkeys tucked tightly into a shelf at the last bottleneck of Wadi Dhayka before the gorge opened out onto the coastal plain. Flood waters crested higher here than anywhere else because of the bottleneck. As they watched, the flash flood peaked a few feet lower than the shelf on which they were perched. At that point, the great volume of water became almost silent as it rushed by. Suddenly it was over. The crest passed and the flood level receded steadily.

As the waters swirled below them, Wells was reminded of the *Daily Light* book of devotions in his shirt pocket. He took it out and turned to the readings for the day. One was from the Psalms. It said, "Lead me to the rock that is higher than I, for you have been my refuge."[4] He read another passage to Qumber, "Thou art my rock and my salvation."[5]

[4] Psalm 61:2.
[5] Psalm 62:2.

Sur, sailing ships' home port, ca. 1952 (WWT)

They sat for a while as if in disbelief at their deliverance from certain death.

Unexpectedly, Qumber blurted out, "I wish to be baptized."

Wells replied, "Are you sure you want to do this?"

"Yes," came the reply. "I am sure."

Several Sundays later, Qumber al Mas was baptized by Rev. Dykstra, enlarging the small circle of native church members in Muscat.[6]

South to Sur and Ja'alan

Always a poor sailor, in the fall of 1941, Wells went by sailing ship with Qumber, Merook, Walook, and others to Sur, located near Oman's southern tip that jutted into the Arabian Sea. Sur had been a major center of Omani shipping and international trade for centuries because it had the best natural harbor at the toe of the Arabian Peninsula. Although the weather was very hot, this was the time of year that men who pursued the long-distance sailing trade returned home to refit their ships, relax, and make ready for their next voyage. While Wells and his entourage were in Sur, the wali provided him a house for lodging and for doing clinical work. The people eagerly welcomed the team and lined up for medical attention. Together, Wells and his colleagues performed about three hundred operations during their short stay.

Wells returned to Sur two years later. During this visit, he received an invitation from the amir of Bilad Beni Bu Ali. Wells was told he should come as soon as possible because the amir was ill. Hastily Wells,

---

[6] See endnote 21:6, p. 395.

Qumber, and Walook mounted camels for the trip inland. Wells was amazed at the size of the oasis and the hospitality of the amir, a soft-spoken man who evinced the epitome of courtesy and good manners. This surprised Wells because the men of Ja'alan who visited Muscat were wild and boisterous. The amir was anxious to make Wells feel at home and wanted to carry on long discussions on diverse questions like: "What keeps an airplane up in the air?" and "Why should a war in Europe affect innocent people in Ja'alan who do not care who wins so long as they have rice to eat?"

While the war raged outside Oman, internal rivalries were a constant reminder that war in some form was not far away. Writing from Bilad Beni Bu Ali while visiting the amir, Wells was again reminded of this reality:[7]

> Amir Ali rules only two-thirds of all Ja'alan, the tribe of Beni Bu Ali. A rival tribe, Beni Bu Hasn, has their own shaykh. These two tribes keep up an interminable feud. The territory of Beni Bu Ali borders upon that of Beni Bu Hasn. On the outer limits of each tribe's territory stand high towers and from them snipers keep a close lookout for a chance to pick off members of the rival tribe that may venture into range. All day long as we worked, and sometimes even at night, we would hear the rifle shots and at times bullets would whistle overhead. We were assured it was all in fun and that no one ever got hurt. Judging from the number of wounded men we treated, we decided that one need not join the army medical corps in order to bind up wounded soldiers.

A return to the Wadi Sama'il and Nizwa

In 1944 Wells went with Qumber and other hospital assistants to Jinah in the Wadi Sama'il. They were hosted by Shaykh Hamid bin Hamid al Rushdi, whose people kept them very busy with operations and treatments. The imam received word that Wells was in Jinah and requested he come to Nizwa. In short order, Wells and Qumber mounted camels and proceeded to Birkat al Moz at the head of the Wadi Sama'il, where stood the home base and imposing fort of Shaykh Sulayman bin Hamyar, whom Wells was getting to know better. Wells carried out a number of eye operations at Nizwa and was about to leave for Tanuf (Shaykh Sulayman's traditional capital) when the imam requested a consultation with him.

---

[7] See endnote 21:7, p. 395.

Shaykh Hamid bin Hamid and son, 1949 (JK)

Upon arriving at the imam's mejlis, Wells discovered the imam wished to discuss world affairs. The ever-important coffee ritual accompanied by Omani halwa came first. Wells, being the only non-Arab in the imam's reception room, discovered that the imam—although concerned about world affairs—saw the world quite differently than did the European Allies. The imam believed it was God's plan for the *kafirs* to destroy each other in this war. His concern was that it was not fair of God to deprive Omanis of their supply of rice from India as a consequence of this World War. His question was age old: Why do the innocent suffer in the process of God fulfilling His plan for humankind?

Wells did not try to provide a theological rebuttal. He may have been troubled by questions regarding "God's plan" for the world too. He personally could not know the "mind of God," and he did not want to get into a "my God says versus your God says" debate. The gospel of love to which Wells subscribed did not fit wartime, much less the conditions of total war. War was more a sign of human failure in applying Christian principles to world affairs. Wells was a New Testament Christian rather than an Old Testament one. (Is an "Old Testament Christian" oxymoronic, or worse, heretical?) Wells was not a declared pacifist; he likely subscribed, regretfully, to the idea of a "just war," then emerging among theologians and philosophers in the West. Besides, he was so busy relieving suffering among Omanis, it was neither the right time nor the right place to explore such theological nuances and details.

"Yes," he said to the imam. "Britain and France are fighting Germany. The United States has also been drawn into the war with Germany and Japan. It is not entirely a question of one 'Christian' nation versus another 'Christian' nation, or a 'Christian' nation fighting a 'heathen' nation, even though it is tempting to think in simple nationalistic terms."

Wells, like most Americans, thought of the United States as a Christian nation then, although he might have had his doubts about Britain. Certainly, Germany's Adolf Hitler was not a Christian leader, nor was the Nazi political system Christian, even though Germany was the Christian land of Luther, Bach, Buxtehude, Barth, and Bonhoeffer (the opposition of this last pastor to Hitler came at the price of his life). Japan, by definition, focused on its own non-Christian religious tradition. Wells believed the imam's parochial view did not comprehend that this war was, indeed, worldwide and would consume everyone, Muslims included, if so allowed.

Wells said he was sure Britain and the United States were not fighting this war only to protect their own narrow self-interests (although they certainly had clear self-interests). Undoubtedly, Germany and Japan both had postwar plans for the colonial possessions of the British Empire, and Japan had already appropriated America's Asian empire (even though Americans thought of their empire through a lens of "American exceptionalism"; that is, it was America's destiny to rule territories like the Philippines for their own good). This was a war against Germany and Japan to insure freedom of all people from domination by these two aggressors. Wells suggested all this to the imam. He further suggested Britain and the United States were fighting for Arab freedom as well and that it was likely that Arabs would be enslaved to one or the other enemy if Germany and/or Japan won the war.

Wells noted, "This was too incredible a thought for the imam to digest, and the meeting broke up soon afterward."

Wells continued by camel to Tanuf, where Shaykh Sulayman bin Hamyar had invited him to come once a year to the Jabal Akhdhar (the Green Mountains) to treat his people during the hottest summer months.

That evening, dinner was served by a poised, articulate woman, who turned out to be Sulayman bin Hamyar's wife. She said to Wells,

"Was not your father a doctor here before you? My mother told me a doctor of the same name as you came here long ago, before the Agreement of Seeb cut off our communication with Muscat. We remember him as a very kind man and an excellent hakeem. In any case, we welcome you and hope you will return many times."

"Yes," said Wells, "my father was a doctor here in the time of Sultan Sayyid Faisal bin Turki, before the time of the present imam. My father was in Oman only a few years, but in that time, he came to the interior several times to treat people." Wells was amazed that memories still existed of his father and of those times more than three decades earlier. It was heartwarming.

The prospect of a regular return to the Jabal Akhdhar was a happy one, but there were always too many opportunities and invitations to take advantage of. Wells juggled visits to the imam—now requesting medicines in Nizwa—with visits to the towns of the Batinah coast, including Sohar and beyond, and trips south to Dhofar, Sur, and Ja'alan. He also needed personal rest and recuperation away from the constant needs of the Omanis and the unremitting pressure of keeping the mission hospitals growing and functioning, as well as time to update his medical expertise.

CHAPTER 22

Headwinds and Tailwinds of War

Several times during the past year I have asked myself whether I was doing my duty by staying here. At times, the call came very strongly to volunteer for war work.

Medical shortages

World War II brought even greater hardship than expected to Wells' medical work in Oman and to the Thoms family. Several years later, Wells told his new missionary colleague, Rev. Jay Kapenga, about the impact of the war on his practice:

> I knew I would to have to scramble to maintain the medical work in the face of wartime shortages. I could hardly imagine what was going to happen when Germany invaded Poland, and then the Dunkirk disaster and its aftermath in Britain. Medical supplies were needed for the war effort. This made it more difficult to purchase supplies for civilians on the open market. A further complication was that ships that normally would carry our supplies were either seconded for the war effort or torpedoed. When Japan got into the war, medical supplies and drugs from Asia were cut off. After Pearl Harbor the US became fully committed to fighting Japan and Germany. Our supplies from the US dwindled to almost nothing. Reordering supplies was a

nightmare because postal censorship slowed the international postal system down, and civilian telegraph service was subject to long delays.

When India went on wartime footing in response to Britain's promise of India's postwar independence if it joined the war effort, we found things even more difficult. We had to do business with smugglers and the black market to keep going. I was desperate for medical supplies and for food and drugs to treat our very sick patients. We had to improvise in so many ways.

Wartime tensions spread widely. Food, particularly rice from India on which Omanis depended entirely, arrived in the suq irregularly at inflated prices. BI ships were commandeered to transport troops and war materiel. Consequently, Oman's wooden fleet of *baghalas* and other large sailing vessels could smuggle irregular supplies of rationed foods like rice and sugar into Oman from India. Non-food commodities of all kinds were very scarce. The war yielded handsome profits to the sailing-ship owners. The war probably prolonged the life of the sailing fleet into the postwar era when it no longer made financial sense to build new, large sailing vessels for the long-distance trades.

When he realized that World War II was going to continue for years, Wells debated with himself whether he should volunteer for US military service or stay in Oman. Deeply conflicted, he summarized his thoughts by the end of 1942:[1]

> Several times during the past year I have asked myself whether... I was doing my duty by staying here. At times, the call came very strongly to volunteer for war work. Thousands of my medical colleagues in America and among them several of my professors have volunteered for overseas work and many of them have already arrived in Egypt, Iraq, and Persia to take up their new tasks.
>
> In India, many British and American medical missionaries are serving with the forces.[2] What right did I have to remain in this quiet, out-of-the-way place when so many others of my profession were serving on hospital ships, in field hospitals, and with ambulance corps?

---

[1] "Matrah and Muscat Medical Report for 1943," unpublished typescript.
[2] His own brother-in-law, Dr. Galen Scudder, CMO of the Ranipet (Tamilnadu) hospital, did so.

This hospital serves an area bigger than Michigan, with a population greater than Grand Rapids. I don't believe anyone would suggest, even in the face of the greatest need elsewhere, the United States would send its surgeons overseas and close its [own] hospitals.

I realize what it would have meant if the [Mission] hospital had not been open during the past year. Almost 10,000 patients suffering from malaria, dysentery, trachoma, leg ulcers, and other ravaging diseases would not have been treated. Over 400 patients, some of whom came from a long distance for treatment in the hospital, would not have [had] hospital care.

I know that the ones who came with intestinal obstruction, severe traumatic hemorrhage, acute mastoiditis, strangulated hernia, and gangrene of the foot would have died if the hospital had been closed. Over 60 cataract cases would not have received sight. About 200 patients with trichiasis and twelve with bladder stones would have had to endure terrific pain for another year. These are the things that convince me that my duty lies here.

There were no newspapers, magazines, or radio stations in Oman. Newspapers and magazines from abroad arrived irregularly, long outdated. Shortwave radio reception was from poor to nonexistent. Wells' receiver was extremely good at intercepting Morse code from ships and at picking up "intergalactic" whines and shrill squeals. Their friend Mr. Toprani, the merchant, had better radio reception high up in his fourth-story aerie on the seafront. He loyally penciled a summary for Wells of each evening's BBC news broadcast during the war years. His notes often required further decoding because the news accounts pressed the limits of his English.[3]

World War II also put stress on family life. Wells and Beth sent their children to Highclerc School in Kodaikanal, South India, the boarding school they had attended as children before World War I. Nancy, Peter, and Norman traveled several thousand miles to and from their boarding school, journeying by the wartime's infrequent and crowded ships and packed Indian trains The charcoal-burning buses that took them up and down the Kodai mountain were equipped with

---

[3] It was entirely understandable that Mr. Toprani's notes on BBC news broadcasts would include the occasional typographical error. It took time and imagination to make sense of Toprani's famous "flea of Hess" note. The flight of Rudolph Hess to Scotland remained a puzzler for days. Any source of humor was welcome in the worrisome World War II years.

rear-mounted gas generators that replaced scarce gasoline supplies with low-grade, combustible fuel.

In "normal" years, the children would arrive in Matrah at the end of October and return to school in India in early January. In the late summer of 1940, Nancy (just turned nine) and Peter (seven) enrolled in Kodai's Highclerc Boarding School. Norman joined them when he turned seven in January 1942. Each would see their parents twice a year, for no longer than three or four months in total; the other eight or nine months they spent with their classmates under the supervision of school housemothers and fathers. In addition to "winter break," between late October and early January, the children would be reunited with their parents for five or six weeks in the summer when Beth and Wells would arrive to vacation at Dar Es Salaam (their cottage). Beth would stay longer than Wells, who had to return to service in the Matrah hospital.

World War II was a disruptive problem. Travel arrangements were so difficult to make that the children stayed in Kodaikanal during winter break for several years consecutively, beginning in 1942. Beth and Wells always arrived in Kodai by Nancy's birthday in September. Beth would either stay through Christmas or make a return trip to place another child in boarding.

In late 1944, having retired from her Baghdad Girls School, grandmother May Thoms came to Kodaikanal to look after the children so that Beth could be with Wells in Oman until after Christmas when Beth would return to leave Lowey in the boarding school after her seventh birthday in February 1945.

Mail from India was slow, made even slower by the wartime inspection and censorship of all letters. Wells and Beth had no idea what their children were experiencing on a day-to-day basis or even where they were. In the spring of 1942, Wells and Beth received a much-delayed terse letter from the school reporting that their children had been evacuated to safety from an anticipated Japanese naval invasion of southern India. Like Singapore and Burma before them, India was virtually undefended, so this was a potent fear.

When Wells, Beth, and Lowey arrived in Kodaikanal in the late summer of 1942, they got the details that the postal censors had clipped from letters sent home. Nancy, Peter, and Norman had been sent on a three-day train trip to Miraj and then on to Panhala near Kohlapur, Maharashtra, on the west coast of India. Responsibility for their care had been dumped on already overworked and bemused missionaries of other Christian denominations. Wells and Beth were besieged with the children's account of the evacuation.

"Yes," the children reported, breathlessly breaking in on one another to tell their parents what fun it had been. "We had no pencils, no books, no teachers for three fun weeks in Panhala!"

"Kodai merchants and other men marched on Bendy Field[4] with sticks for pretend guns. Even though they didn't have any uniforms or equipment, everybody was really excited!"

"The high school boys helped dig trenches below the high school boys' dormitory, and we played war in them. We even invented our own secret message codes."

"We had air-raid drills and blackouts."

"We had such fun in Panhala climbing the banyan trees and chasing the monkeys. We had a wonderful time."

"Norman broke his arm when he fell off a roof and they put his arm in a splint with bandages. But his arm didn't heal right. Dr. Goheen in Miraj rebroke it and set it again. It's okay now. A couple of kids who were watching fainted, but I didn't." As the kids revealed this deep, dark secret, Wells very solicitously inspected both of Norman's arms.

Finally, it became clear the Japanese had overextended themselves trying to create the Greater East Asian Co-Prosperity Sphere. The Japanese invasion fleet retreated to the east side of the Bay of Bengal never again to mount a full invasion of India. The school reassembled its students and teachers and resumed operation.[5]

From 1941 to 1945, the children stayed in Kodaikanal throughout the school year. During the summers, Beth traveled to Kodai with Lowey until she was old enough to enter dormitory life. Because of the very irregular ship connections between India and the Gulf, Wells stayed in Matrah most of the year to keep the hospitals functioning.

In late 1945, booking sea travel was particularly difficult. The children arrived in Matrah on Christmas Day, having been looked after by a doctor friend on India's west coast. They had to return to school two weeks later. This was a precious time together.

With wartime shortages of gas and tires, Wells and Beth decided on a family-affirming medical tour by donkey from Matrah to Afi. They needed six donkeys for the family, several more for medical and food supplies and camping gear, and even more for Qumber, the

---

[4] The soccer field for Highclerc School.
[5] Block, "The Big Scare of 1942."

hospital staff, and the donkey men. Lowey, as the youngest child, not yet eight years old, feared falling off her donkey as it trotted along, and she soon lagged behind the ones urged on by her brothers. Eyes closed, she recited again and again Psalm 23, with special emphasis on "even though I walk through the valley of the shadow death, Thou art with me!" She soon caught up with the rest of her siblings and breathed a prayer of thanksgiving.

All too soon, the children had to board the ship bound for school in India. Wells and Beth felt marooned.

One afternoon, Wells and Beth went to Saih al Malih beach, swam, and collected fresh oysters from the rocks. As they sat watching the sunset, Wells gave voice to their loneliness, "It is just not fair or right to be separated from our children this long. The censors hold up the mail, so we are way behind knowing what they are experiencing. Loving and nurturing them at such a distance doesn't feel right. If this is the way things are going to be every year, perhaps we should not return to Arabia. Maybe we should apply for a position in home missions in the United States where we wouldn't be separated from our children."

"I agree, Wells," said Beth. "You know how difficult I've found it to send our children off to school, even though that is how we grew up. It is so extremely difficult to sit here not knowing what they are doing and experiencing. I just want to see, hear, and hug them!" She put her head on his shoulder in mute desperation amid tears of love and loneliness.

Reflecting on the war years sometime later, Wells said to Jay Kapenga,

> I rattled around in the big doctor's house at the hospital while Beth and the kids were gone. I didn't have anyone to talk to except Shembi, our cook. I couldn't supervise him closely because I was at the hospital so much, and he became lackadaisical about cooking. Once he must have dozed off while baking bread.[6] The bread looked pretty good, but the loaf was hard as a rock! It was inedible, except to make into breadcrumbs, I suppose. I was so overworked, frustrated, and lonely, I threw it at him! It couldn't

---

[6] There was no commercial bakery that made yeast-raised bread. Arabs and others ate only flat breads. White flour, when available, was not very good for baking yeast-raised bread and came from the soft wheat grown in South Asia or the Middle East. Loaves did not rise high. Yeast for baking bread had to be ordered from abroad and, long expired, it would lose much of its leavening power.

hurt him because it was mostly air. It surprised him more than anything.

I had this big house, and there were others caught here because of the war who didn't have housing. One of them was Mr. Pavlicek, from Czechoslovakia, who ran a fish-processing business, whom the British declared to be an enemy alien. He was not an enemy, a spy, or a soldier. He was just a very small-time businessman who had only a decrepit room to stay in while he was stuck in Matrah. I offered him a room in the house and food in return for him repairing and maintaining our hospital equipment. This arrangement allowed for a degree of sociability and conversation.[7] He was very well mannered and convivial and a good problem solver.

Medical matters always pressed in, sometimes demanding unique innovations in this time of scarcity. As Wells recounted:

Paul Harrison discovered infected ulcers healed readily by spreading applesauce on them. But, of course, they didn't heal overnight with this treatment. When supplies of cod liver oil became scarce, I thought shark liver oil could substitute as a source of vitamin A, and D. Pavlicek suggested buying shark livers at Matrah's seafront fish market, putting them in 5-gallon tins on the roof of our house, and letting the heat of the sun "cook" the oil out of the livers. This worked pretty well. The oil would rise to the surface, where we could skim it off. The applesauce and shark liver oil shrank ulcers, so healthy skin could grow anew. Those ulcers gave off a terrible smell, though. Only Nubi, who had no sense of smell, could treat ulcers hour after hour, day after day. We had lots of ulcer cases because so many people were undernourished then, and the ulcers were associated with fairly advanced malnutrition.

For the remainder of World War II, Wells abandoned making medical tours up the Batinah. As he explained to Jay, "Fuel was too expensive. Our car tires had worn completely through, and the car's motor had seen much better days. Once, it went over the side of the road and crashed. Oman did not have a body shop to remove dings,

---

[7] Others with whom Wells communed included Royal Navy personnel trapped on their non-air-conditioned salvage tug in the Muscat harbor for half a year.

HMS Salviola, *salvage tug, 1946* (WWT)

dents, and scrapes—but these were only cosmetic problems. During the war, no tires or auto parts were available in the suq."

SS *Dahpu* and HMS *Salviola*

After a pause, Wells continued his wartime narrative to Jay:

In 1943 a Japanese submarine launched a torpedo into Muscat's port from the open sea, straight through the narrow gap between the British consulate and Fort Jalali, hitting the SS *Dahpu*. It must have been high tide. No one knew torpedoes could be aimed so accurately. Everyone thought the *Dahpu* was secure deep inside Muscat's harbor, but the ship sank where she was anchored. The harbor was a mess. For three years, the ship's masts protruded above water, reminding everyone of that fateful day. Finally in 1946 a Royal Navy salvage ship arrived to raise the *Dahpu*, tow it out of the harbor, and let it sink again out on the open sea.

The salvage tug, the HMS *Salviola*, was configured for divers using old-style helmets, cumbersome diving suits, pressurized air hoses, and lead-soled shoes to keep the divers upright under water. The crew worked for hours at a time under water. Their job was to refloat sunken ships just long enough to move them to deep water. The divers had to be able to work at considerable depths, where the water was cold, and then return to the tremendous heat at the surface. They labored under great stress.

Beth was away in India with the children through the hot summer, and she stayed in India through the Christmas season. I couldn't get passage on a ship immediately after WWII ended, so I stayed in Matrah.

The weather was steam-bath hot in summer but delightful in winter. I invited the *Salviola*'s master to occupy a bedroom in the house while the *Dahpu* was being raised. I also invited some of his officers to occupy other empty bedrooms. This gave them some relief from heat stress and from depression, since the house was big and slightly cooler than the ship, and they could walk around on dry land as much as they wanted. The remaining crew would have more room onboard the ship as a result.

When the whole crew went nearly "stir crazy" from being on board the small vessel too long, I invited them to the hospital for volleyball and tea. In the bargain, I found them more than willing to give blood, because we had no blood bank in Oman. Ultimately another salvage vessel arrived to raise the sunken merchant ship and tow it out to sea to let it sink in deep water, out of harm's way.

Unintended consequences

One benefit of the war came from motorized military vehicles arriving in the Arabian Gulf. At war's end, the US Army Air Force that staffed the Masirah Island air base was directed to sell off their equipment at a discounted price to the sultan. The sultan, in turn, could decide whom he deemed worthy to receive the limited supply of surplus trucks and jeeps. Few paved roads existed in Oman, so four-wheel-drive vehicles were required to negotiate the unpaved,

Exit the camel and donkey age, 1941 (WWT)

Enter the motorized age—WWII surplus, ca. 1947 (WWT)

unimproved tracks. Motor vehicles would soon enough replace camels and donkeys, but that was still in the future.

The sultan offered Wells a war-surplus Dodge Power Wagon weapons carrier for five hundred dollars. Wells accepted, thinking it came in fully working order. When he took delivery, he discovered it did not come with tires. These he had to purchase from the black market in Kuwait.[8] Despite this ignominious beginning, this rugged vehicle served well for the period immediately following the war.

Wells soon observed that the sultan had discovered how to turn his largesse with war-surplus vehicles to political advantage. Sultan Sayyid Sa'eed gave a war-surplus jeep to Shaykh Sulayman bin Hamyar of the Jabal Akhdar as a gift. A prestigious vehicle, the only one in the imam's territory of the interior, it required expensive gas and lubricants. Paying for the upkeep of the jeep threatened to bankrupt the shaykh. Yet the shaykh could not dispose of this precious memento from the sultan either. It was a mechanical "white elephant," that is, a method of gifting invented by unknown potentates in an earlier age.

Traffic to the hospital also increased in surprising ways. Shaykhs from Abu Dhabi, along with Shaykhs Shakhbut and Sa'eed bin Maktoum bin Hasher Al Maktoum of Dubai, showed up unannounced in Matrah, having driven their war-surplus jeeps all the way from those northern ports to get medical treatment at the Matrah hospital.

Later, Shaykh Shakhbut of Abu Dhabi invited Wells to open a hospital either in Abu Dhabi or Buraimi.[9] Wells noted that these surprise

---

[8] These purchases were arranged by Wells' brother-in-law, Dr. Lewis R. Scudder Jr.
[9] Owing to his mission's financial constraints, Wells could not do this. Instead,

Dubai's Shaykh Sa'eed bin Maktoum bin Hasher Al Maktoum, Matrah, 1947 (WTC)

Dubai shaykh's Jeep, Matrah hospital, 1947 (WTC)

visits by the rulers of the Trucial Oman unsettled Sultan Sayyid Sa'eed, for he seemed to realize motorized transportation opened his domain to potential invasion from the north. He recognized that he might need more protection from the British to hold onto his kingdom—an unpleasant thought. Motorized transport changed the reach of every monarch in the region.

---

he introduced the shaykh to the Drs. Kennedy at the Buraimi Oasis, and the Kennedys started a hospital through their mission connections.

CHAPTER 23

Coastal Epidemics

I got up this morning to come to work. It was just a mild fever last night; I thought maybe it was a recurrence of malaria. This morning, I had a high fever. I'm tired. When I tried to walk, I couldn't. My knees wouldn't hold me up. People are calling it "kundoo."

A modern Sinbad story

Wells and the al Mas brothers—Mohammed, Mubarak, and Qumber—wedged into the heavily loaded Model T and headed northwest.[1] The paved road ended on the outskirts of Matrah, and then the sand-and-gravel road ran on to the Ruwi customs gate, where a rutted desert trail began. The car lumbered through the customs gate at Ruwi and plunged into the desert. When the trail petered out, they headed for the beach, crossed the sand dunes on deflated tires, and nosed onto the hard-packed beach sand. They whizzed up the coast on reinflated tires to receive a hearty welcome from the people of Seeb. Most of the residents of Seeb were subsistence fishermen who also cultivated seaside date gardens.

As the medical team returned to Matrah from a successful day at Seeb, they were relaxed and convivial. Conversationally, Wells asked Qumber, "How did you and your brothers come to work in Matrah?"

---

[1] Wells made medical sorties of short duration up the Batinah coast until WWII when there was a shortage of tires and parts for the car. See also, endnote 23:1, p. 396.

"I came because my brothers already worked for Dr. Harrison. They wanted me with them because I got mixed up in mischief in Bahrain where we lived for a while. Originally, of course, our father came from Baluchistan, across the water, opposite Oman."[2]

"Why did he leave Baluchistan?"

"Pirates kidnapped my oldest brother in Baluchistan. My father was determined to get him back and moved to the 'Pirate Coast' to find him. My father became a pearl diver. He was employed by a tyrannical *nakhoda*, who treated all his divers and rope tenders like slaves. Eventually, my father led a successful mutiny and took the pearling ship to Bandar Abbas in Persia. They left the captain for dead, but he did not die. Somehow, he found his way back to Dubai. When my father returned to Dubai to collect his wife and family, he was arrested. Mutiny is the worst crime on the Pirate Coast, and my father was going to be executed. His friends helped him escape.

"My father said to his friends, 'On me is responsibility for getting up into the window of the fort prison when the tide is high at midnight and jumping into the sea with all my irons attached. On you is responsibility for fishing me out of the deep water quickly, for the irons will sink me.' That night, at high tide, there was a splash. Men in the waiting boat went over the side, hauled the man with the irons up to the surface, and rowed him to a sailing ship headed for Bahrain. My mother was already aboard. Two days later, they were in Bahrain, where my father became a pearl diver again."

"Did your father ever find your oldest brother?"

"No. It was not the will of God."

"How did you come to work in the hospital in Matrah?"

"My brother Mubarak received schooling at the Mission School in Bahrain. He was mischievous; perhaps the British administrator of Bahrain sent him there to learn to behave. He learned enough to work as a 'house boy' in a British household, and he traveled with a British family to India and to Kashmir. When he returned to Bahrain, he got a job in the mission hospital and liked it. Dr. Harrison hired and trained him. When Hakeem Harrison came to Oman, he brought Mubarak with him. Mubarak learned to inject Salvarsan intravenously, almost without pain, and other techniques, and he learned enough English to become a good compounder."[3]

---

[2] Until 1959, Gwadar, on the Baluchistan coast, was an exclave of Oman. BI ships made courtesy calls there and carried Baluchis to Oman and up the Gulf.

[3] Pharmacist.

"My other brother, Mohammed, became a pearl diver like our father, but he started as a rope puller, which meant that he was paid less than the divers. He had bad luck. In his first pearling season, a big storm sank many boats. My brother was one of the few who survived. He was sleeping on deck, and everyone below was drowned. He and three others swam on the surface and grabbed a floating spar. One by one, each of his shipmates weakened and went to 'the mercy of God.' My brother was about to do the same. At the moment of his death, he was lifted onto a boat, and someone forced hot tea between his lips. Soon he was 'a son of Adam' again. Mohammed never returned to pearling, even though there were no other good jobs. Some years ago, he joined Mubarak here at the hospital. As you know, he is good at engine and auto repair and electrical work, too.

"I had a job as interpreter to the British consul in Bahrain. The consul was a 'big man' in town. I was responsible for caring for his horses, and I could do many tricks on those beauties. He abruptly left Bahrain because of some questionable business dealings. He left me with forty thousand rupees to keep for him—which I did. He wanted me to go to Baghdad as a reward, but my father said no.

"Then I got a job with the shaykh of Bahrain. But there was a palace revolution, and the shaykh's son replaced his father, so I lost my job.[4] After that, I got a job with a lesser shaykh. I swear I did nothing very wrong, but before long, I was in jail." Qumber pondered this memory silently and then continued.

"My brothers arranged with the shaykh for my release, and I came to Oman so I could work in the hospital, too.[5] Except for one eight-month trip with Dr. Storm when we traveled around the interior of Arabia, I have been here in Oman ever since."[6]

Smallpox on the Batinah coast

Wells' medical sorties ranged farther and farther up the Batinah. On every trip up the coast, he took smallpox vaccine and vaccinated as

---

[4] Traditional leadership titles were used in Sa'udi Arabia and Bahrain. Abdal Aziz bin Sa'ud was first called a shaykh, then imam, then amir, then finally king. Leadership titles in Bahrain progressed from shaykh to hakim to king. Investing Western monarchical title on the ruler also implied an aristocracy with more extensive rights to property than in traditional Arab society.

[5] Harrison, *Doctor in Arabia*, 77-90. This account is also supplemented by Harrison, *Before Oil*, 159-61.

[6] An account of this trip is in Janet Storm Pengelley's biography of her father, *William Harold Storm*, and *Neglected Arabia* 176 (1937), 3-14.

many people as possible. As far as Wells knew, there had been no epidemic of smallpox for more than a decade. His biggest disappointment came at Khor Fakkan, an exclave of the emirate of Sharjah, just across the border from the emirate of Fujairah. Wells had never previously tried to vaccinate the residents of Khor Fakkan, so they were ripe for a big epidemic that could wipe out a third or more of their population.

The wali of Khor Fakkan was coldly polite to Wells' offer of free treatment for his people. When Wells asked if he could vaccinate them against smallpox, the wali turned negative. Wells assured him that vaccination was a medical treatment well recognized in Arab tradition. Recalling the book he had been given by the Pakistani pearl merchant, Wells pointed out that none other than the great Islamic physician-philosopher, Abu Sina,[7] recommended vaccination, not only for people but also for protecting sheep from anthrax. The wali was unmoved. Finally, he muttered, "All is in God's hands, and it is not for mankind to play God," and waved his hand in dismissal. No further argument would change his mind. Wells reluctantly retraced his route to Matrah with his hospital team.

When they reached the Batinah plain near the Wadi Sama'il, the team encountered a man staggering along the road, scarcely able to put one foot in front of the other. Something was desperately wrong. His gait suggested an alcoholic; but how likely was it that he could be inebriated at midday?[8]

The Model T pulled up beside the man, who looked at them with fever-glazed eyes. They sat him on the running board, checked his vital signs, and noted his symptoms. The patient's fever was high, and he had red spots in his mouth that were turning to sores. There was no question: he had smallpox, and if something was not done and soon, he could become "smallpox Harry," spreading the disease along the coast.[9]

Wells said to Qumber, Mubarak, and Mohammed, "Quickly. We'll build a small hut in the thicket over there. That will give him

---

[7] Ibn Sina (or Abu Ali Sina) was the Persian polymath and physician who lived between 980 and 1037 AD.

[8] This story is true, but I have inserted it earlier in Wells' Oman medical career than it occurred. Wells never knew what medical problems villagers would present when he and his staff toured outside Matrah.

[9] An allusion to "typhoid Mary," an Irish immigrant to the US who transmitted typhoid to others in her occupation as a cook. Mary remained presymptomatic of typhoid herself, in contrast to this man, who could transmit smallpox only after he had contracted the disease.

shade. We'll make a bed for him and give him food. He must stay there in complete isolation for the next several weeks until the scabs on his body fall off, the pus dries up, and his temperature returns to normal. We will instruct the shaykh of the next village to bring him food and water and leave everything outside his hut. No one may visit inside the hut under any circumstance. We have no idea where he contracted smallpox. We'll do the best we can to contain this outbreak." Once they had constructed a rough lean-to, Wells turned to the man.

"Brother, you are very sick. Your illness can spread to other people. It is not written on your forehead that other people should die because of you. We built you a small *barasti* right here. You must stay inside. People will bring you water and food that they will leave at the doorway. While you have fever, you may not have coffee with visitors. You must stay inside, and they must stay outside. When your fever is gone and you are better, you can rejoin your friends and family. They and your shaykh will thank God you followed our instructions." The man indicated he understood. Before further conversation was possible, he collapsed on the pallet inside the little hut and lost consciousness.

"We must vaccinate everybody in nearby villages because we don't know where this man came from, where he contracted the disease, or if he came ashore from a boat. With luck, very few people will get smallpox, and if we are extremely lucky, there may be only a few deaths." What Wells did not say to the al Mas brothers was that, if they were not lucky, the disease could spread like wildfire to villages along the coast.

Having given instructions about the care of the man in the hut and having used all their vaccine on those living in the immediate vicinity, the team returned to Matrah. Wells said to the brothers, "We'll stock up with more smallpox vaccine and go back up the coast in two days. In the meantime, the clinic will open as usual tomorrow at 8 a.m. Get a good sleep, for the day after tomorrow, we'll vaccinate people beyond where we vaccinated today."

When no reports of smallpox arrived in the next weeks, Wells realized the Batinah coastal villages had been lucky. He and his team had stumbled across the patient just in time. An epidemic that likely would have produced many deaths had been prevented.

There was no guarantee they would be in the right place at the right time in the future. What Wells would give for a proper public health program. He thanked God for mercifully sparing these villagers and relieving the hospital staff of yet another major crisis. It stuck in the back of his mind, though, that the hospital had no good way of dealing with widespread epidemics. They had no effective way of isolating patients afflicted with rampant communicable diseases. He pondered ways to make an institutional firewall, so that a few infected patients would not spread their maladies to everyone else.

Flies

"Flies! Flies! They're driving me crazy!" said Wells shooing them away with his hands. He was talking to Mr. Toprani, the can-do man of all trades. "Have you noticed the flies here in Matrah? They are everywhere. They cluster around moisture and standing water. Hordes of them land on people's eyelids, noses, and lips. They land on exposed food in the suq that has sugar or moisture in it. They are in all the houses and the hospital. They land on cooked food before people can take a bite. This can't be good. If we could just improve the conditions of public health by getting rid of these pestilential insects, I'm sure we would have many fewer patients with gastrointestinal ailments."

"Flies will be there, of course," said Mr. Toprani, somewhat philosophically, as one who had accommodated himself to the realities of life in Oman. "But my wife, Shantibhai, says we are not having too many flies at our house. On the corniche of Matrah Bay, my house is four stories high. Maybe we are too tall for many flies, but maybe the sea breeze is keeping them away. Perhaps they are not liking sea breezes."

"Perhaps," said Wells doubtfully, reflecting on the location of the mission's inland hospital location in relation to Toprani's seaside mansion. "The hospital grounds are outside the city wall and up the wadi a bit. The area next to the hospital is where garbage from the town is dumped, and it is an open field for people to answer the call of nature. That's it, Mr. Toprani," said Wells excitedly. "You live far from the main breeding ground for flies in Matrah, which is next to the hospital. Who owns that garbage-dump property?"[10]

"The sultan owns it. There is no real estate market here as in Karachi and Bombay. There they have brokers who link buyers with sellers. Here the land is the sultan's until he grants someone the right to build, and then it is the new owner's. In due time, if the owner dies or abandons his property, everyone is knowing. The building deteriorates

---

[10] Matrah had no treated water supply or sewage disposal service then, and it also meant that many people answered the call of nature outside the city walls. The town dump was a natural place to do this because no one lived there, and it was an easy walk beyond the walls. Dr. Harrison had observed that human feces decaying in the open air was a principal source of flies in this desert environment.

slowly, and its stones are taken away to be used for other buildings. After a while, a local road may go through that property. There is no town planning here."

"Are you suggesting we convince the sultan to give the property to us for a good purpose?" Wells queried. "I thought so. I'll ask him to donate the land for a contagious diseases hospital to isolate patients who need to be separated from the community. This could include tuberculosis and leprosy patients, and it could have space to isolate patents suffering from smallpox, typhoid, or cholera that might mushroom into epidemics. Then the property could no longer be the town dump; it would have to be cleaned up, and fewer flies would breed. This would be good for the whole town and for the hospital. How can we get the sultan to give the property for this purpose?"

Toprani responded, "If you are already having one plan for the property, if someone is giving funds for buildings, then the sultan is also finding it easy to give the land." After a pause he continued, "How much would it cost to put up buildings? Are you needing equipment, or is it mostly buildings cost?

Wells ruminated for a few minutes. "Very little equipment would be involved. Patients need only beds and bedding. In the beginning, they could sleep on the floor as they do at home, but it is easier to keep clean if there are beds."

"In that case," said Mr. Toprani, "I am giving you funds to defray the cost of the buildings. I am thinking you will not need more space than for two dozen patients."

"Thank you! That would be perfect. You are most generous," said Wells. "I will raise the matter with the sultan when the time is right. We are not going to rush; we will 'make haste slowly.' We'll talk more of it later and decide the cost of the buildings before starting construction. You won't need to give the money all at once, since it will take time to put the plan into action."

Further plans for a contagious diseases hospital were, indeed, put on hold as Wells waited for the opportune moment to broach the issue with the sultan.

"Kundoo"

"Where are Yacoob and the others today?" Wells asked Qumber one morning.

"Yacoob is at home, sick with a high fever. He didn't come to work."

"It's good he stayed at home if he's not feeling well. We don't want our staff making people ill when they come to the clinic. Where are the others?"

"They are sick, too."

Strange, thought Wells. Most unusual. We don't have labor unrest here as sometimes in the United States, so it's not a "sick out." People are not staying away from work just to make a point about their pay or working conditions.

To Qumber, he said, "I'm going to visit Yacoob. We need to find out about the others. Can you check on them? Don't go inside their houses. Talk to them from outside. I don't want you to come down with whatever they may have contracted."

Wells grabbed his doctor's bag and shot out the door. He found Yacoob at home with a high fever. "Hmm, 105 degrees. How long have you had this fever, Yacoob? Has it been high very long?"

"No, Hakeem," came Yacoob's answer. He had come down with the fever only after work yesterday. This morning it was really high.

"What else can you tell me about your illness?"

"I got up this morning to come to work. It was just a mild fever last night; I thought maybe it was malaria again. This morning, I had a high fever, and I don't have any energy. I'm tired. When I tried to walk, I couldn't. I don't think it was my balance, but my knees wouldn't hold me up. There are others in the neighborhood experiencing the same thing. People are calling it 'kundoo.'"[11]

"Kundoo? That's not Arabic. Are you talking about possession by an evil spirit, or is it something else?"

"It's something else. This neighborhood is mostly Baluchi people from the northern side of the Arabian Gulf. Kundoo is Baluch for 'weak knees.' Everybody around here has kundoo and can't walk without help."

"Everyone has it?" asked Wells incredulously.

"Well, not everybody. Maybe a third or half the people have it. Quite a large number, though."

"Yacoob, I'm leaving aspirin with you. Take two tablets every four hours. Make sure you drink a lot of water. Coffee might be too strong, but you can have it if you feel up to it. Get plenty of rest and sleep. I will look in on you every day to see how you are. In the meantime, I have to find out more about kundoo."

---

[11] *Kundoo*: "weak knees," a mysterious disease that debilitated many Omanis.

A house call to Sur Lawati, Matrah, mid-1950s (RB)

Kundoo developed into a major crisis throughout Matrah, the largest commercial seaport in Oman. At the height of the epidemic, Wells made twenty house calls a day. Fortunately, the number of people at the clinic dwindled as news of the disease frightened people enough to stay home. Wells suspected that mosquitoes were, once again, behind this ailment.

Patients reported semiparalysis in one leg and one arm. It was not like a nervous system disorder, more like a severe soreness of muscles. It reminded Wells of polio in its acute stage. Patients, however, recovered in about four days and were listless for a week afterward. There were few deaths, except among the very young. Kundoo did not always involve the same muscles, although headache, backache, and numbness, together with weakness of the legs, with pain, were characteristic. None of the patients had a bad cold or cough. If there had been colds and coughs, Wells might have thought it was a recurrence of the Spanish influenza pandemic of 1918. As it was, only a few patients complained of chest pain, sore throat, or a cough. Not everybody experienced high temperatures; some had temperatures as low as 101 Fahrenheit. They all had weak knees and could not walk unassisted.[12] The only treatments that seemed to help were salicylates, aspirin, and sedatives. Quinine, sulphadiazine, and antibiotics did not provide relief.

Wells inquired of Wali Ismail Rasassi, the Palestinian governor of Matrah, for information about the origin and spread of the disease.

---

[12] Post hoc identification of this epidemic is not possible, but its symptoms were consistent with a West Nile virus-like contagion.

He learned that kundoo had suddenly shown up. Never before had there been reports of this ailment, now so widespread. There were no accounts of kundoo coming from inland or from up the Gulf. In fact, the disease seemed to be spreading the other way, starting in Matrah and moving into the interior and up the coast. There were grim rumors of people lying by the roadside unable to continue walking home.

Then a report came that the disease was first experienced in Sur, down the coast toward Ras al Hadd. This suggested that kundoo may have been brought by an Arab trading ship that had sailed into the harbor of Matrah from Sur, the center of Oman's long-distance sailing-ship fleet that welcomed vessels from throughout the Indian Ocean and the Gulf. Perhaps one or more of these ships had brought the infected mosquitoes. If so, it would have been easy for kundoo to spread since few houses were screened.

Giving credence to the notion that kundoo had arrived from outside Oman was the fact that the outbreak had begun in September. Many of the sailing ships would return from East Africa during the summer and then move up the Gulf, selling their wares and purchasing products to carry on to India and Africa in the winter season. Sailing vessels were not required to pass quarantine inspection. If the ships' crews had contracted kundoo, it would have been months earlier, and the carriers would have been long gone by the time the outbreak was widespread.

But then, suddenly, kundoo subsided as quickly as it had begun. The incoming tsunami of an illness had arrived without announcement, reached its climax, and then subsided and passed on up the Gulf and into the interior. Wells realized Oman had just survived a contagious disease epidemic. Perhaps from one-third to one-half of the population was visibly affected, but there was no way of knowing how many had actually contracted the disease because public health records did not exist. Wells did not have time to reflect on kundoo any further, except to note it in his annual hospital report.[13] The queues at the hospital clinic never shortened during the duration of the malady, except for a week or two when patients were reluctant to leave home. In the end, Wells was unable to identify the disease with any specificity.

---

[13] There was no ministry of health to which to send reports of the contagion.

CHAPTER 24

Dhofar

Can you put three or four fish in the other wells?

Discovering Dhofar, 1944

Sultan Sayyid Sa'eed bin Taymur requested that Wells attend his mejlis at his Muscat palace from time to time. Wells dressed formally since he never knew ahead of time the reason for his summons to the palace. The sultan began one of Wells' court appearances with an invitation: "Would you come to Dhofar to treat my people there? I'll be happy to host you. I'll have the British fly you to Masirah Island, and from there, you can come the rest of the way by my fast launch. You and your wife will both be welcome and also the medical workers you would need."

"Thank you very much for the invitation," Wells responded. "Would it be possible to come during the hot summer in Muscat because many fewer people come to the hospitals then? That way we can provide medical assistance to as many people as possible in both places."[1]

---

[1] No tourism to Dhofar was possible in those days, whereas today Dhofar receives many tourists during the summer rainy season.

"Yes, certainly," replied Sultan Sayyid Sa'eed. "You'll be the first surgeon to come to Dhofar since Harold Storm almost fifteen years ago, and he was the first surgeon ever to visit. I think there will be plenty for you to do. We've never had an eye surgeon there. Shall we plan for you to stay in Salalah for a month? Or longer? It will be the rainy season, for Dhofar is the only part of Arabia to experience summer monsoon rains. It is a welcome contrast to the rest of my kingdom."

"No longer than a month, I'm afraid," said Wells. "My wife and I want to go to India for a month to see our children in school there. It is not that they miss us, but rather we miss them so very much. Also, we need relief from the intense heat of Muscat-Matrah. Our staff needs relief, too, and they go to date gardens up the Batinah. We shouldn't be away from the hospital in Muscat too long."

"Excellent! We'll plan accordingly. Please let my clerk know the dates that are best for you, and we will work it out. I plan to host you in Salalah personally and look forward to entertaining you and your wife. Of course," the sultan added conspiratorially, "I'll have to have my British 'keeper' along. It makes me feel a bit of a zoo specimen. Everyone is so suspicious about Americans taking advantage of the situation now that they are in both the war and the oil business. I'll try to arrange for an American military officer to keep my keeper company.'"

"The more the merrier," replied Wells. "If they know some medicine, I could put them to work. They will be good company and add to our conviviality in any case."

"Incidentally, Khatoun Jauhara will be the second Western woman ever to visit Dhofar. The first was Lady Mable Bent, wife of the archaeologist Theodore Bent, who visited in 1895 before either of us was born. Mrs. Thoms will be a curiosity to Dhofari women, but I imagine she, too, is used to being a zoo specimen." Wells chuckled and nodded in agreement.

The sultan continued, "I am always relieved to retreat to Dhofar. Financial times have been difficult ever since I assumed power from my father. Sayyid Taymur bin Faisal accumulated substantial debts and couldn't extricate himself from them. Since the loans were incurred while he was head of state, I had to take responsibility for them. On the advice of the British consul and Sir Percy Cox, I hired a British financial manager, Bertram Thomas, to help manage my affairs." Sultan Sa'eed grunted as he recalled that episode. "Thomas turned out to be a fair-weather sailor and left me in worse shape than before. All he could do was dream about crossing the Empty Quarter before any other Westerner. Because of his failure, I had to resume managing my own affairs.

"Living in Dhofar saves me money. I say this not to shock you, but so you will understand. I own basically everything in Dhofar, including most of the people. I have many slaves. Don't worry! I take care of them well. I do not abandon them in old age. I am not cruel. Dhofar is wonderfully productive—a garden of delight. My people produce almost everything. I don't pay cash salaries or provident fund payments. It costs just about the same if I live there or not or if I have guests. By living in Dhofar, I save the extra funds I would expend here in Muscat, where I don't have very many slaves or productive plantations and where I must purchase almost everything. In Muscat, I also must give substantial cash gifts to visiting shaykhs. It is expensive, but it is how I build alliances and strengthen my kingdom.

"I do all this to pay off the debts incurred by my father and grandfather. You know those Indian moneylenders. At least the British kept them from imposing their normal interest rates of 25 percent, per month, or I would never be able to pay off my debts. Yet, I am determined to do so. The British stopped every other way my father and grandfather could accumulate wealth. They stopped the slave trade—a real money maker in its time—and the arms traffic—which would still have been a great source of revenue without their interference.

"So I let the British view me as a puppet on a string. What choice do I have? In return, they defend my kingdom, guard my rights, and guarantee my debt. There will come a time when I will become less dependent and be able to return to Oman to the grandeur of my namesake, Sultan Sayyid Sa'eed the Great. Oman was prominent once. It could be a self-respecting state again.

"In the meantime, I would like you to treat my people in Salalah and the surrounding area. Although it is beautiful there, in no way can one confuse it with Paradise. Besides treating the people, I need you to survey their health problems so improvements can be made."

In due course, Wells, Beth, Qumber, and their medical troupe arrived by launch off the Dhofar capital of Salalah. Together with Capt. Richard Ernest Byrd, the British consul in Muscat, and Lieutenant Murphy, a representative of the US Army, they were brought by the sultan's fast launch.

Dhofar is a little green crescent of well-watered coast facing the Arabian Sea next to the Hadhramaut province of Yemen. Salalah, the principal city, lies on this lowland plain. In the dry Qara Mountains beyond this strip lies the land of *mughur*[2] trees. Frankincense trees do not grow on the well-watered plain but on the dry, inland side of the mountains. Frankincense is harvested from the sap that oozes from cuts in the bark and is widely used for religious rituals in Christian communities. More popularly, its smoke deodorizes the clothes of women guests in prosperous Arab homes and contributes to health as an ingredient in medicines. The coastal strip forms a stark contrast with the remainder of Arabia, for just here, the monsoon winds provide a rainy season every year. Elsewhere, rain falls sporadically and unpredictably.

Shortly after the Thoms' launch dropped anchor in the Salalah harbor, a large rowboat, paddled by eight men, put out through the surf. Having transferred the visitors and their luggage, the oarsmen started paddling shoreward. As the swells grew higher, they synchronized their strokes with the cresting waves. Suddenly, at the critical moment, they paddled furiously, so the boat rode on the crest of the tumbling surf until it came to a grinding, crunching halt on the beach. Wells, the officers, and the men hopped off and waded through the last few feet of the surf onto the beach. Beth was just about to do the same, when two slaves ran through the surf holding above their heads an armchair lashed to two poles. This they brought to the gunwale of the rocking boat and motioned her to sit in it. She did so, whereupon they turned and carried her back to the beach with the poles on their shoulders. Once beyond the surf, they deposited her like a queen on dry land, splashed by not one drop of salt water.

An imposing figure greeted them: "Welcome to al Baz, the sultan's guest house. My name is Mahmoud. I hope you will be comfortable here close to the sea. The rest of your group will stay in another house nearer Salalah, on the other side of those coconut palms. That house is big. They can live on the top floor where they can cook and eat. You can treat patients on the first floor and run your clinics on the ground floor. The staff has stocked water, coffee, utensils, staples, vegetables, and primus stoves for cooking and pressure lamps for light. They will also bring you meat and fish. Coffee and halwa are coming, so please sit on the verandah and take your rest. My staff will bring your luggage." With that, the sultan's chief slave swept away, drawing the rest of the medical crew with him.

After inspection of the beach house, Beth was impressed and declared: "This house is clean and bright, Wells. The bedroom is simple

[2] Frankincense.

with two solid *charpoys*,[3] a cotton mattress, cotton sheets and towels, and mosquito nets. The bathroom has soap, a big water tank, and good space for a 'pour bath,' and a squat toilet. This is most progressive and hygienic for being a million miles from anywhere."

"Yes, indeed. This sea breeze is wonderful, too. I am feeling less queasy already; sorry to have been such a terrible sailor. I hope some of this air wafts far enough inland to air-condition the other house. We will use the clinics to get an initial feel for people's health problems. Then later, we can explore and stop in villages and gardens to see what 'normal' people are like here, and if there are diseases not presented in clinic. The sultan said he would provide a car and driver, and he has given us permission to travel about Dhofar as we please."

By the time they had hiked over to the house allocated for the clinic, Qumber and the others had settled in comfortably and were cooking supper, a delicious *ma'raq* and rice. Over dinner, they talked about the coming days.

"We are going to be busy. We'll start with a clinic in the courtyard downstairs in the morning. We'll need everyone to help. Fortunately, there is a medic here. You know Dr. Shafiq, Qumber. He worked in our hospital when Dr. Harrison was here, and then he took additional training in Bahrain. We'll ask him to give shots and such. If this is like the Batinah, there will be ulcers, and somebody will have to treat them. Others will help in different ways. Khatoun Jauhara will help with the women at clinic and treat their eyes with eyedrops and zinc ointment.

"Qumber, you will have to do the sterile preps and autoclaving of instruments starting in late morning. We will try to limit ourselves to minor operations and do them all from afternoon into the early evening. Then supper, relaxation, and bed. I expect it will be the same schedule every day, except we also need to check on our patients postoperatively to know their progress. If we do this for six days, we will rest on the seventh, Sunday, to worship, relax, and explore Dhofar. Then we should be rested to begin another six-day cycle." Wells paused to make sure he was understood.

"Beth, we'll need some ladies doing laundry every day. I expect a slave or two will be assigned this duty. I know people are very skittish about washing bloody cloths. So, Khamees, you will need to rinse thoroughly every bloody cloth, sheet, towel, and item of clothing, or they won't get laundered. We can't have a shortage of clean clothes and supplies. If we all do our part, it is going to be very smooth and

---

[3] Beds with interwoven webbing tape in lieu of springs.

harmonious, and we shouldn't have an ounce of trouble from our patients or the Dhofari staff assigned to us."

They all agreed, each expecting to add his or her nuanced wrinkle as the days progressed. They had run their own makeshift field hospital many times, so the staff knew the routine. "One more thing," said Wells. "Even though Dhofar looks like Paradise, it is still hot and humid. We must maintain our fluids throughout the day. Beth, can you ask Mahmoud for pitchers of fresh limeade with sugar for us in place of midmorning coffee—and another limeade break in midafternoon? We'll be so much more efficient if we're well hydrated, and I won't get the shakes from hypoglycemia. We'll also need to boil water for drinking. Who knows what might be in the water that comes directly from the plantation wells."

Evening interlude

After an evening hymn, Wells and Beth walked back to their beach guest house. "It is such a nice evening," said Beth. "Let's sit on the verandah and watch until twilight." It was serenely peaceful in the soft light, with a few people gliding along the beach, returning home at day's end. All sounds subsided, except for the breaking waves. Presently, the land-sea breeze waned as the interior beyond the mountains cooled.

Suddenly Wells blurted out, "What the . . . what's going on? I've got the hungriest mosquitoes swarming all around me. What about you?"

"There's a squadron of them buzzing and biting like crazy! Quick, Wells, get the FLIT!" Beth squealed, swatting at the air.

"There are way too many of them to spray Flit everywhere,[4] and we have only a limited supply of it to sterilize our operating room," responded Wells. "We are living semioutdoors here, with windows and doors opening onto the verandah, which has no screens to protect us. No bug spray could get rid of them all. Let's jump into our beds and get those mosquito nets down, pronto! I'm really, really itchy."

They raced to ready the *charpoys*, tucked nets under the slim mattresses, and slid into their beds while trying to keep the mosquitoes out. "Argh," said Beth. "One got inside! There! Got it, I think! Nope." Slap. "There!"

"Whoo," sighed Wells in relief. "I didn't bring a torch inside the net with me, and it's too dark to read. I brought along Theodore Bent's

---

[4] Flit was the leading—and nearly only—insecticide of its day; 5 percent DDT was added to it in the late 1940s.

account of Dhofar from fifty years ago. I thought we could read aloud from it at the end of the day, but it's outside, over there, and I don't want to get it with those mosquitoes flying-in-wait. We'll just have to meditate, lick our bites to stop the itching, and then say our prayers and fall asleep. I don't know what we can do about these mosquitoes. There are so many of them. I've never seen anything like it. So much for Dhofar being Paradise. I'll bet there's tons of malaria here."

Ordinary little fish

Wells was first to pop out of bed in the morning. He had a pour bath, shaved, dressed in clean whites, and headed outside into the cool breeze to look around. Where did those voracious flying beasts come from? Where was there standing fresh water? There had to be a lot for so many mosquitoes. He found nothing until he looked in the sultan's coconut grove between the guest house and Salalah, and then he heard the whine of mosquitoes under the palm fronds.

There they were—in five freshwater wells irrigating the palms. The first four he looked in were alive with "wrigglers," mosquitoes hatching from larval stage. From each, there was a cloud of newly hatched mosquitoes rising from the surface of the water and flying into the plantation. Hmm, he thought. Might as well look at the last well; it probably won't be any different. When he looked in, he saw no "wrigglers" at all. The water was as crystal clear as a good well should be. Then he looked more closely. Feeding languidly at the surface were several plump fish. He saw they were nibbling the "food" on the surface, the wrigglers.

Wells turned and spoke to the gardener slave. "Do you see those fish right there?"

"Yes, sir."

"What kind of fish are they? Where did they come from?"

"I don't know, sir. They are just ordinary little fish. They must have come from one of the streams flowing down from the mountains. We don't catch them or eat them, they're too small."

"Can you catch more of these fish from one of the streams, and put three or four in each well? Incidentally, Brother, what is your name?"

"I am Hassan. Yes, I can do that, but it would be better to have my brother catch them because he is the sultan's fisherman."

"Well, Mr. Hassan, do a good job, and the sultan will reward both of you."

"Immediately, sir," said Hassan as he strode away intent on his new mission.

That evening, as they sat again on the verandah watching the sun set and the passersby plodding home, Wells said to Beth, "I checked the wells tonight again. Hassan was as good as his word. There are a couple of fish in each well. We'll see what effect that has. There may be so many other breeding sites around Salalah that it probably won't make a perceptible difference."

Wells grabbed the volume from the nearby table. "Let's see what Theodore Bent had to say about Dhofar in 1895. Let's do it before the 'skeeters' dive bomb us." He passed the book to Beth and said, "Would you read? It has been a long day." Beth got through the introduction to Bent's narrative before Wells drifted off. She continued to read to herself:

> Dhofar and the Qara Mountains that encircle it form a quite abnormal feature in the otherwise arid coast of southeastern Arabia. We here find a long narrow stretch of flat alluvial soil at the foot of the mountains, very little raised above the level of the sea. This plain is never more than nine miles wide, and at the eastern end, it is reduced to an exceedingly narrow strip. Water is here very near the surface. The plain is very fertile and capable of producing almost anything.
>
> [There are] many groves of coconut palms, tobacco, cotton, Indian corn, and various species of grain. In the gardens, we find many of the products of India flourishing—the plantain, the papaya, mulberries, melons, chilis, brinjals,[5] and fruits and vegetables of various descriptions.
>
> Dhofar and the Qara Mts. may be termed one large oasis by the sea. The Qara Mts. are full of water [and] are decked to their summits with rich vegetation, and this will account for the fertility of the plain of Dhofar and the strange contrast it forms to the rest of the coastline of Arabia.[6]

No wonder the sultan loved this place, Beth thought as she closed the book. She and Wells had come to love it, too, despite the "skeeters."

---

[5] Eggplant.
[6] Ethel Thoms wrote about this incident in an article that appeared some years later: "Women of the Frankincense Country." The quotation appears on page 7 of that article.

Then she abruptly realized what was happening in the air around her and called out: "It's mosquito time, Wells. Wake up! Time to get in bed! The mosquitoes are here in droves."

"Right, right," he mumbled as he climbed groggily into bed and tucked the net under his mattress. "What a day! I don't know. Maybe four hundred people in clinic. . . . It's a big blur. I'm bushed." In an instant, he was out cold.

The pattern repeated every day. When the Dhofaris realized that the medical team was staying for a month, daily attendance at clinic stabilized at about two hundred. Operations went smoothly in the afternoons. The staff was fulfilled but fatigued.

Four days later, the sultan, Lieutenant Murphy, and Consul Byrd came for late afternoon tea at the guest house. Conversation was pleasant and polite, if not particularly personal. The sultan asked after everyone's wellbeing. The dying afternoon breeze soughed through the palms. As the light dimmed, the breeze stopped.

When Sultan Sa'eed was about to bid adieu, he sat upright, quite startled, and said, "I haven't been bitten by a single mosquito yet tonight, and always there are thousands to pester me here! How is that possible?"

Wells told him about his experimentally putting fish in the wells, and that it seemed to be working even better than he expected. "Sunset can now be enjoyed," he said. "No sound of one hand slapping an exposed neck or face."

"Yes, yes, doctor. You amaze me with your ingenious solution to what we thought was insoluble! Just like that, too," and he snapped his fingers. "Moreover, it has not cost anything. A wonderful solution. Tomorrow, I will order all my wells to be stocked with these fish, and then I will extend my command to every well in Dhofar."

Wells took this conversation as a cue to report on some of his findings about public health. "We have plenty of evidence that malaria is a major health problem here, Your Highness. With help from God and the little fishes, malaria rates may drop in time. As a result, people will then be more able to work and earn a living, and with more people healthy, it will save on the escalating costs of quinine, too." Wells sensed that the sultan was especially pleased with the prospect of saving money.

Sultan Sayyid Sa'eed observed that Wells and Beth and the hospital staff were hard at work, while Captain Byrd and Lieutenant Murphy had little to do. "Since tomorrow is Sunday and your Christian day off, I'm sending the car and driver for you. Take the day to explore Dhofar and take Consul Byrd and Lieutenant Murphy with you. I'll send a guide and guards out to meet you at Khor Rori beyond Taqah. From there, you can go up into the mountains and have a picnic. I think it is really the nicest part of all Arabia; it is certainly the nicest part of my Arabia. Your staff will have the day off in Salalah too. I'll send a sheep for my people to roast for your British picnic and another one here for your staff."

As they climbed into the car the next morning, Byrd trilled, "Good show! I've brought my field glasses. I think we can give H. H. a day off for good behavior.[7] He is almost at his wit's end figuring out what to do with us, don't you think, Murphy?"

"Yes, it'll be great to get out of town into the country. I brought some SPAM. Made in Minnesota, my home state. It's our gift to the world. I have a can of cheese and some dill pickles my mom sent, too," he said holding them aloft delightedly.

Beth said, "Yum! Delicacies we don't often get. We shouldn't serve the SPAM to our Dhofari hosts, though. It has pork in it, doesn't it?"

"Who knows for sure," replied Murphy. "Some of the guys claim it's 'meatloaf that didn't go to basic training.' We get it all the time at the base. Get hungry enough, you'll eat it. The best part is it doesn't need refrigeration."

Looking through the picnic supplies, Beth enthused, "We have wonderful fresh Arab bread, the very thin Bedu-style *khubs rakhaal*, tough and unleavened. We can have cheese and SPAM or mutton sandwiches. They'll be perfect with the fresh drinking coconuts the sultan sent along."

The party drove eastward to the end of the road at Khor Rori, then the largest lake in Arabia. It was about a mile wide and three miles long with a sand bar separating it from the ocean.[8] The Bents reported that an ancient city (mentioned by Ptolemy) had been located here. The visitors discovered some ancient fort-like walls, but the ruins revealed no clue of their age.

Wells and Beth and the others walked along the lakeshore until it turned into a wadi, where a feathery waterfall cascaded. As they climbed above the falls, the landscape changed dramatically. Against all expectations, they found cows grazing contentedly on a rolling grassy tableland. There were acacia and wild fig trees and another

---

[7] "H. H." stands for "His Highness."
[8] Khor Rori is much smaller in size today.

Beth overlooking the Dhofar coastal plain, 1944 (WWT)

lake. This was truly Arabia Felix, Happy-Fortunate Arabia. They knew, however, that Arabia Deserta, the land of water scarcity, lay just beyond the nearby ridge.

After their sumptuous picnic, some Qara cattle herders wandered over to visit. Their Arabic was strange, if indeed it was Arabic. Completely unintelligible to Wells and Beth, it was Jabali,[9] a hill dialect, understood only by the Wells' guide-translator who helped them converse.

The Qara asked why the visitors were there. Wells replied they had come to see the beautiful lake, to which the Qara snorted in disgust. That could not possibly be the reason. What was there to see? But they became more interested when they learned Wells was a doctor. Conversationally, he asked after their health. One of the older men said he had constant pain in his joints. Wells gave him two aspirin. In short order, the elder's pain began to subside, and as the afternoon wore on, he exclaimed about the miraculous disappearance of his joint pain. Wells gave him a small supply of aspirin to last for a week with explicit instructions. "Do not to take all the pills at once. Two pills after morning prayers and another two pills after noon prayers. This medicine is strong." He made his patient repeat the treatment with sign language holding two fingers up for each dose. Taking the pills

---

[9] Since *jabal* refers to hills or mountains, *jabali* would be "[someone] from the mountains."

The mughur *tree, source of frankincense, 1944* (WWT)

all at once could hurt him, explained Wells. The Qara man nodded to indicate he understood. By the time they returned to Taqah, the word had spread that there was a doctor in their midst, and many people wanted to see the hakeem for treatment.

Dhofari women considered Beth a great curiosity—as the sultan had predicted—a living zoo specimen. They were truly surprised to discover she could speak Arabic. The women clapped their hands, jumped up and down excitedly, smiled and laughed, and wanted to touch her again and again to make sure her skin color would not come off. After that, they had no problem communicating. Beth found their horizons severely constricted, just like the *"kinder, kuche, kirche"*[10] mindset of Midwestern immigrants from the "old country." *Am I ever lucky to live in this time,* she thought.

Beth was fascinated by Dhofari society as she explored it. In Salalah, there were very few Arab Omanis other than the members of the royal family, government officials, and their immediate attendants. A likely majority of the visible residents, both slave and free, seemed to be of African descent. This may have been because Arab women were not allowed to move about in public, while African women had more freedom to be unaccompanied in public. Of the Africans, the best dressed and healthiest appeared to be H. H.'s slaves. Moreover, they seemed secure, happy, and—if possible—contented with their lot. They seemed to love the sultan. Many freely admitted that they were slaves of the sultan and believed they were superior to others. Few of the hill

---

[10] Children, cooking, church (Dutch).

Female slave patient, Salalah, 1944 (WWT)

people, the Qara, were seen in Salalah or elsewhere on the plain. The mountain folk who infrequently visited the city appeared to be ill at ease around Arabs, as well as the slave and free Africans.

At the end of their pleasant stay in Dhofar, Wells gave H. H. the grim and cautionary report of his medical survey as follows:

1. Nonvenereal syphilis was common in Salalah along the plain as far as Taqah. Wells treated more than two hundred cases with bismuth injections during his visit. Return treatment should occur. After the war, there will probably be new and improved drugs to contend with this malady.
2. Leprosy was extensive. There was no short-term cure. Wells suggested H. H. start a leprosarium on his experimental farm in Dhofar. Patients could be treated there and work at the leprosarium to defray part of their treatment cost.
3. Malaria was endemic. Perhaps the "small fish" in the well treatment could bring down its incidence by reducing the number of disease-bearing mosquitoes.
4. Dysentery was also found across the region. This suggested the need for better sanitation and water supply protection to decrease the contamination rates.
5. Tuberculosis was also widespread, as in other parts of Oman. Better diets, together with preventive measures in the home, could decrease its incidence.
6. Since they did not have a microscope in Dhofar, it was not possible to assess the extent of hookworm. It appeared,

however, to be rife, as indicated by the halting gait of many farmers that Wells observed walking and working.

The short summary report was that preventive medicine and better sanitation were likely to return benefits many times their cost. A more sophisticated report would have to await the time H. H. had a real health department and hospitals and clinics with doctors and nurses. Then they would need to maintain reliable health statistics. Wells could not imagine when that day would come, given the sultan's ongoing debts and well-known tightfistedness. Undaunted, Wells could still dream of and work toward that day.

Return to Dhofar, 1950

At the sultan's invitation, Wells and Beth visited Dhofar again in 1950—this time with their children, Peter, Norman, and Lowey. They traveled by the sultan's boat on a three-day, seven hundred-mile cruise and again landed on Salalah's beach by surfboat cresting the breakers. Beth and Lowey were carried ashore as Beth had been years before. The two arrived without so much as a splash, each held aloft by the sultan's slaves, who lifted them high above the waves in an armchair on poles.[11]

As they settled into their Dhofari routine, Beth was reminded that the inhabitants lived in a three-tiered society. First came the relatively few Arab Omani rulers, next the slaves of African descent, and finally the tribesmen from the hills who spoke their hybrid language. Once again, she noted that those of African descent—a majority of the people in Salalah—were well-dressed and proudly announced that they were servants of the sultan.

Three of the sultan's children, two daughters and a son, lived in Dhofar. The sultan had married the daughter of a Qara tribal chieftain, and their children were raised in Dhofar. Wells attended the medical needs of the sultan's son, Qaboos, who would one day rule in his father's stead.[12]

As in his previous visit, Wells was overwhelmed by hundreds of patients every day. He carried out another medical survey and discovered that malaria was the most common ailment, followed closely by trachoma, intestinal parasites, and *tair,* a nonvenereal form

---

[11] This section is based on Wells Thoms, *Knox Memorial Hospital Annual Report 1950-51* (unpublished typescript), and Thoms, "Women of the Frankincense Country."

[12] Sultan Sayyid Qaboos bin Sa'eed bin Taymur did in fact come to the throne through a palace revolution in 1970. He reigned benevolently for fifty years until his death in January 2020.

Qaboos with the Thoms commoners, Salalah, 1950 (WWT)

of syphilis that was spread from mothers to their children. Wells indicated to the sultan that two men—a sanitary engineer and a public health specialist—could transform the health of the people of Dhofar.

The status of slaves intrigued Beth as she moved freely among the womenfolk. As she had learned, the sultan's palace slaves formed the elite among those with slave ancestry. Beth noted that the slaves seemed to be remarkably contented. She wrote about them in a *Neglected Arabia* article:

Thoms family portrait, photographed by Sultan Sayyid Sa'eed bin Taymur, Salalah, 1950 (SST)

Wells and Beth with H. H., Salalah, 1950 (SST)

The women dance on many occasions. They dance to exorcise the devil. They dance at weddings, and they dance in procession when they carry full water pitchers on their heads to replenish the tanks in the palace bathrooms. Always the dance is done to chanting and beating of drums. The leader of the bathing chorus was one of our major surgical cases. Wells was loathe to operate on her under [medical] touring conditions and tried to persuade her to come to Muscat for surgery. However, her determination to be rid of her abdominal tumor without further delay, and her absolute confidence that she would recover, won him over to doing it.

When we brought her out of the operating room and returned her to her bed, she was borne triumphantly by several of her stalwart male relatives past a large group of her fellow dancers. Most patients were content with a mat on the floor, but she saw to it that she had a bed [that] she had furnished with mosquito net, sheets, and woolen blankets. During her rapid convalescence, she was never without a ring of male and female visitors who brought her presents of food and incense.[13]

The elite women dancers and musicians appeared to have occupied the top rung of the palace's slave society. A slave woman was assigned to do Wells and Beth's laundry. She was clear about what she would do and what was out of her realm of responsibilities. She carefully paced her duties, insisting that she would wash clothes on one day and then iron them on the next. Extra work, such as caring for linens from the clinic or from surgical operations, was beyond her writ and required extra pay. On no account would she wash clothing, cloths, or bandages contaminated by blood. Slave society had its own established rules and precedents, mirroring the rest of Omani culture.

---

[13] Thoms, "Women of the Frankincense Country," 10.

CHAPTER 25

Hospital Snapshots, 1942–69: The Sharon Thoms Hospital for Contagious Diseases

Shahrbanoo, a Baluchi woman abandoned by her husband, became the leprosarium's star resident. Her husband had expelled her from her family, house, and town to live on the margin of society outside the city wall.

Mr. T. F. T. Sa'eed, 1942

In early 1942, Mr. 'T. F. T. Sa'eed' visited his homeland of Muscat and Oman for the first time since abdicating the throne in 1932.[1] Omanis were delighted to see him, as was Wells. The ex-sultan, Sayyid Taymur bin Faisal, arrived on a BI ship and alighted at the customs pier in Muscat. A great crowd had assembled, and Wells stood patiently in line with the throng of happy Omanis waiting to meet their former monarch. When Wells' turn came, Sayyid Taymur greeted him warmly and addressed him using his Arabic name: "It is good to see you again, Ameen! It has been such a long time since we last met."

Wells subsequently invited Sayyid Taymur and Sultan Sayyid Sa'eed bin Taymur to a dinner in Matrah. Father and son came to the mission home and had a wonderful evening recollecting life in Oman in days long gone by. The assembled party included other colorful

---

[1] "T. F. T. Sa'eed" is an Anglicized abbreviation of his name in Arabic—Sayyid Taymur bin Faisal bin Turki al Bu Sa'eed or Taymur [son of] Faisal [son of] Turki [of the] Sa'eed family.

characters who regaled each other with interesting stories of the al Bu Sa'eed family and Omani history, and Wells recounted some of his experiences with other rulers up the Gulf. Sultan Sayyid Sa'eed was very relaxed at that initial gathering.

As the weeks progressed and his father extended his stay in Muscat, Sultan Sayyid Sa'eed's enthusiasm waned. Wells speculated that Sayyid Taymur's visit was considerably more expensive than Sultan Sayyid Sa'eed had anticipated, in particular because of the gifts and food the sultan was expected to dispense to palace visitors. Wells wondered if the sultan was also worried about his father's widespread popularity. Sayyid Taymur was an extrovert who had friends throughout the community. His son, Sultan Sayyid Sa'eed, was certainly intelligent, but he was quiet and introverted. Would there be a misguided effort by his father's friends to place Sayyid Taymur again on the throne, even though he had expressed no desire to rule? During his reign, Sultan Sayyid Taymur had been very generous, with the result that his kingdom had fallen deeply in debt. Were Oman's finances again being sucked dry by the ex-sultan's lavish entertaining and generous gift giving to visiting shaykhs? Sultan Sayyid Sa'eed clearly did not intend to plunge his treasury back into the red. In time, "Mr. T. F. T. Sa'eed" returned to his exile, and fiscal normalcy returned to the kingdom.[2]

In November Sultan Sayyid Sa'eed wrote Wells a letter granting the mission land next to the hospital designated for a contagious diseases hospital. This was in response to a request from Wells, who had long envisioned such a medical facility and who had waited for the propitious moment to make his request. The plot of land, about one hundred meters by one hundred meters, was a gift that cost the sultan little. He had no use for that parcel of scrubland, rubble and trash strewn as it was. On the other hand, Wells was grateful for the gift and immediately started cleaning up the plot and planning one ward for tubercular patients and another for leprosy patients.

In 1944 Wells announced that construction of the new hospital would begin soon. Two stone tablets, carefully engraved in both English and Arabic, would be placed on either side of the entrance gate,

---

[2] Wendell Phillips was perhaps the only historian-commentator who interviewed Sayyid Taymur while he was living happily after he had abdicated. See his, *Oman: A History*. Notably, while in exile in India, Sayyid Taymur said to Phillips, "I'm free. Sa'eed is in prison now." Monarchical leadership isolates and imprisons its own.

explaining the purpose and patronage of the new facility. The English script read:

> THE SHARON THOMS MEMORIAL HOSPITAL
> FOR CONTAGIOUS DISEASES.
> 1945
> Dr. Sharon Thoms started the fight
> against contagious diseases in Mutrah
> in 1909. He died here in 1913.
> This hospital is dedicated to carry
> on the task which he started.

The Arabic text acknowledged the sultan's seminal role in the establishment of the hospital:

> His Highness SAYYID SA'EED BIN TAIMUR,
> THE SULTAN OF MUSCAT AND OMAN
> granted this land to
> THE AMERICAN MISSION HOSPITAL
> requesting that it be used for
> the isolation and treatment of
> patients suffering from
> contagious diseases.

It took several years to clear the site and build the isolation wards for tuberculosis and leprosy patients. Finally, in 1948, the sultan cut the ribbon, marking the official opening of the mission's third hospital in the capital cities area. The engraved tablets were proudly displayed at the hospital gate.

In short order, Wells reported that the tuberculosis ward of the hospital had treated twenty-three patients with pulmonary tuberculosis in its very overcrowded seven-bed ward. When they were admitted, all the patients were sputum positive, showing evidence of active pulmonary tuberculosis. Four were discharged as sputum negative after a few months on streptomycin and collapse therapy,[3] which involved collapsing the infected lung by injecting air or nitrogen or by severing a nerve. One patient died. Eleven returned home with improved health after two months. Two returned home unimproved. Four of the five remaining inpatients had shown good prognosis, but one patient was going "downhill." Wells noted that streptomycin

---

[3] Also called artificial pneumothorax or phrenicectomy.

Sa'eed, a long-term Hansen's Disease patient, late 1950s (RB)

usually gave some initial benefit but unless combined with rest and collapse therapy, it did not produce a cure.[4]

In 1949 a leprosarium for patients with Hansen's Disease was also built in Matrah. Mr. Toprani, true to his promise of years earlier, contributed significantly to the cost of the building and supervised its construction. The ward included four, two-bed rooms for inpatients, a treatment room, and a waiting room for outpatients. Construction materials on order would add a kitchen and bathroom. Three leprosy patients were soon admitted.

Shahrbanoo, a middle-aged Baluchi woman became its star resident. When her husband discovered she had contracted leprosy, he quickly divorced her and expelled her from their family, house, and town to live on the margins of society, outside the city wall. There she had subsisted in poverty, scratching out a precarious living by begging.

Six months into her treatment, Shahrbanoo showed improvement, having received Diasone by mouth; sterile dressings for the many, runny, open ulcers on her hands and feet; and aureomycin in cod liver oil instilled into both eyes, twice daily. Wells reported that she had gained weight, become cheerful, cooked her own food, and kept her veranda and room neatly swept. Her once almost blind eyes were

[4] Rest, with an adequate diet, was essential. This meant long-term residence in the tuberculosis isolation ward—something that many patients found difficult to do because of expense, lack of patience, or loneliness. In Europe and the US, tuberculosis isolation hospitals operated in many cities until the late 1950s.

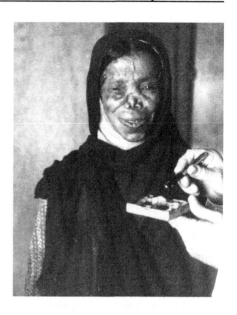

Shahrbanoo, patient with visibly pronounced symptoms, late 1950s (RB)

seeing more clearly. The fiery sensation in her limbs had cooled. She was making remarkable progress.

How different it was to have the Sharon Thoms Hospital for Contagious Diseases functioning. Wells remembered how powerless he had felt to help leprosy patients when he first arrived in Oman. His thoughts returned to that woman whose plight was similar to Shahrbanoo's.

She had sat for hours in front of the Matrah hospital weeping and calling out, "Help me, help me! No one will help me!" She, too, had been expelled from her family and community because she was considered "Unclean! Unclean!" She had been ruthlessly cast out to fend for herself with nowhere to go. Finally, completely distraught, she staggered up the wadi leaving her begging bowl on the ground outside the hospital. When Wells saw she had gone but left her bowl behind, he ran out of the hospital, picked up her empty bowl, and chased up the valley to return it to her. Even this small act of mercy shocked his employees. To have admitted her to the hospital in those early days would likely have resulted in a community boycott of the hospital. How times had changed.

With the opening of the contagious diseases hospital, the sultan's government announced its intention to move its isolation camp for lepers from far distant Seeb to an empty area up the wadi, beyond the hospital, away from the city wall. He decreed that the lepers could come to the Sharon Thoms facility for regular treatment and be treated as outpatients.

Not satisfied with his "on-the-job training" for treating leprosy, Wells spent several months of his 1948-49 furlough at Carville, Louisiana, where the US Public Health Service maintained the United States' only leprosarium. Wells wanted to see if there were lessons to be learned from this model facility that could benefit the contagious diseases hospital. He enlisted as a volunteer at Carville in place of one of its pastors. While he was there, he met patients as well as pastors and doctors appointed to run leprosaria in South America and Africa.

In retrospect, Wells considered the Sharon Thoms Hospital for Contagious Diseases the most important achievement of his thirty years in Oman. It filled a gap explicitly designed to help "the least of these my brethren,"[5] for whom there was no safety net of care or treatment. It was testimony to the lasting impact of a young boy's walk beyond the suq with his father so many years before.

---

[5] Matt. 25:40.

CHAPTER 26

Relief, Rest, and Relaxation

A rogue wave slammed into the ship's port side, and the vessel rolled dangerously. The wave engulfed the superstructure and cascaded down the lee side of the vessel "like Niagara encaving us." She saw Maisie's green blouse flash by in the water.

Homelife

In Kuwait, Bahrain, and Muscat/Matrah, Wells and Beth lived simply. At home, they preserved a semblance of emotional and familial privacy, separate from the pressures of their daily routine, the social crises of the hospital staff, and the grimness of medical trauma. Wells and Beth subscribed to Bumpus & Co.'s book-lending service. And as in Dhofar, their last ritual before sleep every night was to take turns reading one precious chapter aloud. In this way, they absorbed the adventures of all the European explorers of the Middle East—Burton, Burckhardt, Cox, Doughty, Stark, Bell, Philby, Lawrence, Thesiger, Blunt, and Wellsted.[1] They read books by their friend Lowell Thomas,[2] various British and American novelists, and Christian theologians, commentators, and philosophers. They liked early European writers

---

[1] See endnote 26:1, p. 396.
[2] Thomas, *With Lawrence in Arabia*.

on Asia and the Middle East, including Carsten Niebuhr (1792) and other early naturalists and doctors like Grose (1772) and Ives (1773).[3]

Corresponding with friends and family was a major avocation. Wells and Beth wrote copious letters, he with a portable typewriter and she in her fastidiously crafted handwriting. Wells wrote his stepmother weekly, regardless of heat or humidity or press of work at the hospitals. His epistles were models of clarity, as if he had brushed his hair and put on a clean shirt before writing her. She saved many of his letters, and they provide valuable insight into those times. In addition to communicating with their widely scattered families, Wells and Beth maintained a worldwide network of friends and acquaintances with whom they regularly shared information about life in Oman.

Wells had a highly developed aesthetic sensitivity, and from childhood on, he exhibited a great interest in nature. He was amazed at how unpromising plants would suddenly bloom with beautiful flowers and colors. He loved to draw and paint. As a student at Kalamazoo College, he was the art director and editor of the yearbook. Beth and he always tried to maintain a garden, both in Arabia and India, where vegetables and flowers coexisted. They found special satisfaction in flower gardening at their Kodai cottage.[4] Wells sketched and painted his way from Jerusalem to Iran—with the places where his work schedule was heaviest being least represented.

Besides social networking through letters, Wells and Beth waged their own continuous cribbage tournament. In Oman, they played bridge with the Chauncys, although no more than a half dozen times a year.[5] Trips to the beach (Saih al Malih or Qurm) offered retreat from the hurly burly of hospital and town life in Matrah. Tennis was popular in Oman, and friendly matches engaged teams made up of American Mission staff, Omani hospital staff, British expatriates, Sayyid Taroiq bin Taymur and Sayyid Thuwaini (of the royal family), and other influential Omanis. No matter how tired, Wells was always game for a tennis match. Volleyball was another group sport played

---

[3] Niebuhr, *Travels Through Arabia*. Grose, *A Voyage to the East Indies*. Ives, *A Voyage from England to India*. Ives was a doctor, and Wells loved his description of the elephant as having "a foot like a cat."

[4] The garden was a riot of colors and species, including verbenas, roses, delphiniums, zinnias, African violets, nasturtiums, dahlias, azaleas, and a pond with water lilies.

[5] Chauncey was British consul in Muscat for a decade and then became Sultan Sayyid Sa'eed's wazir. His wife was a colonial grande dame, a *burra memsahib* of the old style.

Thoms family in Kodai, ca. 1944 (WTC)

on the hospital grounds, and Wells organized a hospital team to play other local clubs and visiting Royal Navy squads.

High teas, receptions, and dinners completed Muscat's limited social "whirl." Teas were held weekly among the mission personnel, and monthly business "meetings" afforded relaxed community time, often overwhelmed by daily demands. Dinners were organized for important holidays and national days, as well as for visiting dignitaries. All these were insufficient to offset the grindingly inexorable enemy—the unrelenting heat and humidity of Gulf and Oman summers.

By the peak of Oman's summer weather, temperatures in the operating room approached 125 degrees Fahrenheit, a veritable sauna. There was no air-conditioning to relieve the stifling mugginess. As operating room temperatures rose, Wells found it more and more difficult to maintain his extensive schedule of afternoon operations. Despite precautions, it was always a challenge to prevent perspiration of the operating room staff from dripping into open incisions. Wells was probably thirty or more pounds lighter than he would have been because of the extreme heat.

At night, in mosquito-repelling, screened-in cages, Wells and Beth slept under the stars on the roof. As the weather approached roaster temperatures, they would hang wet sheets and towels as improvised evaporative coolers. But these fabrics dried so quickly Wells and Beth would have to continually remoisten them. As the summer progressed, the humidity rose so high that wet sheets and towels produced little cooling, for the water no longer evaporated. It seemed as if the surrounding hills radiated back as much humid heat at night as they absorbed from the sun during the day.

When Wells and his staff could no longer tolerate the heat, they stopped operating. His staff retreated to date gardens up the Batinah in search of relief from heat stress. There, the cooler ocean breeze and the gentle lullaby of the pounding surf were a world away from the urban oven of Matrah and its surrounding hills. Meanwhile, Beth and Wells would retreat to the hill station resort of Kodaikanal in South India.[6]

Kodai retreat

Beth and Wells relished the cool air of Kodai. They were grateful for its seven thousand-foot elevation, high above the mosquito-laden, malaria-infested plains below. In Kodai, the Thoms family and other Arabian Mission folks found a full complement of recreation and entertainment—conferences, tennis and bridge tournaments, plays, and concerts. Missionary families from throughout India, Ceylon, and even Burma would vacation in Kodai. It was a "Chautauqua Plus," an exhilarating time of renewal.

Most importantly, this was a time for reunion with children who attended Highclerc School. Frequently, the summer denizens of Kodai went on camping expeditions with their children to the rolling grasslands of the Palani Hills and in the remnant forests in the moist valleys.[7] The verdant vistas from the many outdoor walks scattered in the hills around Kodai's artificial lake formed a welcome contrast to Oman's dry browns and grays. Longer hikes into the hills beyond Kodai refreshed and energized vacationers.

Wells and Beth were especially fortunate when they went to Kodai. In the 1930s, Paul and Monty Harrison, posted to Oman, volunteered to serve elsewhere in the Gulf if Wells and Beth would take their place in Oman. The exchange was made, and the Harrisons expressed their appreciation by kindly offering to sell the Thomses their little Cotswold-like Kodai cottage named Dar Es Salaam.[8] Beth

---

[6] Crossette, *The Great Hill Stations of Asia*. Dickason, "The Indian Hill Station." "Kodaikanal" is pronounced (in Tamil) "ko-day-con-al." Westerners shortened it to the colloquial "Kodai."
[7] See endnote 26:7, p. 396.
[8] Realm of peace.

Beth (left), Ida. S. Scudder (center), and Ida B. Scudder, Dar Es Salaam, 1947 (WWT)

and Wells could recover from Oman's heat, regain some lost weight, and observe their children's progress in school from the comfort of their own mountain lodge.

Along with Dar Es Salaam, in the Indian colonial tradition, the Thoms family also "inherited" the property's cook/caretaker and family retainer, Mr. P. Soosainathan, "Soosai" for short. One of nature's noblemen, Soosai was loved by every generation of Dar Es Salaam residents for more than fifty years. Moreover, he was widely respected in Kodai's Indian community. Much of his charm came from his mixing American slang ("those guys") with contemporary British and Indian English. He sported a white, cotton *dhoti*, draped in traditional style around his waist and legs; a copious turban, loosely wound around his head; and a cast-off, Harris tweed jacket over a collarless white shirt. All of this was augmented by a stubble of beard, from five days to two weeks old. Soosai was Roman Catholic; his sweet-tempered son Stanislaus—named by Soosai's Polish priest-confessor—also helped as needed at Dar Es Salaam. Because the name "Stanislaus" sucked too much oxygen out of the Tamil language and sounded abrasive, everyone called him Thani, or Little Brother.[9]

---

[9] It would have been pronounced something like "es-stan-iss-los," perhaps pronounceable for Hindi speakers of the north but totally unsatisfactory to Tamil speakers of the south.

Mr. P. Soosainathan in his garden, 1946 (WWT)

Soosai reigned supreme in his windowless, smoky kitchen. From the ancient, broken-down, English, cast-iron, wood-and-coal-burning stove emerged unimaginable feasts. Since there was no refrigerator in Dar Es Salaam, Soosai purchased vegetables and meat in the bazaar daily. All dishes were prepared from scratch. Most difficult was the traditional American, after-church, Sunday-noon feast. There was hardly enough time for Soosai to prepare and cook everything, even if he started before breakfast. His fruit pies were a triumph of lattice-work or meringue tops with artistic scenes. Often, he would render, quite innocently, a pie decorated with a rendering of his beloved Roman Catholic church. This affront to a decidedly Protestant family did not go unnoticed, but Beth, mistress of the house, let it go unremarked upon since she recognized the positive influence of Soosai's faith on his conscientious service.

Kodai grocery stores stocked comparatively few prepared foods beyond powdered Ovaltine and Horlicks malted milk; powdered, evaporated, and condensed milk in tins; bitter Seville orange marmalade; Britannia biscuits; black tea; Marmite; tinned Australian butter; and Kraft cheese. Wells and Beth bought these from Hamidia's "grocery store." Yeast-raised bread came from the local King George bakery, but Soosai baked excellent rolls and cakes. The culinary magic was all his. In addition, Soosai was a prize-winning flower gardener. Dar Es Salaam snuggled into its flowerbeds like any Cotswold cottage should.

The children liked Spencer's and Pereira's for their hard candies, such as barley sugar and "goose eggs," and for tins of condensed milk

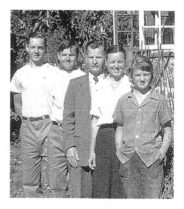

Five Thomses in Kodai, 1950 (WWT)

that could be caramelized by being submerged in boiling water for several hours. In addition, there was always the corner halwa man from whom "tastes" could be cadged in order to verify quality before purchase. As they grew older, the Thoms boys made excursions into the bazaar, called "the Budge," where they could acquire fireworks from Shri V. T. Pillai. His hardware store supplied the entire school population with firecrackers, bottle rockets, and "flowerpots."

V. T. took much ribbing from the schoolboys, who would ask for "left-handed screw drivers" and "red, white, and blue-striped paint," among other mythical products. V. T.'s invariable response to these imaginary objects was to scratch his head or smooth his mustache and declare, "Well, Mistair, I am not having in stock at present. Next week, I am going to Madurai, and I am definitely inquiring. Now, I am having available very good bottle rockets from Tenkasi, and other things also." Juvenile arsonists could not resist his pitch; they were drawn to V. T. Pillai like luna moths were drawn to the mercury vapor streetlamps at the Five Corners intersection outside Kodai School's main gate. He took the teasing in good humor and never raised his prices beyond what the traffic would bear.

The Thoms boys went to the Budge for their haircuts, next door to the Kodaikanal Cooperative Stores, Ltd. There, a young man, Mr. N. Muthu, clipped their manes with style, always including a razor shave of their sideburns and around their necks. At some point, the calm, enterprising, and self-possessed Muthu was allowed to come to the school's compound on Saturday mornings to administer haircuts outdoors. As a result, boys did not have as many opportunities for mischief as they had had in the Budge. Muthu became modestly wealthy from his moppet-clipping monopoly and bought orchards and land below the town. The only difference between a school haircut and

Hiking at Marian Shola, 1943 (WTC)

the real thing was that school clients did not receive the surprise, right-to-left head snap of their neck vertebrae, the *de rigeur* final move of any self-respecting Indian barber in the Budge.

When they were very young, Beth and Wells' children—Nancy, Peter, Norman, and Lowey—all attended Kodai School as day scholars when the family vacationed in nearby Dar Es Salaam. As soon as the children were old enough, usually at age seven, they entered dormitory life. The school was small, with most grades enrolling fewer than twenty-five students.

Since other children of missionary, business, and diplomatic families also commuted to the boarding school in Kodai, the Thoms children believed it was "normal" to live far removed from their parents. They even took to traveling on chaperoned and unchaperoned journeys for as long as a week in each direction, to and from school. The Thoms children formed lifelong friendships there. Indeed, it shocked many parents to discover that their children welcomed the prospect of leaving home in January to be with their friends for the long school year. That attitude attested to the well-run nature of the school and its highly principled staff. For the Thoms children, there was the reassuring security of having a family home in Kodaikanal where their parents came each year.

En route to Vandaravu (a thirty-five-mile hike), 1949 (WWT)

The school's anchor was Carl Phelps, an impeccable embodiment of a New England, Christian-school headmaster. Balding and short, every day he strode masterfully from his picturesque lakeside residence to the main gate of the school, resplendent in his three-piece suit and tie, cane in hand, declaring with undeniable body language that a steady, no-nonsense, leader was at the helm and fully in control. The school offered an American and Eurocentric college preparatory curriculum.[10]

During World War II, the teaching staff was enriched by the numerous "enemy aliens" stranded in India. These civilians would be released from British internment camps in India if they could find employment. Fritz Kolb, an Austrian mountaineer, trapped in India when war broke out, became a physical education instructor at the school.[11] Alois Musil, a gifted Czech linguist, taught ancient and modern European languages, particularly Latin and French, but also German, Spanish, Greek, Hebrew, and Russian.[12] A Swiss expatriate,

---

[10] It did not admit that India and Asia were legitimate areas of study. Students did not benefit from field projects into the local communities, nor did the school prepare students for Indian, British, or German higher education. Students from those countries were at a distinct disadvantage upon returning to the United Kingdom or Germany.

[11] Kolb became Austria's ambassador to Pakistan and later served as director of the Institute of Advanced Studies in Laxenburg, Austria.

[12] Musil's fluency in Latin was such that he conversed regularly with the student priests at the Jesuit College in Shembaganur, four miles below Kodai School. Latin was the common language for the five hundred Jesuits in training.

Madame Caspari, taught piano and was a lifelong proponent of Madame Montessori's teaching philosophy and methods. Mario DiGiorgio, an Italian from Trieste, was a gifted violinist. He and his small chamber orchestra were touring the Orient, playing in hotels and upscale restaurants, when World War II erupted. He took charge of Kodai School's orchestra and vocal music programs.[13]

The student body was also partly composed of children of "enemy alien" families, especially of German Christian missionaries in India. After initially interning these families at a prisoner of war camp, British authorities realized the children threatened no one and should be able to go to school rather than be home schooled inside the internment camp. A special dormitory was set up with German house parents for these students. Names like Helms, Speck, Meyer, Tauscher, and Jungjohann were common on class rosters, and the Germans added richness to campus cultural life and sports.[14]

The boarding school experience was more difficult for Beth and Wells than for their children. To send their children off by ship every January, knowing they would not see them for five or six months, was emotionally difficult. Wells and Beth looked forward immensely to their mid- and end-of-year family reunions. Their strong bonds with the peoples of the Gulf and their children's love of their school community in India kept them from resigning from the Arabian Mission and seeking Christian medical service in the United States.

Furlough and the journey "home"[15]

In 1948 the Thoms family was overdue for leave in the United States.[16] Nancy graduated from high school in May and, along with four of her classmates, planned on returning to the States to enter college in September.[17] Long-haul air flights did not yet exist, so an ocean voyage

---

[13] See endnote 26:13, p. 396.

[14] The school's female physician, Dr. Rosenthal, was a Jewish emigre from Germany, one indication of how the school evinced an environment of toleration among staff and students.

[15] This account comes principally from Beth Scudder Thoms Dickason's written account and Maisie Korteling's detailed letters to her parents and to Lowey and David Dickason.

[16] Furloughs were awarded like sabbaticals—every seven years. Furloughs allowed for the reunion of extended families, health care, continuing education, fundraising from supporting churches, speaking tours to churches, and rest (if time remained). The Thomses were on furlough in 1939, 1948, 1956, and 1962.

[17] Nancy was to enter Oberlin College. Her classmates were Bob Carman, Hal Closson, Marian (Maisie) Korteling, and Margaret DeValois.

was the default option for travelers. Arranging ship's passage was difficult in the years after World War II because so many expatriates wanted to return to either Europe or North America. Some families had to split up, sailing on different ships. As an alternative to dividing missionary families, Jack DeValois, an RCA missionary working in India, secured passage for the DeValois and Thoms families on the MV *Taurinia*,[18] a slow-moving Italian freighter. They were accompanied by three of Nancy's classmates and the school's Italian teacher, Madame Caspari, and her husband.[19]

The *Taurinia* was a tramp freighter capable of hauling a variety of cargoes. She was among the war's "floating wounded," having been sunk in Naples harbor in 1945 and then refloated, repaired, and equipped with two well-worn diesel engines. Her previous name was SS *Ipanema*, suggesting a South American heritage. She would take forty-eight days to reach Naples from Madras, India, with port calls at Colombo, Ceylon; Aden; Djibouti, French Somaliland; Massawa, Eritrea; Port Said, Egypt; and Beirut, Lebanon.

There were fifteen people in the Thoms-DeValois entourage, and ten more travelers completed the passenger manifest of the *Taurinia*. Most notable was the keeper who accompanied the caged live animals stored at the stern of the ship. He was transporting wild animals (including a python, a deer, a baby elephant, a baby leopard, and various wild cats) to restock Milan's zoo after World War II. The elephant drank a bucket of milk a day. The baby leopard was handled by the children until it became a convinced carnivore.

Several days into the Indian Ocean voyage, Beth was surprised when family and friends raucously sang "Happy Birthday" to her, and the chief steward proudly proffered a custom-baked birthday cake. It was all the more surprising when they discovered that the cake literally oozed cognac. After polite nibbles from the teetotaling missionary adults and faces of "icky" disbelief from the underage younger set, the birthday celebrants passed the cake on to the crew who demolished it with delight—appreciative of the birthday girl's generosity. More birthdays were to come. No matter how much the travelers protested, the cakes always came saturated with cognac. The Americans, however, did find that the daily spaghetti ration was delicious and came cognac-free.

---

[18] A girl's name, meaning "female bull."
[19] See endnote 26:19, p. 397.

Monsoon mayhem

The annual southwest monsoon set in with gusto as the *Taurinia* grumbled, sputtered, and vibrated westward through the Indian Ocean. The ungainly freighter labored sluggishly in the heavy seas, propelled by only one ailing diesel engine that belched a cloud of greasy black smoke. The captain set a southwesterly course, head on into the wind and waves, a passage that sufficed as long as they were able to head southwest. Eventually, however, to enter the Red Sea, the ship had to cut diagonally northwest in a path guaranteed to nauseate passengers while the ship pitched and rolled across the blustering wind and the angry ocean. Indeed, the ship did buck, yaw, roll, and plunge. Travelers with delicate stomachs, including Wells, fell into their bunks. Beth and a hardy few remained upright, trying to control their queasiness, and held on tightly to stanchions and railings when on deck.

One particularly wretched morning, Maisie Korteling, Lowey, and a young English girl walked behind the bridge for fresh air. The girls soon went below, but Maisie stayed outside to watch the breakers. Suddenly a rogue wave slammed into the ship's port side, and the vessel rolled dangerously. The wave engulfed the ship's superstructure and cascaded down the lee side of the vessel, looking to Beth "like Niagara encaving us." As she and her friend were singing "My Bonnie Lies over the Ocean," Beth saw Maisie's green blouse flash past in the surge of water cascading off the upper deck.

Horrified, Beth ran to the bridge shouting, "Man—woman—girl overboard!" When women on deck saw Maisie bobbing in the water, they threw emergency life rings over the side. Being white, the rings were invisible in the white frothy foam. Fortunately, one red ring was easier to see, and they hoped Maisie would find it. Crew members clambered aboard a lifeboat and released it from its davits. The sea was so rough that the lifeboat slammed against the hull as it was lowered toward the swirling brine, endangering its crew.

The captain and first mate, already on the bridge, decided at once to hazard a rescue. The *Taurinia* turned precariously across the huge waves. In midturn, the ship canted at a treacherously steep angle before slowly righting itself. Finally, the 180-degree turn was completed. Now everyone crowded the deck wondering where the teenager was in the immensity of the tumultuous sea.

Surprised at being swept overboard, Maisie immediately started treading water.[20] As the ship receded into the distance, she knew there

---

[20] This section comes from Maisie Korteling's account.

was no way she could catch it, much less climb back aboard. She knew the propellers would be dangerous if she got sucked into the ship's wake. At the bottom of the deep troughs, she was afraid the high mountains of water around her would drive her under. She bobbed like a cork as the waves passed under her. She had lost her glasses. Squinting through the darkness, she could see only the ship's masts, and then she was alone in the steely gray, warm sea. It was pointless to thrash around. Watching the ship disappear out of sight was profoundly disheartening. The wind and spray blinded her, so she did not know if she was crying. Even if she was desperate, what was the point of screaming? She rolled over, turned her back to the waves, and floated in the maelstrom.

Within minutes of their precarious 180-degree turn, the officers on the bridge sighted the red life ring and brought the ship to a stop. Less than a hundred feet away was Maisie, improbably bobbing on the surface. A rope ladder was dropped over the side and a sailor descended.

Suddenly, miraculously, Maisie became aware of the ship rolling, pitching, and yawing almost beside her. Although she had lost her spectacles, she could see well enough to swim toward the ladder. She had been unaware of the ship until it was almost on top of her.

As she neared the ladder, a sailor scooped her up, placed her on the bottom rung, then lifted her slowly, step by step, making sure she did not lose her grip or fall back into the sea. Time stood still. When Maisie reached the deck, the officer on the bridge noted it had been just seventeen-and-a-half minutes since the great wave overwhelmed the ship. Virtual "death-and-resurrection" in seventeen-and-a-half minutes. Now all they had to do was turn the ship around once again onto their intended course. Outstanding bravery and seamanship had completed a miraculous, midocean rescue. The English-speaking passengers spontaneously started singing the doxology.

Maisie, dazed from slamming her head on the railing when she went overboard, had suffered a deep scalp wound. Wells sewed her up and put her to bed. Understandably, she was in shock, claiming she was just fine when, in fact, she was completely drained by this life-threatening experience. Sleep was the best therapy. Everything had happened so quickly that she did not have time to ponder her predicament. She was encapsulated entirely in the moment.

"What were you thinking when you were out there in those big waves all by yourself?" asked one of her companions the next morning.

"Well, I'm short sighted. I lost my glasses, so I couldn't see the life rings. The ship was so big, I couldn't really miss it, but it was amazing how close it came. I'm a poor swimmer, so I decided to tread water. I didn't give up hope that the ship would come back. Then when it did appear, I thought, 'Boy, will I have a good story to tell my children!'"

"What a feat of outstanding seamanship! What convinced the captain and first mate to swing the ship around in such dangerous conditions?" asked another.

A knowing teenage voice responded, "The first mate is sweet on Maisie. He calls her 'Ze Maisie' and is always on the lookout for her. After the rescue, he hugged her and said, 'I'm so thankful!'"

To celebrate her rescue and to eclipse her trauma, the travelers composed a song and held a games tournament as the *Taurinia* labored onward. In a class by herself, Maisie won the swimming prize.

Animals in turmoil

Amid all the turbulence of the ocean, the animals on board had been thrown around violently. Cages popped open, and terrified animals careened about on deck. Rumor quickly spread that a "boa constrictor" had escaped.[21] A baby elephant ran down a passageway and got wedged headfirst in Peter and Norman's cabin, stuck between the bunks. When found, she was squealing for her mom. Ultimately, a bucket of milk and some of alfalfa calmed her down and coaxed her out.

The sambhar deer also required attention. He had fallen and broken his right foreleg below the knee. His keeper came to Wells in distress, claiming this accident to have been the disastrous "last straw" of the voyage. Could Wells splint the leg of this beautiful animal? Wells searched the infirmary and found bandages and plaster of paris. He mixed the plaster, soaked the bandages with it, and then wrapped the deer's immobilized leg.

A month later, before arriving in Naples, Wells and the keeper went to remove the cast and discovered it was gone. The deer had eaten it. The bone had knit, but the keeper was upset. "My beautiful animal is deformed. See this unsightly bulge on his leg."

Wells consoled him, "It could be much worse. People will understand that he, too, has a war wound. He could have died. Cheer up. Your sambhar deer is alive and well and has four good legs. With his three-tined antlers held high, he can still lead his herd." Wells thought

---

[21] That it was a boa is unlikely since that species is from South America. More likely, it was a Burmese python or a reticulated python. Both species grow to more than eighteen feet long.

he might have set a precedent for treating fractures—edible casts. There were no takers.

The escaped snake was the biggest concern to the sea-bedraggled passengers. Panic spread. Two English spinsters refused to come out of their stateroom for fear of it and demanded that their meals be delivered to their door. Cabin doors remained shut to limit the big snake's progress. A day later, it was found comfortably wrapped up in a coil of rope at the bow of the ship. Apparently, snakes get seasick too.

Jack DeValois recommended that Maisie send her parents a telegram letting them know of her ordeal bit by bit. As a first message, he suggested she send the telegram: "Glasses lost overboard. Send prescription." Then when they reached Interlaken, Switzerland—far from the sea after her worst memories faded—she wrote her parents so they would not first get the full story by grapevine.

Once back home in Holland, Michigan, Maisie shared her story with her church's youth group. A day or two later, while driving to Holland from Grand Rapids, Wells and Beth picked up two teenage hitchhikers. One of the boys said to the other: "You know, there was a gal who spoke on Sunday to our class at church. She said she had been washed overboard into the Indian Ocean and was picked up again. It sounded like a tall tale to me."

Wells looked over his shoulder and said, "Young man, you can believe every word she said. We know that brave girl. We were there when it happened. I sewed up her scalp wound. It was a miraculous rescue, and we praise God for it."

"Home"

Furlough came every seventh year. This was a precious time for bonding anew with family and friends in the United States. It was also a time for the Thomses to re-establish links with the churches that supported them with prayer and by pledging donations. Wells and Beth, like all other missionaries, made the circuit of as many RCA churches as possible to update and motivate them for the missionary enterprise.

At the same time, their children needed to attend school, but Wells also wanted his children to see and learn as much about the United States as possible, especially its natural wonders. To accommodate their school timetable, short trips occurred during the school year, and longer trips were scheduled during summer vacation. Their summer trips frequently included marathon drives, usually wrapped around speaking engagements. They would often arrive at a worried pastor's door very late on a Saturday night, barely in time for a short night's sleep before Sunday services and mandatory socializing.

The Thoms kids loved the summer mission-fest days when their family threaded its way across Iowa, a bastion of Dutch Reformed Calvinism. Church potluck dinners always seemed to finish with perfectly ripe, sweet melons and refreshing vanilla ice cream—heaven to those who had been ice cream starved for the previous six years. The kids heard their father speak many times and playfully counted how often he told the same stories. Wells was entirely aware of what they were doing and tried to vary their listening diet, but he found that good stories were worth retelling, even if they did garner youthful teasing.

An unexpected feeling would universally sweep through returning missionaries. Shortly after arriving in the United States, they would realize that it no longer felt like "home." Yes, of course, it was their familial and national "home," but it was not really their "flesh-and-blood" home anymore, even though their flesh-and-blood relatives lived here. They were caught in a fog of culture shock. For Beth and Wells, America was somehow different now than it was when last they were here. It was even more different from the way it had been when they first went to the mission field. This sense of dislocation always made them eager to return to Arabia.

For the children, public schooling in Grand Rapids was bearable, but they also suffered from the loss of their familiar places and routines. Their new school was not a substitute for their boarding school in India and the intimate friendships they had formed there. Although the United States was their ancestral home, it was not their "real" home—the one of warmth, love, and intimacy they thrived on. No matter how hard they tried, they could not see themselves as part of the local community. If not consciously cosmopolitan, they had become global citizens, and the provinciality of West Michigan was disconcerting.

Happily, the furlough concluded at the end of 1949, and with gratitude, the Thoms family—minus Nancy, who remained for college—returned to Oman, and the children excitedly proceeded to boarding school in South India. The rhythm and pace of mission life resumed once again.

CHAPTER 27

Hospital Snapshots: Transition and Development

The [prime] minister asked if Wells believed in the existence of heaven.

The end of "Old Oman"[1]

World War II greatly changed life in Oman. Under Britain's security umbrella, the sultan continued to rule, at least titularly, the *diras* of many nearly autonomous tribes—with the interior under the imam's flag being almost completely autonomous. These areas were linked to the sultanate by the modes of transportation that had been used for centuries. On land, people walked, rode donkeys, or used camels and camel caravans for passenger and freight travel. On water, sailing ships linked coastal towns and villages as they had done for centuries. Only a few shipping companies connected key ports in the Gulf, such as Matrah, with the wider world. No ports could handle large ships of the motorized age, so people and cargo were transshipped to shore by small boats and barges. Civilian air transport was of little importance in Oman.

Despite this seemingly ageless tapestry, war had triggered rapid developments, and change was in the wind. World War II brought motor transport to Oman in the form of surplus army trucks, jeeps, and motor

---
[1] See endnote 27:1, p. 397.

Camel caravan, 1950s (RB)

launches. At their arrival, few realized the impact they would have on the tribes' isolation. Although day-to-day community life remained unchanged, the greater ease of reaching other communities expanded the knowledge and choices open to individuals and communities. Symbolic of this change was the Land Rover that soon occupied a secure niche in Omani life. As long as roads were not built, camels could compete disadvantageously with Land Rovers. At first, the Omani camel had nothing to fear except the sound of growling truck engines and clashing gears that pierced the quietude of the desert. After roads were built, however, the age of the camel and donkey passed quickly, and Oman's world changed.

An example of the changes in store occurred in 1947 when Shaykh Sulayman bin Hamyar heard Wells was attending to the imam. Shaykh Sulayman raced up to Nizwa Fort in a US Army surplus jeep given to him by the sultan. Against the imam's complete opposition to modern technologies in his realm, Shaykh Sulayman's appearance was unique and tradition shattering. At that time, the only petrol (gas) station in all of Oman was on the coast at Riyam, between Muscat and Matrah. There gasoline, lubricating oil, and kerosene could be purchased in five-gallon cans. Initially, these cans were hauled by camel into the interior for Shaykh Sulayman, who soon saw to it that Land Rovers regularly brought the supplies to him. In such small steps, the modern world intruded into the interior of Oman.

Cholera-like dysentery?

In September 1949, a messenger on a fast camel (with another fine, smooth-riding camel in tow) brought an emergency request from Shaykh Sulayman bin Hamyar of the Bani Riyam. An epidemic of dysentery had broken out in Tanuf and Nizwa. The shaykh's son was sick and near death. Many others were afflicted. Could Wells come immediately?

Dr. Lakra had just returned from his annual leave in India, and the Dykstras were away. If Wells went to the interior, Beth would have to manage church worship and preaching, the school teaching tasks, and the hospitals—a heavy load on top of her own duties teaching women to read and write Arabic. Wells had hoped to take Beth with him to the interior, but this was not the right time. Wells immediately departed by camel for Tanuf with four assistants—Qumber, Mallalah, and Qumber's two sons (Husain and Ali)—and a large supply of medicines on this nineteen-day round trip.

Upon arrival in Tanuf, they found the shaykh's son emaciated and feverish. Two people had already died from fulminating diarrhea before he arrived, and other babies and adults had also died. Wells was concerned the outbreak could be cholera. Careful assessment of others who had contracted the bloody flux convinced Wells that they presented the Shiga strain of bacillary dysentery instead.

Wells recalled in his annual report:

> We had plenty of heavy ammunition to throw at the disease, Sulfasuxadine and Sulphaguanadine as well as vitamins in ampoule form as well as tablets. Several bottles of intravenous glucose and normal saline came in handy. We spent nine days passing out medicines to all and sundry who came to our temporary dispensary, and in the afternoons doing minor eye operations. By giving out the sulfa drugs in generous amounts free of charge to a large number of people in Tanuf and nearby Nizwa, we seemed to have stopped the force of the dysentery epidemic. Over one hundred operations were done. A good supply of atebrine for malaria and sulphaguanidine for dysentery were left with the shaykh to give out to sufferers of these diseases after our departure. Shaykh Sulayman bin Hamyar became a fairly keen diagnostician and enthusiast of the new medicines.

The shaykh's son soon began to improve, as did many who were not *in extremis* when Wells arrived. Wells surmised the disease must have contaminated oasis water channels, the *felejes,* with feces of sick people. People normally drank the canal water without boiling it, so canals were direct conduits for the waters of life to turn into the waters of disease, pestilence, and death. Since the outbreak extended southward, those with dysentery must have either traveled to or affected the zone as far south as the canal of the Felej Daris in Upper Nizwa, the largest in Oman.

During one afternoon's operations, Shaykh Yasser, leader of the Janaba tribe, appeared at the operating room doorway saying he needed Wells to treat a sixteen-year-old Bedu boy in a distant encampment. The boy had been stabbed. Shaykh Sulayman bin Hamyar was anxious to help others of his Ghafiri tribal coalition and volunteered the use of his jeep. In less than an hour, the two shaykhs, the jeep driver, and Wells were on their way to the small oasis of al Hubi near the Rub al-Khali. Their route went through Bahla, with its great twelve-mile circumference wall and fortress, and on to the impressive castle at Yabrin seven miles farther. There the car stopped so that the shaykhs and jeep driver could attend to their evening prayers. While they were doing so, Wells explored the castle and was impressed by the six-story, forty-room fortress with walls twelve feet thick at the base and three feet thick at the top. Its teak doors were termite-proof and beautifully made, and its ceilings were sumptuously patterned in the designs of a Persian carpet. Wells thought artisans may have been brought from India to build it. He thought to himself, there were giants in the land in those days.

They continued driving through Bisyah and Fil, crossing ancient, abandoned irrigation ditches and wheat fields. They eventually found the encampment at al Hubi and were welcomed by scores of rifle shots from enthusiastic tribesmen. To have two great shaykhs and a foreign doctor visit at the same time was cause for celebration.

Wells found his feverish patient with a deep abscess in his back, the result of the infected stab wound. Wells incised the wound, drained it, and packed it with iodoform gauze. The young man was given morphine and Procaine penicillin. By the time they departed in the middle of the night, the patient was sleeping peacefully, and his temperature had returned to near normal. With a few hours of sleep on soft cool sand and a fine meal of roast goat and rice, they started their return trip to Tanuf and arrived just as the sun's first faint glow touched the eastern sky.

As they alighted from the jeep, Shaykh Yasser expressed in amazement, "If we had gone by camel, the whole round trip of one hundred miles would have taken us five days. We left here after asr prayers yesterday afternoon, and here we are back again before the fejer'athan prayer this morning. I used to be opposed to automobiles in my *dira*. Now I'm going to ask the Ingleez to give me one."

If camels could have understood him—particularly since he was one of the more conservative leaders of the interior—they would have groaned in alarm. Bedu life was about to change fundamentally for the first time since the domestication of the camel. The door had just slammed on the Camel Age. The Motor Age had begun without ceremony. *Sic transit gloria mundi.*

First cataract

Wells had received a number of communications from the imam since their initial meeting. The imam's eyes were deteriorating in association with developing cataracts that Wells had examined at that time. By 1953 the imam's sight had worsened to the point he could no longer read. In desperation, he twice requested Wells to come. His attitude toward modern medicine was softening as he saw the benefits of Wells' eye surgery on other patients in Nizwa and Tanuf.

Communications with the imam and the interior of Oman were increasingly controlled by the sultan after Wells had gone into Oman's interior in the early 1940s. The letter from the imam in 1953 requesting Wells operate on his cataracts came directly to Wells, but Wells believed it was necessary to consult the sultan to gain official permission to go into the interior for this purpose. The sultan's first answer was firmly negative; Wells could under no circumstance treat the imam. Second thoughts, however, prevailed, and Wells received a countermanding letter authorizing him to go to Nizwa to operate on the imam. Whether this was a decision of Leslie Chauncy or the sultan, Wells could not tell. It seemed to reflect the understanding that the imam was elderly,[2] that he no longer presented a significant threat to the sultan, that there was little likelihood of a new strong imamate forming again after the imam's death, and that cultivating diplomatic relations between coast and interior was useful.[3]

The press of hospital work in Matrah, however, prevented Wells from heading for Nizwa for almost fifty days after the imam's requests

---

[2] The imam's strength had failed, and he was barely able to stand.
[3] The British Foreign Office was very sensitive about this trip. See endnote 27:3, p. 398.

Beth, Wells, and Lowey in Arab dress, 1953 (WTC)

arrived. It must have seemed an eternity to the imam. Fortunately, the letters were written by the imam's personal secretary, Hilal bin Ali, his nephew. The letters requested Wells and his party, including Beth and Lowey,[4] to come dressed in Arab garb, and they did so.[5] When they arrived at the great round tower of Nizwa's fortress after their several-day camel trip, they climbed up to meet the imam in his mejlis in the tower.

After the usual pleasantries and refreshing coffee, Wells presented a three-volume version of the Holy Bible to the imam, who accepted it graciously, saying he would read it after regaining his sight. The imam was mannerly and polite toward Beth and Lowey, addressing them by their Arabic names, Khatoun Jauhara and Atiya.[6] In an exception to the normal greetings toward women, the imam shook Beth's hand gingerly through his cloth-covered fingertips. Even though he could

---

[4] In 1951 Wells took his two sons, Peter and Norman, along with Beth, into the Jabal Akhdhar and beyond to Bahla and Yabrin. He wanted them to see the interior; his sons, having graduated from secondary school, were soon to return to the US for their collegiate studies. They did not visit the imam on this trip.

[5] In fact, they always dressed in Arab garb when in public on multiday tours outside Muscat or Matrah. They also carried Western clothing in case an occasion required it.

[6] *Atiya* means "a gift."

not see well, he lifted four pomegranates from a bowl and proffered them to Lowey with a smile saying, "A gift for 'a Gift.'"

Wells examined the imam's eyes again and found the cataracts to have "ripened," ready for excision. A room in the fort was prepared as an operating room, and several days later, Wells operated on one of the imam's eyes. The imam's qadi said he had found a verse from the Q'uran that indicated man's responsibility is to take care of his health to the best of his ability, implying that Wells' treatment was now approved in the imam's domain. The surgery was a success, and the imam agreed Wells should return in six months to repair his other eye. Wells would have agreed with the theology, expressed widely in Nizwa, that all healing comes from God and that Wells was only His channel (*sebab*). In the meantime, the imam's restored sight in one eye helped him greatly.

In conversation, the imam raised the issue of Wells' gift of the Christian Scriptures being given away for free in Nizwa. He noted that there was resistance to distribution of Christian Scripture. Other Muslim religious leaders had objected.

As they talked, the imam suggested, "Why cannot your Scriptures be sold for a small price? You are "People of the Book." It is alright if our people do not wish to pay the price asked for your Scriptures. It is not the same as giving Scripture free to anyone whether they want it or not." The imam recalled for Wells that in his boyhood Christian colporteurs from Syria occasionally came through the interior selling Christian Scriptures, and that people then were eager to buy portions because there were few books of any kind available locally. Nobody had found fault with the colporteurs then, perhaps because they were not from the Arabian Peninsula but also because they were not Westerners.

Wells wanted to take a photograph of the imam before operating. Being an antimodernist, the imam refused to pose and turned away from the camera. He said, "In the Quran it says 'Those who make likenesses of living creatures must, in the day of Judgment, give them life.'"

Wells pointed out that many Muslim Arab governments required their subjects to have a photograph taken for their passports. Even the sultan's government in Muscat issued passports for all from the imam's domain who traveled internationally.

The imam replied, "I do not consider people who do such things [to be] Muslims; rather, I think they must be *kafirs*." When pressed, the imam admitted to having seen his own reflection in a mirror several times, but he had a low opinion of the vain men and women who regularly looked at themselves in mirrors. The imam was not a narcissist.

When Wells said, "I would still very much like to take a photo of you," the imam demurred again. "If I take the picture of you, the blame will be on me," Wells assured him.

Rock solid in his convictions, the imam rejoined, *"Ma'awanak bi-sharr"*[7]

In the wake of the imam's death

In 1954 the imam died before Wells could return to remove his second cataract. His death marked the end of the thirty-four-year-old Agreement of Seeb, the truce between the tribes loyal to the imam and the tribes loyal to the sultan. That agreement had divided Oman into two pseudostates separating the interior from the coast.

What would happen now that the imam was gone? Questions abounded. Would the *tamimas* and shaykhs of the interior tribes assert their power to select a new imam? If so, who would measure up to the standards of Ibadhi tradition?[8] Would Sultan Sayyid Sa'eed bin Taymur want a renewed Seeb-like agreement? Would the British? Would Britain continue to back the sultan indefinitely? Would Shaykh Sulayman bin Hamyar, now the dominant *tamima* of the interior, be content with an old-style imamate? Did he really consider himself a rival to the sultan by claiming to be the "King of the Nabahina and Lord of the Green Mountains," as he titled himself in his letters to Wells? Did he fancy carving out his own, independent kingdom, funded by oil royalties or Sa'udi support, as preferable to a loosely structured traditional imamate?

A workable solution to these vexing questions would require lengthy negotiations. Whatever Oman was to become politically, it was going to be difficult to squeeze Humpty-Dumpty back into the form of the old tribal alliances. Wells speculated to himself that Sultan Sayyid Sa'eed—far from an ideal candidate—would somehow

---

[7] I will not help you in doing evil.
[8] Numerous treatises describe the Ibadhi and their differences from other Islamic groups. The Ibadhi trace their origins to the earliest days of Islam. Their imam of the early twentieth century was distinctive for his opposition to modernity and inanimate energy-powered technology. A devout and learned man, he ruled in the tradition of benevolent dictators. His concern was for the wellbeing and sustainability of the Muslim community. He was entirely above moral reproach and was an exceptional spiritual leader.

prevail either as the new imam or as a postimamate ruler. Wells had no special knowledge or information on which to base his hunch, but he knew most of the potential leaders personally and was a good judge of character.

Sultan Sayyid Sa'eed had no intention of allowing the initiative to pass to the interior's influential tribal personalities. In an unprecedented raid, he and mobile troops riding World War II surplus army vehicles invaded the interior from the south. He moved before organized resistance could be mounted, and he was joined by other troops from the coast. Sultan Sa'eed had the advantage of both modern alliances and ancient traditions. He was the sultan with whom many tribes were already traditionally aligned. For the short term, he cut a deal with the leading interior shaykh, Sulayman bin Hamyar, reaffirming the Seeb Agreement-based rights of Sulayman to the Birkat al Moz Fort at the head of the Wadi Sama'il. Finally, the British, on whom he had always depended when confronted by worst-case scenarios, backed the sultan. Together, these measures secured the sultan's influence, for a time, as ruler of the entire country.

Even so, it was not assured that Sultan Sa'eed would prevail in the long run. He was known as a reluctant ruler and as one who was bakhil, a skinflint. He had never erected more than a minimalist state, and what did exist functioned in a very limited way. Many of his key administrators were non-Omanis—from his personal wazir and head of the armed forces, who were both British, to the director of Customs, who was Pakistani, to the wali of Matrah, who was Palestinian, to the Baluchi mercenaries, who were the backbone of his armed forces. Only his minister of the Interior, Sayyid Ahmad bin Ibrahim, who was the de facto prime minister when the sultan did not reside in Muscat, was Omani. Sayyid Ahmad was one of the sultan's distant cousins and had the job of collecting *zakat*[9] and receiving information from walis and qadis throughout the sultan's domains. Who paid their *zakat*, and into which *bayt al mal*[10] they paid it, defined political allegiance in the absence of votes and party politics.

On top of that, some Omanis perceived the sultan to be too Westernized. He had been educated in British India and was fluent in English, which supported the perception of his Westernization. Moreover, he was not a fervent Islamic leader. Until or unless he was

---

[9] Religious tithes.
[10] Treasury or bank.

Drs. Das, Bosch, Thoms, and Draper, ca. 1960 (WTC)

perceived to be a sufficiently conservative Muslim ruler, his future was in doubt.

Expansion of medical mission

Until the mid-1950s, there was usually only one mission doctor in residence at the Matrah and Muscat mission hospitals. The death of the imam, who had been reluctant to allow his subjects to visit the mission hospitals, and the subsequent invasion of the interior by the sultan, brought about the end of mobility restrictions on Omanis. This unleashed a much-expanded volume of work on the mission hospitals. Consequently, more mission doctors were appointed to Oman. Wells initially contracted with able doctors from India. In later years, several of these Indian doctors, who had started their careers in mission service, continued to serve nobly in other Omani government hospitals. There were also many other doctors who visited Oman for limited tours of duty, extending from a few weeks up to one year.

Wells wrote about the resulting expansion of services:

> We now have an obstetrical unit in Knox Memorial Hospital, a group of four rooms underneath [Dr.] Lakra's house. The old garage and storeroom [have] been remodeled so now we have a clean, lighted delivery room, a four-bed ward, one private room and two kitchens, a bathroom, and a toilet, all enclosed in a walled-in compound so that it is a separate unit to be used exclusively for obstetrics.[11]

Until the early 1950s and the arrival of Jeanette Boersma, no American mission nurse was appointed to Oman.[12] In order to meet

---

[11] Medical report for 1952-53.
[12] Elizabeth Cantine and Mrs. Van Peursem had run clinics in Muscat earlier.

Matrah hospital staff, 1950s (WTC)

the demand of the hospitals, Wells contracted with Indian nurses (men and women) to provide nursing services, such as with Nurse Mary. By the late 1960s, missionary nurses from Denmark and the United States were working in the hospital, and the missionaries had begun training Omani hospital staff in more complex duties.

Tanuf revolt

After the death of the old imam in 1954, matters in the interior were in flux. Although Sultan Sayyid Sa'eed had sent troops into the interior to claim it under his jurisdiction, the shaykhs of the interior wanted to continue the imamate and appoint their own candidate. But they failed to find someone who had a reputation of integrity to match that of the old imam. At the same time, Shaykh Sulayman bin Hamyar had visions of autonomy (if not total independence) from both the imam and the sultan.

As a symbol of his independence, Shaykh Sulayman invited the mission in 1957 to send a medical tour to the Jabal Akhdhar and Tanuf. The group was large and included many new doctors and nurses of the hospital, as well as Wells and Beth. They traveled via motor vehicles along the road to the interior constructed by Petroleum Development, Oman (the PDO), the recently created agency to oversee the development of the oil industry. The medical team spent a month in Tanuf, saw many patients in clinics, and carried out many operations. For trichiasis alone, they operated successfully on more than one thousand people.

Such a lengthy and productive period at Tanuf must have improved the reputation of Shaykh Sulayman bin Hamyar among his

---

Jeanette Boersma arrived in 1952. Others arrived in 1958 and 1959, with a regular supply of mission-appointed, short-term nurses beginning in the mid-1960s.

own people and other tribes of the interior (and possibly emboldened him to push for even more autonomy). The shaykh shared none of his grand plans with either Wells or the mission team. Shortly after they returned to the capital, civil war in the Jabal Akhdhar broke out. Ultimately, the sultan's forces won, assisted by British aircraft and troops. Shaykh Sulayman bin Hamyar, the would-be Imam Ghalib, and others fled to Sa'udi Arabia. The sultan had won the day. To cement his victory, his country was renamed the Sultanate of Muscat and Oman.[13]

Not long thereafter, the mission learned of new rules affecting their travel inside the country. Wells and Beth were limited to traveling within a seventy-five-mile radius of the capital cities (Muscat and Matrah). Other mission employees were limited to a twenty-five-mile radius of the capital cities. In these zones, they could circulate freely. Beyond these zones, they needed official approval from the sultan. These new regulations stopped the extensive medical tours up the Batinah, to Sur, Ja'alan, Dhofar, and the Sharqiyya, as well as into the interior. Medical tours were approved to noncontroversial regions under the sultan's control. This regulation marked the end of the mission's extended medical tours into Oman beyond Muscat and Matrah.

The sultan's regulations did not, however, decrease the medical workload at the mission hospitals. Personnel there and in the hospitals were busier than ever because patients increasingly came from the interior and up the coast by Land Rover. No longer was there an antimodernist imam inhibiting motor travel. Motor traffic to the capital cities increased rapidly.

Because of the sultan's rule, the medical staff was more effectively segregated from Omani life. They could not be used by opposition interests, as Shaykh Sulayman bin Hamyar had tried to do, to advance their self-interests within the interior. The newer medical staff did not realize that being sequestered on the coast kept them from fully understanding Omanis and seeing how they lived and worked in the towns and villages beyond the capital cities region. They did not have the same opportunities that Wells and Beth had had in previous decades to know the Omani people. Only after Sultan Qaboos came to the throne a decade later was this rule rescinded, for it was no longer necessary to the survival of the kingdom.

---

[13] Tanuf was reduced to rubble in retribution and its people scattered.

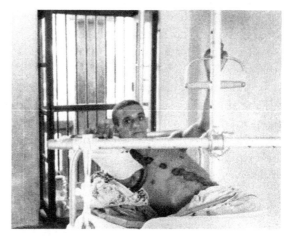

Patient previously cauterized, Matrah (WWT)

Struggles continue in the interior

Separatist political insurrections reemerged in the interior in 1957 as Shaykh Sulayman bin Hamyar made alliance with a new, but less accomplished, imam and sought to wrest autonomy for his *dira* in the Jabal Akhdhar.[14] An active resistance to the central government erupted, resulting in an all-out civil war. Once again, the sultan called on British troops to occupy the highlands and suppress the uprising. This was a new, more intense form of land warfare than previously staged, and it introduced munitions new to the Green Mountain highlands—particularly land mines. Ultimately, the leaders of the failed insurrection, including Shaykh Sulayman, fled to Sa'udi Arabia. The highlands were successfully occupied by the sultan's forces, which had never before fully controlled the mountains.[15]

In order to reconstruct the devastated highlands economy, the sultan began providing wheat and Klim (powdered milk) to the mountain folk. He then asked Wells to survey the medical needs of highland tribes. Along with other researchers, Wells was flown to Jabal Akhdhar and undertook conversations with the indigenous tribes. He had treated a large number as patients during his previous tours to the interior, so he knew many of the leaders in that remote region, and they trusted him.

---

[14] Earlier, Sulayman had exiled himself to Sa'udi Arabia in anticipation of this separatist strike. In retaliation, the sultan had Sulayman's capital at Tanuf destroyed.

[15] This was a period of great unrest throughout the Middle East. See endnote 27:15, p. 398.

Wells recalled the humor of one conversation with a mountain shaykh. Wells had asked, "What would it take to restore your community? How many goats would you need, and how much seed to cultivate wheat and other crops?"

The shaykh responded, "Oh, it's alright. It is not necessary. Please tell the sultan to just keep the 'Klim' and bags of wheat coming, as in recent months. That would be just fine." Life had always been difficult and tenuous in the mountains, and never before had there been assured food supplies for everyone. The shaykh, however, was more than happy to receive free handouts in perpetuity from Sultan Sayyid Sa'eed.

More changes come to the hospitals

In the late 1950s, air-conditioning was installed in the operating room of the Matrah hospital for the first time. With air-conditioning fully functioning, Wells no longer dreaded the prospect of conducting operations at very high room temperatures, and there was a much decreased risk of cross infection of wounds now that the perspiration of the doctors and medical personnel would no longer drip into open wounds.

Two other rooms of the hospital were also air-conditioned. Lower temperatures alone seemed to cure some patients. For example, septic prickly heat had brought Grey Mackenzie's shipping agent to near collapse with high fever and the pain of hundreds of boils on his skin. Four days of air-conditioning restored him. The toddler grandson of the minister of the Interior had had a fever and persistent diarrhea and was listless, without appetite. Putting both the infant and his mother in an air-conditioned room gave them excellent, restorative sleep. In two days, the child's diarrhea had stopped, and he began eating well again.

Cessation of the Civil War in the interior had brought ever-more patients to the hospitals. This increase occurred despite the opening of clinics and dispensaries in outlying towns as a result of British aid, British petroleum exploration, and enterprising entrepreneurs. The development program, led by the sultan's British adviser, Col. Boustead, recommended opening a new hospital in Matrah, located one-and-a-half miles from the mission hospital. It was conceived as a brick-and-mortar project to enhance the economy and health conditions of the local community, and a British hospital consultant was hired to assess the project's prospects.

Women eye patients post-op, ca. 1960 (RB)

When he arrived in Oman, the consultant was surprised to learn that there was a mission hospital nearby and visited Wells and the hospital. He was very favorably impressed by what he saw. The mission hospital was busy and well run. Morale was high. Patients were happy. Outcomes were excellent. He was most impressed by Wells' personality, whom he called an "able, virile, well-balanced, and good-humored Christian, highly regarded in the locality." Ultimately, the consultant recommended against building another hospital, for it was likely to be understaffed and poorly run. He did not think it wise for the sultan's government to run competition with the mission hospital and come in second.[16]

Wells was beginning to feel uneasy about the increasing load on medical services in the hospitals. Hospital records for 1958 note that more than three hundred additional, very sick patients had come directly to the mission hospital from the interior, many with a previously unseen medical complaint. A typical case arrived one day when a Land Rover stopped at the hospital gate, and men ran into the hospital with a preteen-aged boy on a litter. Wells examined him and could imagine what had occurred, but he wanted to hear the young man's story. "What happened, Little Brother?" he asked.

---

[16] See endnote 27:16, p. 399.

An overly full hospital, late 1950s (WTC)

Grimacing, the boy said, "I was herding goats in the *jabal*. Then, BANG! And I fell and couldn't use my left foot. It was bleeding; some of it was gone, but it hurt a lot then, like it does now. I crawled back to the village." The boy's foot had been mangled by a land mine.

"Where is your family?"

"They couldn't come. They are too poor. They said you would help me. They brought me as far as Tanuf by donkey. Others got me a ride. Now it is just me."

"Qumber! Khoda Rasoon! Quickly. There is no time to spare. We need to get young Yasir here ready for an operation. He may need blood. If we have none in stock, I can give a pint since I've not given blood for ten days. Let me know."

Wells discovered how extensive the damage was when the boy was placed on the operating table. To reconstruct the foot seemed impossible, for it was a tangled mess of bone splinters, blood vessels, and flesh. As Wells and Dr. Maury Heusinkveld consulted about the boy, Maury observed that amputating the foot would handicap the boy for the rest of his life. If at least half his foot could be saved, he might be able to walk with a cane. Wells observed the lad would need a customized shoe to accommodate his partially restored foot. In the course of time, the foot was saved and protected by a rough-hewn shoe. Even so, thought Wells, the boy is not going to be able to walk long distances. Several weeks later, Yasir had made a remarkable recovery due to his youth and resilience.

Now, thought Wells, how do we get him home? Even if we pay for his travel in a for-hire Land Rover, it cannot take him all the way. The end of the navigable track is Tanuf, and there are no roads into

Landmine survivor and his donkey, 1959 (WWT)

the mountains. How would he return to his home from Tanuf? It did not take long to come up with an idea. What the young man needed was a donkey to carry him home and through the mountains. Lacking money, this solution seemed to be a fantasy.

Wells spoke to his fellow missionaries and to the other members of the local congregation. "Perhaps we can all make small contributions. If we can buy him a donkey, Yasir can go home, and he and his family will have a means of transportation in the *jabal* for a few years. A donkey is hardy and can always find food there." Yasir became the hospital's poster boy. The idea caught on with the church, whose members contributed toward the cost of the donkey. Soon enough, Yasir was delighted with the good-natured donkey that was his new transport, and he headed happily toward the customs gate at Ruwi and then home, riding proudly astride his beast. The hospital staff and church had the satisfaction of knowing they had gone the "second mile"[17] for this innocent youngster.

To accommodate the ever-increasing patient load, the hospital hired more staff. As the numbers grew, it was frustratingly difficult

---

[17] Matthew 5:41. In this quotation, Jesus says: "If one is compelled to go one mile, go with him two." The reference is to an unjust Roman law taxing local people to provide free labor and Jesus' injunction to carry the load twice as far as Roman law required. It is the opposite of "an eye for an eye" principle.

Dr. Kennedy (left), Shaykh Shakhbut, and Wells Thoms, Buraimi (WTC)

to maintain the personal relationships that Wells had previously maintained with patients. On the one hand, it was wonderful that the hospital could meet the medical needs of more Omanis. On the other hand, the doctors and nurses included a new breed of managers and specialists practicing ever-more specialized medicine. There were increasingly complicated issues of staff coordination and deployment. Most new expatriate hospital personnel did not know Arabic and needed the help of translators. Even newly minted RCA missionaries were not trained in Arabic, a dramatic shift in policy from past practice in the Arabian Mission.

The hospitals were becoming so busy that taking medical tours outside Matrah was increasingly difficult, except for periodic, small group trips for a few days or a weekend. Was this what Wells had striven for these past twenty years? The medical work was everything Wells had hoped it would become, and yet it felt less satisfying. More people were being served, but fewer personal relationships were being established and maintained.

In the spring of 1959, Wells and Beth spent a few days in Abu Dhabi as guests of the ruler, Shaykh Shakhbut, whom Wells had previously treated. Out of this meeting, the ruler invited Wells to set up a hospital in Abu Dhabi and expressed his willingness to grant land for this purpose. Unfortunately, Wells could not accept the shaykh's generous offer because the Arabian Mission's financial resources were hemorrhaging, and it could not commit to another station.[18] The shaykh also wanted a doctor to visit the Buraimi oasis once a year to treat his people. Wells contacted Dr. Kennedy and the TEAM mission that had established a hospital in Sharjah.

Encouraged by his British advisers, Sultan Sayyid Sa'eed reluctantly agreed to organize a municipal council for Muscat and Matrah. This deliberative body was chaired by the wali of Matrah, Ismail Rasassi, and Wells was invited to serve as public health adviser. Various schemes of municipal development were discussed, but all of them ran aground on the question of financing. Even the idea for a privately subscribed Matrah electric power company foundered.

At this late date, there was still no effective national educational system and no public health or medical service in Oman. The institutions that did exist were run mostly by private entities, without significant governmental oversight or intervention. The Arabian Mission hospitals and its own school filled an important niche in the "unorganized" government services sector. Because the sultan did not approve of educating his people, the prospect for expanding the mission's coeducational school, Al Amana (trans. "integrity"), was out of the question.[19] Enrollments were limited mostly to children of hospital and church workers, as well as a few Muscatis.

Many of the older members of the mission community in Oman believed they had a de facto leader in Wells, a widely respected senior associate who could represent their views to the sultan and his government better than any other emissary. For this group, Wells fit the roles of shaykh and colleague both, even though the Arabian Mission functioned officially as a decentralized group and took votes at meetings democratically. It was, however, difficult for younger missionaries to view Wells simultaneously as shaykh and colleague. When were they talking to Wells as a shaykh? When as a colleague?

Wells' long term involvement in Oman's life gave him recognition by and access to the local community that few others in the mission could enjoy. Indeed, the mission hospital was popularly known as the Mushteshva-Tome-iss—Thoms' Hospital—as if it were his private

---

[18] The decline in the Arabian Mission's financial resources became clear within five years. The hospitals in Kuwait closed. The hospital in Bahrain remained open only with the support of the king. Promised resources from the RCA never materialized. See Scudder III, *The Arabian Mission's Story*.

[19] Sultan Sayyid Sa'eed was not shy in telling the British that they had "gone wrong" by giving India modern education.

domain. He chafed at this appellation, but to little effect. Such was the trust Omanis had placed in him. He and the hospital had been there for two decades through thick and thin, and they had saved countless lives. To his patients, he was an hakeem, the ultimate physician-healer. Because they trusted him, it seemed as if he had a larger-than-life healing touch.

Matrah hospital staff, late 1960s.[20] (*WTC*)
1. Waleed Ramdthan; 2. Peter Thoms; 3. Sa'eed Sinon; 4. Ahmed Jengan; 5. Hamza Haider; 6. Ali Yusef; 7. Ahmed Salem; 8. Moh'd. Khamees; 9. Ahmed; 10. Yahyah; 11. ___; 12. Moh'd. Khamees; 13. Abdulla; 14. ___; 15. Khalfan Aziz; 16. Moh'd. Taleb; 17. Sa'eed Nassir; 18. Ibrahim Moosa; 19. Moosa; 20. ___; 21. Mr. George; (unnumbered: Jim Dunham, Anne DeYoung, Beth Thoms, Wells Thoms, Don Bosch, ___, Habl Das, ___, ___, Khoda Rasoon); 22. Moh'd. Kassem; 23. Ali Moh'd.; 24. Hamed Sa'eed; 25. Mahmood; 26. Moh'd. Esa; 27. ___; 28. Abdulla Nassir; 29. Othman Pesi; 30. Abdul Rahman; 31. Mahmood Habieb; 32. Ali Khamees; 33. Khamees Salim; 34. Moh'd. Tuchey; 35. Khadeeja; 36. Amina; 37. Marium; 38. Beebee; 39. Santhamma; 40. Qumbar; 41. Panamma; (Carolyn Johnston, Wilma Thoms); 42. Mr. Lhondi; 43. Hamed Nassir 44. Ahmed Janel; 45. Yohannan; 46. Diyab; 47. Yusef Rasoon; 48. Alladad; 49. Hamed; 50. Rashid Moh'd.; 51. Ali Moh'd.; 52. Salem; 53. Mabarah Najman; 54. Hamed; 55. Salem Moh'd.; (Marcia Newhouse); 56. Khamees Nubi; 57. Dawood; 58. Juma; 59. Shahoo; 60. Moh'd. Abdullah; 61. ___; 62. Salem; 63. Mubarak Tayseer; 64. ___; 65. Jamail Tayseer; 66. Ahmed Ibrahim; 67. Abdul Wahab Abdul Latif; 68. Mansoor; 69. Dashook; 70. Ghulam Abdullah; 71. Ali Abdul Latif.

[20] In January 1970, twenty-five years after she retired as business manager of the hospital, Khatoon Jauhara (Beth Thoms) numbered and identified most of the Omani hospital staff; she could recall all but a few names (blank entries). Some faces were insufficiently visible for Jauhara to identify. Not all staff members were present to be photographed since the hospital functioned on a twenty-four-hour schedule.

Ahmad bin Ibrahim, Wells, and retainers, 1959 (WTC)

A clandestine patient

The hospital telephone rang one morning in December 1959. The caller was the wazir, Col. Leslie Chauncy, and he wished to know if the hospital could accommodate a VIP. An accident had occurred, and the patient needed immediate care. Calls of this type were rare, but Wells responded they would have a room awaiting the arrival of the mystery patient.

Wells swung into action, instructing Khoda Rasoon to prepare for emergency treatment of a VIP who would be arriving shortly. It could be anyone from a crew member of a tanker at sea, to a member of the sultan's armed forces or an employee of the petroleum exploration company. There was an outside chance it was someone from the royal family, but this was not likely, since under British advice the royal family was usually treated in India or England.

The entourage motored to the hospital within the hour. The mystery patient was none other than the minister of the Interior, Shaykh Sayyid Ahmad bin Ibrahim, the second-ranking Omani official after the sultan. This caused a stir among the staff because government officials seldom used the hospital. This, however, was an emergency, and there was no other choice.

Sayyid Ahmad had been India bound via the BI ship *Dwarka* for a medical check-up in Bombay. When he boarded ship, he went directly to his first-class cabin. After the ship had departed Muscat harbor, he decided to take a nap. Something about the bed was uncomfortable, though, so he put his pillow at the opposite end of the bed and lay down again. Suddenly, a loud explosion boomed at what had been the head of the bed. Someone had tried to assassinate Sayyid Ahmad. The bomb burned his feet, ankles, and lower legs instead of his head, neck, and upper torso. The ship returned to Muscat, and he was brought to the mission hospital for immediate care, skin grafting, and other necessary treatment.[21]

Sayyid Ahmad made steady progress and soon recovered from the shock of the assassination attempt. When Wells visited him in the morning and evening, Sayyid Ahmad wanted to turn the discussion in the direction of religion. At some point, the minister asked if Wells believed in the existence of heaven. Wells' antennae were always alerted when conversations with ranking officials turned from the mundane to the eternal. The Christian community was well aware that Sayyid Ahmad, under orders from the sultan, had directed security guards to surround the church at Sunday worship times. The presence of guards discouraged native Christians from attending public worship and provided tangible evidence to the sultan's detractors that he was a protector of Islam. Wells knew that a possible trap lay behind the seemingly innocent question about the afterlife.

How could Wells know whether Sayyid Ahmad was asking a religious question of great personal interest to him, or was looking instead for evidence of a Christian openly proselytizing a Muslim? If the latter, then Wells could open the Arabian Mission to the charge of illegal proselytization, and the mission could be expelled from Oman.

Wells said to Sayyid Ahmad, "Please wait. I'll be right back. I want to show you something." Wells ran home and returned with a book. He said, "This is my own Bible. Its cover is olive wood from Palestinian olive trees. It is in Arabic and in two parts. The oldest and longest is the Hebrew 'Bible.' The shorter part is the 'Injeel' that comes to us from the Prophet Isa and His followers. These are the Scriptures of the 'People of the Book.' Please read it for yourself and see what you think about heaven and other matters. It is my gift to you, and it is the most

---

[21] Unknown to most in Oman were two attempts on the life of Sultan Sayyid Sa'eed in 1963 and 1966. Because these occurred in neighboring Dhofar, news of them did not spread widely throughout the rest of Oman. Beth and Wells did not know of these events at the time, but their last twelve years in Oman were beset by growing political instability. Few had any idea where it would lead. Tensions intensified.

Sayyid Ahmad bin Ibrahim, de facto prime minister from 1939 to 1970 (photo, 1959, RB)

valuable book I own. You may keep it, but right now, I must complete my rounds to see my other patients."

Sayyid Ahmad returned many times for check-ups of his legs and feet. He seemed to appreciate Wells' sage response and never raised, even obliquely, the matter of proselytizing again. As the months passed, fewer guards showed up outside Muscat's Sunday worship services.

On one of his hospital visits, Sayyid Ahmad expressed concern that sultan Sayyid Sa'eed had now been in Dhofar continuously for three years. His absence from Muscat was remarked on openly by Omani commoners, who also noted many jobs were available in other countries up the Gulf, but very few were available in Oman. They expressed growing discontent at the lack of job opportunities. Sayyid Ahmad averred it was difficult to communicate all this emphatically enough by radio-telephone to the sultan via his wazir, Col. Chauncy.[22]

Perhaps Sultan Sayyid Sa'eed had ruled too long, Sayyid Ahmad suggested. He ruled over a politically somnolent country where change occurred slowly. The Agreement of Seeb had locked the country's recalcitrant antimodern leaders into the interior. The divide produced a devoutly religious state in the interior and a passive but not very secular one on the coastal fringe. Rule had been passed peacefully from generation to generation in the al Bu Sa'eed family—quite unlike the

---

[22] There was only one radio-telephone channel connecting the wazir in Muscat with the sultan in Salalah.

situation in Kuwait, the Emirates, and Sa'udi Arabia, where violence was more the norm. Perhaps the sultan did not realize how rapidly British power and influence were waning during his rule. The sultanate was growing weak, and the British had lost patience with the sultan. Wells and Beth understood only the broad outlines of these changes, for it appeared Oman had an almost infinite capacity to drift from day to day and season to season. He listened carefully to Sayyid Ahmad but offered no advice.

In the early 1960s, political instability rose again in southeast Arabia. A civil war broke out on the borders of Dhofar led by a left-wing, largely socialist movement aimed at overthrowing the sultan. News of this insurrection was muffled in Matrah, and specifics were not publicized. Two attempts were made on the sultan's life in Dhofar, where he had sequestered himself in his palace, protected by barbed wire and guards—a prisoner in his own fiefdom. In response to these events, he strengthened his militia into a much more formidable and competent armed force.

At the same time, revolution also broke out in the colony of Zanzibar, long a treasured province of Oman. Arab Omanis, in power there for more than a century, were displaced. Some Zanzibari Omanis returned to Oman, hoping to re-establish a niche in their homeland, but they often proved to be destabilizing elements as they sought positions of importance within the country because of their education and modernity. As a component of their modernity, they were not as easy going as other Omanis, and their presence rankled longtime residents.

Tragedy strikes the mission

One evening, the worst imaginable event occurred in the mission community. Dr. Maurice Heusinkveld, a veteran mission physician who had served in Iraq and Bahrain, was temporarily replacing Wells, on leave in the United States. As Dr. Heusinkveld returned home in the dark of the night, an unidentified attacker shot him. Seriously wounded, Heusinkveld stumbled into his house. Another mission doctor was called to see what could be done. It soon became clear Heusinkveld was so badly wounded, he would not survive. Before he died, knowing the end was near, he repeated the phrase of Jesus on the cross before His own earthly death, "Father, forgive them for they know not what they do."[23]

---

[23] Luke 23:34.

Distraught by this sad turn of events, Wells and Beth raced back to Oman from their furlough. They found mission colleagues fearful and full of questions. Was the murder of Heusinkveld purposely intended? Or had Wells been the target since the Heusinkvelds were living in the Thoms' house? Was this an act of personal vengeance or of political import? The Arab-Israeli War of 1967 had occurred recently; was this murder somehow in reprisal for American involvement in that catastrophic loss? A dud hand grenade had been lobbed onto the roof of the hospital earlier that year. Were these isolated events, or did they form a pattern? Was the civil war in Dhofar spreading into Oman proper, and was the mission a prime target?

The missionaries looked for signs of overt animosity toward them from Omanis. Much to their relief, they saw nothing of the sort. Omanis and expatriates alike were uneasy. Law enforcement in Oman could not help with the investigation of Heusinkveld's death. The personal tribal law that had obtained for so many generations was ill suited to the sleuthing that was needed in this case. Criminal investigations were rare, and the procedures, even though known to the British, had never before been employed in Oman. When a crime was committed, it was usually clear who the perpetrator was, and retribution was handled by custom rather than by law.[24]

For Wells personally, the loss of his cherished colleague opened the scarred memory of losing his own father so many years before. He was especially concerned for the Heusinkveld family: Eleanor, Maurice's widow, and their three sons. He remembered how his own life had changed, how his family had packed up and returned to a new, not particularly happy, life in the United States after his father's death in 1913. He feared the same awaited the Heusinkveld boys.

Others in the mission had no similar tragic loss and were not sure how to deal with it. Wells tried to communicate his thoughts compassionately—in effect, saying he understood personally how traumatic this loss was. Wells was especially disturbed because the murder violated Wells' understanding of the best of Omani culture. He had never felt physically threatened in all his years in Oman.

Wells and Beth had much to ponder. The Oman they knew was changing. Their own medical mission had already changed profoundly.

---

[24] The murder of Dr. Heusinkveld was never officially solved. Legal issues abound. The principle of extraterritoriality governed all foreigners in Oman then. The British consul was the magistrate in extraterritorial matters. Violence between a Muslim and a (Christian) foreigner had no precedent in Islamic law or in Oman. The case fell "in the crack" between tradition and modernity.

They were grateful for their many peaceful years practicing Christian diplomacy and health care for all. They had come to know, respect, and love many Omanis. They had expressed through their daily living the "more excellent quality" of Christ's way. They wondered now what their future should be.

Part III: Love

"Nothing we do, however virtuous, can be accomplished alone; therefore, we are saved by love."*

---

* Reinhold Niebuhr, *The Irony of American History*, 63.

CHAPTER 28

The Other Wise Man

*May the Lord bless you and keep you.
May the Lord make his face to shine
upon you and be gracious unto you.
May the Lord lift up his countenance upon you and give you peace.*
Numbers 6:24-26

Christmas 1969

Wells walked to the front of the humble Muscat church as he had done many times before. He rarely preached, but on the last Sunday of every year, he led the worship service and always in the same way. In Arabic—for few of the Arab parishioners knew English—he delighted the worshippers with the same story that had enriched their memories from the previous year.[1] Wells told the familiar tale in a characteristically "Arab" manner—complete with colorful repetitions and florid gestures.

"When I was young," he began, speaking slowly and reflectively, "I lived in Persia, across the water there." Wells pointed out the window to the north, where Iran loomed beyond the distant horizon. Although they knew they could not see Iran, several parishioners glanced out the window. "Remembering those days now seems like a dream from deep

---

[1] The short story that Wells paraphrased was adapted from Van Dyke, *The Story of the Other Wise Man*. It has been said that Van Dyke's story was, at one time, more popular than Charles Dickens' *A Christmas Carol*.

within me," Wells resumed. "Nothing seemed impossible then, for I was active and young and at the peak of my powers."

As his listeners warmed gradually to his tale, Wells spoke more rapidly and dramatically.

> I received the best of everything as a young man. In return, I was expected to give back to my community by learning the entire body of wisdom regarding religion, science, and medicine that my forebears had developed. I studied the stars for hints of the future. I read books on astronomy, the holy scriptures, and medicine. How the celebrated sages of the past, the hakeems, we would call them today, came to their vast knowledge, I do not know. I wanted to understand their wisdom and pass on their knowledge to the next generation of our people. What a privilege. I had a great and worthy calling in life.
>
> Then one night, my reading of another tradition's Scripture, one brought to Babylon from distant Jerusalem, caused me to search the heavens for a guiding star. What I saw prompted me to call together the learned elders of my people. We gathered at the darkest time of night—the best time for star gazing, for studying the heavens, and for worshiping the supreme God of Purity and Light.
>
> I shared with the gathering of elders a prophecy in the foreign Scriptures about the birth of a new king and of a star that would lead sky watchers to the place of the child's birth. Although they were intrigued by my tale, many of the elders offered excuses for why they could not accompany me on a quest for the babe. One claimed he was too old and frail; another said he was too physically weak to make the trip; others pointed to responsibilities they had that would keep them from leaving their families. Three of them, however, decided to join me in following that star.
>
> I knew we had to leave very quickly because I had seen two very bright stars converging in the heavens, and I did not know how long they would move together. This was undoubtedly the sign of the impending birth of a very great person. Exactly who he might be or where he was to be born, we did not know.
>
> Before I could complete my own preparations, my three comrades slipped out into the night, and I bid them farewell. I did not know when or if I would see them again. We hoped to

meet within ten days near the Temple of Seven Spheres in the far reaches of the great rivers, the Tigris and Euphrates. If I should be late, they would have left, and I would have to travel alone, always chasing their trail across a dangerous and lonely land.

This would be an adventure of a lifetime, so I prepared carefully. I sold all my land and goods, turning the income into traveling necessities. In addition to these items, I carried three portable gems that I could sell as needed for emergencies along the way. They were small and easy to hide. Sewn into my clothing was a beautiful, huge blue sapphire; a many-faceted, gorgeously tinted ruby; and a large, round pearl of great price that glowed in iridescent colors.

The further Wells progressed in his story, the more he seemed to become the Persian wise man from days long past. In earlier years, he had read the story, but by now, he had told it so many times, it was deeply embedded in his memory, and he could retell it as if it was his own personal story.

Before dawn brightened the sky the next morning, I was on my way. I rode Vasda, my stately steed, who was ready and eager to get underway. The first few miles flew by as Vasda settled into an energy-saving canter. I was euphoric to be on the road, intent to push hard every day so that I could connect with the caravan of my friends.

On the next-to-last day of this trip, we traveled late into the night. Vasda grew increasingly tired, and when she was near exhaustion, I had to dismount and walk for a time before remounting. After dark, Vasda suddenly pulled up short. Something was wrong. In the middle of the trail in front of us lay a lifeless form. Was this person sleeping? Sick? Dead? I had to check. At first it seemed to be a dead man. I wondered if I should bury him or just leave him in the desert according to the religious practice of the Zoroastrians.

I let go of the man's arm after trying to find his pulse. It dropped back on to his chest, and he let out a ghostly exhalation. As I turned away, his hand gripped my robe convulsively. He wasn't dead or a ghost. He was very ill. As an hakeem, I could not leave him to die out in the open roadway, so I tended to his fever and then loaded him onto one of our pack animals. We continued along our journey, following the star that led us west.

In the meantime, we talked, and I told him about my quest. He was delighted and picked up quickly on my story.

The man explained his situation in this way. "I am a Jew—one of many who live in exile from Jerusalem in this part of the world. The prophecy you mention is in our holy writ, and it says that the King of the Jews, whom we call the Messiah, is to be born in a little town, Bethlehem of Judea, not far from Jerusalem. You should seek your newborn baby there."

After several days, the traveler was well on his way to a remarkable recovery. When he turned to go on his way, he thanked me for nursing him, and I thanked him for verifying my quest. I then resumed my own delayed journey. By the time I reached the Temple of the Seven Spheres, however, it was empty, just a ruin on the landscape. My friends were no longer waiting, but I found a note instructing me to follow them across the desert.

This I tried to do. I was entering country unsuited for my exhausted mount and pack animals, so I had to backtrack to Babylon to sell my beautiful Vasda and my precious sapphire in exchange for a train of camels loaded with supplies needed to traverse the western wasteland. There was no other way to continue my quest. I regretted falling farther behind my companions. Only God, the Merciful, knew whether I would be able to rejoin my companions because I had stopped to show mercy to the fallen Jew.

I pressed on across the burning desert, trying with every sinew to shorten the distance between my wise colleagues and myself. I trudged over shifting sand dunes and rocky plateaus strewn with sharp stones everywhere. There was little water to be had, and wild animals threatened my way. Finally, I came to the other side of the wilderness. Damascus and then Mt. Hermon beckoned. Then the glistening Sea of Galilee, sheltered in the arms of jutting cliffs. I followed the star's direction down along the Jordan River and then up into the hills of Judea, to the town of Bethlehem. It had been a long and arduous journey, but I hoped I had finally arrived at my intended destination.

The streets of Bethlehem were virtually deserted. It appeared as though the citizens had abandoned their town. As I wandered through the empty streets, I heard the voice of a woman singing a lullaby to her swaddled child. I was drawn to her house and knocked. I asked if three strangers had come to the village recently, and she nodded her head in reply.

"Yes," she said. "Three foreigners came to the place where Joseph of Nazareth was staying with his young wife and new baby. They did not stay long. Indeed, they didn't even stay for a full night. They left as mysteriously as they had arrived. Joseph and Mary, too, disappeared in the middle of the night, along with their infant. All were gone by dawn. We are not sure where they went, but some think the family headed south, toward Egypt."

Her baby cooed and wriggled happily. I realized that such a child could be the king I sought. When I extended my hand, he grasped my finger trustingly.

"They say the Roman soldiers are on their way from Jerusalem to levy a new tax," she continued. "That is what censuses are all about, taxing people. Our men have taken our flocks to the hills in order to avoid the tax collectors."

As we talked, we heard loud shouting and cries coming from the other end of the village. "Help! Help! They are killing our babies!" Hysterical and distraught mothers ran from house to house warning parents elsewhere.

The sounds grew louder as panicked citizens advanced on the house where I was speaking with the young mother. From their pitiful pleas, I could hear babies and young boys being slaughtered. At first, I didn't know what to do, but then it seemed I had no choice. I had to try to save this woman's child from the vicious cruelty of the soldiers. House by house, King Herod's troopers approached. When the leader arrived at the front door, I blocked the way.

Standing my ground, I said to him, "There is no one here but me. I am alone and am waiting to give this jewel to the prudent captain who will leave me in peace." I extended my open palm, and the brilliant ruby glowed crimson for him to see.

The captain was shocked at first, never having seen such a magnificent thing of beauty before. Then, when he realized it was real and could be his, he snatched it out of my hand and called out, "Move on. There is no child here. The house is quiet." On his command, the soldiers retreated into the distance.

When I realized what I had done, I was filled with remorse. I admitted to God that I had told a deliberate falsehood in order to save the child. Moreover, I had second thoughts that I had expended the second of my three treasures to save the baby. What had I done? What kind of man would this child become? Would he be worthy of such a great price? Would I ever be able to find the prophesied baby-king?

As I left the crude home, the voice of the woman weeping happy tears followed me. "Because you have saved the life of my little one, 'May the Lord bless you and keep you. May the Lord make his face to shine upon you and be gracious unto you. May the Lord lift up his countenance upon you and give you peace.'"[2]

Wells paused and took several deep breaths before continuing. His audience was so raptly attentive that no sound came from them. Then he rejoined the narrative.

I searched year after year, everywhere from Egypt in the south to Judea and Jerusalem in the North. A rabbi in Alexandria told me to search in the neighborhoods of the low born, since *this* king would not be an aristocrat or one from the ruling class. He would not be like the Joseph of old, the dreamer who became vizier [wazir] of Egypt. Everywhere I looked, there was poverty and pestilence. As an hakeem, I was compelled to do my best for the afflicted that I met, whether in their homes or in prisons. Indeed, that is how I earned my daily bread, by tending the ill.

As the years passed, I became old and stooped. My flowing black hair turned snowy white. Yet, no one I asked had any idea where to find the prophesied king. At last, after more than three decades of wandering, I found myself back in Jerusalem. Exhausted and penniless from my travels, I knew this would be my last chance to find the king I had long sought.

There seemed to be a lot of excitement on the streets when I arrived in Jerusalem. Men and women spoke excitedly with each other and then set off on foot to the west of the city. I stopped a passing baker and asked him what was going on. His response was that people were heading out of the city walls to a cave-strewn quarry known as Golgotha. There was to be the execution of three miscreants that day—two known criminals and a man who had done many wonderful deeds. He had the nerve to call himself the Son of God and had earned the wrath of the chief priests and their religious advisors. Pontius Pilate, the Roman

---

[2] Numbers 6:24-26.

prefect, had condemned him to death for posing as the King of the Jews, a direct threat to Caesar and the Jewish ruler, Herod.

I thought, "Maybe this is the king I've been looking for all these years. Perhaps I can use my beautiful pearl, my final gem, to buy his pardon." Just as I thought this, a squad of soldiers escorting a captive girl marched by near where I stood. Suddenly the wretched girl broke away from them and fell on her knees in front of me, grabbing my gown.

She had recognized my clothes, my style of dress, and said, "Help me! I am one of you, who believe as you do. Have pity on me, for the sake of the God of Purity and Light. My father was a Parthian merchant. He died yesterday, and I have been seized to pay his outstanding debts. Without money, I am to be sold as a slave. Save me, save me, please."

What was I to do? I had already parted with my other two treasures and my beloved Vasda. If I gave up the pearl for the desperate girl, what would I have left to ransom the king? I would be empty handed if I found him. Yet, I could not ignore her pitiful plea. She was real, and her fate hung in the balance. She was someone I could assist immediately; the king was still unfound.

It was as if I could do nothing else. I had to save her. In that moment, I realized that paying for her release would be a true deed of love for another. Is not love the light of the soul? So, I gave up the pearl, my pearl of great luster and value. I said to her, "Take it. I had saved it for a king, but you may have it. It is the last of my treasures."

At that moment, the sky darkened, and there was an earthquake with dust and rocks raining down on all of us. The soldiers ran away. The young girl and I were the only ones left huddling under the eaves of a home. What had I to fear anymore? My quest was over. I had failed. I had not found my prophesied king. It would not have mattered if I had died right there. Despite these somber thoughts, I also knew that if I had to live my life over again, I would live it the same way.

Suddenly there was an aftershock of the earthquake. It loosened a roof tile that fell and hit me on the head. I crumpled to the ground. As she cradled me in her lap, the girl looked up as if she had heard someone speaking. I heard it, too, and replied: "Not so, my Lord. For when did I see you hungry and feed you?

Or thirsty and give you something to drink? When did I see you a stranger and take you in and shelter you? Or find you naked, and clothed you? When did I see you sick or in prison and come to you?[3] For thirty-three years I have searched for you high and low, and I have not found you or ministered to you, my king."

I was exhausted and fading fast, but I heard a musical voice, as if from a distance, say: "Verily, I say unto thee. Inasmuch as thou hast done it unto one of the least of these my brethren, thou hast done it unto me."[4]

Upon hearing these words of reassurance, I lay back in peace. I had no strength left. I could go now, knowing that my life journey had been completed. My treasures had been accepted. I had caught up to the other wise men and found the king.

Wells lowered his head a moment, and then returned in silence to his seat in the chapel. Sitting down, he closed his eyes in prayer and reflection. He looked every bit the aging missionary, the hakeem, the wise man of the Arabian Mission in Oman.

In a way that always caught them by surprise, the rich meaning of the story broke over the congregation of Omani parishioners and fellow missionaries. Unlike times in the past when Wells had resumed his pew, however, this time his listeners wept openly and uncontrollably. They would never hear the tale told in this way again. The story was a metaphor for Wells' life—and their own. Although they had often become so absorbed in their daily routines that they lost sight of their primary mission, this retelling reminded them of the passion that undergirded their efforts, their callings. The missionaries had come to Oman motivated by Christ's injunction to go into all the world to tell others of His most excellent way. It had not always worked out as they had hoped or expected. Too often, they had misunderstood their own calling—just as the fourth wise man had done. Yet, their Christian acts of grace and service to Omanis and others in Arabia had really been acts of worship offered to God. Christ's second Great Commandment was nestled in His first. Love of and service to others was *truly* love of and service to God.[5]

---

[3] Matthew 25:37-39.
[4] Matthew 25:40.
[5] Matthew 22:37-40 (RSV): "You shall love the Lord your God with all your heart and with all your soul and with all your mind. This is the great and first commandment. And a second is like it: You shall love your neighbor as yourself. On these two commandments depend all the Law and the Prophets."

CHAPTER 29

Epilogue: Journey's End

Silver and gold have I none;
but such as I have, give I thee.[1]

An hakeem's impact

Dr. Wm. Wells Thoms—Hakeem Tome-iss—was the last of the superbly skilled physician-surgeons, doctor-diplomats, manager-administrators, teacher-trainers, flexible-adaptable creative problem solvers, and inspiring team leaders who served in the RCA's Arabian Mission. These were the skills required of solo pioneer physicians in the age before oil. Because these pioneers worked alone, they had to be competent multifunctionally. The pioneer physicians included not only Wells but also his parents, Sharon John and Marion Wells Thoms, as well as Paul Harrison, Stanley Mylrea, Harold Storm, Eleanor Calverley, Sarah Hosmon, Arthur and Christine Bennett, and Louis Dame. Each left an enduring mark on the Arab communities they served. These hakeems served with great compassion. Working with evangelists, educators, and technicians, as well as with loyal hospital

---

[1] Acts 3:6 (KJV): "Then Peter said, 'Silver and gold have I none; but such as I have, give I thee. In the name of Jesus Christ of Nazareth, rise up and walk.'"

aides from India and the Gulf, they built strong, high-functioning, Christian-Muslim hospital teams founded on the love of Christ. In this, they profoundly affected Gulf Arab society. Medicine evolved so immensely during World War II that doctors who came to Arabia after the war with narrowed medical specialties were trained to work only as part of a team.

In addition, as the first modern eye specialist in Arabia, Wells concentrated on trachoma and trichiasis because these blinding infectious diseases were so widespread. Over the course of thirty years in Oman and the Gulf, he carried out thousands of operations to preserve and restore sight. After he retired, Oman's Ministry of Health recognized a continuing need to reduce the damage done by trachoma and trichiasis and created a government-sponsored effort to take up his cause. A lasting testament to Wells' tireless ministry is that the World Health Organization in 2013 declared Oman to be trachoma-free. Oman is the sole Gulf Arab country to have eradicated this dread disease. When Wells arrived in Oman, it was rare to find an adult Omani with two good eyes. To encounter an Omani adult today without two good eyes is rare.

Wells began his war on eye diseases earlier in the Gulf when serving in Bahrain, Sa'udi Arabia, Qatar, the Emirates, and Kuwait. He built on the prior contacts of pioneer mission physicians and established personal relationships with the rulers of each country (Sa'udi Arabia, Bahrain, Qatar, Abu Dhabi, Dubai, Sharjah and the lesser emirates, and Kuwait). In so doing, this "soft diplomat" knew and treated the rulers of all the Gulf Arab countries whose descendants retain power today.

Wells' most important achievement in Oman—the opening of the Sharon Thoms Hospital for Contagious Diseases—became so successful after 1970 that the contagious illnesses of tuberculosis and Hansen's Disease (leprosy) have disappeared from Oman. Other epidemic and endemic diseases have also been significantly reduced.

Final convulsive changes to Oman

In his later years in Oman, as political and social tensions intensified prior to the oil era, Wells knew Oman was in turmoil. He would have had to be deaf and blind not to notice. The dissatisfaction people felt toward the old sultan, Sayyid Sa'eed bin Taymur, was palpable. They were especially upset that the sultan resisted making beneficial changes in education and agriculture. From time to time, this dissatisfaction expressed itself in uncharacteristic public violence.

In 1964 Oman's ex-province of Zanzibar succumbed to revolution, cutting that island loose from Arab overlordship. The sultan's British advisors pushed him to institute more than "band-aid" development schemes to stave off similar uprisings throughout Oman; some he approved reluctantly, like the municipal council for Muscat and Matrah. Even these limited changes were not enough, and their ineffectuality was foreboding, considering Britain's planned withdrawal from Oman in 1971. Wells despaired of future prospects in Oman.

From their mejlis in the Arabian Gulf, Wells and Beth also despaired of changes they saw in American society. They observed with growing concern the consumerist transformation of the United States in the post-World War II decades. The "gospel of wealth" that wooed so many Americans away from traditional Christian faith and the values of self-sacrifice and service troubled them. These new trends flew in the face of their years of sacrificial giving and caring. Although they did not know if the sudden flood of wealth into the Arab world would have the same corrupting effect, they did know that newfound affluence would bring about major changes, and not all of them desirable. The "conflict" they foresaw was not between Islam and, in their way of thinking, the "more excellent way" of Christianity. The greater conflict would be between economic materialism on the one hand and spiritual values at the heart of both Christianity and Islam on the other hand. In this conflict, they surmised, Muslims and Christians would align on both sides; some Muslims and Christians would unabashedly pursue wealth and self-interest, while other Muslims and Christians would promote spiritual virtues.

A fraught farewell

In the face of these uncertainties, Wells and Beth retired in 1970, thirty years after they had landed in Oman, forty years after Wells had arrived in the Gulf as a physician, sixty years after he had first traveled to Oman as a boy, and seventy-two years after his parents had made the Gulf their home.

They departed from Oman weeks before a palace coup replaced their old associate Sultan Sayyid Sa'eed bin Taymur as Oman's supreme ruler. To the throne came his son, Sultan Sayyid Qaboos bin Sa'eed bin Taymur bin Faisal al Bu Sa'eed.[2] Oman has not been the same since.

---

[2] Sultan Sayyid Qaboos bin Sa'eed bin Taymur, in turn, died in Oman on 10 January 2020. His successor is Sultan Haitham bin Tariq bin Taymur. In a style analogous

Au revoir, *1970* (WTC)

After four decades of adventure in Arabia, Wells and Beth planned to live modestly in retirement in the United States, enjoying beautiful summers at their rustic cottage in the White Mountains of New Hampshire. They had purchased a simple place on Stinson Lake, similar to the one they had honeymooned in forty years earlier. They anticipated modernizing their fully furnished retirement *pied-a-terre*, installing electricity and plumbing. They were eager to make use of the boat and canoes waiting in the boat shed.

A few short months after delivering his valedictory rendering of "The Fourth Wise Man," Wells and Beth flew from Oman to England and traveled for a few weeks through Scotland. The vibrant greens of the hills and the contrasting browns of the moors, the long walks across heather-topped landscapes, the feel of the bracing air, the cadence of the melodious Scots brogue, the good humor and courtesy of Scots people, and the changing patterns of the sea and sky, all reinvigorated them.

On returning to London, they hoped to visit their old associate, ex-Sultan Sayyid Sa'eed. The deposed ruler of Oman was now residing in an upper floor of the posh Dorchester Hotel in London. Wells wanted

---

to the British monarchical tradition, we may say, "The old sultan is dead. Long live the new sultan."

to greet the ex-sultan, express condolences at the loss of his kingdom, and wish him well. Wells wanted to say that he, too, had retired and left Oman. Sadly, that encounter was not to be. Sayyid Sa'eed's aide told Wells that the ex-sultan would not meet with him.

What a shock. Sayyid Sa'eed, a man Wells deeply respected and had known since he was a "little nipper," whose hospitality Wells had received and returned on so many occasions, whose own health and wellbeing and that of his family Wells had assured, and whose countrymen Wells had served so selflessly for three decades, refused to meet with him. The rebuff wounded. Clearly the self-absorbed ex-ruler was grieving his losses.

Sayyid Sa'eed was not the only one who grieved. Wells grieved as well. He had voluntarily handed to others the work and the people he had loved so dearly. Would they continue the compassionate vision of his heart? The two of them, the ex-sultan and the compassionate hakeem, were both exiles now. One was among the most loved men in all of Oman, a voluntary exile. The other, among the most reviled in Oman, was an involuntary exile. In his grief, Wells reminded himself that what he had done in Oman and the Arabian Gulf, he did for God and the people, not for the acclaim of earthly powers and principalities.

Shortly after Wells and Beth departed for Heathrow Airport, a telephone call came to their London hotel. It was from the Dorchester Hotel saying that ex-Sultan Sayyid Sa'eed would be pleased to see them for tea that afternoon. But it arrived too late. Wells and Beth were already on their way to the United States. Wells never again saw Sayyid Sa'eed, nor did the reclusive ruler ever contact his faithful hakeem.[3]

Requiescat in pace

On October 25, 1971, barely a year after Wells and Beth had returned to the United States, Wells succumbed to rapidly spreading melanoma cancer, a disease for which there was then no cure. Since his return, he had dictated his memoirs, undergone and recovered from surgeries, and spent cherished time with his family in Michigan and New Hampshire. When his youngest daughter commiserated with him about being so sick, he consoled her lovingly by saying, "A flower is beautiful and all the more precious because it does not last forever. This is true for all living things."[4]

---

[3] Sayyid Sa'eed died in London in October 1972.
[4] As if prolonging the beauty of this flower, Wells donated his body for anticancer

The earthly remains of William Wells (Ameen) Thoms, MD, FACS, were interred at the seaside New Naval Cemetery in Shaykh Jabbar Cove, Muscat, Oman, in good company. Others of his family and immediate circle of Arabian Mission friends who are buried nearby include his father, Sharon John Thoms, MD (1913), and beloved wife Beth (Jauhara) Scudder Thoms Dickason (2002), Maurice M. Heusinkveld, MD (1967), Rev. James Dunham (2007), and his wife, Joyce Dunham (2012). Saints all.

Tread softly, ye who enter that simple seaside cemetery. This is the earthly resting place of heroes of Oman and of the Gulf. In the style of the legendary Hakeem Tome-iss, they did not view themselves as heroes or saints. Together with the rest of the Arabian Mission personnel, working in the hospitals and congregations of Muscat and Matrah, they constituted a merciful force, acting heroically for the benefit of all Omanis and Gulf residents whether they were Christian, Muslim, Hindu, or other.

For all of them, the blessing inscribed on Wells' grave is an apt epitaph: "Such as I have, give I thee." Wells brought healing, despite all odds. In retrospect, we see and understand how improbable and unconventional his success was. Through unfaltering compassion for others, his journey of faith, hope, and love brought immeasurable benefit.

To God be the glory.

---

research.

Afterword

"No virtuous act is quite as virtuous from the standpoint of our friend or foe as it is from our standpoint. Therefore, we must be saved by the final form of love which is forgiveness."*

Praise God.

Al Hamdulillah.

---

* Reinhold Niebuhr, *The Irony of American History*, 63.

Endnotes

1:1. Chapter 1 is based entirely on Thoms family diaries, letters, photographs, and the oral tradition of family and friends. In addition, in his retirement, Wells produced cassette tape recordings of his life prior to their arrival in Oman in 1939. These were essential documents for this biography.

Wells served in Panama at Gorgas Memorial Hospital during the late 1920s and made a photographic record of that time, as well as written accounts of selected experiences there. These do not include his unfolding romance with the mysterious Alma (whose surname we do not even know).

In later years, Beth Thoms wrote recollections of her life until moving to Oman in 1939. She referred to Alma obliquely in her diary and identified her by first name only once but did not dwell on the full story. Other details of this episode have been preserved as recollections of Michigan relatives.

Wells' simultaneous double engagement deeply embarrassed him, and Alma was referred to only once or twice in family discussions with him. Of the many stories recounted in the family, this one remained off limits. Only Wells knew how he untied his first betrothal, and he did not talk about it.

The wedding of Beth and Wells in the little church in New York is documented in photos and was witnessed by Beth's Sapphire Club classmates from Oberlin College. Also in attendance were several RCA dignitaries, stand-ins for both sets of parents.

In this chapter, Wells' final letter to Alma is fictional. He must have written her such a letter since she had already returned to Panama. He was an honorable young man who never intended to play Beth against Alma. He had to terminate his relationship with Alma to follow the calling he felt compelled to pursue. She was in Panama, he in Michigan. Long communications by telegram and telephone were impossible then—all communication was by letter. He did not retain a draft of his farewell to Alma.

1:2. "Hill stations," in the age before modern air-conditioning, were hilltop destinations where British colonials went to vacation and recover from the heat, humidity, and maladies contracted in their workaday careers in "the plains" of India. At an altitude from five- to seven thousand feet, these stations were from seventeen to twenty degrees cooler than the plains below and out of range of malaria-bearing mosquitoes. The cooler temperatures gave the feeling of being in a European climate. In the age after railroads made travel to the hills easier for families, British colonial functionaries built Cotswold-like cottages in these stations, with names suggestive of home. Boarding schools were built so children did not have to be sent to Europe or America for a proper (Western) education. This way, children would be separated from their parents for only a few months in the hills instead of enduring year-long separations.

2:1. Handley Page aircraft—the HP-42 in particular—are documented on various websites, including that of British Air on its historical page: https://www.britishairways.com/en-us/information/about-ba/history-and-heritage, accessed 2/7/17. For Imperial Airways flights to the Middle East, see Pirie, *Air Empire*. Seaplanes connected Imperial Airways to remote corners of the British Empire. They flew to the southern tip of Africa and landed on the Nile River, the rift valley lakes of Africa, and in saltwater harbors. They also replaced the HP-42 on flights to the Orient and Australia. See Pirie, "Passenger Traffic," which verifies that Wells and Beth must have been very early passengers on HP-42 flights from Lake Tiberias to Baghdad. Higham, *Britain's Imperial Air Routes 1918 to 1939*, 407, corroborates the early hub at Lake Tiberias as the link to HP-42 flights to Baghdad.

Information on flying the furrow can be found in McGregor, "Flying the Furrow." Narratives of the Nairn buses connecting Baghdad with Syria/Lebanon are recounted in Munro and Love, "The Nairn Way." *Popular Mechanics* featured both the Handley Page HP-42, in "The World's Largest Airplane" (March 1931), 394, and the Nairn bus enterprise in "Streamline Bus Replaces Camel in Desert" (March 1934), 400, in graphic articles. The railroads in French and British Mandate territories were of post-World War I vintage. The Jezreel Valley line was of the Ottoman gauge; at 1,050 mm, it was slightly wider than meter-gauge rail lines. The author has found neither a reference to the May DePree Thoms photos (taken nearly a century ago) in other online repositories nor documentation of the photos' existence in other archives. May founded a girls' school in Baghdad and probably knew many people in the expatriate community there in consequence.

3:1. Acquiring fluency in a foreign language is demanding and seldom exciting. It is a mark of the seriousness of the RCA that they invested from 5 to 10 percent of their missionaries' careers in acquiring facility in Arabic. When Wells and Beth went to the Gulf, English was not nearly the dominant international language it is today. Investing the first two years of a missionary's career in learning Arabic assumed a missionary was making a lifelong commitment to serve in the region.

On Gertrude Bell, see Wallach, *Desert Queen*. See also, Gertrude Bell's letters (online). Her British Parliamentary Paper on the British occupation of Iraq after World War I (*Review of the Civil Administration of Iraq*) still stands as a compelling product of its time. In it, Bell suggests a model for education in Iraq that seems based on the Van Ess schools in Basrah. At the time, this may have seemed flattering to the Van Esses and their colleagues. These schools had remained strong until they were nationalized by the Baath government in the late 1950s, by which time, it may have been that schools so highly praised in the British-dominant era would be viewed quite differently in the later self-consciously nationalist age.

Following the lead of Van Ess, the Arabian Mission operated schools in each of its stations. Edwin Calverley opened the first school in Kuwait with a modern curriculum, and its graduates were instrumental in Kuwaiti government service in the early post-World War II era. The Al Raja' School in Bahrain continues to this day and has provided education in modern subjects for many decades, thereby playing an instrumental role in the evolution of modern Bahrain. In Oman, the mission operated Al Amana School in Muscat from the 1930s to the 1980s. Until the era of Sultan Sayyid Qaboos bin Sa'eed, this school educated some of the royal family and many others of all social strata in modern subjects. Today the Al Amana Centre (Matrah) focuses on Christian-Muslim dialogue to enhance mutual understanding.

On the Van Esses, see Van Ess, *Pioneers in the Arab World*, 188. For Harry J. Wiersum's recollections of learning Arabic, see "First Experiences in Arabic."

Neglected Arabia is a good, but far-from-perfect, source of information about the knowledge, attitudes, and motivation of Arabian Mission personnel. Before it was officially renamed *Arabia Calling*, it was issued as the *Quarterly Letters from the Arabian Mission*. The early letters have the freshness and candor associated with the "early launch stage" of any adventurous, but amateur, enterprise. In later years, *Neglected Arabia* took on a more institutionalized quality. Authors wrote to no one in particular. They depicted Arabs and Arabia and the Gulf as needy in material and spiritual ways. After all, the Arabian Mission's goal was to make a very big change in the spiritual orientation of Gulf Arabs, and if possible, also Arabs of the deep interior of Arabia. *Neglected Arabia*'s audience was church members of the RCA—people who were already convinced of the rightness of Protestant (Calvinist) Christianity for the whole world. Missionaries were sponsored by a congregation (or several congregations) in the RCA, and they returned to the United States every five to seven years. *Neglected Arabia* was intended to keep church members in touch with the progress of the Arabian Mission. It was not intended to accentuate the difficulties, challenges, or roadblocks confronting missionaries. The readership of *Neglected Arabia* became so broad that authors could not know everyone who would read their articles. The impersonality of the articles, therefore, introduced a degree of denominational political correctness, without resorting to fiction or gratuitous hyperbole. In the last two decades, academics have discovered *Neglected Arabia* to be a valuable source of information. Yale University has preserved this documentary series.

3:15. The BI had other local names dating from the beginning of steamship service up and down the Gulf. The "fast" ship made only a few, scheduled stops as opposed to the "slow" ship that had a flexible schedule and stopped in any port of the Gulf with passengers and cargo to either load or discharge. The BI linked Gulf kingdoms into the British Empire and was one of the reasons the British considered the Gulf to be their own "English Lake."

3:17. T. E. Lawrence was famously known as "Lawrence of Arabia." Cox, Wilson, and Philby were British colonial dignitaries. Philby attended Sunday worship when in Basrah. He did so to savor John Van Ess's magnificent Arabic, despite having himself converted to Islam in order to marry his second, Arab, wife. He reverted to Christianity after settling again in England in his later years.

3:18. Of the Van Esses, Gertrude confided in letters to her parents, "I spent the whole of yesterday talking to Mr. Van Ess, the American missionary. He is the most invigorating companion; he knows the place as no one else does" (March 24, 1920). In another letter, she wrote: "I get rather tired of seeing nothing but men. My great standby is Mrs. Van Ess, the wife of the American missionary. I like them both, and she is particularly nice. I see her often. He has an unexampled knowledge of the country and gives me a good deal of help. He speaks Arabic better than any foreigner I ever heard" (31 May 1916). Dorothy Firman Van Ess was one of the best educated of Arabian Mission appointees. A missionary in her own right, Dorothy was one of many Swarthmore College graduates to enter mission service overseas and was well equipped to deal with the challenges of running her own girls school in the Ottoman imperial age. Gertrude Bell thought the Van Esses to be the only other Western intellectuals in Iraq.

4:1. An excellent source on the Van Ess years in Basrah is Charles Gosselink's, *Dear Folks at Home*. Charles' father, George, wrote these edited letters to his Iowa family during the 1920s. At the time, George was a short-term missionary in Basrah assisting John Van Ess in the Boy's School of High Hope. Van Ess could not have done what he did without the valuable support of George Gosselink. Charles noted in conversation that, although George saw to the day-to-day functioning of the school, he left it to John Van Ess to make interpretive statements on life in Iraq, the Gulf, and Middle East. Van Ess was the recognized authority.

5:1. The pearling industry is described by a number of contemporary observers: Zwemer and Zwemer, *Zigzag Journeys*; Belgrave, "Pearl diving in Bahrain"; Mylrea, "The Pearling Industry"; Hopper, "Slaves of One Master," 2008 and 2015; Carter, "The History and Prehistory of Pearling in the Persian Gulf."

Some of this chapter is fictive. Smethers is entirely fictional, but he represents the views of British imperial and commercial interests that were prevalent throughout the Gulf region. Wells would have learned of these matters over dinners and receptions with imperial administrators and businessmen. This narrative device shows the veneer of the British Empire that had been built on the base of Gulf economies and society.

During his final years of service, Wells' missionary colleagues invented an award for him. He was given a "lifetime experience award" as the Arabian Mission missionary who knew the most about the BI's agents and business processes, for he was the one who had traveled the most extensively on BISN ships. He also knew the most about moving baggage and equipment through the port customs offices in the Gulf.

5:14. Unfortunately, most of these "Bahraini" freshwater springs on the island and in the sea have dried up. The increased demand for potable water due to population growth, the disruption of underground aquifers associated with construction and land reclamation, and the heightened use of water from these aquifers on the Sa'udi Arabian mainland have either sucked them dry or plugged them up. The Al-Hasa Oasis is fed by aquifers on the Arabian mainland and continues to be Sa'udi Arabia's best naturally watered agricultural area.

5:17. This author was fortunate to be invited to the bridge on several BI vessels in both monsoonal and calm weather. The ethereal silence and calm on the bridge of a ship—far removed from creaks and groans as the superstructure and its furnishings and cargo shifted and distant from the vibration of the steam valves, pistons, and gears of the engine room—must be experienced to be understood. The bridge, situated near the rotational center of the ship, is the most stable and quiet place on the ship. In return, it demands the greatest resolve and determination in driving the ship safely to its destination.

6:1. The Jarman, *Historic Maps of Bahrain* collection shows the growth of Bahrain before and after the 1930s. Readers will note that the mission hospital complex (including the church and Al Raja' School) sat at the southern edge of Manama. Beyond it were the cemeteries edging the built-up city. The Marion Wells Thoms Hospital for Women became a residence for hospital personnel and has now reopened as the Samuel Zwemer Clinic. The entire enlarged medical complex continues today under the patronage of the king of Bahrain and the visionary leadership of Dr. George Cherian, CMO of the American Mission Hospital.

6:5. Mechanical air-conditioning had been developed in India for the British. The *punkah* was a large, horizontal fan pulled rhythmically on a rope running through the wall to a human puller outside. Bahraini labor was not as cheap as Indian labor, and Muslim society was more egalitarian—save for the institution of slavery (and missionaries did not have slaves). The other air-conditioner was the "thermantidote," a desert cooler that pushed a blast of (dry) air across a pan of water. The problem in Bahrain was that its sultry summer air was so humid, it could not be cooled further by moisturizing it. The hospital was dedicated in 1903, but none of the mission's buildings used the indigenous, very effective wind towers ("windcatchers" in Arabic) for relief of heat stress.

6:7. Homeopathic patients received small doses of poisons (as if consuming "the hair of the dog that bit you"). Its modus operandi was similar to India's *ayurvedic* medicine. Homeopathy became popular after the Civil War as part of the Christian Science practice championed by Hahnemann. The University of

Michigan ran two medical schools at the turn of the twentieth century. (The Homeopathic school closed about 1920. The allopathic medical school was a leading medical school in the US.) Sharon enrolled in the allopathic medical school, and Marion enrolled in the homeopathic school. Students took some courses in common, and it was in one of these classes that Marion and Sharon first met. Other allopathic medical students agreed Marion was fully capable of doing an allopathic medical degree, and she assisted one of its medical school professors in his research and teaching, but she never practiced surgery.

6:15. The grief of the Zwemers must have been overwhelming. They left Bahrain a year after they had buried their two children there. They returned to Bahrain in 1912, only to withdraw again after less than a year. Samuel Zwemer took an appointment in Cairo and founded the journal, *Muslim World*. Nowhere is the loss of their children mentioned in surviving letters, documents, or biographies. We are left to infer that their departure from Bahrain came because of their deep, possibly inconsolable, grief.

7:1. This chapter is based on Wells' tape recorded recollections made during his last year of life. He wanted his family to know what had happened in the family reunion in Garbutt, New York. A typescript of the letter S. J. sent to Seth and Etta Wells is among letters in the Wells Thoms collection of correspondence. Seth Wells' experience in the Civil War is corroborated by New York state Civil War service rosters, as is the service and death of his brother Will. Other family details are revealed in the research of Paul Armerding, who has reviewed the Thoms family letters in Michigan. See also, the University of Michigan's historical record of its homeopathic medical school that closed after World War I.

Many Civil War veterans probably experienced what we now call post-traumatic stress disorder (PTSD). One of the best known cases is featured in Winchester's, *The Professor and the Madman*, who may have manifested other mental illness as well. The "mad" man, a doctor, was pensioned for life by the Union Army because of his deeply disturbing extramedical duties that involved punishing rebellious recruits by branding them on the face. Incarcerated for life in a British mental institution for murder, the doctor became the most prolific volunteer contributor to the *Oxford Unabridged Dictionary of the English Language*.

7:4. "Behold, I tell you a mystery: We all shall not sleep, but we all shall be changed, in a moment, in the twinkling of an eye, at the last trump: for the trumpet shall sound, and the dead shall be raised incorruptible, and we shall all be changed. For this corruptible must put on incorruption, and this mortal shall put on immortality. But when this corruptible shall have put on incorruption, and this mortal shall have put on immortality, then shall come to pass the saying that is written, Death is swallowed up in victory. O death, where is thy victory? O death, where is thy sting? The sting of death is sin; and the power of sin is the law: but thanks be to God, who giveth us the victory through our Lord Jesus Christ. Wherefore, my beloved brethren, be ye steadfast, unmovable, always abounding in the work of the Lord, forasmuch as ye know that your labor is not in vain in the Lord" (I Cor. 15:51-58, American Standard Version, 1901).

7:9. Until 1915 a network of short-line interurban electric trolleys extended from New York City as far west as St. Louis. These "light rail" lines connected villages and farms with market towns and linked the countryside with cities, hauling passengers and freight from farm to market. Legislative changes in 1915 and the growing use of the automobile spelled the end of this independent, electric-rail network.

8:1. C. Dalrymple Belgrave, who had served as the ruler's wazir for thirty years (the ruler was known at different times as hakim, shaykh, and king), was a great stabilizing influence in Bahrain until the era of Arab self-determination took hold. Belgrave's papers and journals are as interesting as those of any British resident or consul in the Gulf. His oversight and regulation of the pearling industry protected the interests of the low-income divers and their colleagues. He limited the transfer of divers' debts from one generation to the next.

Janet S. Pengelley's biography of her father, *William Harold Storm*, recounts the life of the adventurous Dr. Storm, who served most of his career in Bahrain.

8:5. "Compounder" was the term used for a pharmacist. At that time, few prescriptions were premeasured into pills or capsules by pharmaceutical manufacturers. The compounder combined the chemical ingredients of the prescription for patients to take in powder form. In earlier times, pharmacies were also known as "chemist's shops" because the compounder needed knowledge of chemistry. These powders often were quite bitter or distasteful. Sometimes the powdered prescription was put into a soluble capsule. In the nineteenth century, some pharmaceutical firms made their powders into pill form. Most of the pills, however, proceeded through patients' digestive systems without dissolving and thus did not accomplish their purpose. Perhaps the first company to successfully make a soluble pill—known as "friable"—was the Upjohn Company of Kalamazoo, Michigan.

9:8. In "Story of a Book," Thoms elaborates on the provenance of this treasured volume:

Avicenna wrote the *Canon* in Persia in the early part of the eleventh century, during the golden age of Arabian medicine. Stored in his mind were the philosophical and medical writings of the Greeks, which had been translated into Arabic by Hunayn bin Ishaq and other Christian scholars of the Jundi Shapur school of medicine. He was also a scholar on the theology of the Q'uran, which he knew by heart. To him the body, mind, and soul made up the whole personality of man. To Avicenna, there was no mortal conflict between science and religion or between religion and philosophy, but all three were parts of the whole— Ultimate Truth. His philosophy was essentially that of the Greeks—Aristotle, Hippocrates, and Galen—his religion that of a Moslem mystic, his attitude toward natural phenomena that of the modern scientist. He not only passed on to his students and to posterity a compendium of the knowledge of the past, but also, when his own observations differed from those of the ancients, he boldly stated his theory in opposition to the traditional one.

To further emphasize the lasting importance of Avicenna's tome, Thoms cites the comments of "Cyril Algid," probably Dr. Cyril Elgood—sometime physician to the Shah of Iran—who published *A Medical History of Persia and the Eastern Caliphate*, and several other major works on Persian medical history. As Thoms reported it, Elgood maintained that the importance of the *Canon* could not be overestimated.

With the composition of the *Canon* (about 1020 CE), Avicenna placed the coping stone to the arch that bridges between the medical system of Hippocrates and Galen and that of Harvey and modern medicine. There was to be from that moment a standard by which medical practice and scientific theory could be tested. Could or could not such a theory be deduced from the writings of Avicenna? Galen was rivaled, if not actually displaced. The *Canon* became, by means of its Latin translation, the textbook of all the universities of Europe.

Original observations lie scattered throughout his works. He discovered and described the insertions of the intrinsic muscles of the eye. He suggested that certain diseases were waterborne, the cause being minute animals that lived in the water, too small to be viewed by the human eye. He was the first to attempt to differentiate between obstructive and hemolytic jaundice. Some of his clinical descriptions are excellent, especially the sections on nervous, cutaneous, and genitourinary diseases. His dietetic and therapeutic directions are admirable. He was far in advance of his age in his condemnation of astrology and magic and in his attempt to divorce them from medicine.

Abu Sina's *Qanun* resides now in the Rare Books Collection of the University of Michigan, where I examined it in 2015. Its condition is excellent, with tight binding, firm cover boards in red leather, and clear Arabic imprint on high quality paper that has deteriorated very little. Handwritten notes in the margin are still legible, and there is no visible water damage. The towwash's family that owned it had treated it well over the centuries. Probably it was wrapped tightly in cloth so that it would not be damaged in transport.

In the 1930s, the price for a rare book was modest. Wells accepted this book in payment for the hospital bill. Then he paid the Unani doctor-towwash's hospital bill himself since the hospital would have had no use for the *Qanun*. Even at the time he gave the book to the University of Michigan, it likely had a low resale value.

9:13. With a specialty in eye surgery, Wells was particularly interested in the history of science and medicine dealing with light and vision. While studying Arabic in Jerusalem, he carried out eye surgeries and learned the methods Arab medical practitioners had developed to operate on trichiasis (the inward turning of the eyelashes that can score the cornea and blind those with this early stage of trachoma). He improved these methods to save

9:14. As far as Wells could determine in 1957, no one had translated any of it from Arabic into English since Dr. O. Cameron Gruner of Montreal had translated the first book of the *Canon* in 1930. A later note on the history of medicine indicates that Dr. Harvey Cushing of Massachusetts General Hospital was eager for his colleague, Paul Harrison, to acquire old Arabic medical manuscripts. Harrison was unsuccessful in this. But the significance of Wells' acquisition of Hakeem Abu Sina's five-part *Qanun* impressed Paul Harrison's children who were also research-oriented doctors, and they published an article on it; see Harrison and Harrison. "My Dear Paul."

10:9. Jarman, *Historic Maps of Bahrain* is an invaluable source of information regarding the evolution of the topography and cultural landscape of Bahrain.

Awali reached its peak development as a look-alike American suburb in the 1950s, resplendent with movie theater, school, restaurants, and other services. The mission offered medical services there into the 1960s. The mission relationship with BAPCO was nurtured by Dr. Harold Storm, the CMO of the hospital that succeeded Louis Dame. Storm had a house in Awali, as well as in Bahrain. His daughter, Janet, married Bruce Pengelley, a BAPCO oil man. See Janet Pengelley, *William Harold Storm, M.D.* Revenues from BAPCO to the hospital terminated when Dr. Storm retired. This change in hospital revenue brought the hospital to a budget crisis. Ultimately, the hospital was restructured with an autonomous board in Bahrain. Under the patronage of the king of Bahrain, the hospital continues to thrive to this day.

12:2. Beth was supportive of Wells but not endlessly so. Between his spiritual quagmire and her raising three young ones largely alone since he was consumed by his work, she came nearly to her wit's end. One day, when she could take it no longer, she dressed the children (Nancy, Peter, and Norman) in their best clothes, put on her most formal Sunday clothing (dress, hose, shoes, pillbox hat with small veil not covering her face, and gloves), and

the sight of thousands of Arabs during the next forty years. He noted, but could not explain, why people of African ancestry, slaves and their descendants, did not contract trichiasis.

took her family to sit in line with those waiting to see the doctor (Wells). The Arab families also waiting knew something was up but did not know its meaning. When it was their turn to see the doctor, Beth brought the children and said to Wells, "I want you to meet your children, in case you have forgotten them and me. This is Nancy. This is Peter. This is Norman." Nancy, detecting the tension, withdrew into her mother's skirts while smiling, wiggling nervously, and saying in loving delight, "Daddy-y-y!" Peter being younger, lunged forward and hugged his father's knee squealing in equally loving delight, "Daddy-y-y!" Norman being a toddler in his mother's arms, looked on approvingly. Wells got her message. This episode may have marked the beginning of a new and deeper, lasting relationship between Beth and Wells. They needed and loved each other and their family.

12:4. Cantine went on to argue in a missiological tour de force:

Our individual attainments or the attainments of the Christian Church and Christian nations in knowledge, in riches, or in power are not in themselves persuasive. These things that are known as the fruits of Christianity will not lead many Moslems to desire to be engrafted into the true vine. Neither, I think, has our superior theology been the means by which Christ has approached the hearts of most converts from Islam.

The Moslem heart is not different from yours or mine. What would appeal to us will appeal to him. It must be the heart that touches the heart. The things of the heart—love, joy, peace, long suffering, gentleness, goodness, and the like—are what the heart esteems worthwhile the world over. The way, then, for him who would enter the door is to bring of these gifts which the heart always craves. If it were enough to tell of them [the gifts] and the Source from which they spring, it would be simple. But the human heart demands more than this, else had the Gospel ended for us with the story of the disciples. There is only one way to prove to our Moslem friend that Christ can and will give to him now these blessings and that is to show him that He has given them to us. We must not alone ask him to listen to us speak and read about them but also to examine and prove them, and this can only be done as they are exhibited in our lives.

To use an analogy, which will be familiar to many, we are as commercial agents, persuading merchants to trade with the Firm which we represent. We have an abundance of printed appeal at hand, clear and convincing, but in addition to this, there is need of the living epistle. We must show our samples, and these, for us missionaries, are nothing less than the fruit of the Spirit in our own lives. We say to him, "Believe in the Lord Jesus Christ, and He will give you blessings of peace and joy and holiness." At once he replies, "You have believed; I will judge of the worth of your belief by what you have of these blessings." And so, we are very particular about these samples of ours. We are not introducing our goods where there are none like them but rather do we have to show that we have, that our Head can supply, a better article than has been before known. The Moslem has something of all those things that we would offer to him with Christianity, and unless he is convinced that we have in our own characters and lives more than he—more of love and benevolence, more of brotherliness and pity, more of true prayer and true submission to God—our progress will be slow indeed. There are things in the Moslem faith of which he is proud and justly so. We must show him that in these, we are better Moslems than he. There are things in which his faith is lacking. We must show him these our riches, that he may recognize his poverty. It is just in showing this, the evidential value of Christian love and pity, that our hospitals are such a help in reaching the heart. It is the opportunity given for brotherly help wherein is the present value of our schools.

This all means that the nearest way is the hardest way for us. We have first to know the Moslem heart and the things he holds dear. We cannot know, understand, appreciate, without first loving. We have to touch his heart with our hearts, to come into intimate contact with his life. For this we want no flattering tongue nor imperfect means of communication. We want to enter into his life and forget the things in which we think our own civilization is superior. In short, we must approach him just as Christ approached the people in Judea and Galilee. And it is only by such a way of self-denial and service that we can get near enough to show, to *show forth* those things that commend our faith and will lead our Moslem brother in God's providence, to accept it as his only comfort in life and death. (Italics his.)

A newsprint version of Cantine's essay was carefully clipped and preserved among Wells' letters and memorabilia; see Cantine, "The Nearest Way to an Arab Heart."

12:6. One God with three forms dates from antiquity and has been a source of controversy for some Muslims. God the Father is God. Jesus Christ is God made manifest to humans in history, the Son. The Holy Spirit was early termed God's "Holy Breath," the continuing presence of God among humans. Wells believed these terms of human origin failed to fully grasp the essential oneness of God that is beyond human linguistic expression and understanding. Every word that reduces God to human comprehension is itself inadequate because God cannot be contained in human words. For discussion of Muslim acceptance of the triune nature of God, see Roberts, "Trinity vs. Monotheism." See also, Volf, *Do We Worship the Same God?*

12:7. Some Muslims thought that Wells used "magic" to cure people. Of course, humans in many societies—parts of Arabia included—believed/still believe in both "white" and "black" magic. Wells would have said there was no truth that he used magic. The Holy Spirit was almost palpably present to him in every operation, inspiring and carrying him forward, as it sustained each patient, too. The Holy Spirit was miraculous, not the magical trick of a conjuror. Furthermore, he knew he could not control the Holy Spirit or conjure its presence. It was the gift of God's love offered to all in that instant, regardless of whether they were believers or nonbelievers. He attributed the high success rate of patient outcomes, both inside and outside the hospital, as much to the Holy Spirit as to the natural immunity of his patients, his use of sterile techniques, the constancy of hospital hygiene, and/or his surgical skill and compassion for his patients.

12:10. Wells' family did not come from the Dutch Reformed Church tradition nor were they Dutch. His father had been raised a Methodist Episcopal. Beth's family was not Dutch, either, although they had been in the Reformed Church for generations. The Scudders were originally Congregationalists. The Protestant mission enterprise often brought together people of different denominations. On the mission field, many missionaries discovered ecumenism since the divisions of the many Christian denominations hardly made sense in cultural and religious settings where most people adhered to non-Christian religious beliefs and practices. Those of divergent Christian theological beliefs served together as colleagues in the Arabian Mission. Their commonality was a commitment to share their understanding of the Christian faith with others. Therefore, attributing singleness of doctrinal view to missionaries in the same denominational mission is unhelpful.

14:18. Wells' conversation with King Abdal Aziz dovetails with the account of Karl Twitchell, one of the early American petroleum prospectors and negotiators. Abdal Aziz had signed the papers for a first oil concession much earlier, but it had expired. In 1933 King Abdal Aziz signed over a second oil concession to ARAMCO (a consortium of American companies). Abdal Aziz was mindful he could be much more vulnerable to criticism from his "orthodox" Wahhabi countrymen for having signed a second treaty with such "infidels"—the first concession having been signed because there was no alternative except to depend on a foreign company to search for oil in Arabia. A repetition, however, could be construed among the more conservative as a major mistake and an expression of greed, love of wealth, and/or loss of faith in allowing non-Muslims access to Arabia. Until after 1938, when King Abdal Aziz met with President Roosevelt in the Suez Canal, there were no American embassies or consulates in Sa'udi Arabia. King Abdal Aziz had crafted his story into easily remembered sound bites so that shaykhs visiting his mejlis in Riyadh would be able to retell this news again and again on return to their tribesmen. Couched in specifically religious terms, the statement reiterated the fact that much more revenue would accrue to King Abdal Aziz who, as absolute monarch, constituted the newly minted Sa'udi state. Abdal Aziz's story also made for good press outside Sa'udi Arabia. Wells could not have known in advance that Abdal Aziz would use him as a foil for spreading this new information inside Sa'udi Arabia.

15:1. Col. Harold R. P. Dickson and his wife, Violet, left an indelible imprint on the literature of Kuwait and its surroundings with *Kuwait and Her Neighbours*, a six-hundred-page archive of information. *The Arab of the Desert* is another six-hundred-page volume. Each has an extensive glossary and multiple maps and diagrams folded into the back cover. Freeth's *Kuwait Was My Home*, is yet another view from the Dickson family perspective. Mylrea's draft, *Kuwait Before Oil* (in a slightly altered version as *Before Oil Came to Kuwait*, also from 1952), was never actually published but was edited by several people, most notably Rev. Samuel Zwemer and Mrs. Dorothy Van Ess. The original manuscript is not extant. A synthesized memoir compiled by D. G. Dickason, consisting of Mylrea's edited manuscript(s) and other published and unpublished essays, is forthcoming. Calverley, *My Arabian Days and Nights*, is the memoir of a woman doctor missionary colleague of Mylrea. Much of her story was compiled from Mylrea's daily journal, now also lost to posterity. Allison, *Doctor Mary in Arabia*, follows on Calverley's accounts of treating women in Kuwait.

The Wells Thoms stories in this chapter come directly from his tape-recorded recollections. Some of these stories were told again and again at the dining room table. Howell, *Strangers When We Met*, gives an account of the Arabian Mission in Kuwait. It does not cover the material in this chapter, although it does briefly mention Wells and Beth Thoms. Beth trained the first Kuwaitis to carry out laboratory tests so that the mission doctors would be free to treat patients. Lewis R. Scudder III's excellent volume also provides a detailed coverage of the Kuwait Mission.

15:16. Years later, Wells returned to Kuwait. While there, he visited A. at his home. Over coffee, Wells exclaimed, "A., you have changed! You have had an operation to repair your cleft lip! The doctor did a good job. I suggested repairing your lip when you were in the hospital with your broken leg. And you would have none of it. You refused. What happened?"

"Oh, back then, I didn't think it was necessary. I had lived with it all my life, and it had not stopped me. But some years ago, I wanted to get married and take another wife. The girl was very nice, and I was drawn to her. But the idea of marrying me did not appeal to her. She said she absolutely would not marry a 'camel'!" A.'s nickname, because of his harelip, had always been "camel." "That did it. I changed my mind and decided to have the operation so she could no longer say no."

"So, you married again?" asked Wells. "Has it been a good marriage?"

"Yes, and yes, thanks be to Allah," said A. "Today she is the mother of three sons. God is generous."

15:17. Dickson's suspicions that Arabian Mission personnel were agents of the United States (or other European powers) is documented in Tuson, *Playing the Game*, 266. He was especially suspicious of those of non-English origin, particularly those with Dutch last names. The Arabian missionaries were an eclectic lot, being drawn from Australia, the United States, the Netherlands, England, Switzerland, and elsewhere. Samuel Zwemer, John Van Ess, Maurice Heusinkveld, and Fred Barny all spoke Dutch fluently. There was no basis for his suspicion, but Dickson was simply being a loyal servant of the empire that possessed somewhat paranoid sensitivities.

16:1. See the letters in the archives held in New Brunswick Theological Seminary of S. J. Thoms to and from the RCA board. These cover his acceptance in Muscat and the need for State Department intervention with the Court of St. James regarding the United States Treaty with Muscat. The mission's *Neglected Arabia* quarterly newsletter (variously titled but running from the 1890s into the 1960s) gives tantalizing hints of what was happening in Oman. The Freed Slave Boys School is also treated there briefly, together with photographs of the boys in their early adult years. See also, Landen, *Oman Since 1856*; Graves, *The Life of Sir Percy Cox*; Phillips, *Oman*; Peterson, *Historical Muscat*; and Zwemer and Cantine, *The Golden Milestone*.

16:13. The letter reads: "Mascat, October 8, 1913. My dear Mrs. Thoms, You will no doubt be sorry to read the death of my beloved father, H. H., the Sultan, after a short illness on the 4th instant [October 4, 1913]. At the same time, you will be glad to note that I am placed on the throne of Mascat & Oman. My best salaams to your good self, dear Saida, Kamila, and Ameen [the Thoms children, Frances, Lois, and Wells]. Yours Sincerely, Sayd. Taimoor [*sic*]." The letter was postmarked the same date in Muscat. Sultan Sayyid Taymur bin Faisal had been on the throne perhaps two days when he conveyed this news to the family of his friend and fellow Mason. The Oman to which Taymur refers was probably that of the Batinah Coast, for the interior of Oman was in hands hostile to the al Bu Sa'eed rulers of Muscat.

17:1. Paul Harrison wrote two books on his experiences in Arabia, drawing on his service in many parts of the Gulf and Sa'udi Arabia. The first was *The Arab at Home*; the second was *Doctor in Arabia*. Often, they are quite humorous in comparing Arab and Midwestern American viewpoints. In their time, they were popular with American readers. Harrison's second wife, Monty (under her first name, Ann), wrote Paul's biography, *A Tool in His Hand*. His son, Dr. Timothy Harrison, supplemented these books with *Before Oil*.

Ronald Wingate relates fully the Agreement of Seeb story in his memoir, *Not in the Limelight*, including the role of his butler Etisham. Karen Armstrong relates the anecdote about the Prophet Muhammad in her biography of him, *Muhammad: A Prophet for Our Time*.

18:8. Diekema saved the teenaged Wells from a brush with the law. When Hope College's basketball team beat Michigan State's team on the same night a Hope student won a national speech contest, Wells—then enrolled at the Hope Academy—and other boys celebrated. The father of one of the boys was a minister of a Reformed Church in town, so they said, "Let's ring the bell in your father's church!" People throughout the town heard the boisterous clangs and became alarmed, thinking there might be a major emergency. A police officer arrested the boys as they exited the church. Hope College's Pres. Dimnent recruited Diekema to defend "his boys."

Diekema reviewed in court the breaking-and-entering charge after the prosecution had made its case. "Now, what happened?" asked Diekema. "Some college boys became very happy—maybe too happy—over big victories for Hope College and for the whole city. Did they go to a saloon to celebrate the team's big win or the speech champion? No! They went to church! Since when has it been illegal to go to church? They didn't even break a window! Yes, they disturbed the peace. These young men should have asked permission. They should apologize. For that, I'd like to request the church members to retract their complaint."

Put on the spot, the churchmen reluctantly agreed to drop all charges. Wells and his buddies apologized and were grateful for Diekema's sage intervention.

18:10. The *Pictorial Review* advertised fashionable patterns for women's clothes. Patterns in the magazine could be bought in local department stores, together with fabrics, needles, and thread. Wells contacted local merchants indicating his impending sales blitz. If the merchant provided Wells and his partner introductions printed in the local paper, they would tell new subscribers where they could buy the dress patterns. By summer's end, both men had saved $800 beyond their hotel, food, and car costs—a huge sum of money in the 1920s, when most workers did not earn more than $6 per day.

19:2. The General (Men's) Hospital was officially named Knox Memorial Hospital, after its American donor. This was Wells' primary focus every day. After inpatient rounds and prayers early every morning, an outpatient clinic ran the rest of the morning (unless Wells carried out lab tests). Upward of 250 people might come to the clinic for diagnosis and treatment in a single morning. In the afternoon, Wells undertook major and minor operations and procedures. These were followed by evening rounds of inpatient visits. It was normal for him to be called out on at least one house call every day. Only the highlights of the developments in the hospital during Wells' first fifteen years are noted in this chapter. After 1970, Knox Memorial Hospital was renamed Ar Rahma [Mercy] Hospital.

19:16. Wells wrote in his Muscat and Matrah Medical Report for 1943 (unpublished typescript) about the car:

> One of our greatest needs is a new touring car. The one we have now has taken some awful punishment. It went to places such as Kuriat and Nakhl before roads of any kind were built and was the first car to visit many inland towns, carrying doctor, preacher, medicines, and the Gospel to out-of-the-way places. When the speedometer broke three years ago, the car had gone 50,000 miles, and it has gone at least 20,000 since. When it fell down the mountainside two and a half years ago, we thought it would never run again, but it was soon put into running order, although fenders, doors, and other accessories looked as if they had been in a wreck. The motor had not been seriously damaged. A few months after the accident, we went 250 miles up the coast to Khor Fakkan to vaccinate the entire population of that city, and last summer, it went there again to rescue the Dykstras. On the return trip, it cracked up at a place called Khaboorah. Mohammed has been able to get it running again so that it can still carry us about on short local hauls, but its days as a touring car are done. We will have to postpone regular touring up the Batinah.

19:22. In 2009 this author visited Nizwa and met a merchant in the old suq. When asked if he had met Dr. Thoms, the merchant said, "Oh yes. I fell down a well headfirst and got all ripped up around my ears and face. It was awful. Everything swelled up very big. Dr. Thoms examined me and said there was a medicine that would help me. I asked him how much it was going to cost. He said 200 *baisas*. I said, what if it doesn't work? He said it would work. I said, okay, Give me the medicine, and if it works, I'll pay you 200 *baisas*." That was their bargain. The medicine worked, and the merchant was still alive to tell about it in 2009.

19:24. One of the hospital's medical team said (40 years after Wells had retired), "Dr. Thoms was more a father to me than my own father. I was thirteen years old when I asked him for a job. He wanted to know what skills I had—what I could do. I told him I could sign my name, and I could count to thirteen. That was it—*bas*. He hired me anyway, and I learned how to help in the hospital from him and from others.

"But I was just thirteen years old. I was hot headed. One day, I got into a big fight, and the *askaris* [tribal guards] arrested me and threw me into Fort Jalali's dungeon. Somehow, Dr. Thoms had heard that I had gotten into trouble and been arrested. He came to Fort Jalali and spoke with the wali. He said, if the wali would release me, he [Dr. Thoms] would guarantee nothing like this would happen again. It was difficult for the wali to say 'no,' as this is exactly how Omani shaykhs intervened and negotiated punishments and paroles for their tribesmen who got in trouble. I was very grateful. Who knows what would have happened to me otherwise."

20:3. As conservative evangelical Christians, Sarah Hosmon, Fanny Lutton, and Nurse Mary gave of themselves endlessly to the community. Fanny was a "buzz saw" of energy. Sarah, a competent doctor for her times, had had major health problems. She had a wooden leg (prosthesis) and could always be heard when approaching. If anything, this endeared her to the women she served. She had an indomitable spirit and expressed great love and care for them. Nurse Mary was the one who came to homes in times of greatest stress. The three were supported in their efforts by the Dykstras; Minnie was also religiously conservative. Muscat was inhabited by determined Christian women bent on conversion. All realized the challenges of making converts from Islam. The church, run by Rev. Dirk Dykstra, subjected any would-be converts to exacting cross-examinations. It did not accept converts who were "rice Christians" who converted in order to be fed. Besides, the church had very few jobs to offer converts. The Ibadhi Muslim women of Muscat admired and loved these women for their sincerity and purity of commitment to Christian belief.

21:1. We cannot say with full confidence that this photo is of the imam in his Nizwa Fort mejlis. Since there are no other photographs of the imam, this one is accepted provisionally on circumstantial evidence only. The mejlis room is consistent with the layout of the Nizwa Fort mejlis (as reconstructed in modern times). The array of people in the room is also consistent: *askaris* on either side; the petitioner (probably a shaykh) with back to camera, facing persons against the wall; a scribe with his back to the wall (possibly grandfather to Oman's current minister of *awqaf* and religious affairs or the imam's personal secretary); and the elderly chief figure in profile and white turban (possibly the imam). If truly a photograph of the imam, it must have been taken about 1952—when the imam was nearly blind from cataracts (hence his pose) and when petroleum companies were negotiating security for their oil prospecting teams from interior tribes, such as the Duru.

The photo is a large glossy print in the Thoms photo collection. It was probably not taken by Dr. Wells Thoms himself. The oversize glossy print is consistent with photo prints taken by professional (commercial) photographers in those days. (The only other large glossy photos in Wells' collection are souvenir reminders of visiting naval vessel receptions on board their ships.) Wells kept this print with his other photos; he never mentioned its provenance. In any case, it is consistent with the mode of governance then carried out within the imam's domain. If not an actual photograph of the imam, it is entirely consistent with the manner in which he transacted business in Nizwa.

The account of the flash flood in the Wadi Thayka comes from an undated account of it by Beth Thoms, as told to her by Wells. It was probably written in Oman, interleaved on the same kind of paper with worship materials she used there.

21:2. According to Sharia law, the Abrahamic principle (Ex. 21:24), also found in Judaism (and taken from the Babylonian Code of Hammurabi)—"an eye for an eye, and a tooth for a tooth" (Matt. 5:38)—meant that a family could require a murderer be put to death for his crime. Alternatively, "blood money" could be negotiated. In fact, Ibadhi Islamic justice was quite lenient, and a murderer might be imprisoned for some years until his shaykh would vouch that the murderer would not repeat the crime. Major Anderson, head of the Muscat Garrison in Fort Mirani, when questioned about punishment of murderers, said, "I provide the family with a properly working rifle and fresh ammunition. There is nothing more cruel than seeing an old muzzle loader misfire at such a time" (personal communications, 1965). In fact, Major Anderson did not expect to provide a rifle. In the period 1925-70, there was only one time in Muscat and the Batinah under the sultan's rule when a murderer was executed, and he was a slave who had killed his master.

21:6. There were two branches of one indigenous Christian church, one in Muscat and one in Matrah. The former was mostly Arab. The other was mostly of Baluchi and Persian descent. These did not include the few expatriates who attended from South Asia, Europe, and the US. (Sunday evening worship services were in English.) After the hospitals were taken over by the Oman government in 1973, the indigenous Christian members were distributed widely throughout Oman. It became difficult to maintain each church autonomously with padres from Egypt. Ultimately, through deaths of senior members and reversion to Islam, few indigenous members remained. To the end, Qumber al Mas remained adamantly a Christian. He said, "If it was good enough for the Doctor [Thoms], it is good enough for me!"

21:7. Although MASH units (Mobile Army Surgical Hospitals) were not created until after World War II, much of Wells' efforts to bring medical assistance to people in their villages was similar in concept. The difference, however, was that his field unit had only one doctor and several illiterate medical assistants whom he had trained on the job. Even in the Matrah hospital, he had to exercise constant triage (also a post-World War II term); patients who could be saved took priority over others who could not. His medical practice was not at all unlike that of an ER surgeon, except he also had to cover many other functions to keep the hospital working.

23:1. Much of this chapter is assembled from Wells' annual reports of the medical work in Oman. Not all the annual reports were saved since there were no photocopy services. Any surviving transcript is a carbon copy. Perhaps the reason the reports survived in Wells' records is that he sent copies to his mother, and she retained them, along with many of his letters. The RCA archives does not have the annual medical reports from Oman, nor does it have annual medical reports from Bahrain, Kuwait, Basrah (while the hospital functioned there), or Amarah (until the hospital was nationalized). Brief reports of the medical work can be found in *Neglected Arabia/Arabia Calling*. Unfortunately, these distilled records lose most of the human interest and detail that appeared in the individual hospital annual medical reports.

26:1. Burton, *Goa and the Blue Mountains*, is a personal narrative of a pilgrimage to El Medinah and Meccah. See bibliography for: Burckhardt, *Travels in Arabia*; Wellsted, *Travels in Arabia*; Palgrave, *Narrative of a Year's Journey to Central and Eastern Arabia*; Blunt, *A Pilgrimage to Nejd*; Doughty, *Travels in Arabia Deserta*; Lawrence, *Revolt in the Desert*; Stark, *The Southern Gates of Arabia*; Thomas, *Arabia Felix*; Thesiger, *Arabian Sands*; Bell, *Persian Letters*; and Philby, *Arabian Days*.

26:7. Reserved forest bungalows were built in the age of the British Raj as circuit-house residences for the British forestry officer to stay in. These could be reserved for private use. Most popular were the sites of Vandaravu, Marion Shola, Kukkal (but preferably camping some miles away at Kukkal Cave), Poombarai, and Berijam Lake (Fort Hamilton). Campers hiked from thirteen to thirty-five miles from Kodai to these sites. The reserved forests were natural *sholas* (copses of rain forest), much reduced today. The intervening high-country grasslands have also been replaced by plantation forestry, and forest workers occupy the highlands in much larger numbers than sixty or seventy years ago. Some large animals have also returned to these areas, particularly the *gaur* (India's equivalent of a bison or Cape buffalo).

26:13. DiGiorgio found in the school an adoptive home and never left; much beloved, he died there in harness. Musil left only when near retirement to assume another post in Colorado. Together, with many other dedicated teachers, these "aliens" gave the school uncommon continuity and dedication to excellence in teaching and learning. Kodai School provided an excellent education for talented students. On the other hand, facilities and strategies for teaching those with educational disabilities were almost nonexistent. Indeed, most schools in the US did not have programs for children with learning limitations. Kodaikanal International School survives today as one of India's premier International Baccalaureate-granting private secondary schools, based on the foundation established under Carl Phelps and others.

26:19. Madame Caspari and her husband, both Italian-speaking Swiss citizens, were caught in India during World War II after visiting Tibet. Inexplicably, given Switzerland's neutrality, the British Raj considered them "enemy aliens" but yet allowed them to take jobs in India. Madame Caspari taught piano at Kodaikanal School, and her husband oversaw the grounds and maintenance. While in Kodaikanal, Mme. Caspari met Mme. Montessori, who had founded a Montessori school in Kodai. Mme. Caspari became a foremost proponent of Montessori education, and she actively promoted Montessori schools into her late nineties (she lived to age 101).

27:1. This chapter is based on the numerous histories and contemporary accounts of Oman in the post-World War II period. Among these are excellent volumes by Peterson and Rabi. This chapter does not intend any revision to Omani history, except for the ways that Wells Thoms and the Arabian Mission Hospitals interleaved with it in those times.

Arabian Mission personnel resisted engaging in the domestic politics of the countries they served. Individuals like Wells Thoms, however, were reluctantly drawn into its periphery simply because of their long-term acquaintances and friendships with Omanis who sided either for or against the sultan or imam. Wells was always wary of Shaykh Sulayman bin Hamyar, as he was of other leading shaykhs of the interior. The former played "both sides of the street" politically for many years before his separatist intentions became clear. Wells believed he had little choice but to work with the leaders in power (no matter their attitudes or biases) rather than with those whom he preferred to be in power.

27:3. In a declassified communication between Muscat and London are the following handwritten remarks: "I wonder if we shall find out what Sulayman bin Hamyar said to the Doctor. To meet the imam is an achievement; to the best of my knowledge, no white man has ever previously done so. He was always said to dislike Americans" (R. C. Blackham). "I think we can rely on Chauncy to find out at least a part of what Thoms learnt." "One must hope that the imam's anxiety about his sight is the main reason for seeing Dr. Thoms and, with that, his aversion to foreigners has in his case been overcome by the prospect of gain." (Written in a different hand.)

This report refers to a message from Consul Chauncy, who stated: "I have received private report from Nizwa. Thoms and family in Arab dress have met the imam. One of the latter's eyes has been treated, and the other is to be done in six months. Report adds that Thoms is to return via Jebel Akhdar and has already met Sulayman bin Hamyar in Tanuf." If there is any surprise in these communications, it is the implication that the British consulate (particularly Leslie Chauncy, who had served as British consul first and the sultan's wazir later) seemed unaware of Wells' earlier trips to the Jabal Akhdhar and Nizwa. The Thomses and Chauncys were, after all, tea, tennis, and bridge chums, and they celebrated Western holidays together—including Boxing Day.

Wells' familiarity with interior shaykhs and even the imam was enough to give any servant of the British Empire the "heebie jeebies." Right under their noses, "agents" of rival empires were functioning with impunity. Just as they had suspected and tried to prevent for decades, their deeply rooted fears bubbled to the surface over a simple act of Christian charity.

27:15. The Suez Crisis of 1956 marked pivotally the decreased influence and control that Britain and France exercised in this region. Britain accordingly made plans to abandon its "English Lake" by 1971. Bahrain and Kuwait became independent from Britain's protectorship. Oman's relation to Britain was different, but it was intended that British influence should decline there about the same time also. There was an implicit expectation of separation from Oman. At the same time, Iraq underwent its own transformation when the king was assassinated and the Kassem government came to power in 1958. In the early 1960s, there also occurred the Zanzibar revolution, and some Omani Arabs returned to Oman. They, thus, added a dimension of uncertainty to Oman's domestic political arena.

27:16. In 1959-60 a proposal was fielded under Col. Boustead's development initiative to construct a sixty-bed hospital in Matrah (less than two miles from the mission hospital) and a thirty-bed hospital in Nizwa. The idea for a new hospital in Matrah was attributed to the sultan. Dr. Daniel Thomson, from the British Ministry of Health, consulted on these plans. In his official report, Dr. Thomson wrote: "The long-established American Mission Hospital provides extensive medical care, although, admittedly, it could not be contended that it entirely meets the need, especially of the Muscat hinterland. Still, in a country otherwise well-nigh bereft of medical provision, it seems to me unjustifiable to construct a second hospital within a mile and a half of the existing one." See Thomson's evaluation, *Report on Medical Services and Projects in Muscat and Oman*, reproduced in Trench, *Arab Gulf Cities*, 209-12.

Glossary of Foreign Terms

Arabic/Indian Term	English Translation
Abui	dear father, literally, "my father"
agal	rope "crown" used to secure kaffiyas, usually black
Ahl I Kitaab	People of the Book; Christians and Jews
ahlan wa sahlan	welcome
akhui	my brother
al Amana	integrity, name of mission school in Muscat
al hamdullilah	praise God
al khokha	the little gate for pedestrians set within the larger door; also known as the "eye of the needle"
Allah	the one God in Islam
Allah kareem	God is generous
ambar	storeroom
ameen/Ameen	trustworthy; Peter and Wells Thoms' Arabic name

amir	title of ruler; precursor to the title "king"
asr prayer	fifth prayer of the day in Islam
As Saada	name for women's hospital in Muscat; happiness
askaris	tribal guard; militia
Astaghfirullah	I seek the forgiveness of God
awqaf	department of religious endowments; responsible for the poor
ayah	nanny, nursemaid
baghala	deep-sea sailing vessel; large dhow
bajal	syphilis-like disease, often passed from children to mothers
bakheel	stingy, tightfisted
baksheesh (Indian)	tip, small sweetener for services; an Indian term widely used among Arabs
Barakat el Messiya	A blessing of Jesus (be upon you)
barhi	succulent dates, especially grown in Basrah area
barash	syphilis-like disease, often passed from children to mothers
barasti	house or hovel, often made of reeds and palm branches
bas	no more; that's final
bayt al mal	treasury or holding bank
Bedu, Bedouin (pl.)	Arab nomads dependent on goats and camels; some Bedu owned trees at the margin of settled cultivation
beitna beitkum	Our home is your home
bejel	syphilis-like disease, often passed from children to mothers
beladiyya	municipal office building
baisa	low-level currency coined by sultan for business in the suq
bisht	cloak or outer garment
boom (boum, bum)	large, double-ended sailing craft used for long ocean voyages; with lateen sails
burra mem or burra memsahib (Indian)	wife of highest-ranking Britisher in government service; key to social networks in the colonial period

charpoy (Indian)	bed with interwoven webbing tape in lieu of springs
chit (Indian)	handwritten note; often official permission
coolie (Indian, used by Arabs)	day laborer
cum	get up
cumshaw	gift, inducement; bordering on a bribe
dakhil	literally, "inside." It entails the implication of required hospitality toward and protection of strangers.
Dar Es Salaam	Realm of Peace; name given to the Thoms family cottage in Kodai
dhoti (Indian)	cloth wrapping used by men in India to cover their legs and abdomen
dhow	an Arab sailing ship; "dhow" is probably originally an Indian word, but it is used widely throughout the Indian Ocean region to refer to large sailing ships. In Arabic, different types of sailing vessels are distinguished by separate names, e.g., baghala, boom, sambuq, jalbut, shuai—each with its own design, rig, and sail configuration.
dira	a tribal region controlled by a shaykh
dishdasha	long robe, usually white, worn by men throughout the Middle East
djinn, jinn	genies or spirits, most often malicious, that can possess people
Eid al-Adha	most sacred holiday in the Muslim calendar
Eid Mubarak	Happy Eid (holiday)
fi man Allah	God go with you
finjan	small cup for coffee
firman	an official government permit in Islamic countries (particularly the Ottoman Empire)
gahwa	coffee
gaur	Indian bison or Cape buffalo
gelebiya	full-length gown worn by men
ghawwa	pearl diver
habara	buzzard; large game bird

Hadith	traditions attributed to Muhammad
Hajj	Muslim pilgrimage to Makkah in the last month of the year. A faithful Muslim who has made this pilgrimage may use the honorific "hajji."
hakeem	wise man, physician, philosopher; a title accorded to a distinguished member of the community
hakim	ruler; to be distinguished from "hakeem"
halal	meat slaughtered according to Islamic law
halwa	a sticky, sweet form of candy; perhaps a variant of Turkish delight
hareem	women's quarters in a home
Hassawi	native of Al-Hasa
hawa-i-jahazz (Persian)	sailing vessel; literally, a "ship of the air" (or wind)
huri	light, canoe-like boat paddled by one or two men
Ibadhi	Dominant branch of Islam in Oman; an early offshoot from the root of Islam. Their jurisprudence is broadly similar to that of Sunni Islam of Arabia.
ijlus hina	sit here
Ikhwaan	the Brethren (not to be confused with the Muslim Brotherhood, an Egyptian movement) of Sa'udi Arabia; traditional nomadic warriors that assisted Abdal Aziz bin Sa'ud to consolidate the Arabian principalities into Sa'udi Arabia.
imam	prayer leader in a mosque; title of Muslim leader of a high order
insha'Allah	if God wills
Ingleez	English; refers to British and Americans who speak English
Injeel	the Gospels
Isa	Jesus
Isa bin Miriam	Jesus, the son of Mary
jabal	mountain or hill
Jahiliyya	Age of Ignorance; the time before Mohammed arrived

jalbut	type of sailing boat; a lifeboat
Jauhara	Gem Lady; name given to Beth Thoms by Arab women
jett	alfalfa
jezail	long-barreled, muzzle-loaded musket
kaccha (Indian)	inferior, low quality, not good
kaffiya	head cloth worn by a man
kafir	infidel; nonbeliever in Islam
kelb	Bedu dog, usually unclean and reviled by most Muslims
khalas	the finest dates produced at Al-Hasa
khanjar	dagger with sheath
khatoun	woman of nobility or high status; honorific title for a respected woman
Khawarij	dissenters, those early in Islamic history who disagreed with Sunni and Shi'ah views on leadership succession in Islam
Khoja (Persian)	honorific meaning pious; most are Sunni
khubs rakhaal	unleavened bread baked by the Bedouins; coarse, thin, and round
kundoo (Baluchi)	"weak knees"; description of mysterious disease that debilitated many Omanis
Kuttab	basic or primary schools that teach only the Q'uran
La Allah il Allah wa Muhammad rasul Allah	"There is no god but Allah, and Muhammad is his prophet." Opening call to prayers from the muezzin.
Ma sh'Allah	What hath God wrought
ma'raq	Arab stew more lightly spiced than the curried dishes of India
Ma'adan	Marsh Arabs of Iraq; derived from the root word for Eden
ma-baap (Indian)	mother-father (mom-pop)
madhab	Islamic school of jurisprudence
mai abyadh	cataract of the eye; literally, "white water"
mai aswad	glaucoma; literally, "black water"
mai lumi	Limeade
maistry (Indian)	manager; construction foreman
maulvi	a teacher of Muslim law

mejlis	reception room in home; hall for official gatherings
Min barakat al Masih ana shafait	By the blessing of God, I am well.
Mu'allim at-Thani	"Second Teacher," i.e., Avicenna; Aristotle was the "First Teacher"
mu'allim	teacher; used as a title
mudhif	reed-constructed, arched-roof mejlis of the Marsh Arabs
muezzin	man who calls the faithful to prayer five times a day; often from minaret
mufti	a Muslim legal expert
mughur	tree; source of frankincense
Muharram	first month of Muslim calendar when warfare is banned; literally, "banned"
mullah	learned theologian, religious leader
mushteshva	hospital
Muslim; Muslimin (pl.)	one who submits to the will of God
muttawi, muttawiyun (pl.)	enforcer of the religious standards of Islam
najis	syphilis-like disease, often passed from children to mothers; literally, "dirty" or "filthy"
nakhoda	captain of Arab sailing ship
namaz salah	prayers
naqib	governor
Nasrani	"Nazarenes," after Jesus of Nazareth, i.e., all Christians
neem	a mahogany tree; sometimes known as the Indian lilac or margosa
pace kachem dhoti (Indian)	man's long cotton cloth, draped as if it had separate legs
pakka (Indian)	many-faceted word: proper, good, right, established pillar of community (when referring to a person), either male or female; re: food: good, pure, proper, superior
pani (Indian)	water
pani-jahazzi (Indian)	water-sailing vessels, water tankers
punkah (Indian)	a fan; originally a board or cloth swung overhead in a room by a servant outside via a rope and pulley; an electric fan

qadi	a judge, highly qualified in Islamic law
Qanun	Canon; specifically applied to the work of Avicenna
qasr	castle, mansion
Q'uran	scripture of Islam, in which the Prophet Isa features prominently as the only perfect man
Rais al Khalij	Resident British agent for the Gulf (or Oman); literally, "Head of the Gulf"
Rifa'a	the hill country in Bahrain; a raised place
saaman	gear, luggage
Sa'eed	Norman Thoms' Arabic name; happy
sahib (Indian)	title given distinguished men
saif	pearl diver's rope tender
salaam alaikum	peace be upon you
sambuq	two-masted sailing vessel with square, windowed sterns; patterned after old European vessels with lateen sails and no jib
Semakh	a town in Palestine; fish
Sharia	Islamic law based on Q'uran
Shatt al-Arab	River of Arabs; the river in the south of Iraq created by the confluence of the Tigris and Euphrates Rivers
shaykh, sheikh	tribal or village/town leader; often a principal landowner
shaykhdom	artificial Arabic/English term for the realm of a shaykh
Sherif of Makkah	ruling family of Mecca and Medina
Shi'ah	branch of Islam found principally in Iran and Iraq; perhaps 15 percent of all Muslims; recognizes Ali as legitimate successor to the Prophet Muhammed
shola (Indian)	copses of rain forest; especially found throughout South India
souk at-towwash	pearl merchant's market
Sunni	the Way; the main sect of Islam
suq, souk	bazaar, marketplace
ta'al	come here
Tabib, cum. Ta'al.	Doctor, get up. Come.

tair	nonvenereal form of syphilis spread from mothers to children
tamima	paramount shaykh of a tribal confederacy in interior of Oman
tao	syphilis-like disease, often passed from children to mothers
tiffin	light snack, often taken at midday
towwash	pearl merchant who carries sieves to sort pearls by size; literally "siever"
Unani	Ionian, i.e., Greek; description of medical practices
wadi	valley; usually with no flowing water, in a dry stream bed
Wahhabi	conservative Muslim movement that helped Abdal Aziz rise to power in Sa'udi Arabia
wali	governor; official representative of the sultan
W'Allah	by God
wallah (Indian)	person, merchant, seller of goods
wazir	a ruler's principal advisor, often British
wilayat	province or state (such as the Basrah Wilayat)
ya tawil al 'amer	honorific; "Oh Long of Life"
zakat	2.5 percent tax payable according to Islamic law for charitable use
zar	malicious spirit that can possess people, like a djinn

Bibliography

Acman, Andre. "How Memoirists Mold the Truth." *New York Times Sunday Review*. 6 April 2013.
Admiralty Naval Staff. Geographical Section of the Naval Intelligence Division. *A Handbook of Arabia*. Vol. 1. General. London: His Majesty's Stationery Office, ca. 1920.
Al Busaidi, Yaqoub Salim. "The Protection and Management of Historic Monuments in the Sultanate of Oman: The Case of Historic Buildings of Oman." *Proceedings of the Seminar for Arabian Studies* 34 (2004), 35-44.
Al Hajri, Hilal. *British Travel Writing on Oman: Orientalism Reappraised*. Oxford: Peter Lang, 2006.
———. "Through Evangelizing Eyes: American Missionaries to Oman." *Proceedings of the Seminar for Arabian Studies* 41 (2010), 121-31.
Al Naim, Mashary. "The Dynamics of a Traditional Arab Town: The Case of Hofuf, Saudi Arabia." *Proceedings of the Seminar for Arabian Studies* 34 (2004), 193-207.

Al Nakib, Farah. "Revisiting Hadar and Badu in Kuwait: Citizenship, Housing, and the Construction of a Dichotomy." *International Journal of Middle Eastern Studies* 46 (2014), 5-30.

Al Rashoud, Claudia Farkas. *Kuwait's Age of Sail: Pearl Divers, Sea Captains, and Shipbuilders Past and Present.* Kuwait: Husain Mohammed Rafie Marafie, 1983.

Al Salimi, Abdulrahman. "Different Succession Chronologies of the Nabhani Dynasty in Oman." *Proceedings of the Seminar for Arabian Studies* 32 (2002), 259-68.

Al Sayegh, Fatma. "American Missionaries in the UAE Region in the Twentieth Century." *Middle Eastern Studies* 32 (January 1996), 120-39.

Al Tikriti, Walid Yasin. "The South-east Arabian Origins of the Falaj System." *Proceedings of the Seminar for Arabian Studies* 32 (2002), 117-38.

Allfree, P. S. *Warlords of Oman.* A. S. Barnes and Co., 1967.

Allison, Mary Bruins. *Doctor Mary in Arabia: Memoirs by Mary Bruins Allison, M.D.* University of Texas Press, 1994.

Andriyanova, Olga. "Some Observations on Women in Omani Sources." *Proceedings of the Seminar for Arabian Studies* 41 (2011), 1-12.

Archer, J. C. "Basrah, City of Sinbad." *Neglected Arabia* 105 (April, May, June 1918), 3-6.

Armstrong, Karen. *Muhammad: A Prophet for our Time.* Harper-Collins, 2006.

Arnold, David. "The Indian Ocean as a Disease Zone: 1500-1950." *South Asia: Journal of South Asian Studies* 14 (1991), 1-21.

Bakker, Roelphine. "The Arab Patient." *Neglected Arabia* 194 (Oct., Nov., Dec. 1941), 5-7.

Bandopadhyay, Soumren. "Diversity in Unity: An Analysis of the Settlement Structure of Harat al-Aqr, Nizwa, Oman." *Proceedings of the Seminar for Arabian Studies* 35 (2003), 19-36.

Beeston, Alfred Felix Landon. "Functional Significance of the Old South Arabian 'Town.'" *Proceedings of the Seminar for Arabian Studies* (2005), 87-88.

Belgrave, Sir Charles Dalrymple. *Papers of Sir C. Dalrymple Belgrave, 1926-1957.* www.scribd.com/document/16225787/Papers-of-Charles-Dalrymple-Belgrave-1926-1957.

———. "Pearl diving in Bahrain." *Journal of The Royal Central Asian Society* 21 (1934), 450-52.

———. *The Pirate Coast.* London: G. Bell & Sons, 1966.

Bell, Gertrude. "Letters." Gertrude Bell Archive, Newcastle University. gertrudebell.ncl.ac.uk.
———. *Persian Letters*. London, Ernest Benn Limited, 1894.
———. *Review of the Civil Administration of Mesopotamia*. London: His Majesty's Stationery Office, 1920.
Bennett, Arthur K. "Wards of Busrah Hospital." *Neglected Arabia* 69 (April, May, June 1909), 6-9.
Bennett, Christine Iverson. "In the Women's Ward." *Neglected Arabia* 83 (Oct., Nov., Dec. 1912), 11-13.
———. "Pen Pictures of Women's Medical Work." *Neglected Arabia* 89 (April, May, June 1914), 18-20.
———. "Sketches of Women's Medical Work in Arabia: Busrah, 1895-1914." *Neglected Arabia* 90 (July, Aug., Sept. 1914), 14-18.
Biehler, Dawn Day. "Flies, Manure, and Window Screens: Medical Entomology and Environmental Reform in Early Twentieth-Century US Cities." *Journal of Historical Geography* 36 (2010), 68-78.
Blake, George. *B. I. Centenary 1856-1956—The Story of the British India Steam Navigation Co. Ltd*. London: Collins, 1956.
Block, Nancy Thoms. "The Big Scare of 1942: How Kodai School Kids Got a Long Spring Vacation." Unpublished typescript.
Blunt, Lady Anne. *A Pilgrimage to Nejd*. 2 vols. London: Frank Cass & Co., 1881.
Boersma, Jeanette. *Grace in the Gulf: The Autobiography of Jeanette Boersma, Missionary Nurse in Iraq and the Sultanate of Oman*. Eerdmans, 1991.
———. "Nurse Mary of Muscat." *Arabia Calling* 241 (Autumn 1955), 11-12.
Bosch, Donald T. *The American Mission Hospitals in Oman: 1893-1974*. Muttrah, Oman: Mazoon Printing Press, 2000.
———. "Towards a Grade A Medical Program." *Arabia Calling* 232 (Summer 1953), 13-14.
Bosch, Donald, and Eloise Bosch. *The Doctor and the Teacher: Oman 1955-1970; Memoirs of Dr. Donald and Eloise Bosch*. Muscat: Apex Publishing, 2000.
Burckhardt, John Lewis. *Travels in Arabia*. London: Henry Colburn, 1829.
Burrough, Bryan. "When Commerce and Illness Intersect." *New York Times*. 2 Feb. 2013. Book review of Mark Harrison, *Contagion: How Commerce Has Spread Disease*. London: Yale University Press, 2012.
Burton, Sir Richard. *Goa and the Blue Mountains: Or, Six Months of Sick Leave*. London: Richard Bentley, 1851.

———. *Personal Narrative of a Pilgrimage to El Medinah and Meccah*. London: Longman, Brown, Green, Longmans, and Roberts, 1855-56.

Calverley, Edwin. "Kuwait Today, Yesterday, and Tomorrow." *Muslim World* (1920), 39-47.

———. "Where *Mullahs* are Doctors." *Neglected Arabia* 105 (April, May, June 1918), 14-17.

Calverley, Eleanor T. "The Arab Woman and the Lady Physician." *Neglected Arabia* 126 (July, Aug., Sept. 1923), 3-5.

———. "In the Steps of the Great Physician." *Neglected Arabia* 108 (Jan., Feb., March 1919), 3-8.

———. *My Arabian Days and Nights: A Medical Missionary in Old Kuwait*. Thomas Y. Crowell Co., 1958.

Cantine, Elizabeth De Pree. "Daily Work at the Hospital." *Neglected Arabia* 48 (Oct., Nov., Dec. 1903), 10-12.

———. "The Lepers in Muscat." *Neglected Arabia* 75 (Oct., Nov., Dec. 1910), 11-13.

Cantine, James. "The Boys of the Freed Slave School." *Neglected Arabia* 57 (Jan., Feb., March 1906), 15-21.

———. "Fresh Impressions of Muscat." *Neglected Arabia* 52 (Oct., Nov., Dec. 1904), 4-10.

———. "The Nearest Way to the Moslem Heart." *Neglected Arabia* 80 (Jan., Feb., March 1912), 6-7.

———. "The New House at Muscat." *Neglected Arabia* 47 (July, Aug., Sept. 1903), 13-17.

———. "Sharon J. Thoms, M.D.: An Appreciation." *Neglected Arabia* 85 (April, May, June 1913), 3-4.

———. "Tour in Oman." *Neglected Arabia* 44 (Oct., Nov., Dec. 1902), 20-24.

Carter, Robert. "The History and Prehistory of Pearling in the Persian Gulf." *Journal of the Economic and Social History of the Orient* 48, no. 2 (2005), 139-209.

Carter, John. "Tribal Structures in Oman." *Proceedings of the Seminar for Arabian Studies* 7 (1977), 11-68.

Chatty, Dawn, and John E. Peterson. "Oman." In *Countries and Their Cultures*. Edited by Carol R. Ember and Melvin Ember. Macmillan Reference USA, 2001, 3:1681-89.

Cheesman, Robert Ernest. "Philby of Arabia: Review." *Geographical Journal* 111 (1948), 250-54.

Colamaria, David. "The United States Navy—A Sailor's Life in the New Steel Navy: Working with Coal." http://www.steelnavy.org/history/exhibits/show/steelnavy/hardlife/coal, accessed 22 February 2017.

Costa, Germana Graziosi. "The Ships' Names of Muscat Bay." *Arabian Studies* 7 (1977), 105-27.
Cox, Major-Gen. Sir Percy. "Some Excursions in Oman." *Geographical Journal* 66 (1925), 193-226.
Crossette, Barbara. *The Great Hill Stations of Asia*. Basic Books, 1998.
Dahl, Erik J. "Naval Innovation: From Coal to Oil." *Joint Force Quarterly* (Winter 2000-2001), 50-56.
Dalenberg, Cornelia. "One Day in the Life of a Visiting Nurse." *Neglected Arabia* 175 (April, May, June 1936), 7-11.
———. *Sharifa*. Eerdmans, 1983.
———. "Unforgettable Patients." *Arabia Calling* 217 (Summer 1949), 12-15.
———. "The Women's Hospital Bahrain." *Neglected Arabia* 189 (July, Aug., Sept. 1940), 6-8.
Dame, Louis P. "Arabs Met at Baharain Hospital." *Neglected Arabia* 194 (Oct., Nov., Dec. 1941) 9-11.
———. "Intolerance in Inland Arabia." *Neglected Arabia* 117 (April, May, June 1921), 9-14.
———. "Pen Pictures of a Doctor's Travels." *Neglected Arabia* 133 (April, May, June 1925), 12-15.
———. "Touring Inland Arabia." *Neglected Arabia* 130 (1924), 3-6.
Daniels, John. *Kuwait Journey*. Luton, UK: White Crescent Press, 1971.
Dearden, Seton. *Burton of Arabia: The Life Story of Sir Richard Francis Burton*. National Travel Club, 1937.
Dickason, Beth Scudder Thoms. "The Taurinia Trip to Italy When Maisie Korteling Fell Overboard." Unpublished typescript.
Dickason, David D. "The Indian Hill Station." *Geographical Review* 65 (1975), 115-17.
———. "The Nineteenth-Century Indo-American Ice Trade: An Hyperborean Epic." *Modern Asian Studies* 25 (1991), 53-89.
Dickason, Lois Thoms. "My Adventure to Nizwa." Unpublished typescript.
Dickson, H. R. P. *The Arab of the Desert: A Glimpse into Badawin Life in Kuwait and Sau'di Arabia*. London: George Allen & Unwin, 1949.
———. *Kuwait and Her Neighbours*. London: George Allen & Unwin, 1956.
Dieulafoy, Jane. *A Suse: Journal des Fouilles, 1885-1886*. Paris: Librairie Hachette et Cie., 1888.
Doughty, Charles. *Travels in Arabia Deserta*. N. p., 1888.
Doumato, Eleanor Abdella. "An 'Extra Legible Illustration' of the Christian Faith: Medicine, Medical Ethics and Missionaries in

the Arabian Gulf." *Islam and Christian Muslim Relations* 24 (2002), 377-90.

———. "Receiving the Promised Blessing: Missionary Reflections on 'Ishmael's (mostly female) Descendants." *Islam and Christian Muslim Relations* 19 (1998) 325-37.

Drake, Christine. "Oman: Traditional and Modern Adaptations to the Environment." *Focus* (Summer 1988), 15-20.

Dykstra, Dirk. "A Study in Reinforced Concrete." *Neglected Arabia* 171 (April, May, June 1935), 3-6.

Dykstra, Minnie. "Our Muscat School, 1891-1952." *Arabia Calling* 229 (Autumn 1952), 3-7.

Edgell, H. Stewart. "The Myth of the 'Lost City of the Arabian Sands.'" *Proceedings of the Seminar for Arabian Studies* 34 (2004), 105-20.

Eickelman, Christine. "Fertility and Social Change in Oman: Women's Perspectives." *Middle East Journal* 47 (1993), 652-66.

Eickelman, Dale F. "The Coming Transformation of the Muslim World." *Middle East Review of International Affairs* 3 (1999), 78-81.

———. "From Theocracy to Monarchy: Authority and Legitimacy in Interior Oman 1935-1957." *International Journal of Middle East Studies* 17 (1985), 3-24.

———. "Religious Tradition, Economic Domination and Political Legitimacy: Morocco and Oman. *Revue de l'Occident Musulman et del la Mediterranee* 29 (1980), 17-30.

Elgood, Cyril. *A Medical History of Persia and the Eastern Caliphate.* Cambridge University Press, 1950.

Elmahi, Ali Tigani. "Traditional Fish Preservation in Oman: The Seasonality of a Subsistence Strategy." *Proceedings of the Seminar for Arabian Studies* 30 (2000), 99-113.

———. "Traditional Methods of Food Preservaton in Oman: A View to the Past." *Proceedings of the Seminar for Arabian Studies* 28 (1998), 45-47.

Enck, Paul, and Winfried Håuser. "Beware the Nocebo Effect." *New York Times Sunday Review* (11 August 2012).

Ewald, Janet. "Crossers of the Sea: Slaves, Freedmen, and Other Migrants in the Northwestern Indian Ocean, c. 1750-1914." *American Historical Review* (Feb. 2000), 69-91.

Farah, Caesr E. "Anglo-Ottoman Confrontation in the Persian Gulf in the Late 19th and Early 20th Centuries." *Proceedings of the Seminar for Arabian Studies* 33 (2003), 117-32.

Flexner, Abraham. *Medical Education in the United States and Canada: A Report to the Carnegie Foundation for the Advancement of Teaching.* Carnegie Foundation for the Advancement of Teaching, 1910.

Freeth, Zahra. *Kuwait Was My Home.* London: George Allen & Unwin, 1956.

Fromkin, David. *A Peace to End All Peace: The Fall of the Ottoman Empire and the Creation of the Modern Middle East.* Avon Books, 1989.

Fuccaro, Nelida. *Reviews in History*, 2009. http://www.history.ac.uk/reviews/review/726. Review of James Onley, *The Arabian Frontier of the British Raj: Merchants, Rulers, and the British in the Nineteenth-Century Gulf.* Oxford University Press, 2007.

Garba, Roman, and Peter Farrington. "Walled Structures and Settlement Patterns in the South-Western Part of Dhofar, Oman." *Proceedings of the Seminar for Arabian Studies* 41 (2011), 95-99.

Gosselink, Charles, ed. *Dear Folks at Home: Letters from Iraq 1922-1925—George Gosselink.* Boat House Books, 2008.

Graves, Philip. *The Life of Sir Percy Cox.* London: Hutchinson & Co., 1941.

Grose, John Henry. *A Voyage to the East Indies.* London: Printed for S. Hooper, 1757.

Hamblin, Dora Jane. "Has the Garden of Eden been located at last?" *Smithsonian Magazine* 18, no. 2 (May 1987). https://www.scribd.com/document/268191039/Hast-the-Garden-of-Eden-Been-Located-at-Last-Smithsonian-Magazine-May-1987.

Hamilton, Alastair. *An Arabian Utopia: The Western Discovery of Oman.* Oxford University Press, 2010.

Handbook for Travellers in India, Burma and Ceylon. 5th ed. London: John Murray, 1911.

Hankin, Nigel B. *Hanklyn-Janklyn or A Stranger's Rumble-Tumble Guide to Some Words, Customs and Quiddities Indian and Indo-British.* New Delhi: Banyan Books, 1992.

Harrison, Ann M. *A Tool in His Hands.* Friendship Press, 1958.

Harrison, Madaline B. and Timothy Harrison. "My Dear Paul: Letters from Harvey Cushing." *Surgery* 119:558-67.

Harrison, Paul W. "The Appeal of Oman." *Neglected Arabia* 120 (Jan., Feb., March 1922), 13-15.

———. *The Arab at Home.* Thomas Y. Crowell Co., 1924.

———. "The Challenge of Oman. *Neglected Arabia* 145 (April, May, June 1928), 8-10.

———. *Doctor in Arabia.* John Day Co., 1940.

———. "The Doctor's Greatest Opportunity." *Neglected Arabia* 99 (Oct., Nov., Dec. 1916), 3-4.

———. "Early Medical Touring." *Neglected Arabia* 182 (July, Aug., Sept. 1938), 16-18.

———. "Hospital Assistant." *Neglected Arabia* 183 (Oct., Nov., Dec. 1938), 17-18.

———. "Medicine and the Bedouin of Kuweit." *Neglected Arabia* 91 (Oct., Nov., Dec. 1914), 12-15.

———. "Medical Practice in Arabia." *Neglected Arabia* 100 (Jan., Feb., March 1917), 12-14.

———. "Medical Work in Oman." *Neglected Arabia* 77 (April, May, June 1911), 10-13.

———. "A Trip to the Pirate Coast." *Neglected Arabia* 109 (April, May, June 1919), 3-6.

———. "War and the Hospital." *Neglected Arabia* 204 (Oct., Nov., Dec. 1944), 3-6.

Harrison, Timothy S. *Before Oil: Memories of an American Missionary Family in the Persian Gulf, 1910-1939.* Rumfordbooks, 2008.

Hay, Sir Rupert. *The Persian Gulf States.* The Middle East Institute, 1959.

Heilbrun, Carolyn G., and Joan M. Weimer. "Is Biography Fiction." *Soundings: An Interdisciplinary Journal* 76 (1993), 295-314.

Heusinkveld, Maurice. "A Day in the Life of a Mission Doctor." *Arabia Calling* 221 (Autumn 1950), 8-10.

Heusinkveld, Elinor. "Whatsoever Things Are of Good Report: Annual Report, Muscat." *Arabia Calling* 246 (Autumn 1958), 12-15.

Heusinkveld, Paul, *Margaret's Mission to Arabia, Africa, and India 1965-2010.* Van Raalte Press, 2021.

Higham, Robin. *Britain's Imperial Air Routes 1918 to 1939.* G. T. Foulis, 1960.

Hogarth, David George. *The Penetration of Arabia: A Record of the Development of Western Knowledge Concerning the Arabian Peninsula.* Frederick A. Stokes Co., 1904.

Holes, Clive. "The Arabic Dialects of Arabia." *Proceedings of the Seminar for Arabian Studies* 36 (2006), 25-34.

Hopper, Matthew S. "Slavery and the Slave Trades in the Indian Ocean and Arab Worlds: Global Connections and Disconnections." *Proceedings of the 10th Annual Gilder Lehrman Center International Conference at Yale University,* 2008.

———. "Slaves of One Master: Globalization and the African Diaspora in Arabia in the Age of Empire," Proceedings of the 10th Annual

Gilder Lehman Center International Conference at Yale University, 2008.

——. *Slaves of One Master: Globalization and Slavery in Arabia in the Age of Empire*. Yale University Press, 2015.

Hosmon, Sarah. "The Woman Doctor in Oman." *Neglected Arabia* 125 (April, May, June 1923), 14-15.

Howell, W. Nathaniel. *Strangers When We Met: A Century of American Community in Kuwait*. New Academia Publishing, 2016.

Hubers, John. "Samuel Zwemer and the Challenge of Islam: From Polemic to a Hint of Dialogue." *International Bulletin of Missionary Research* 28 (2004), 117-21.

Hudson, Ellis H., and Agnes L. Young. "Medical and Surgical Practice on the Euphrates River: An Analysis of Two Thousand Consecutive Cases at Deir-ez-Zor, Syria." *The American Journal of Tropical Medicine and Hygiene* 11, no. 4 (1 July 1931), 297-310.

Hyslop, Jonathan. "Steamship Empire: Asian, African, and British Sailors in the Merchant Marine c. 1880-1945." *Journal of Asian and African Studies* 44 (2009), 49-67.

Ives, Edward. *A Voyage from England to India in the Year 1754*. London: Edward and Charles Dilly, 1773.

Jarman, Robert L., ed. *Historic Maps of Bahrain, 1817-1970*. Cambridge, UK: Archive Editions, 1996.

Johnstone, T. M., and J. C. Wilkinson. "Some Geographical Aspects of Qatar." *The Geographical Journal* 126 (1960), 442-50.

Joseph, Suad. "Patriarchy and Development in the Arab World." *Gender and Development* 4 (1996), 14-19.

Joshi, Sanmukh R., Shahnaz N. Shah al-Bulushi, and Thamina Ashraf. "Development of Blood Transfusion Services in Sultanate of Oman." *Asian Journal of Transfusion Science* (2010), 34-40.

Joyce, Miriam. *The Sultanate of Oman: A Twentieth Century History*. Praeger, 1995.

Kapenga, Marjory. "The Arabian Mission Dream." Unpublished typescript.

Kelly, John Barrett. *Sultanate and Imamate in Oman*. Chatham House Memoranda: Royal Institute of International Affairs, December 1959.

Kennedy, John. *The History of Steam Navigation*. Liverpool: Charles Birchall, Ltd., 1903.

Kirmayer, Laurence J. "The Cultural Diversity of Healing: Meaning, Metaphor, and Mechanism." *British Medical Bulletin* 69 (2004), 33-48.

Kunzru, Hari. *New York Times*, 5 April 2013. Review of Leslie Hazlton, "The First Muslim: The Story of Muhammad." Riverhead Books, 2013.

Landen, Robert Geran. *Oman since 1856: Disruptive Modernization in a Traditional Arab Society*. Princeton University Press, 1967.

Lawrence, Thomas Edward. *Revolt in the Desert*. George H. Doran Co., 1927.

Limbert, Mandana E. *In the Time of Oil: Piety, Memory, and Social Life in an Omani Town*. Stanford University Press, 2010.

Lindsay, Harry, Abdul Rahman Halaissie, R. A. E. Bagnold, and A. E. Lees. "Desert Borderlands of Oman: Discussion." *Geographical Journal* 116 (1950), 169-71.

Lindsay, Harry, and Robert Ernest Cheesman. "A Further Journey across the Empty Quarter: Discussion." *Geographical Journal* 113 (1949), 45-46.

Lorimer, John Gordon. *Gazetteer of the Persian Gulf, "Oman, and Central Arabia."* 6 vols., incl. maps and genealogical tables. Calcutta: Superintendent of Government Printing, India, 1915.

Luhrmann, Tanya Marie. "How Skeptics and Believers Can Connect." *New York Times Sunday Review* (7 April 2013), 12.

Mackenzie, John M. "Empires of Travel: British Guide Books and Cultural Imperialism in the 19th and 20th Centuries." http://mudrac.ffzg.hr/~dpolsek/sociologija%20turizma/MacKenzie_Empires%20of%20Travel.pdf.

Madineh, Seyed Mohammad Ali. "Avicenna's Canon of Medicine and Modern Urology. Part 1: Bladder and Its Diseases." *Urology Journal* 5 (2008), 284-93.

Malone, Joseph J. "America and the Arabian Peninsula: The First 200 Years." *Middle East Journal* 30 (1976), 406-24.

Maloney, Clarence. *The Evil Eye*. Columbia University Press, 1976.

Marineli, Filio, Gregory Tsoucalas, Marianna Karamanou, and George Androutsos. "Mary Mallon (1869-1938) and the History of Typhoid Fever." *Annals of Gastroenterology* 26 (2013), 132-34.

Mason, Alfred DeWitt, and Frederick J. Barny. *History of the Arabian Mission*. Board of Foreign Missions, RCA, 1926.

McGregor, Alan. "Flying the Furrow." *Saudi Aramco World* (March/April 2001), 24-31.

Melamid, Alexander. "International Trade in Natural Gas." *Geographical Review* 84 (1994), 216-21.

———. "The Jebel al-Akhdar (Oman)." *Geographical Review* 82 (1992), 470-72.

———. "New Oil from Arabia." *Geographical Review* 78 (1988), 76-79.

———. "Qatar." *Geographical Review* 77 (1987), 103-5.

———. "The United Arab Emirates." *Geographical Review* 87 (1997), 542-44.

Mershen, Birgit. "Settlement Space and Architecture in South-Arabian Oases: Preliminary Remarks on the Division of Space in Omani Oasis Settlements." *Proceedings of the Seminar for Arabian Studies* 29 (1999) 103-10.

Miller, John J. "The Unknown Slavery: In the Muslim World, that Is—and Is Not—Over." *National Review* 54 (2002), 41-43.

Moerdyk, William J. "A Glimpse into Kodaikanal School." *Neglected Arabia* 177 (Oct., Nov., Dec. 1936), 14-15.

Moldenke, H. N., and A. L. Moldenke. *Plants of the Bible*. Chronica Botanica Company, 1952.

Monroe, Elizabeth. "The Shaikhdom of Kuwait." *International Affairs (Royal Institute of International Affairs)* 30 (1954), 271-84.

Morin, Richard. "Indentured Servitude in the Persian Gulf." *New York Times* (14 April 2013), 4.

Morison, Samuel Eliot. *Maritime History of Massachusetts*. Houghton Mifflin Co., 1921.

Morris, James. *Sultan in Oman*. London: Faber and Faber, 1957.

Morton, Michael Quentin. "The Third River." *Liwa: Journal of the National Center for Documentation and Research* 5 (2013), 32-56.

Moyse-Batlett, H. *The Pirates of Trucial Oman*. London: Macdonald, 1966.

Multhoff, Anne. "A Parallel to the Second Commandment." *Proceedings of the Seminar for Arabian Studies* 39 (2009), 295-301.

Munro, John, and Martin Love. "The Nairn Way." *Saudi Aramco World* (July/Aug. 1981), 19-24.

Muttrah Mission Hospital. "Diagnoses of Inpatients for Year 1972 [with Deaths]." Unpublished typescript. Drexel University Archives.

Mylrea, Bessie. "Arab Superstitions about Diseases and Quackery in Medicine." *Neglected Arabia* 126 (July, Aug., Sept. 1923), 12-14.

———. "A Morning in the Women's Clinic in the Mason Memorial Hospital, Bahrain." *Neglected Arabia* 73 (April, May, June 1910), 10-11.

———. "Quackery and Medical Superstition in Arabia." *Neglected Arabia* 96 (Jan., Feb., March 1916), 20-22.

Mylrea, Charles Stanley Garland. *Before Oil Came to Kuwait.* Unpublished typescript, 1952.
———. *Kuwait before Oil.* Unpublished typescript, 1952.
———. "Kuweit Medical Work, 1915-1916." *Neglected Arabia* 102 (July, Aug., Sept. 1917), 15-18.
———. "A Month in Oman." *Neglected Arabia* 67 (Oct., Nov., Dec. 1908), 3-6.
———. "Muscat-Matrah and Oman, Then and Now." *Neglected Arabia* 200 (July, Aug., Sept. 1943), 3-10.
———. "The Opening of the Olcott Memorial Hospital." *Neglected Arabia* 186 (July, Aug., Sept. 1939), 3-7.
———. "The Pearling Industry." Unpublished essay, 1938.
———. "Some Rewards of the Doctor." *Neglected Arabia* 142 (July, Aug., Sept. 1927), 3-6.
Nash, Harriet. "Stargazing in Traditional Water Management: A Case Study in Northern Oman." *Proceedings of the Seminar for Arabian Studies* 37 (2007), 157-70.
Nicolini, Beatrice. "Historical and Political Links between Gwadar and Muscat from 19th-Century Testimonies." *Proceedings of the Seminar for Arabian Studies* 32 (2002), 281-86.
Niebuhr, Carsten. *Travels through Arabia, and Other Countries in the East.* 2 vols. Translated by Robert Heron. Edinburgh: G. Mudie, 1792.
Niebuhr, Reinhold. *The Irony of American History.* Charles Scribner & Sons, 1952.
Nordland, Rod. "In Surprise, Emir of Qatar Plans to Abdicate, Handing Power to Son." *New York Times* (25 June 2013).
Ochsenslager, Edward. "Life on the Edge of the Marshes." *Expedition* 40 (1998), 29-39.
Onley, James. "Britain's Informal Empire in the Gulf, 1820-1971." *Journal of Social Affairs* 22 (2005), 29-44.
Onley, James, and Sulayman Khalaf. "Shaikhly Authority in the Pre-Oil Gulf: An Historical-Anthropological Study." *History and Anthropology* 17 (2006): 189-208.
Owen, Roderic. *The Golden Bubble.* London: Collins, 1957.
Pachter, Henry M. *Magic into Science: The Story of Paracelsus.* Henry Schuman, 1951.
Palgrave, William Gifford. *Narrative of a Year's Journey to Central and Eastern Arabia.* Macmillan and Co., 1865.
Paterson-Smythe, J. *A People's Life of Christ.* London: Hodder & Stoughton, 1921.

Pengelley, Janet Mable Storm. *William Harold Storm, M.D. Missionary Doctor in Arabia: A Life and Times*. Woodlands, West Australia: Janet Pengelley, 2005.

Percot, Marie. "Indian Nurses in the Gulf: Two Generations of Female Migration." *South Asia Research* 26 (2006), 41-62.

Peterson, John E. "The Arabian Peninsula in Modern Times: A Historiographical Survey." *American Historical Review* 96 (1991), 1435-49.

———. "Britain and the Gulf: At the Periphery of Empire." In *The Persian Gulf in History*. Edited by L. G. Potter. London: Palgrave Macmillan, 2009.

———. "Britain and 'The Oman War': An Arabian Entanglement." *Asian Affairs* 7 (1976), 285-98

———. *Defending Arabia*. St. Martin's Press, 1986.

———. *The Emergence of Post-Traditional Oman*. University of Durham Institute for Middle Eastern and Islamic Studies Papers, 2005.

———. *Historical Muscat: An Illustrated Guide and Gazetteer*. Leiden: Brill, 2007.

———. "The Kingdom of Enigma." *Survival* 48 (2006), 147-56.

———. "The Nature of Succession in the Gulf." *Middle East Journal* 55 (2001), 580-601.

———. "Oman: al-Ghafiriyah and al-Hinawiyah Tribal Confederations." *Arabian Peninsula Background Note* APBN-001. Published on www.JEPeterson.net, September 2003.

———. *Oman in the Twentieth Century*. London: Croom Helm, 1978.

———. "Oman's Diverse Society: Northern Oman." *Middle East Journal* 58 (2004), 31-51.

———. "Oman's Diverse Society: Southern Oman." *Middle East Journal* 58 (2004), 254-69.

———. "Oman: The 1966 Assassination Attempt on Sultan Sa'id b. Taymur." *Arabian Peninsula Background Note* APBN-004. Published on www.JEPeterson.net, August 2004.

———. "Oman: Three-and-a-Half Decades of Change and Development." *Middle East Policy* 11 (2004), 124-37.

———. "The Revival of the Ibadi Imamate in Oman and the Threat to Muscat, 1913-1920." *Arabian Studies* 3 (1976), 165-88.

———. "The Shi'ah Dimension in Gulf Politics." *Arabian Peninsula Background Note* APBN-005. Published on www.JEPeterson.net, July 2007.

———. "Tribes and Politics in Eastern Arabia." *Middle East Journal* 31 (1977), 297-312.
Philby, Harry St. John Bridger. *Arabian Days.* London: R. Hale, 1948.
———. "Two Notes from Central Arabia." *Geographical Journal* 113 (1949), 86-93.
Phillips, Wendell. *Oman: A History.* London: Longmans, Green & Co., 1967.
———. *Unknown Oman.* London: Longmans, Green & Co, 1966.
Pirie, Gordon. *Air Empire: British Imperial Civil Aviation, 1919-39.* Manchester University Press, 2009.
———. "Passenger traffic in the 1930s on British Imperial Air Routes: Refinement and Revision." *Journal of Transport History* 25, no. 1 (2004), 63-83.
Popper, Sir Karl. "Historical Explanation." *University of Denver Magazine* (1966), 4-7.
Rabi, Uzi. *The Emergence of States in a Tribal Society: Oman under Sa'id Bin Taymur, 1932-1970.* Brighton: Sussex University Press, 2006.
Radionov, Mikhail. "The Jinn in Hadramawt Society in the Last Century." *Proceedings of the Seminar in Arabian Studies* 38 (2008), 277-81.
Rajab, Amer, and M. A. Patton. "A Study of Consanguinity in the Sultanate of Oman." *Annals of Human Biology* 27 (2000), 321-26.
Reeler, Claire N., Nabiel Y. Al-Shaikh, and Daniel T. Potts. "An Historical Cartographic Study of the Yabrin Oasis, Saudi Arabia." *Proceedings of the Seminar for Arabian Studies* 39 (2009), 351-57.
Rennell of Rodd, Lord, B. P. Uvarov, and Wilfred Thesiger. "Across the Empty Quarter: Discussion." *Geographical Journal* 111 (1948), 19-21.
Roberts, Nancy. "Trinity vs. Monotheism." *The Muslim World* 101 (2011), 73-93.
Rogers, Naomi. "Germs with Legs: Flies, Disease, and the New Public Health." *Bulletin of the History of Medicine* 63 (1989), 599-617.
———. "The Proper Place of Homeopathy: Hahnemann Medical College and Hospital in an Age of Scientific Medicine." *Pennsylvania Magazine of History and Biography* 108 (1984), 179-201.
Ruschenberger, William Samuel Waithman. *A Voyage Round the World Including an Embassy to Muscat and Siam, in 1835, 1836, and 1837.* Philadelphia: Carey, Lea & Blanchard, 1838.
Salvatore, Nick. "Biography and Social History: An Intimate Relationship." *Labour History* 87 (2004), 187-92.

Sadnovnikov, Slava. "Escape, From, Freedom: The Refutation of Historical Interpretations in the Popperian Perspective." *Dialogue* 43 (2004), 239-80.

Schiff, Stacy. "The Dual Lives of the Biographer." *New York Times Sunday Review*, 24 November 2012.

Schreiber, Jurgen. "Transformation Processes in Oasis Settlements in Oman; 2005 Archaeological Survey at the Oasis of Nizwa—A Preliminary Report." *Proceedings of the Seminar for Arabian Studies* 37 (2007), 263-75.

Scudder, Dorothy Jealous. *A Thousand Years in Thy Sight: The Story of the Scudder Missionaries in India*. Vantage Press, 1984.

Scudder, Ida B. "Dr. Ida." Unpublished typescript.

Scudder, Lewis R., II. "Doctoring the Great and the Poor." *Neglected Arabia* 200 (July, Aug., Sept. 1943), 13-14.

———. "Kuwait Hospital Carries On." *Neglected Arabia* 203 (July, Aug., Sept. 1944), 12-14.

Scudder, Lewis R., III. *The Arabian Mission's Story: In Search of Abraham's Other Son*. Eerdmans, 1998.

———. "A Personal Vision of Mission in the Middle East." Unpublished typescript, 2003.

Searle, Pauline. *Dawn over Oman*. London: George Allen & Unwin, 1975.

Segal, Erin. "Merchants Networks in Kuwait: The Story of Yusuf al-Marzuk. *Middle Eastern Studies* 45 (2009), 709-19.

Seland, Elvind Heldaas. "The Indian Ships at Moscha and the Indo-Arabian Trading Circuit." *Proceedings of the Seminar for Arabian Studies* 38 (2008), 283-87.

Skeet, Ian. *Oman: Politics and Development*. St. Martin's Press, 1992.

Skinner, Raymond Frederick. *Ibadism in Oman and Developments in the Field of Christian-Muslim Relationships*. Durham Theses: Durham University, 1992.

Smith, Richard. "Oman: Leaping Across the Centuries." *British Medical Journal* 297 (1988), 20-27.

Stark, Freya. *The Southern Gates of Arabia*. London: Murray, 1934.

Stark, Laura. *Journal of Sociology* 119 (2014), 1777-80. Review of Owen Whooley, *Knowledge in the Time of Cholera: The Struggle Over American Medicine in the Nineteenth Century*. University of Chicago Press, 2013.

Steel, Frances. *Oceania under Steam: Sea Transport and the Cultures of Colonialism, c. 1870-1914*. Manchester University Press, 2011.

Stevens, J. H., and R. King. "Bibliography of Saudi Arabia." Working paper. University of Durham, UK, 1973.

Storm, Harold. "Present Touring Conditions in Oman." *Neglected Arabia* 160 (Jan., Feb., March 1932), 11-13.

———. "A Tour to Dhofar." *Neglected Arabia* 165 (July, Aug., Sept. 1933), 3-7; 166 (Oct., Nov., Dec. 1933), 4-8.

"Streamline Bus Replaces Camel in Desert." *Popular Mechanics* (March 1934), 400.

Takriti, Abdel Razzaq. *Monsoon Revolution: Republicans, Sultans, and Empires in Oman, 1965-1976*. Oxford University Press, 2013.

Tamm, Abdal-Malak Khalat. *The Arabian Mission: A Case Study of Christian Missionary Work in the Arabian Gulf Region*. Thesis. University of Durham, 1977.

"The World's Largest Airplane Provides All Modern Luxuries for Forty Passengers." *Popular Mechanics* (March 1931), 394. https://archive.org/details/PopularMechanics1931/Popular_Mechanics_03_1931/page/n115/mode/2up.

Thesiger, Wlfred. "Across the Empty Quarter." *Geographical Journal* 111 (1948), 1-19.

———. *Arabian Sands*. London: Longmans Green, 1959.

———. "Desert Borderlands of Oman." *Geographical Journal* 116 (1950), 137-68.

———. "A Further Journey across the Empty Quarter." *Geographical Journal* 113 (1949), 21-44.

———. "A Journey through the Tihama, the Asir, and the Hijaz Mountains." *Geographical Journal* 110 (1947), 188-200.

———. *The Marsh Arabs*. London: Longmans Green, 1964.

———. "A New Journey in Southern Arabia." *Geographical Journal* 108 (1946), 126-45.

Thomas, Bertram. *Arabia Felix*. London: Cape, 1932.

Thomas, Lowell. *With Lawrence in Arabia*. Century Co., 1924.

Thoms, Beth Scudder, "Forty Years of Remembering." Written for the women of the Chicago Classis. Promotion and Communications, RCA, 1970.

Thoms, Ethel Scudder. "October 15 in Matrah." *Arabia Calling* 238 (Winter 1954-55), 9-13.

———. "Our Neighbors." *Neglected Arabia* 193 (July, Aug., Sept. 1941), 4-8

———. "The Story of the Year." *Arabia Calling* 245 (Winter-Spring 1956-57), 3-15.

———. "The Summer That Is Coming Will Be Fun." *Arabia Calling* 228 (Summer 1952), 9-13.

———. "Women of the Frankincense Country." *Arabia Calling* 224 (Summer 1951), 7-12.

Thoms, Sharon J. "The Hospital at Bahrain." *Neglected Arabia* 44 (Oct., Nov., Dec. 1902), 12-16.

———. "Medical Tour of Sharjah (Sharga)." *Neglected Arabia* 42 (April, May, June 1902), 5-8.

———. "The People of Matrah." *Neglected Arabia* 82 (July, Aug., Sept. 1912), 6-7.

———. "The Plague at Bahrain." *Neglected Arabia* 46 (April, May, June 1903), 8-11.

———. "Ups and Downs of Medical Work." *Neglected Arabia* 56 (Oct., Nov., Dec. 1905), 6-8.

Thoms, William Wells. "Building Bridges in Arabia." *Neglected Arabia* 184 (Jan., Feb., March 1939), 20.

———. "The Desert Shall Blossom Like a Rose." *Arabia Calling* 232 (Summer 1953), 8-11.

———. "From a Doctor's Journal." *Neglected Arabia* 180 (Oct., Nov., Dec. 1937), 6-13.

———. *Muscat Medical Reports.* Unpublished typescripts, 1942, 1944, 1952-53, 1955-56, 1957-58, 1958-59, 1959-60, 1960-61.

———. "Over the Green Mountains to Oman." *Neglected Arabia* 201 (Oct., Nov., Dec. 1943), 3-6.

———. "Second Generation Speaks." *Neglected Arabia* 183 (Oct., Nov., Dec. 1938), 4-6.

———. "Story of a Book." *Michigan Alumnus Quarterly Review* (Winter 1957), 115-19.

———. "The Substance of Things Hoped For." *Arabia Calling* 225 (Autumn 1951), 3-6.

———. "Touring DeLuxe." *Neglected Arabia* 204 (Oct., Nov., Dec. 1944), 6-8.

Thomson, Daniel. *Report on Medical Services and Projects in Muscat and Oman.* In *Brief for Political Resident on Long-Term Civil Development Measures in Sultanate of Muscat and Oman, 1960 [FO 371/149147].* Reproduced in *Arab Gulf Cities: Muscat and Matrah.* Edited by R. Trench. Cambridge, UK: Archive Editions (1994), 209-12.

Tobi, Yosef. "Salom (Salim) al-Sabazi's (Seventeenth Century) Poem of the Debate between Coffee and Qat." *Proceedings of the Seminar for Arabian Studies* 38 (2008), 301-10.

Townsend, John. *Oman: The Making of the Modern State.* St. Martin's Press, 1977.

Trench, Richard, ed. *Arab Gulf Cities:* vol. 1, *Kuwait City;* vol. 2, *Muscat and Mattrah;* vol. 3, *Doha, Abu Dhabi, Dubai, and Sharjah;* vol. 4, *Manama.* Cambridge, UK: Archive Editions, 1994.

Tuson, Penelope. *Playing the Game: Western Women in Arabia*. London: I. B. Taurus, 2003.

———. "Scholars and Amazons: Researching Women Travellers in the Arabian Gulf." *Liwa: Journal of the National Center for Documentation and Research* 5 (2013), 15-31.

Tuson, Penelope, and Emma Quick, eds. *Arabian Treaties (1600-1960)*. 4 vols. University of Virginia Press, 1992. Vol. 4, *Saudi Arabia*.

Twitchell, Karl S., with Edward J. Jurji, *Saudi Arabia: With an Account of the Development of Its Natural Resources*. Greenwood Press, 1947.

Vanderwerf, Lyle. "Mission Lessons from History: A Laboratory of Missiological Insights Gained From Christian-Muslim Relationships." *International Journal of Frontier Missions* 11 (1994), 75-79.

Van Dyke, Henry. *The Story of the Other Wise Man*. Harper and Brothers, 1895.

Van Ess, John. *Meet the Arab*. The John Day Company, 1943.

Van Ess, Dorothy F. *History of the Arabian Mission: 1926-1957*. Unpublished typescript. 1958.

———. *Pioneers in the Arab World*. Eerdmans, 1974.

———. *Who's Who in the Arabian Mission*. RCA Board of Foreign Missions, 1939.

Van Peursem, Gerrit D. "America in Kuwait." *Neglected Arabia* 142 (1927), 7-8.

Vogelaar, Harold. "Abraham the Archetype of Faith; 'There is No God but God!'" *Word and World* 16 (1996), 169-72.

Volf, Miroslav, ed. *Do We Worship the Same God? Jews, Christians, and Muslims in Dialogue*. Eerdmans, 2012.

Wallach, Janet. *Desert Queen: The Extraordinary Life of Gertrude Bell—Adventurer, Adviser to Kings, Ally of Lawrence of Arabia*. Anchor Books, 1999.

Watt, George. *The Commercial Products of India*. London: John Murray, 1908.

Webster, Douglas. "The Foreign Missionary Today." *Theology Today* 41, no. 4 (Jan. 1960), 504-11.

Webster, Roger M. "The Bedouin in Southern and Southeastern Arabia: The Evolution of Bedouin Life Reconsidered." *Proceedings of the Seminar for Arabian Studies* 22 (1992), 121-34.

Wellsted, James Raymond. *Travels in Arabia*. London: John Murray, 1837.

West, Sheila K. "Trachoma: New Assault on an Ancient Disease." *Progress in Retinal and Eye Research* 23 (2004), 381-401.

Wiersum, Harry J. "First Experiences in Arabic." *Neglected Arabia* 33 (Jan., Feb., March 1900), 6-8.
Wilkinson, John C. "The Background to the Political Geography of South-East Arabia." *Geographical Journal* 137 (1971), 361-71.
———. "Bayasira and Bayadir." *Arabian Studies* 1 (1975), 75-85.
———. *The Imamate Tradition of Oman*. Cambridge University Press, 1987.
———. *Water and Tribal Settlement in South-East Arabia: A Study of the Aflaj of Oman*. Oxford, UK: Clarendon Press, 1977.
Wilson, D. "Memorandum Respecting the Pearl Fisheries in the Persian Gulf." *Journal of the Royal Geographical Society of London* 3 (1833), 283-86.
Wilson, Dorothy Clarke. *Dr. Ida*. McGraw-Hill, 1959.
Winchester, Simon. *The Professor and the Madman*. Harper-Collins, 1998.
Wingate, Sir Ronald. *Not in the Limelight*. London: Hutchinson, 1959.
Woodberry, Robert D. "The Missionary Roots of Liberal Democracy." *American Political Science Review* 106 (2012), 244-74.
Woodward, Catherine S. "The Discourse and Experience of the Arabian Mission's Medical Missionaries, Part I: 1920-39." *Middle Eastern Studies* 47 (2011), 779-805.
———. "The Discourse and Experience of the Arabian Mission's Medical Missionaries, Part II: 1939-1960." *Middle Eastern Studies* 47 (2011), 885-910.
World Health Organization. *Trichiasis Surgery for Trachoma*. 2nd ed. Geneva, Switzerland: WHO Press, 2015.
Yaccob, Abdol Rauh. "British Policy on Arabia before the First World War: An Internal Argument." *Proceedings of the Seminar for Arabian Studies* 38 (2008), 319-25.
Yule, Henry, and Arthur C. Burnell. *Hobson-Jobson: A Glossary of Anglo-Indian Words and Phrases, and of Kindred Terms, Etymological, Historical, Geographical and Discursive*. London: J. Murray, 1903.
Zeigler, H. C. *A Brief Flowering in the Desert: Protestant Missionary Activity in the Arabian Gulf, 1889-1973*. PhD diss., Princeton University, 1977.
Zinsser, Hans. *Rats, Lice, and History*. Little, Brown and Co., 1935.
Zwemer, Amy E., and Samuel M. Zwemer. *Zigzag Journeys in the Camel Country*. Fleming H. Revell, 1911.
Zwemer, Samuel M. "Across the Threshold to Hassa." *Neglected Arabia* 53 (Jan., Feb., March 1905), 12-16.
———. *Arabia: The Cradle of Islam—Studies of the Geography, People and Politics of the Peninsula with an Account of Islam and Mission Work*. Fleming H. Revell, 1900.

———. "Three Journeys in Northern Oman." *Geographical Journal* 19 (1902), 54-64.

———. "The Use of Amulets among Moslems." *Neglected Arabia* 72 (Jan., Feb., March 1910), 6-10.

Zwemer, Samuel M., and James Cantine. *The Golden Milestone: Reminiscences of Pioneer Days Fifty Years Ago in Arabia*. Fleming H. Revell, 1938.

INDEX

A

Abdal Aziz bin Sa'ud. *See* Abdulaziz bin Abdul Rahman bin Faisal
Abdallah bin Jiluwi bin Turki al Sa'ud, 133-36, *137*
Abdul Rahman bin Faisal bin Turki, 91
Abdulaziz bin Abdul Rahman bin Faisal, 49, 67-68, 91, 118, 131, 133-34, 137-38, 140-41, 143-45, 147, 149-52, 157, 159-61, 168, 179, 388
Abdullah bin Hijji, 165-66, 170-71, 181
Abdullah bin Jassim bin Mohammed Al Thani, 111-16, 118-22, 179
Abdur Rahman Qasebi, 120, 133-34, 137, 140
Abu Dhabi: Shaykh Shakhbut invites Wells to, 346-47

Ahmad bin Ibrahim, 337, 349-52, *349, 351*
air travel: flying the furrow, 22-25, 375; Imperial Airways 20, HP-42 (Hanno), 21, 374-75
Ajaji, Mohammed, *137*
Alexander, John, 5, 7-8
Ali bin Abdullah Al Hamudah, 264-65
Ali, Hilal bin, 334
Ali, Isa bin, 261
Allison, Mary Bruins, 164, 389
Alma, 3, 6-11, 373-74
American Export Line, 187-88
Amir Abdal Aziz. *See* Abdulaziz bin Abdul Rahman bin Faisal
Amir Ali, 264-65
Anderson, Maj., 395
anemia: pernicious, 98-99
Ann Arbor (Michigan), 1-12, 226

Arabic language study: in Basrah, 27-35, 375-76; in Jerusalem 17
Armerding, Paul, 380
Armstrong, Karen, 391

B

Bahrain, 85-110; and the "Bahrain Blues," 123-28; and BAPCO (Bahrain Petroleum Company), 110, 128-29; and cataract surgery, 118-19; and death of Marion Wells Thoms, 189; and death of Zwemer children, 189; first patient in, 89-90; hospitals: Marion Wells Thoms, 69; Mason Memorial (American Mission Hospital, AMH), 70; and hospital orientation, 85-89; mission staff, 67-68; and payment in kind, 97-101; stresses of medical practice in (e.g., spiritual, psychological, economic, bureaucratic), 123, 127-30, 384-85; and "two seas" (fresh/salt), 58-59, 378; Wells' first medical post in, 49-59, 65
Balasundram, Mary, 190, 196, 204, 247-50, *251*, 253, 339, 393
Balfour, Arthur, 18
Banerji, Dr., 120
BAPCO (Bahrain Petroleum Company), 110; Arab employees of, 128-29
Bargouti, Mu'allim, 17
Barny, Esther, 222
Barny, Fred 164, 197-98, 390
Barny, Margaret, 164
Batinah coast: and medical tours, 230
Belgrave, C. Dalrymple, 95, 108, 378, 381
Belgrave, Marjorie, 108
beliefs, religious, of Wells Thoms: family background, 387-88; Holy Spirit, 387; Jesus Christ, the Great Physician, 129; love of God, 126; spiritual revival, 127; Triune God, 387
Bell, Gertrude, 29, 33-34, 45, 375, 377, 396
Bennett, Arthur, 164, 365
Bennett, Christine, 365
Bennett, Jessie, 74-75
Bent, Mable, 292
Bent, Theodore, 292, 296, 298
births, Thoms family: Lois Ethel (Atiya) Thoms, 172; Nancy Fisher (Sharifa) Thoms, 18; Norman Wells (Sa'eed) Thoms, 94; Peter Scudder (Ameen) Thoms, 94
Blackham, R. C., 398
Bob, the dog (*kelb*), 231-32; meets a shaykh, 232-34
Boersma, Jeanette, 250, 253-54, 338, *251*
bones, broken (femur), 176
Bosch, Don, *338*, *348*
Boustead, John, 342, 399
Brinckman, Harry, 3
British India Steam Navigation (BISN), 19, 49, 377
Byrd, Lt., 293, 299-300

C

Calverley, Edwin, 180, 376
Calverley, Eleanor, 169, 179, 365, 389
Calvin, John, 18, 127, 225
Canon [Qanun] of Medicine (Abu Ali ibn Sina, Avicenna), 98-101, 382-84
Cantine, Elizabeth DePree, 189, 190-91, *195*, 248
Cantine, James, 42, 47, 81, 93, 125-27, 179, 189-95, *191*, *195*, 198, 200, 248, 385-86, 390
career options, of Wells: Plan A (Arabia), 5, 6-7; Plan B (Michigan), 7-8
Caspari, Mme., 322, 323, 397
Chamberlin, Neville, 187
Chauncy, Frederick Charles Leslie, 314

Chauncy, Leslie, 333, 349, 398
Cherian, George, 379
Chloromycetin, 243-44; equally used, on all classes, 245
Christian churches in Oman, Muscat, and Matrah, 395
Churchill, Winston, 188
Conrad, Joseph, 61
Cox, Percy, 32, 34, 192-94, 292, 377
Curzon, George, 200
Cushing, Harvey, 7, 206, 384

D

dakhil (interior, inside), 39-42
Dame, Elizabeth, 68-69
Dame, Louis P., 49, 67-68, 90-93, 103-4, 107-11, 114-15, 128, 138, 144, 160, 365, 384
Das, Dr. Habl, *338*
De Gaury, Gerald Simpson, 178
De Young, Anne, 245, *348*
death: of Marion Wells Thoms, 72-74, 77-81, 82-84, 380-381; of Zwemer, Fatima, and Ruth, 75; of Jesse Bennett, 75
DePree, May, 77, 79-82, 84, 222, 225, 244, 248
DeValois, Jack, 323, 327
Dhofar, Oman, 291-306; and Qara Mts. excursion, 299-302; residences in, 294-95; Salalah medical tour in, 293-304; and second medical tour, 304-6; and slaves, status of, 305-6; society of, 302-4; swarms of mosquitoes in, 296-97, controlled by fish, 298-99; and treatment of Qaboos, Sultan's son, 304
Dickason, D. G., 389
Dickson, Harold, 32, 166, 171-74, 178-81, 388-90
Dickson, Violet, 32, 166, 172-74, 178, 182, 388
Diekema, Gerrit John, 198, 226, 391
DiGiorgio, Mario, 322, 396

Dimnent, Edward D., 391
diseases: anemia, 99, 233; ascaris worms, 103-4; cellulitis, 91; bilharzia, 92; cholera, 92; dysentery, 92; Hansen's Disease (leprosy), 8, 310, 366; malaria, 92, 132; najis (syphilis- and yaws-like), 132; obliteration of: tuberculosis, 366; Hansen's Disease, 366; epidemic diseases, 366; plague, 92; smallpox, 92; tuberculosis, 132; typhoid, 72
Draper, Bern, *338*
Dunham, James, 348, 370
Dunham, Joyce, 370
Dykstra, Dirk, 203-6, 209, 212, 217, 229-30, 234-35, 247, 250-51, 257-59, 264, 392-94
Dykstra, Minnie, 203-5, 212, 217, 230, 247, *251*, 392-93

E

Elgood, Cyril, 382
epidemics: and dysentery, cholera-like, 331; and felej canals, role of, 332; and kundoo, 287-90; and smallpox, 283-86
Etisham, 208, 391

F

Faisal bin Turki, 179, 193, 197, 199, *200*, 201, 222, 224, 233, 390
Faisal I (Iraq), 29, 33
Faisal, Nadir bin, *200*
fiancées: Alma, 3; Beth, 2, 3-5; and Wells' decision, 9-12; 373-74
flies, as disease vector, 286-87
foreign trade constriction: arms, 293; slaves 293
Fowle, Cumford, 111, 121-22
friendships (of Sharon John Thoms): American consul (Basrajh), 45; Mughsin Pasha, 43-44; Sayyid

Taymur bin Faisal, 199, 202, 224, 307, 390
furlough, in States, 322-28; and feelings of alienation, 328

G

Galen, 382-83
Garden of Eden (Iraq) 37-39
Goheen, Dr., 273
Gosselink, George, 378
Gruner, O. Cameron, 384

H

hakeem: from physician to, 130; relationship to patients of, 129
Hamad bin Abdullah Thani, 112-13, 115
Hamid bin Hamid al Rushdi, 265, *266*
Hamyar, Sulaiman bin, Shaykh, 207, 257, 259, 265, 267, 278, 330-32, 336-37, 339-42, 397-98
Hansen's Disease, 9
Harrison, Monty, 191, 214, 391
Harrison, Paul, 7, 92, 125, 160, 169, 179, 191, 196, 214-17, 229, 234, 242, 244, 258, 275, 282, 295, 316, 365, 384, 390-91
Harrison, Regina, 191n4, 316
Harrison, Timothy, 391
Harthi, Isa bin Salih al, 207, 232-34, 257
Haseena, Ma, 214
heat stress, relief of, 316; and cook-caretaker (Mr. P. Soosainathan), 317-18; at Dar Es Salaam cottage, 316-17; at Highclerc school (Kodaikanal), 320-22, 397; and retreat to Kodaikanal (India), 316-22
heat, oppressive, 242-45
hernia, strangulated, 154-57
Heusinkveld, Eleanor, 353
Heusinkveld, Maurice M., 344, 370, 390; murder of, 352-53
Hill stations (India), 374

Hinge, Walter, 107-8
Hippocrates, 382-83
hobbies: of Sharon John Thoms, 43; of Mughsin Pasha, 43-44
Holland, Michigan, 225-26
Holland, Robert Erskine, 198
home life (Oman) of Beth and Wells, 313-16
home, distancing from life in the US, 328
Hosmon, Sarah, 190, 204, 217, 229, 248, 250, 365, 393
hospital proposal, new government, 399
hospital, contagious diseases (S. J. Thoms Hospital), 308-12; and Hansen's Disease, 310-11; and tuberculosis, 309; and Wells as intern at leprosarium, 312
hospital, women's (Muscat), 247-56; births at, 253; and Dr. Hosmon, 248; and Dr. Vander Zwaag, 255; expansion of (1952-53), 250; and Fanny Lutton, 250; and Jeanette Boersma, 250, 253-54; and midwifery, 249; and Nurse Mary, 247, 249; renamed As Saada Hospital, 255
Huber, Dr., 226
Hudson, Ellis, 132

I

Ibadhi Islam, Shari'a, 395
ice: in air-conditioning, 379; as medical treatment, 73-74
Imam Yahya, 152
imam: approves Christian scripture sales, 335; and cataracts, 333; death of, 336; demonstrates thoughtfulness, 260; discussion with, 266-68; frailness of, 259; and photography, 335; succession of, 336-37; surgery of, successful, 335; welcomes the Thomses, 335

Indianapolis, IN, 225
Iraq (British Mandate of Mesopotamia), 23-25, 27-49; Baghdad, 23, 25; Basrah, 51-52, 379-380; Ctesiphon (Tisphon), 24; Garden of Eden 37-39; Kerbela, 24; and May DePree Thoms, 189; Rutbah Wells (Anbar Province), 23; Shatt-al-Arab, 52
Isa bin Miriam. *See* Jesus Christ
Isa, Salih bin, 207

J

Ja'alan (Bilad Beni Bu Ali), 264
Jarman, Robert L., 384
Jauhara, Khatoun (Beth Thoms), 118, 292, 295, 334, 370
Jayakar, Dr., 199
Jerusalem, 17-18
Jesus Christ, 61, 86, 129, 133, 150-51, 157, 215, 239, 260, 352, 354, 360, 363-64, 366, 381, 385-87
Jiluwi, Sa'ad bin Abdallah bin, 136, *137*
Jiluwi, Sa'ud bin, *138*, 139

K

Kapenga, Jay, 250, *251*, 254, 269, 274-76
Kapenga, Marjorie "Midge," 250, 254
Kennedy, Dr., 278n9, *346*, 347
Khalifa, Isa bin, Shaykh, 108, 179
Khalili, Muhammad bin Abd Allah al, 207-8, 333-36, 338-39
Khamees, 295
Khaza'al bin Jabir, Shaykh, 32, 55-56, 164
Kitaab an-Nejat (Book of Salvation, Avicenna), 98, 100-101
Kodaikanal International (Kodai) School, 320-22; faculty, 396-97
Kolb, Fritz, 321
Korteling, Maisie, 324-27
Kuwait, 163-83; Arabian Mission's impact in, 179; aridity of, 169-70; and battle of Jahra, 169; and Col. H. Dickson, 166, 173-75; and djinn (spirit possession), 167; and Dr. Mylrea, 181, 389; Eid celebrations in, 173; entertaining the ruler of, 178-83; first oil well in, 172; hospital inside wall of, 168-69; and model ship construction, 176-78, 182-83, 389; socializing in, 173, 388-89; and treatment of dental abscess, 165-66, 170-72, 182; welcomed by C. S. G. Mylrea, 165-70, 179-80

L

Lake Tiberias (Sea of Galilee), 19-20
Lakra, Dr., 67, 331, 338
Lawrence, T. E., 32, 377, 396
leprosy, 9
Luther, Martin, 18, 267
Lutton, Fanny, 79, 204, 207, 250, 393

M

Maktoum, Sa'eed bin Maktoum bin Hasher al, 278
maladies, endemic: abscesses (boil-related), 114-16; athlete's foot, 99; cataracts, 113; chronic otitis media, 104; cranio-facial anomalies (cleft palate, club foot), 92; dental abscesses, 171, 181; glaucoma, 113; gout, 114; hernias, 97; non-venereal syphilis-like disease, 132-33; ringworm, 99; scabies, 99; tuberculosis, 132
Malallah, 240, 331
marriage: of May DePree Thoms to S. J. Thoms, 81, 189-90
Marsh Arabs (Ma'adan), 40-42
Mas, Ali al, 331
Mas, Mohammed al, 204, 215, *216*, 217, 230, 238, *241*, 281-85, 392

Mas, Mubarak al, 204, 215, *216*, 217, 233, 281-85
Mas, Qumber al, 204, 212, 215, *216*, 217, 230, 261-65, 281, 283-85, 287-88, 293, 295, 331, 344, *348*, 395
Mason Memorial Hospital, 234, 239-41; and advances in medicine, 243; and al Mas brothers, 281-83; with Beth Thoms as manager, 240-41; oppressive heat of in operating room, 244-45; and training of staff, 246; and wartime complications, 242
Matrah, Oman, 211-18, 219-22, 226, 229-42; and death of S. J. Thoms, 222-25; family auto accident in, 237-38; and Knox Memorial Hospital, 229; travel restrictions during civil war, 342; Wells' arrival in, 212-14; Wells' memories of, 219-22
Merook, 264
Mesopotamia. *See* Iraq
Minot, George R., 99
mission philosophies: of Zwemer, 125; of Cantine, 125-26, 385-86
Moerdyk, James, 70, 80
Mughsin Pasha, *43*, 44-45
Murphy, George P., 99
Murphy, Lt., 293, 299, 300
Musil, Alois, 321
Muthu, N., 319
MV *Taurinia*, 325
Mylrea, Bess, 163, 166
Mylrea, Stanley, 74, 91, 163-66, 168-69, 179-80, 365, 378, 388-89

N

Nahyan, Shakhbut bin Sultan al, 278, *346*, 347
Neglected Arabia (periodical), 376-77
Niebuhr, Carsten, 314
Nizwa: and Birkat al Moz Fort, 259; difficult access to, 258; and interception by guards, 259; reconstruction of Jabal, 341-42; and route via Rostaq and Tanuf, 258-59; Wells' first visit to, 257-61; Wells meets imam at, 259; Wells' second visit to, 265-268; Wells' third visit to, 333-37
non-Western medicine, 100
Nubi, 275
Nurse Mary. *See* Balasundram, Mary

O

oil concession, Sa'udi Arabia, 159-60
Oman: achievements of Wells in, 366; and Agreement of Seeb, 205-10, 393; air-conditioning, installation and effects, 342; becomes trachoma-free, 366; British Agency hospital and Dr. Jayakar in, 199; churches in, 395; and civil war in Tanuf, 339; conversation with Percy Cox in, 192-93; Dhofar, 210, 281-306; Freed Slave Boys School, 191; Ghafiri and Hinawi factions in, 207; and hospital re-opening challenges, 204, 215-18; hospital staff, 393; influence of British in, 200; Jeanette Boersma in, 253-55, 340; and Knox Memorial Hospital, 191, 392-93, 396; and landmine victim from Jabal, 343-45; letter from Sultan Sayyid Taymur to Mrs. M. DePree Thoms, 390; Matrah hospital in, expands services, 338; Muscat, 190, 392; and Muscat women's clinic, 191; Nizwa, seat of imam in, 207, 394, 398; Nurse Mary in, 196, 393; and resistance to mission medical work, 197-98; shaykhs, paramount in, 207; S. J. Thoms Hospital for Contagious Diseases, 307-12; slaves, manumission of, 193-95; and slavery in, 201; sultan's father (Mr. T. F. T. Said)

returns to, 307-8; Wells elected FACS in, 196; Women's Hospital in, 190, 393
other wise man: Christmas story of, 357-64; metaphor for missionary motivation, 364; as embodiment of second Great Commandment, 364
Ottavi, Msr., 192
Ottoman Empire, vestiges of: medical licensing, 46-47

P

Palani Hills, camping at, 320-21, 396
Pavlicek, Mr., 275
pearling, 62-64, 378; chronic otitis media from, 104; Wells' visit to fleet, 104-7; C. D. Belgrave's regulation of, 381
Pengelley, Bruce, 384
Pengelley, Janet S., 381, 384
Peninsular & Oriental (P&O), 19
Pennings, Gerrit, 67-68, 76-77, 86, 90
Pennings, Gertrude, 68, 76, 77
petroleum reserves (Middle East): Iraq-Iran 47-48: Anglo-Persian Oil Company, 49: Burmah Oil (BOC): Bahrain, 57, 107-10, 384
Pettyfer, Maj., 232
Pettyfer, Mrs., 231-32
Peursem, Gerrit Van, 150
Phelps, Carl, 321, 397
Philby, Harry St. John Bridger, 29, 32, 147, 377, 396
Pillai, Shri V. T., 319
placebo treatment for ulcers, 239
prime minister: assassination, attempt and treatment, 349-51; gifted a Bible, 351

Q

Qatar (Doha), 111-22; Ar Rayyan, 113, 120-21; and petroleum concession, 121-22

R

Rabi, 397
Rasassi, Ismail, 289, 347
Rashid, Mohammed al, 145
Rasoon, Khoda, 344, *348*
Rhoades, Ralph "Dusty," 57
Roosevelt, President (Franklin Delano), 388

S

Sa'eed the Great, 293
Sa'eed, Qaboos bin Sa'eed bin Taymur bin Faisal al bu, 304, *305*, 340, 367, 376
Sa'eed, Sa'eed bin Taymur bin Faisal al bu Sa'eed, 199, *200*, 202, 204, 243, 278-79, 291-92, 299, 300, 302-4, 306-9, 336-37, 339, 342, 347, 351, 366-69
Sa'eed, Sayyid Faisal bin Turki al, 268
Sa'eed, Sayyid Mahmood al bu, 250, 255
Sa'eed, Taroiq bin Taymur bin Faisal al bu, 314
Sa'eed, Taymur bin Faisal bin Turki al bu, 179, 199, *200*, 201-2, 204, 207, 224, 292, 307-8, 390
Sa'ud, Sa'ud bin Abdalaziz al, 152
Sa'udi Arabia: al-Hasa (Hofuf), 135-43; Dareen, 131; Katif (Qatif); Ta'if, 49
Sa'udi Arabia: cataract surgery in, 157-58; conversation in about Christ, 150-52; conversation in with the king, 159-60, 390; conversation in with a mullah, 157-58; emergency surgery in, 154-57; and governor of the eastern province, 136; Hofuf (al Hasa oasis), 133-43; imperious slave in, 137-38; and king's jeweler (Shi'ah), 141-44; 144-45; and king's purchasing agents, 137,

140; medical trips in, 131; Riyadh, 147-61, 152-54; and treatment of governor's son, 136-37; and treatment of king, 140-41, 144-45; and treatment of king's daughters, 148-50
Sabah, Ahmad Al Jaber al, 166, 172, 176, 178, 182, 183
Sabah, Ahmad al, Shaykh, 166, 172, 176, 178, 182-83
Sabah, Mubarak al, 32, 164, 168, 179
Sabah, Mubarak the Great, Shaykh, 32, 164, 168, 179
Sabah, Salim al Mubarak al, 168
Sabah, Salim bin Mubarak al, 168
sambuqs (indigenous sailing ships), 105
Scholten, Frances Thoms, 42-44. *See also* Thoms, Frances
Scudder, Ethel "Beth" Talcott, 2-9, 11-13. *See also* Thoms, Beth
Scudder, Ida B., *317*
Scudder, Ida S., 5, *317*
Scudder, Lewis R., III, 389
Shafiq, Dr., 295
Shah, Lt. Col. M. H., 100
Shahrazad, 252-53
Shahrbanoo, 310, *311*
shark liver oil, 239
Sharqiyya medical visit, 261
Sina, Abu (Avicenna), 98, 100, 284, 382-84
slavery: ocean trade of, suppressed by British, 62-64; in Qatar, 116-18
Smethers, Capt. (fictional), 53-56, 58-65, 104
Soosainathan, P. "Soosai," 317, *318*
SS *Barala*, 51-57
SS *Excambion*, 187
Stanislaus S., "Thani," 317
Storm, Harold, 205, 283, 292, 365, 384
Sulayman, 90, 119
Sultan Taymur. *See* Sa'eed, Taymur bin Faisal bin Turki al bu
Sur, Oman: Wells' medical tour in, 264

T

Talib Pasha, 32
Talib, Sayyid, 33
Tanuf, Oman, 267-68
Taymur bin Faisal. *See* Sa'eed, Taymur bin Faisal bin Turki al bu
terramycin, 252
tetanus, 250, 252-53
Thani, Abdallah bin Jassim al, Shaykh, 111-16, 118-22, 179
Thani, Hamad bin Abdallah al, Shaykh, 112-13, 115
Thani, Mohammed bin Jassim al, 111, 116-18
Thani, Mohammed bin Jassim bin Mohammed al, 111, 116-18
Thesiger, Wilfred, 257-58, 396
Thomas, Bertram, 292, 396
Thomas, Lowell, 160-61, 313
Thoms, Beth, 17-21, 23, 25, 28, 31-32, 34, 37, 39, 51, 94-95, 118, 124, 129, 160, 163-66, 169, 172, 178, 180, 183, 187, 189, 195, 198, 201, 203, 205, 211-14, 227, 231-32, 237-38, 240-41, 244, 247-48, 250, 254, *258*, 271-74, 277, 292-96, 298-300, *301*, 302, 304-5, *306*, 313-14, *315*, 316, *317*, 318, *320*, 322-24, 327-28, 331, *334*, 339-40, 346, *348*, 352-53, 367, *368*, 369-70, 373-75, 384-85, 387, 389, 394, 398
Thoms, Frances, 77, 80-82, 158, 195, 221, 223, 225, 390
Thoms, Lois "Lowey" Ethel, 77, 80-82, 172-73, *174*, 187, 189, *195*, *199*, 214, 221, 223, 225, 237-38, 240, 272-74, 304, *315*, 316-17, *320*, 322-24, 327-28, *334*, 335, 390
Thoms, Marion Wells, 43
Thoms, Marion Wells, 68-72, *73*, 75, 77-84, 165, 189, 198, 226, 365, 380

Thoms, May DePree, 187, 190, 193, *195*, 197-203, 272, 375
Thoms, Nancy Fisher, 18, 20-21, 23, 25, 51, 94-95, 173, *174*, 187, 189, 271-72, 274, *315*, 316-17, *320*, 322-23, 327-28, 384-85
Thoms, Norman Wells, 94-95, 173, *174*, 187, 189, 231-32, 234, 238, 271-74, 304, *315*, 316-17, 319, *320*, 322-23, 326-28, 384-85
Thoms, Peter Scudder, 94-95, 173, *174*, 187, 189, 271-72, 274, 304, *315*, 316-17, 319, *320*, 322-23, 326-28, *348*, 384-85
Thoms, Sharon John, 42-44, 46-47, 57, 59, 65, 69-70, *71*, 73-75, 77-84, 89, 92, 99, 111, 164-66, 189-90, *195*, 197-202, 204, 215, 222-27, 253, 268, 309, 370, 380, 390
Thoms, Wells, 1, 2, 4-13, 17-18, 20-23, 25, 27-28, 30-34, 39, 42-45, 47, 49-53, 55, 57-60, 62-65, 67-70, 75, 77, 82, 84-90, 92, 94-95, 97-101, 103-61, 163-67, 170-72, *174*, 175-76, 178-80, 183, 187-90, *195*, 196, *197*, *199*, 203, 205, 210-17, 219-23, 225-26, 229-31, 233-34, 236, *237*, 238-39, *240*, 242-45, 247-48, 250, 253-55, 257, *258*, 259-76, 278, 281, 283-89, 291-305, *306*, 307-14, *315*, 316-18, *320*, 322-28, 330-33, *334*, 335-37, *338*, 339-47, *349*, 350, 352-53, 357-59, 362, 364-67, *368*, 369-70, 373-75, 378, *380*, 382-98
Thomson, Daniel, 399
Thuwaini, Sayyid, 314
Tiberias, Lake, 363
Tiffany, Mary, 68, 70, 76-77, 89, 107
Toprani, Shri Naraindas, 213-14, 217, 221, 271, 286-87, 310
transoceanic travel: American Export Line, 187-88; British India Steam Navigation (BISN), 19, 49, 377; in Gulf (Persian-Arabian), 52-65; MV *Taurinia*, 325; and passenger travel, 55-56, 324-27; Peninsular & Oriental (P&O), 19; SS *Barala*, 51-57; SS *Excambion*, 187; with zoo animals as cargo, 326-27
transport: jeeps, 330; Land Rover, 330; resistance to motor vehicles declines, 333
travel by bus, 19-20, 375
Trench, Richard, 399
Tuson, Penelope, 390
Twitchell, Karl, 388

V

Van Ess, Dorothy (Firman), 27-29, 32-34, 37, 39, 49, 51, 375-77, 389
Van Ess, John, 27-34, 37-45, 47, 51, 112, 375-78, 390
Van Pelt, Mary, 31-32, 164, 172
Van Peursem, Gerrit, 131, 207
Van Peursem, Josephine, 207
Vander Zwaag, Alice, 255
Veldman, Jeanette, 245

W

Wadi Dhayka: flash flood in, 262-64; and Qumber's baptism, 263-64
Wadi Sama'il (Jinah, Birkat al Moz), 265-66
Walook, 264-65
Warnshuis, Mrs., 225
Wells, Etta, 78, 82-84, 380
Wells, Seth, 78-79, 82-84, 380
Wells, Will, 78, 380
Wellsted, J. R., Lt., 258
Western medicine: homeopathy, 71; allopathy, 71; pharmacopeia, 382
Wiersum, Harry J., 30, 376
Wilcocks, Maj., 39
Wilson, Arnold, 32, 34, 377
Wingate, R. E. L., 208, 391
World War II: censorship of mail, 270; consequences of in Oman,

267; disruption of family reunions, 272-73; family life complications, 269; Kodaikanal (India), importance, 270; motor vehicles, impact on, 276; purchase of military surplus, 275-77; relief to Royal Navy personnel, 274-75; and scarcity of drugs, 273; Wells carries on alone during, 273-75

Y

Yacoob, 287-88
Yahya (imam of Yemen), 152
Yasser, Shaykh, 332-33

Z

Zanzibar: in relation to Oman, 210
Zwemer, Amy E., 70-71, 74-75, 189, 378, 380
Zwemer, Fatimah, 75, 380
Zwemer, Peter, 191-92, 195
Zwemer, Ruth, 75, 380
Zwemer, Samuel Marinus, 42, 57, 69-70, 74-75, 80, 93, 125-27, 189, 191, 378, 380, 389-90

Made in the USA
Monee, IL
22 June 2022